Our Ice Is Vanishing/Sikuvut Nunguliqtuq

McGill-Queen's Native and Northern Series
(In memory of Bruce G. Trigger)
Sarah Carter and Arthur J. Ray, Editors

# Our Ice Is Vanishing

# Sikuvut Nunguliqtuq

A History of Inuit, Newcomers, and Climate Change

Shelley Wright

McGill-Queen's University Press

Montreal & Kingston · London · Ithaca

© McGill-Queen's University Press 2014

ISBN 978-0-7735-4462-8 (cloth)
ISBN 978-0-7735-9610-8 (ePDF)
ISBN 978-0-7735-9611-5 (ePUB)

Legal deposit third quarter 2014
Bibliothèque nationale du Québec

Printed in Canada on acid-free paper

McGill-Queen's University Press acknowledges the support of the Canada Council for the Arts for our publishing program. We also acknowledge the financial support of the Government of Canada through the Canada Book Fund for our publishing activities.

Library and Archives Canada Cataloguing in Publication

Wright, Shelley, author
Our ice is vanishing = Sikuvut nunguliqtuq : a history of Inuit, newcomers, and climate change / Shelley Wright.

(McGill-Queen's native and northern series ; 75)
Includes bibliographical references and index.
Issued in print and electronic formats.
ISBN 978-0-7735-4462-8 (bound).–ISBN 978-0-7735-9610-8 (ePDF).–ISBN 978-0-7735-9611-5 (ePUB)

1. Inuit–Canada–History. 2. Sea ice–Social aspects–Arctic coast (Canada)–History. 3. Climatic changes–Social aspects–Canada, Northern–History. 4. Canada, Northern–Climate–History. 5. Canada, Northern–History. 6. Canada, Northern–Social conditions. 7. Canada, Northern–Environmental conditions–History. I. Title. II. Title: Sikuvut nunguliqtuq. III. Series: McGill-Queen's native and northern series ; 75

E99.E7W75 2014     971.9004'9712     C2014-902067-8

This book was designed and typeset by studio oneonone in Sabon 10.2/13

Dedicated to the memory of
Lucien Ukaliannuk, LLD (University of Victoria)
Elder-in-Residence of the Akitsiraq Law School

and

to my mother
Betty Wright

# Contents

# Figures

Unless otherwise noted, photographs are by the author.

# Note on Terminology

The Indigenous people of the Arctic refer to themselves as "Inuit" (people). "Eskimo" is no longer used in Canada. I have sparingly used the word "Eskimo" in historical quotations or where the context makes it appropriate. There are several good dictionaries of Inuktitut in print, as well as websites dedicated to teaching Inuktitut on the Internet. I have listed one of each in the Bibliography. In addition, many books on the Arctic include useful glossaries, including *Uqalurait: An Oral History of Nunavut*, edited by John Bennett and Susan Rowley. I recommend this book to anyone who is interested in Inuit oral history and culture. Whenever I have used an Inuktitut word or phrase for the first time, I have provided a translation. Inuktitut is spoken in several dialects, some of which are reflected in the spelling of different words used in this book. Inuktitut from older sources (such as in Knud Rasmussen's writings) is reproduced with the original English spelling, although much of this is now archaic. My knowledge of Inuktitut is limited, so I have been fortunate in having fluent speakers and writers to help me over the years, including Susan Enuaraq, John Houston, Sandra Inutiq, Piita Irniq, Elisapee Karetak, Alexina Kublu, Mick Mallon, Aaju Peter, Paul Quassa, and Lucien Ukaliannuk.

Whatever errors there are (and I'm sure there are some) are entirely my own responsibility.

The Arctic is ruled by ice. For Inuit, it is the platform on which life is lived. But the ice is melting and becoming dangerous. Late freezing means that travel on the ice is no longer safe until December or even January. Inuit hunters die every year falling through thin ice. In the lead-up to the 2009 Conference on Climate Change in Copenhagen, Mary Simon, former president of Inuit Tapiriit Kanatami and leader of the Canadian Inuit delegation, said there needed to be a 42 per cent cut in emissions by 2020. Kirt Ejesiak, vice president of the Inuit Circumpolar Council, said at the 2011 Conference on Climate Change in Durban, South Africa, that global temperatures must not rise more than 2° Celsius this century. Is it possible for us to change in time?

Inuit are *silaup aalaruqpalianigata tusaqtittijiit* – witnesses and messengers of climate change.

# 1

# Sikuvut: Our Ice

Once they had moved onto the ice no one would dare to sew clothing,
as it was taboo ... They believed that if sewing was done while they were
out on the ice they would not be able to catch any seals, or the ice might
crack up and go to pieces.

Paatsi Qaggutaq[1]

"Arctic Ice Melt in 2012 Was Fastest, Widest in Recent History" trumpeted
a headline in the *Toronto Star.*[2] The big melt of 2012 ended by mid-
September but not before, as the *New York Times* worried, "demolishing
the previous record – and setting off new warnings about the rapid pace of
change in the region."[3] The rapidity of the melting of summer ice in the
Arctic over the past five years is unprecedented, both since satellite records
began to be kept in 1979 and in the much longer oral history of Indigenous
peoples. It appears to be unusual even in the millennia of geological time-
frames. An ice-free summer in the Arctic Ocean was not predicted to occur
until the middle or end of this century. Now, according to some predictions,
it may occur by the end of this decade. Most disturbing is that what was
labelled extreme two or three years ago now seems to be the new reality.
Scientists everywhere are surprised at the rapid rate of Arctic sea ice melting.
Over the past thousand years, despite fluctuations in global temperatures
of about 1 to 2° Celsius, Arctic ice cover has remained relatively stable.[4]
According to Professor Louis Fortier of the University of Laval in Quebec,
"For at least 3 million years, and most likely 13 million ... the Arctic Ocean
has been covered by a thick, floating ice cap, the breadth of which fluctuates
with the seasons and currents." It is now "smaller, patchier and thinner

than ever – and rotten in parts. The extent of the Arctic ice cap has hit a record low [as of summer 2012] and the consequences of what is arguably the greatest environmental change in human history will extend far beyond the North Pole."[5]

Even though the ice melt in the summer of 2013 was not as extreme as the year before, the extent of summer ice was still nearly one-third less than in 1979. On 27 September 2013 the United Nations Intergovernmental Panel on Climate Change released its *Fifth Assessment Report*. Despite a puzzling pause in atmospheric temperature rise over the past few years the oceans and ice are definitely being affected by human-caused, or "anthropogenic," warming: "Human influence has been detected in warming of the atmosphere and the ocean, in changes in the global water cycle, in reductions in snow and ice, in global mean sea level rise, and in changes in some climate extremes. This evidence for human influence has grown since AR4 [*Assessment Review 4*]. It is *extremely likely* [90 to 100 per cent certain] that human influence has been the dominant cause of the observed warming since the mid-20th century."[6]

When the summer ice last disappeared millions of years ago the change happened over tens of centuries. Today it is happening within decades and the effects are being felt now. Hot dry weather in North America and cold rainy weather in Europe during the summers of 2012 and 2013 seem to be connected to atmospheric and ocean patterns created by climate change in the Arctic. Rapid melting is altering the jet stream such that more extreme and longer lasting weather events – persistent rain and flooding, drought, heavy snowfall, severe storms, and (strangely) extremely cold temperatures in winter – are already occurring and may well continue into the future. Longer-term concerns focus on the release of millions of tons of methane (natural gas) into the atmosphere that, for the past hundreds of millions of years, has been trapped in frozen tundra and on the Arctic Ocean floor. Methane has ten to twenty times the greenhouse effect of carbon dioxide. Large-scale releases of this gas into the atmosphere could have a major, possibly catastrophic, effect on global warming. Although melting Arctic sea ice does not raise ocean levels directly, the big melt is being mirrored by major melting of glaciers in Greenland, which will lead to rising sea levels. In addition, as ocean water warms, it also expands, again leading to rises in sea levels worldwide (as measured over the past thirty-five years). Similar melting is occurring around ice shelves in the Antarctic.

Our Earth's climate is ruled by Arctic and Antarctic ice. There is still a glacial plateau the size of a small continent in Greenland calving white mountains of ice into cold blue seas. There is also land-fast ice, or shelf ice, clinging to the margins of Greenland and Ellesmere Island, although this is cracking and splitting away every summer. The broken shelves drift into the Arctic Ocean as great flat islands circling around the polar gyre of ice that slowly rotates clockwise for years before currents and wind sweep them southward. Different again is pack ice, including both annual ice and thick multiyear ice. All this world of ice is melting. Glaciers are spilling melt water as well as giant cliffs of ice into the sea, and the thick permanent pack ice circling the North Pole is disintegrating from the bottom up. Our Earth's climatic fate will be ruled by what happens as the ice melts.

Glaciers, icebergs, shelf ice, and sea ice are made of different kinds of ice. *Glaciers* are plateaus and rivers of ice created from snow that piles up from one winter to the next, hardens, and eventually spills slowly from mountain tops or high latitude land surfaces like Antarctica or Greenland. When the climate is cold they grow and spread, creating great sheets of ice thousands of feet thick and continental in size. When the climate warms up most glaciers melt and shrink. The Greenland ice cap is a remnant of this continental ice – a survivor of the huge ice sheet that once stretched over much of what is now Canada and the northern United States. *Icebergs* are made of ancient fresh water that has been frozen and land-bound within glaciers for tens of thousands of years. As glaciers flow slowly into the sea the ice cracks off in chunks that can range from great frozen cliffs the size of cities to small boulder-sized "growlers" and "bergy bits." Both glaciers and icebergs are fresh water ice.

*Shelf*, or *land-fast* ice lines coastal regions. Around Greenland and the islands of the Canadian Arctic Archipelago this ice clings to shore. If the temperature remains cold enough during the summer it gradually expands into great fixed slabs of thick ice extending out to sea from the land. During spring, leads of water separate the shelf ice and melting pack ice. It is here that the *floe edge* provides a rich marine environment of fish, sea mammals, and their predators – including humans. Farther south, where summer temperatures are warmer, the floe edge will disappear in June or July, returning over the winter for next spring's hunting season. This ice can be treacherous, especially as unexpected spring warming leads to unpredictable melting. Several parties of both hunters and tourists found this out in late June 2013

1.1 Iceberg, Davis Strait

when they discovered that the floe edge had split up and that their camps were on ice that was drifting out into Admiralty Inlet near Arctic Bay. Fortunately everyone made it back to shore safely.[7] When Sam Omik and his brother went on a hunting trip near Pond Inlet around the same time, they nearly fell into the water when they woke up and stepped outside their tent the first morning. Their slab of floe edge had broken off and was drifting out to sea. They also had to be airlifted to safety. Sam's wife, Sandra, says that when he arrived in Iqaluit their little daughter Eve, "was the first to hug Sam when he landed off a rescue helicopter, of course – she pushed herself all through the people to get to him – thank you search and rescue teams from the bottom of my heart."[8]

*Pack ice* is the frozen ocean itself. *Multiyear ice* can be decades old and tens of feet thick. *Annual ice*, which melts in spring and refreezes in the fall, is thinner and more fragile. Much of the multiyear ice in the Arctic is now being replaced by annual ice. Sea ice and fresh water ice freeze differently. Fresh water starts to freeze just above 0° Celsius, forming a thin skim of brittle surface ice that gradually hardens and thickens. Sea water, because of its saltiness, tends to freeze just below 0° Celsius. At first the surface thickens, forming a soupy mixture of glittering jelly. Gradually this hardens to a layer of rubbery grey ice that swells and dips with the motion of waves and currents. As the temperatures continue to plunge the ice thickens and turns white – it is then usually safe to stand on. Annual ice can be 6 or 8 feet thick by spring, before it slowly melts and then refreezes in the autumn. Multiyear ice does not melt in the summer. It may last for ten years or more, gradually becoming a solid underwater ceiling of sculpted ice frescoed with algae that may be 20 feet or more thick.

Polar ice in both the northern and southern hemispheres plays a crucial role in keeping our planet comfortable for a wide diversity of life, including ourselves. Our atmosphere captures energy from the sun and traps it in a warm blanket of heat – the "greenhouse effect" – which is crucial in keeping Earth's surface warm enough for complex life forms to evolve. The glaring white of ice and snow reflects some of the sun's rays back into space, keeping the whole planet at a liveably cool temperature. This is known as the "albedo effect" and is an essential component of our planet's natural thermostat. The polar regions act like giant terrestrial air conditioners that naturally stabilize Earth's average temperature, making life "as we know it" possible. Without the blanket of our atmosphere to warm the planet, the albedo effect of light surfaces such as ice and snow to cool it, and the circulation of wind and water to distribute heat and cold around the whole planet, Earth would be either much too cold or much too hot to support any kind of life like ourselves. As the ice disappears and snow-covered tundra is more and more exposed, the deep blue of the ocean and the browns and greens of the land absorb the sun's radiation, capturing it as heat. This reduction in the albedo effect creates one of the "positive feedback loops" that is accelerating the warming of the planet.

We in the South think of the Arctic as an empty world of pristine white, but it is much more complex than this. It is also a living environment rich with land and marine life. During the spring and autumn millions of migratory birds flood the skies, bringing waves of life that ebb and flow across the Arctic every year. Above the treeline there are still trees – they are simply tiny. Ancient willows no more than a few inches high can be hundreds of years old. The sea, land, and air are teeming with life – belugas, narwhal, bowhead whales, ring seals, bearded seals, walrus, shell fish, Arctic char,

1.2 Arctic cotton, which can be used as the wick in a *qulliq* (stone lamp), Iqaluit

halibut, cod, snowy owls, swans, ducks, geese, ptarmigans, murres, guillemots, gulls, Arctic terns, polar bears, caribou, muskoxen, wolves, foxes,
lemmings. The Arctic is also rich with plant life, from many varieties of
lichens and moss to a garden of summer flowers.

This life also includes human communities that have lived here for thousands of years. People are an essential component of this environment.
"Inuit" means "people." They, their ancestors, and their predecessors have
travelled over the land, ice, and sea of the Arctic from Siberia to Greenland
since before the ancient empires of Egypt, China, and Rome existed, and
they are still here long after the monuments of our ancestors fell into ruins
(or tourist sites). The people of the Arctic developed sophisticated technologies to survive in a harsh environment – the *qajaq* (kayak) and *qamutik*
(dogsled) are just two examples. Caribou clothing is warmer than any product, natural or artificial, developed in the South. The spiralling architecture
of the *igluvijaq* (snow house – the common word "igloo" that most of us
are familiar with simply means "house" and can be built of any material)

uses an architectural design that is unique – both beautiful, practical, and completely in tune with the environment.

Inuit are traditionally nomadic, travelling great distances on land and especially on the sea ice as a highway from one place to another. They have long recognized that the passages through the islands of the Arctic Ocean, frozen for most of the year, are not primarily maritime routes but can be travelled over or even lived on as extensions of the land. Inuit are a unique human community whose culture and technology enrich our own. The Inuit of Nunavut, Labrador, Nunavik (northern Quebec), and the Northwest Territories have helped to establish Canadian sovereignty in the North as Canadian citizens. "They" are also "us."

It has become almost counterintuitive in modern cultures to think of "people" as "an essential component" of any environment. Those of us who live almost exclusively in cities have long since lost any sense of the reality of the natural world. To us "Nature" is foreign – whether it is the exotic beauty of the Arctic or the more prosaic realities of extracting natural resources from the land and sea for our use and consumption. Usually we are so divorced from this reality that we don't think about it. Meat comes neatly sliced and wrapped in plastic. We prefer to ignore the bloody reality of death that makes this possible. Vegetables and fruits are stacked in attractive piles at the grocery store, all fresh, washed, and polished. Most of us forget the dirt, sweat, and hard work that went into planting and harvesting them – not to mention the costs, both economic and environmental, of fertilizers, pesticides, irrigation, land clearing, and the transportation that brought them from land to shelf. When we do think of "Nature," either it might be to see "it" as an inert body "out there" that can be killed, mined, or clear-cut for profit or amusement, or it might be to see our Earth as a suffering victim of human rapacity that needs to be protected or saved. Indeed, the two perspectives are mirror opposites of each other. Those of us who do not live on the land or interact with our follow creatures in a variety of ways may romanticize "Nature," forgetting that humans are inextricably connected to the chain of life on this planet. Climate change skeptics carry this sense of detachment to the point where real human impacts on Earth are ignored or denied.

As Roderick Frazier Nash says in the fourth edition of his classic work *Wilderness and the American Mind*,

Just as fences and dams once proudly testified to our ability to control nature, the protection of wild country now symbolizes our determination to control civilization. The frontier has had its day in the sun. Pioneer, growth-oriented attitudes work[ed] well when the human presence was relatively small and nature seemed vast and inexhaustible. But the evolutionary tide has turned. Growth has turned out to have ironic or self-defeating consequences. The environment is vulnerable. As the new millennium opens before us, it's time for new frontiersmen who understand that what really needs to be conquered is not nature, but ourselves. Wilderness can be an intellectual and a biological starting point for putting human needs into ecological balance with those of our fellow travelers on spaceship Earth.[9]

The concept of "wilderness" is the wild twin of "civilization." Both are human constructs that developed with the creation of pastoral herding, farming, and village life beginning about 10,000 years ago, as indeed Nash himself points out. Both are artificial concepts that too easily ignore the existence of Indigenous peoples (our ancestors as well as those living today) within the natural world as essential components of that world. We have forgotten the ancient wisdom that Inuit and other Indigenous peoples still remember – Earth is not just the foundation of all life; it is itself alive. Either it can be a source of life for all those who have evolved here (like us), or it can destroy.

Part of the problem is thinking of Earth as "it." By doing so we make it easier to objectify and distance ourselves from the source of our own survival and well-being. We ourselves play a role in this drama of life and death whether we recognize it or not. Most Indigenous peoples call themselves "the people" in their own languages, just as Inuit do. We have never developed a word that could help us to define ourselves globally as "the people" of Earth ("Earthlings"?). We forget that the pronoun "we" includes not only humans but also all life on this planet. "We" refers not just to us but also to everything else. This loss, the price of modernity, may be our undoing.

The Arctic can be deceptive in its beauty and power. Whether it is standing at the end of the Road to Nowhere in Iqaluit and witnessing a sunset the colour of yellow primrose or staring upward into a midnight sky filled with pale curtains of glowing northern lights, I am always awestruck by a seemingly timeless and limitless universe around me. But within this natural world of beauty we are never really alone. The life of the land and sea is all around us. Wandering over the flowery tundra on a sunny summer day, you can suddenly find yourself looking down into a downy nest of little ducklings. The Arctic is neither infinite nor eternal. The land and sea have changed and are still changing, whether slowly in the upheaval of continental drift or rapidly in the movement of water, wind, and ice. The Arctic is populated by a rich diversity of animal and plant life. Even in the depths of an Arctic winter polar bear tracks on the sea ice, followed by the catlike prints of an Arctic fox, tell a story of life and community between different species. Animals and people together have lived and breathed, hunted and travelled, raised their young and died on this land and ice for thousands of years.

The vast beauty of the Arctic may be memorable, but the realities of life and death are also confronting and challenging. There is no convenient filter to block out the suddenness of tragedy or the extremes of experience. From the very beginning of my time in Nunavut I was aware of the close presence of death. In July 2001 on my first visit to Iqaluit my hosts and I heard that a small boy had gone missing. The whole town turned out to find him. Every door and porch railing had a small yellow ribbon. He was found but it was too late – he had drowned in a local pond. The closeness of sudden death is a reality in the North, something I never got used to.

But the Arctic also taught me many small town virtues of friendliness, help in times of trouble, humility, humour, and the ever prevalent temptation of gossip. There were times when I was pushed to the limits of what I thought were my boundaries only to discover that those boundaries were wider than I had expected. The North challenges you, pushes you, and then suddenly charms you with something unexpectedly lovely. For an outsider like me, it can never really be home. But the Arctic has the power to draw you back again and again.

I also became aware of how protected we all are in our bubble of civilization. We have imported it to the North – without it we "southerners" (or *qallunaat*, meaning "big eyebrows") would die. This civilization now shields us nearly everywhere we go on Earth, hiding the realness of life and death on our planet. We cocoon ourselves in our cities and forget that, as humans, we are part of nature, not above it or separate from it. Even those of us who are thoughtful and well meaning, valuing the environment and the rights of others, know almost nothing of the realities that await us beyond our comfortable urban surroundings in North America, Europe, Australia, and Asia.

This is true even when we venture out into the "wilderness" with our back-packs, hiking boots, and trail bikes. We are never really alone with the wild-ness of that wilderness. There is usually a safety net, and when there isn't one we can quickly find ourselves lost and in danger. The wild can be deadly for those of us who no longer know how to engage with both the material and spiritual forces of our planet. We have lost the ability to survive as human participants in nature. Even Inuit have lost some of these skills. Fifty years ago drifting ice or a sudden blizzard meant building a shelter and wait-ing out the emergency. Now it requires satellite phones and search and res-cue. We have forgotten the language of Mother Earth and the beautiful terrifying magic that is part of her and our reality. Now we call it science and think we can control it.

That bubble we have created everywhere is slowly trapping Earth in an envelope of increasing heat. We are in danger of suffocating on our own technology. Nowhere is this more obvious than in the Arctic – strange, for this is in so many ways one of the last free places on Earth where humans still remember what it is like to live without a safety net. While politicians and business leaders cling to the old ways, ensuring themselves money and the illusion of power, the reality of climate change is leading us into uncharted waters. The Northwest Passage was ice-free in 2007 for the first time in anyone's memory. Between 6 and 7 July 2010 the Jacobshaven Glacier in western Greenland lost a chunk of ice nearly 3 square miles in size, significantly contributing to the retreat of the glacier inland. A few weeks later a giant ice shelf three times the size of Manhattan broke off the northern tip of Greenland. In the summer of 2011 I transited the Northwest Passage from east to west, something that would have been impossible even five years earlier. In Baffin Bay and Lancaster Sound there were lots of icebergs, including a huge sheet of ice more than 13 miles long that had likely broken off northwestern Ellesmere Island. But in the Northwest Passage itself, there was not a shred of ice.

In late July 2010 the US National Oceanic and Atmospheric Administra-tion issued a report showing that all indicators (melting glaciers and Arctic ice, rising land and sea temperatures, humidity, and snow cover) showed a planet heating up.[10] Climate change is now headline news. On 1 October 2011 the *New York Times* carried this front page headline: "The Threats to a Crucial Canopy: Deaths of Forests May Weaken Controls on Heat-Trap-ping Gas."[11] The article gives a detailed analysis of how a warming climate is creating major problems for the world's forests. These effects include the pine beetle infestation of boreal forests in Canada and the United States, frequent devastating forest fires there and in Siberia, and drought conditions in the Amazon and Australia that have been killing native trees for the past ten years. Dead and dying trees are releasing their stores of carbon into the atmosphere. This in turn leads to rising greenhouse gases and higher temperatures. The forests themselves are carbon "sinks" that store about one-quarter of the carbon dioxide released into the atmosphere. As forests die, another "positive feedback loop" is created. The treeless expanse of the Arctic is directly affected by what happens to forests thousands of miles away.

*Auyuittuq* means "the thing that never melts" – a glacier – in Inuktitut, the language of the Inuit. But the glaciers in Auyuittuq National Park on Baffin Island have disappeared over the past five years, and their brothers and sisters elsewhere are also rapidly retreating. As the ice melts, a way of life that has existed in the Arctic for thousands of years is being forced to adapt to changes occurring at lightning speed.

My own experience in the Arctic began almost by accident. By 2001 I had been teaching in the Faculty of Law at the University of Sydney in Australia since 1988 and before that in Singapore and New Zealand. I had travelled and made many friends in the southern hemisphere. Now, after nearly twenty years away, I was ready to come home to Canada. By one of those fortunate happenstances that come along once or twice in a lifetime I found myself invited to make another long journey – this time to the Arctic, about as far away from Australia as it is possible to get. I had expressed an interest in the new Akitsiraq Law School being established in Iqaluit, Nunavut, and had been asked to consider becoming the northern director. This school was a unique experiment in higher education for Aboriginal students. It was designed to provide a full bachelor of law program for a small group of Inuit students in their own Territory of Nunavut. I dithered a bit but soon realized that this was an offer I could not refuse. After a long telephone conversation with the first northern director, Andrejs Berzins, I decided to get on a plane.

I landed in Iqaluit on a bright sunny day in early July 2001. My first impression was one of surprise and confusion. I felt as if I had landed on an alien planet and was suddenly seized with a palpable sense of strangeness. The airport terminal was a bright yellow building crowded with people coming and going. Most of them seemed to know each other, whereas I felt like a lost stranger – which of course is exactly what I was. Somewhere between

Vancouver and Iqaluit, my luggage had gone missing. The people from First Air were very friendly and assured me it would "turn up." I discovered that I had already missed my first meeting with the chief judge of the Nunavut Court of Justice, Beverley Browne. I realized I was no longer in control of my own destiny and had to resign myself to whatever might come up. I was soon rescued, however, by Gwen Healey of the law school, who proved a cheerful and knowledgeable tour guide. We went on a brief drive around town, enjoying the summer sun. Although not Inuk, Gwen had been raised in Iqaluit and told me she loved it. It was home for her and the best place on Earth!

Iqaluit struck me from the first as a place of contrasts – beauty and ramshackle poverty side by side in disorderly neighbourliness. There was not a real tree in sight, of course, as we were well above the treeline, although still a bit south of the Arctic Circle. The ice had drifted out of Frobisher Bay a few days before, leaving a glittering expanse of blue quickly sinking into the muddy bottom of the massive tide retreating down the bay. People, mostly

1.3 View of icicles from the Akitsiraq classroom at Nunavut College, looking toward Inukshuk High School, Iqaluit

Inuit, were walking around in shirt sleeves despite the fact that the temperature was about the same as a cool winter day in Sydney, which I had just left. There were smiles and friendly hellos wherever we went. The hillsides and ditches were glowing with a rush of Arctic flowers whose names I did not yet know. The sky was a pale blue, the main street was dusty and busy, and every other road was a nameless dirt track (there was no pavement or street names then) spiralling off into the hilly town dotted with wooden houses and ending abruptly in tundra. Government buildings and schools ranged from Inuit-inspired modern design to something that someone must have imagined would have been suitable for a settlement on the moon.

Iqaluit means "many fish" in Inuktitut. It has been the site of Indigenous settlements for hundreds, perhaps thousands, of years. Back in the 1950s Iqaluit (then called Frobisher Bay) expanded its southern population rapidly with the building of a large airbase, hotels, and housing as the Arctic was militarized during the Cold War. Frobisher Bay became part of the DEW Line, or Distant Early Warning system, which tracked the possibility of armed nuclear bombers or missiles heading over the North Pole from the Soviet Union. By the early part of the twenty-first century Iqaluit was still in transition from a small remote community to the "big city" and capital of the new Territory of Nunavut, or "Our Land." Although much has changed since 2001, the city remains an uncomfortable mixture of proud capital and remote northern community.

I met many friendly and interesting people on that first visit, including many of the future law students, with whom I had a rather awkward coffee at Fantasy Palace, then the local version of Starbucks. I stayed an extra week, moving in with Andrejs and Lorraine Berzins, who were welcoming and extremely helpful. I became enthusiastically involved in the start-up of Akitsiraq, which was due to take in a cohort of students in September. I attended a student orientation and welcoming dinner and soon felt very much a part of the team.

But it took a long while for that sense of strangeness to wear off. Like most *qallunaat*, I had little experience and less knowledge of almost everything north of the 49th parallel. I had once briefly visited Alaska and Yukon (where I got married – a story for another time), but that was the extent of my northern exposure. I had not known what to expect of Nunavut, and in many ways I still don't. Was I embarking on a great adventure, or was I simply going north to help Inuit students learn Canadian law? Was this a career-building move, or was I just trying to return home to Canada from Australia the long way round? In fact, I was about to start on a steep learning curve of my own.

One memory that haunted me those first few weeks in Nunavut was that of my father. He had travelled briefly in the Arctic as a young radio officer for the Royal Canadian Air Force (RCAF) in the early 1950s. He was there when the original DEW Line was built in Frobisher Bay as well as at the big US airbase in Thule, Greenland, a smaller RCAF base in Resolute Bay, and other points ringing the Arctic Circle. His flight crew's particular job was to fly over Davis Strait and Baffin Bay in order to check ice conditions for supply ships coming into Thule Air Base as it was being built.

Thule is now under the authority of Denmark, although a tiny US Air Force contingent still remains. The massive, beautiful site is now virtually a ghost town. The Inuit, or Inughuit ("great people"), who used to live in the

1.4  Flight officer Robert E.S. Wright, RCAF station, Greenwood, Nova Scotia, 1950

area were relocated north to Qaanaaq in 1953 to make way for the base. I don't remember my father talking about his experiences there, but somehow his spirit was with me wherever I went in the North. During my first week I travelled on an ATV to a spot above Iqaluit where a lot of the old military base equipment still sits rusting into the tundra. The spot commands a magnificent view of Frobisher Bay and the Sylvia Grinnell River. Like the rusting cans and wires, the names are foreign and the intrusion not particularly welcome in this beautiful ancient land.

Canada began a major push during the early years of the Cold War to protect its sovereignty in the North, partly by moving Inuit around in a massive relocation project that still evokes bitter memories of betrayal and starvation in the North. The old ways were actively and sometimes forcibly discouraged by Canadian government officials and "experts" as Inuit were moved into permanent settlements, dogs were shot by the Royal Canadian Mounted Police (RCMP) under circumstances still controversial to this day, and children were taken away to boarding (residential) schools sometimes many thousands of miles from home. Tuberculosis grew to epidemic proportions, and many Inuit children and adults spent years away from their families in southern sanitariums and hospitals. Many never returned. Inuit traditionally only have one name. They were forced to take second names during Project Surname in the late 1960s and had already been issued numbers on "dog tags," which were used to identify them for government purposes. The fox-trapping industry had collapsed in the 1930s and 1940s, and this one source of income disappeared. Families began collecting children's allowances and welfare, as wage labour was scarce.

Conditions of life in the Arctic remain fraught with serious social and economic problems. Poverty levels are high, as are the associated evils of substance abuse, suicide, early deaths from accident and disease, family violence, homelessness, and dislocation. A colleague of my father who flew with him on those Arctic missions remembers vaguely the government's decision to relocate families to the High Arctic, but neither he nor my father was probably aware of the suffering this experiment caused, just as I was unaware of contemporary problems when I first flew to Nunavut. Unlike my father, I was there long enough to learn more.

The Akitsiraq Law School enrolled seventeen students in 2001 and 2002 in an attempt to meet the need for professionally trained Inuit lawyers in Nunavut as well as to fulfil the requirement for Inuit employment under the

*Nunavut Land Claims Agreement* of 1993.[12] "Akitsiraqvik" means "where one strikes out a wrong – the place where justice is done." There is a specific site in south Baffin Island, a circle of stones near Cape Dorset, that was used up to the early 1920s by Inuit in the area for deciding the most serious cases according to their own law. Few now know exactly where it is. The modern program was taught at Nunavut Arctic College in Iqaluit and offered a full four-year law degree from the University of Victoria in British Columbia. The program was co-managed by the university's Faculty of Law and by the Akitsiraq Law School Society, which was my immediate employer. Almost all of the students were Inuit from many parts of the Arctic, including one young student from Iglulik who, although not ethnically an Inuk, was fluent in Inuktitut and had been raised in the community just like the other kids. The students were mostly women ranging in age from their early twenties to their forties. Most were parents and one was a grandmother. Our lone male graduate was an RCMP constable who later served in Kandahar, Afghanistan, for eighteen months. Not all spoke Inuktitut fluently, although most could at least understand their language even if they were not yet quite comfortable speaking it. Some had lived most of their lives outside of the North and had only recently returned to Nunavut. One was a talented artist and sealskin fashion designer from Greenland who had lived in Iqaluit for many years, whereas others arrived from Nunavik and from Arviat in the Kivilliq region on the western shore of Hudson Bay with little or no experience of life in Iqaluit.

Not all succeeded in becoming lawyers, but in the end eleven students graduated with their bachelor of law degree from the University of Victoria. Graduation day in Iqaluit was 21 June 2005 – National Aboriginal Day in Canada – and it was a memorable and emotional event. Everyone was there, from Governor General Adrienne Clarkson and her husband, John Ralston Saul, to Premier Paul Okalik, our elder-in-residence, Lucien Ukaliannuk, and the chief judge of the Nunavut Court of Justice, Beverley Browne. Akitsiraq graduate Lillian Aglukark's sister Susan sang the national anthem. Professor Ukaliannuk and Judge Browne were granted honorary doctorates of law from the University of Victoria. It seemed like almost everyone in Nunavut had been invited, along with many dignitaries from the South, to celebrate the successful completion of the Akitsiraq program. We made the CBC news program *The National,* and even George Stroumboulopoulos on his talk show, *The Hour*, commented that sometimes the world really does need more lawyers!

But even during such a happy occasion the dark side of life in the North was not far from the surface. A young cousin of one of the graduates was found to have hanged himself the next morning after breaking into the Anglican Church. Alcohol at the graduation dinner played a role in spoiling the occasion for others. One student remained in Ottawa out of fear of a potentially violent spouse, and the governor general's security team was alerted by the university about other potential problems. After it was all over, and I had dropped off former Supreme Court justice Claire L'Heureux Dubé at the airport, a friend of mine and I hugged each other in the parking lot. We didn't know whether to weep for joy over the triumph of the students or in grief for the young life senselessly lost a few days before.

Since the nineteenth century Inuit have had to adapt to changes that have come with the newcomers from the South – from us. These changes have involved all aspects of their lives – cultural, environmental, political, economic, social, spiritual, and personal. This has been especially true for the three generations born since the Second World War. Warming temperatures and melting ice are only the latest in this series of changes. But climate change may be the biggest challenge of all. Not only do Inuit have to adapt to the effects of colonization in the Arctic; now the very foundation of their way of life is disappearing from beneath their feet. For Inuit, not only does *sikuvut nunguliqtuq* ("our ice is vanishing") mean changes to the environment; it also means the opening of the Arctic to greater penetration by southern mining, oil and gas, and other commercial interests. It means that sovereignty has become a hot topic of discussion in which Inuit are not always included. It means a new militarization of the Arctic over which Inuit themselves may have little control. The Arctic in all its complexity, both natural and human, is mutating into something that will affect Inuit and everyone else in ways we cannot foresee. *Sikuvut nunguliqtuq* is a message of deep change at every level. I have no doubt that Inuit will adapt and survive, just as they have in the past. But, as witnessed in 2012 by a young Inuit researcher from Nunatsiavut in Labrador, "As Inuit our lives are tied to nature and for that we have a great respect for mother nature's strength. The land, the sea, and the climate define us as a culture, and our culture will forever be altered because of the changes we are undergoing today."[13]

There are many books and articles dealing with climate change, the history of the Arctic, sovereignty, the Northwest Passage, European exploration, and Inuit. Inuit themselves have also shared their stories. Many of these books, films, and websites are listed in the Bibliography. This book is an attempt to tie some of these threads together into a human history of the Arctic, particularly the eastern Arctic of Nunavut and Greenland, in words and pictures. My purpose is to put questions of climate change, Arctic sovereignty, and economic development within the deeper context of northern history and Inuit life.

In this book I have relied on a variety of sources – traditional, scientific, legal, political, historical (both oral and written), cinematic, visual, spiritual, and personal. I draw on my own experience wherever it is relevant, as well as on the stories, anecdotes, and information I learned directly from both Inuit and non-Inuit northerners. I have included photographs that I took while in the Arctic to give the reader a visual sense of what I experienced, as well as a few archival photographs and the occasional map or chart. I have also included stories about people who played a role in Arctic history. Some of these stories are of people who are still alive, some are of those who have passed away, and some are of people who might be seen as mythical or partly mythical. For the most part these stories are not mine – I am merely passing on what others have told me or what is recounted elsewhere. I have tried wherever possible to obtain permission to tell personal stories or show photographs of people. Some of the archival images may portray people whose descendants are still alive today. My apologies for not being able to identify some of them more specifically. Of course I cannot speak for Inuit or even for those *qallunaat* who have spent their lives working and living in the Arctic. I was there only for a few brief years and since then have returned every year or two for visits. Nevertheless, I feel I have a story to tell about the Arctic and the people who live there that is unique. In some ways this is my own attempt to lay a few ghosts to rest.

The chapters in this book are meant to follow a more or less chronological order, from the origins and history of the Inuit in chapter 2 to both European and Inuit exploration of the Arctic in chapters 3 and 4. This is followed by a discussion of Canadian and Inuit sovereignty in chapter 5. Chapter 6 discusses two of the most troubling episodes in any history of the Arctic: the relocation of Inuit families to places sometimes thousands of miles from their homes and the removal of children to residential schools, both resulting in terrible suffering. Chapter 7 looks at the creation of Nunavut and the contemporary history of the Canadian Arctic. Chapter 8 returns to the major theme of climate change from both an Inuit and a non-Inuit perspective. In chapter 9 I try to draw some of these threads together by focusing on the great iconic image of climate change, *nanuq* (the polar bear). Finally I try to provide some concluding observations about my own experience and what I believe is the much underrated significance of not only climate change in the Arctic but also cultural, economic, and political change for Inuit.

We are all tiny specks on a solitary blue planet circling one ordinary star in a universe of stars. This truth becomes very clear in the Arctic. There is an earthbound yet almost unworldly beauty in the North that can be overwhelming. Transparent air and endless summer days of low-angle light bring out colours and shadows as clearly as if they had never been seen before. When the daylight shortens into the darkness of winter there are long slow sunrises and sunsets of brilliant warm colour and translucent twilight beauty. The tundra in summer is like a pillowy green garden thick with moss, heather, flowers, and ground-hugging willows only inches high. Labrador tea sends up spicy wafts of scent as you walk. As August melts into September the tundra garden turns red and gold, rich with blueberries, crowberries, cranberries, and *aqpiit* (cloud berries). Winter creates a world of white splendour and intense cold silence.

Perhaps it is the treeless expanse of winter white or the deep blue of the summer Arctic Ocean beneath a massive sky that creates this sense of awe. I remember sitting on the beach in midsummer at midnight in Pond Inlet watching the sun circle the sky in a slow spiral that never touched the horizon. I have also watched the full moon slowly tracking around the great darkness of January in Iglulik, again never setting. At times it felt as if I might suddenly take flight so great was the feeling of almost limitless space. I have gone for walks on spring days in April when the ice and snow glow with brilliant blue white and the air is so crisp and clean it feels like cold silk. And I have sat in my apartment in Iqaluit fearing the roof would come off in a winter blizzard. I have been fortunate enough to see walrus and polar bears, ring seals and bowhead whales, Arctic terns and lemmings in their natural environment. I was also lucky in getting to know many Inuit and learning a little about their culture and history. What I learned is completely foreign to most of my fellow Canadian citizens. This book is my attempt to open a door to the Arctic in the hope of providing some insight into the lives of Inuit, the impact of climate change, and the demands that Canada has made and is still making on both the people and the environment of the North.

The ice is melting. A way of life that has existed for thousands of years is changing so rapidly that there is no precedent in either geological or human timescales. Arctic life has always been about the need to respect and adapt to the vagaries of cold, wind, ice, snow, land, and sea. But it is not just Inuit who have to contend with these changes. What happens in the Arctic will change the world for all of us.

I

Iceberg, Croker Bay

Meeka Mike looks on while Qaunaq Mikkigak of Cape Dorset lights
the ceremonial *qulliq* (stone lamp)

4
Old grave marker for Constable Victor Maisonneuve, Dundas Harbour

3 (*Opposite*)
Pangnirtung looking toward Auyuittuq

Abandoned RCMP post, Dundas Harbour

6
*Inuksuk*, Iqaluit

*Aupilaktunnguat* (purple saxifrage), the territorial flower of Nunavut, Pond Inlet

9
Young polar bear, Croker Bay

8 (*Opposite*)
Iceberg, Davis Strait

Matthew Nuqingaq drum dancing as Aaju Peter looks on, Thule site, Dundas Harbour

# 2

# Iglulik: The Place Where There Is a House

It was only because my mother and father went through many hardships that we survived. They only survived because they followed the *maligait* [laws] of the Inuit ... If they hadn't followed the *maligait*, our lives would have been more difficult.

Mariano Aupilaarjuk[1]

## Origins

Although my home was in Iqaluit and most of my time was spent there, I soon realized it was necessary to get out to the smaller communities in order to better understand life in the North. I spent much of my spare time travelling around the Arctic, either on my own or with groups of likeminded travellers. After leaving Iqaluit in August 2005 and moving to British Columbia I tried to maintain contact with the Arctic partly through e-mail and social networking, but also through visits and travel north. In January 2006 I went on a very special visit with a small group of women to the community of Iglulik, located on an island between northwestern Baffin Island and the mainland. It was organized by Carol Heppenstall of Adventure Canada, a company I have travelled with frequently. January is not usually considered a good time to visit the Arctic, but I wanted to experience twenty-four-hour darkness and to celebrate the return of the sun after nearly two months of night. For me it was also a way of overcoming homesickness for the North, although I had never been to this particular place before.

Iglulik consists of about 1,500 people and is about 70° north latitude – well above the Arctic Circle. The hamlet itself was first established by missionaries in the early twentieth century, although the Inuit and those who

2.1 Inside an *igluvijaq* (snow house) looking up, Iglulik

came before them have lived in this area for thousands of years. Inuit of North Baffin Island were encouraged, and in some cases coerced, into moving into the settlement and others like it. Iglulik is known as a centre of Inuit culture and history as well as of scientific research into wildlife. The oral history of the Iglulingmiut ("the people who live in the place where there is a house") is old and rich. Examples of these stories, based on real events in Inuit history, have been shared with the global community through the films of Isuma Productions, based in Iglulik, including the award-winning trilogy of *Atanarjuat: The Fast Runner*, *The Journals of Knud Rasmussen*, and *Before Tomorrow*.[2] The second of these films portrays an encounter between the famous Danish-Greenlandic explorer and anthropologist Knud Rasmussen and Awa, the great shaman of North Baffin, in the early twentieth century. It also shows how Christianity affected the lives of Awa's family and other Inuit in the area, propelling them into the new settlement.

Although some evidence of human occupation going back 25,000 years has been discovered in Siberia and Yukon, there is little or no sign of human occupation of the North American Arctic until about 7,000 years ago. From about that time a wave or waves of small groups of both Inuit and Aleut peoples moved from eastern Siberia to western Alaska. Some moved back to the Russian side of the Bering Strait, where they still live today as Russian Yupiit. Others spread out around Alaska. The Aleuts moved to the long chain of islands separating the Bering Sea from the Pacific Ocean, whereas others moved north. These more northerly groups divided into two cultural groups, each very similar – Yupiit and Iñupiat – both essentially Inuit. Some of these people then travelled across the Arctic beginning about 4,000 years ago. According to Renée Fossett, the first group were "similar in many ways to the people of Siberia's Chukchi Peninsula ... By 1900 BCE they had established themselves along the mainland coasts of Coronation Gulf and Foxe Basin, on most of the Arctic islands, and in northern Greenland. By 1600 BCE they occupied the Labrador coast as far south as Nain. Archeologists, noting their exquisitely crafted microblade technology, which distinguishes them from earlier and later peoples, gave them the name Arctic Small Tool tradition."[3]

Beginning around 2,700 years ago, there was a significant cooling of the Arctic that radically altered living conditions. Another group, known in archaeological circles as the "Dorset culture" or among Inuit as the Tuniit ("the first peoples," "inhabitants before the Inuit," or "beast-like men who lived here before the Inuit"), also travelled east from Alaska from about 500 BC. Pre-existing technologies such as the bow and arrow and the use of dogs seem to have disappeared. The Tuniit developed new technologies such as snow houses and the use of iron and copper. The population of the eastern Arctic decreased during a period of global cooling. About 1,500 years later, around AD 900, the climate again changed, becoming warmer. The Thule people (as archaeologists call the ancestors of modern Inuit) were sophisticated marine mammal hunters based in northeastern Siberia or northwestern Alaska (the exact location is controversial). Beginning about 1,000 to 800 years ago, they moved eastward from Alaska to Greenland and then south to the Hudson Bay region, northern Quebec, and Labrador. These ancestors of the present-day Inuit of Canada and Greenland had redeveloped efficient technologies such as the use of dogs and the *qamutik* (dogsled), the kayak, and the *umiaq* (boat) for hunting and travel on water, as well as the *kakivak* (barbed harpoon head) for fishing and whaling. They quickly spread throughout the Arctic, from far northwestern Greenland to the southern caribou-hunting grounds around Hudson Bay, adapting to regional variations.

Their journey may have been made in several small family groups who followed the changing migration patterns of whales and other animals caused by the warming Arctic Ocean. However, contrary to this gradualist history, it is now suggested that one or more groups swept quickly across the top of the continent from west to east about 800 years ago in less than a decade – perhaps in only two or three years. Robert McGhee suggests that Inuit may have become aware of meteoric iron that had plummeted to Earth in western Greenland[4] or of the use made by Tuniit of volcanic iron in the Disko Bay area, also in western Greenland. The modern-day Inuit remember the Tuniit well, describing them as a large slow people who were also able to run very fast.

The Thule may also have learned about iron implements, especially knives, acquired by the Tuniit in trade with Greenlandic Norse. The Norse were well settled in southern and western Greenland by AD 1200. They may also have had trading posts on Baffin Island. This theory is supported by the archaeological work of Dr Patricia Sutherland:

[I]n October and November 2012, it was reported that archaeologist Patricia Sutherland, adjunct professor of archeology at Memorial University in Newfoundland and a research fellow at the University of Aberdeen in Scotland, had announced new archaeological evidence strongly supporting the presence of a second Viking outpost on Baffin Island.

Sutherland was alerted to the possibility of a Norse camp in 1999, when she discovered two unusual pieces of cord excavated from a Baffin Island site by an earlier archaeologist and stored at the Canadian Museum of Civilization in Gatineau, Quebec, where she worked.

Rather than consisting of twisted animal sinew, the cords were expertly woven Viking yarn identical to yarn produced by Viking women in Greenland in the 14th century.

Sutherland scoured other museums, finding more pieces of Viking yarn and a small trove of previously overlooked Viking gear including wooden tally sticks for recording trade transactions and dozens of Viking whetstones.

The specimens derived from four sites located across a thousand miles of territory extending from northern Baffin Island to northern Labrador. The sites belonged to the Dorset culture, an extinct Paleo-Eskimo people.[5]

The Dorset people, Sutherland says, wore traditional clothing made from hides, whereas the Norse were known to fashion textiles and objects from spun materials. The presence of the cordage artifacts, spun from the hairs of Arctic hare, fox, and dog, has led Sutherland to suggest that the Tuniit may have had more contact with the Norse Greenlanders than previously thought. Some academic theories have the Dorset people disappearing from the Arctic by the eleventh century, but Sutherland believes that the presence of the cordage suggests that the Dorset people survived longer, well after the period of the arrival of the Norse in Greenland in the late tenth century.[6]

Sutherland's work has been featured in *National Geographic*[7] and *Maclean's Magazine*[8] as well as in the documentary film *The Norse: An Arctic Mystery*, which aired as an episode of David Suzuki's television program *The Nature of Things*.[9] If her discoveries and conclusions are correct, much of early Arctic history will need to be reconsidered, especially that related to Indigenous-European contact.[10] However, her efforts to continue her work have been thwarted by the Canadian Museum of History (formerly the Canadian Museum of Civilization), from which she was dismissed in April 2012 for reasons that are very unclear. Her husband, Robert McGhee, one of the world's most eminent Arctic scholars, was also stripped of his emeritus status, which he had held since his retirement from the museum in 2008.[11] There is a possibility that preventing Dr Sutherland from accessing her findings and continuing her work is politically motivated. Some politicians may believe that evidence of long-term contact between Indigenous peoples and the Vikings on what is now Canadian territory may pose a threat to Canadian sovereignty. This is of course nonsense. There is no threat to Canadian sovereignty over land in the Arctic, with one minor exception. What happened to Dr Sutherland fits a pattern of federal government behaviour toward publicly funded science in Canada in the past few years that is very disturbing.[12]

Another interesting theory explaining the outward expansion of the Thule culture is proposed by filmmakers Tom Radford and Niobe Thompson in their documentary *Inuit Odyssey*.[13] They suggest that the expansion was caused by the combination of a rapidly growing population in the Thule homeland in Siberia (partly due to a warmer climate) and the disturbance of East Asian iron-trading routes as a result of the spread of Genghis Khan and the Mongols into China by 1215. This forced the Inuit to find new hunting grounds and the iron ore necessary for their tools, harpoon heads, and especially knives. The Inuit appear to have been both extremely resourceful and, according to Thompson, quite aggressive. Thompson alleges they were in fact a military people who massacred their way across the North, wiping out Tuniit and Greenlanders as they went! Other evidence suggests a much more complex and less bloody history. However, the capacity for news to travel back and forth across the High Arctic does suggest the existence of well-established travel routes by the time Inuit moved east.

## Oral History

The oral histories of the Inuit recount stories of journeys across thousands of miles of land and sea, as well as through the earth, into the air, and under the sea. The adventures of a great shaman such as Kiviuq (whom we will hear more about later) are closely mirrored in the stories of historical shamans and leaders such as Qitdlarssuaq (the Great Qillaq), who travelled from South Baffin to far northwestern Greenland in the nineteenth century, and the famous shaman Awa, who lived in North Baffin Island nearly one hundred years ago and whose descendants live there still. Atanarjuat, the subject of the film of the same name, is a heroic figure who escaped danger and travelled widely, encountering shamans and the spirit world. This man is said to have lived in the area of Baffin Island about 800 years ago. The mythical and the real intersect. It is necessary to pay attention to the echoes of these stories in the wide reach of Inuit history. Through the teachings of elders, the work of filmmakers like Zacharias Kunuk, Madeleine Ivalu, and John Houston, and the written records of travellers such as Knud Rasmussen, the ancient stories of the Inuit are still remembered. These stories are often complex, dramatic, and confronting.

    Throughout the circumpolar region the Inuit have a great story about the creation of the sun and moon, which, although varying from region to region, has strong common themes and characters. The sun is known by Inuit across the Arctic as a woman, Siqiniq, and the moon as her brother, Taqqiq. I and the group of women I was travelling with in January 2006 heard one version of this story in Iglulik (appropriate to our visit to celebrate the return of the sun) as told by Mary Qulitalik, an elder in the community. A similar version was told by George Kappianaq, also of Iglulik, and recounted in John MacDonald's *The Arctic Sky: Inuit Astronomy, Star Lore, and Legend*:

> At this time they would regularly hold festivities in the *qaggiq* (a large igloo built for feasts and ceremonies). While these celebrations were in progress, a person the sister did not recognize, would sometimes come into her birthing place and extinguish the light of her *qulliq* (stone lamp). This person would then fight and fondle her but she never knew who he was. Knowing she would be handled in this manner again, she devised a way to discover the identity of her visitor. So, during the next celebration, she blackened her nose with soot from her cooking pot and waited.
>
> She was sewing or mending something when she suddenly heard a noise and all at once her lamp was extinguished and again she was fondled. Shortly afterwards the aggressor returned to the *qaggiq* and she could hear laughter coming from that direction for the soot on the man's nose had been noticed. She put her boots on and, despite the taboo she was under, having recently given birth, went outside to see who the molester might be. It was her brother, her own flesh and blood. She was devastated by this revelation. In despair she entered the *qaggiq* and exposing one of her breasts through the hood opening of her *amautiq* (women's parka), severed it and offered it to her brother saying "*Tamarmik mamaqtugalunga una niriguk* (I think all of me is tasty so eat this too)."
>
> After she had said these words she took some moss, dipped it in the oil of the *qulliq* and, having lit it, ran outside. Her brother did the same and pursued his sister round the *qaggiq*. The flame on his moss soon went out but his sister's continued to burn brightly and so the chase around the *qaggiq* went on until eventually they both started to ascend into the heavens where she became the Sun and her brother the Moon. It is said that Brother Moon can be seen at night smoldering.[14]

In Arviat on the west coast of Hudson Bay another version of this story has been recorded in a children's book in which various traditional stories have been gathered, translated, and illustrated by the elder Mark Kalluak:

A very long time ago, two pitiful young children, a brother and sister, were abandoned by their parents. They walked for a long time, hoping to find other people. Finally, one night, they saw lights from iglus [houses] flickering on the edge of darkness. They were tired and exhausted, but the children pressed on, stopping only to rest. At last, they neared the lights. The qulliqs burned so brightly that their light drew the children towards them. Eventually, the brother and sister reached the entrance of the iglu and waited to see how the people inside would receive them.

The iglu the pitiful brother and sister entered was a large qaggi (iglu hall), where drum dances and other activities were held. When the people inside noticed the brother and sister, they offered them food. In the qaggi, older men and women, as well as young men and women, had been getting ready to play games after a drum dance.

The brother and sister soon joined everyone in the kissing game – a game where people would snuff out the qulliqs light and walk around and kiss each other in the dark. The young girl decided to find out who she was kissing the most. So she went to the cooking hearth and smeared her nose with black soot from a dead ember.

Then the girl lit her maniq (moss) lamp and went around looking at every face in the qaggi and the adjoining iglus to find out who she had given the most kisses to. After examining each face, the girl realized her brother's nose was the only one darkened with soot. She knew this meant he was the only person she had been kissing during the game. She was so embarrassed that she began rushing from face to face around the qaggi. Gradually, she began to float off the ground and rise into the sky above, all the while she held her maniq lamp in her hand.

When her brother discovered his sister had floated up into the air, he also lit a lamp and gradually floated off the ground in the same way and went up into the sky to follow his sister. The young girl looked back and saw that her brother had almost caught up to her. So she turned to him and blew his flame out, leaving it no more than a soft, glowing, red cinder. But her flame still burned brightly because it had not been blown out.

The pitiful young brother and sister remained in the sky ever since. The brother, with his soft glowing light, became the moon and the sister, with her lamp still brightly lit, became the sun. This is the story Inuit believe and tell about the origin of the moon and the sun.[15]

On one level the two versions of this story might be interpreted as a warning against incest or a lesson about the perils that orphans face. Earth and sky can both be affected by the neglect of family obligations or the breaking of rules. But it resonates at a much deeper level. The tragic imagery of the story matches the darkness of the long winter night. From late November to the middle of January in Iglulik is what the Inuit call *tauvikjuak* ("the great darkness"). Farther north the months of darkness last even longer. As the sun first reappears on the southern horizon after the long winter night, you see a bloody red dome glowing briefly above the flatness of the sea ice. It is as if the sister's severed breast lies briefly before us in the distance until it mysteriously winks out and is gone. It is an illusion – a refraction of Siqiniq's lamp from below Earth's horizon – a trick of the sun's light. Soon Siqiniq shyly appears, a slim golden crescent, and then disappears. She will show more of herself from day to day until in a few weeks she sails fully above the horizon. In the twilight before dawn, the sea ice is deep blue-grey, and the first shadows are long and dim. By noon during the week before the sun returns, the sky is washed with tints of deep cobalt blue and rosy pink. The horizon glows with haunting lavender light that reflects off the snow. The stark world of winter darkness in black and white softens to purple shadows. The snow blooms with the returning light into pastels of pink and mauve. The sky begins to turn from darkness to an opalescent violet blue. Meanwhile Taqqiq slowly creeps around the sky, never setting, his sad white pockmarked face a witness yet again to the return of his sister, whom he can never catch.

The country around Iglulik is mainly flat and surrounded by ice that, during a few brief months in the summer, melts into seawater. By November the frozen sea ice used to be hard enough to travel on, but now it can be unsafe until January. During the winter months the snowy land and ice are indistinguishably connected. Inuit have long lived on the ice during the win-

2.2 Midnight at midsummer in Pond Inlet

ter and spring to take advantage of fishing, seal hunting, or harvesting other marine mammals. During the summer they traditionally migrate inland to look for caribou or take small boats out to the ice floes to hunt for walrus. The film *Before Tomorrow* gives us a glimpse of what that life was like just as European whalers and explorers began infiltrating the area. The spring, summer, and autumn are a brief glorious interlude of sunshine, sudden squally rain storms, and a garden of tundra flowers that quickly turns to the red and gold of autumn-ripe berries. During winter, although the sun may be absent, the sky is still alive with the moon, stars, and (rarely) the northern lights (Iglulik is north of the latitudes where the aurora borealis is most spectacular).

Iglulik has kept a number of traditions associated with the disappearance and return of the sun. Certain games such as cat's cradle should not be played during the long darkness due to the belief that the sun might get tangled up in the strings, delaying her return. The first sunrise in mid-January is celebrated with traditional ceremonies involving the whole community. Children who first see the sunrise must smile only on the left side of their faces, signalling a conditional welcome. Although the sun's return means the worst of the long darkness is over, the cold of winter will continue for many more months. Stone lamps, called *qulliit*, are extinguished, given a new wick and oil, and then relit. Songs greeting the return of the sun are sung.

The Inuit of Canada, as well as of Greenland, northern Alaska, and northeastern Siberia, share many common traditions. These include the Inuit language (with regional dialects), technologies developed to survive in the harshest environment on Earth, and a long culture of resilience and practical innovations developed over at least 7,000 years. Vikings from Norway and Iceland also settled on the fringes of the Arctic during the early Middle Ages, but it was the Inuit who had the skills to survive. Although new waves of Europeans followed, they did not arrive again in significant numbers until the latter part of the twentieth century.

## Modern Elders

There are still elders who remember what it was like to grow up on the land while learning the old skills as they had been passed on for generations, although as time goes by this treasury of knowledge is disappearing. The elder-in-residence of the Akitsiraq Law School, Lucien Ukaliannuk, was born on the land at the end of *tauvikjuak* near Iglulik – probably in an *igluvijaq* (snow house) or *qarmaq* (sod house). He had just one day of formal schooling, but was nevertheless fluent in both spoken and written Inuktitut at a sophisticated level. He had worked with the Igloolik Research Centre before moving to Iqaluit and joining the Law School.

Ensuring that Inuit traditional law and the Inuktitut language were properly integrated into the Akitsiraq curriculum was my first major challenge. The students made it very clear that advanced language skills and culture had to be included. I interpreted this as a test – part of my initiation – and, with the help of Aaju Peter (one of the students), managed to engage Ukaliannuk to teach Inuktitut. It was purely a lucky chance that he was available. From his first day with Akitsiraq it was clear that we had found a wonderful source of knowledge and wisdom. When I asked what their first class with Ukaliannuk was like, the students said "awesome"! However, finding annual funding and housing for him and his family remained an ongoing issue. There was also some controversy over making sure the students weren't expected to learn Inuktitut and Inuit traditional law as "extras" on top of their other law courses; rather the timetable had to ensure that these courses were included in the overall course load they carried. It was something no Canadian law school had tried before. I remain proud that we were able to hire and retain at least one elder of such distinction. Lucien Ukaliannuk eventually became our elder-in-residence and, at the instigation of then deputy minister of justice Nora Sanders, went on to perform a similar role for the Government of Nunavut's Department of Justice.

The role of Inuit elders and leaders has become significantly more difficult as explorers, missionaries, Arctic "experts," and other *qallunaat* have travelled north and insisted on implementing ideas that are often ill-suited to the realities of Inuit and northern life. Where good ideas have been tried, there has been a history of failure to follow through on workable solutions to northern problems. Lack of consistent year-to-year funding, the constant circulation of transient southerners like myself, and inattention by people in the South are often reasons why good solutions get left behind. Patterns of colonial thinking continue despite efforts toward Inuit self-government and northern-based strategies. As the Arctic ice melts, Canada's fragile claim to national authority over the waters of the Arctic Archipelago is subject to greater challenges and increased threats from maritime powers in the United States, Europe, and Asia. In the meantime the Inuit who inhabit these regions must engage with the wider national and global community to protect their homeland. In April 2009 the Inuit of the entire circumpolar region, known as Nunaat, responded to the continuing failure of national governments to consult with and respect their views by adopting a statement regarding Inuit sovereignty in the Arctic (see appendix 1).[16] The Inuit of Nunavut have agreed to accept Canadian sovereignty over their land, but they expect their national leaders and fellow citizens to respect their knowledge and historic presence. It is through the teaching of elders that this knowledge is shared.

There are a number of projects in Nunavut that are designed to record and preserve the knowledge of elders for future generations. One of these is the Tusaqtuut Core Indigenous Knowledge Project, organized by Meeka Mike of Iqaluit. It is an award-winning endeavour not only to record the knowledge of elders from the South Baffin region but also to give them an opportunity to travel and talk to non-Inuit about what they know and can share with people in the South about their traditional knowledge, as they did in 2010 at a seminar hosted by the Arctic Institute of North America in Calgary.[17]

Incorporating the teachings of elders in all areas of northern projects is essential. Ukaliannuk taught the Akitsiraq students advanced Inuktitut language classes as well as three semesters of Inuit traditional law from 2003 to 2005. I sat in on many of the traditional law classes. He taught entirely in Inuktitut, so for those of us who couldn't speak the language, one or more of the students would translate. This led to many fascinating discussions about the meaning of words and about the differences between Inuit and European concepts and culture. I remember one discussion in which Ukaliannuk was asked whether there was any word for "punishment" in Inuktitut. He couldn't think of such a word, nor could anyone else. Instead he stressed that the purpose of dealing with harmful conduct in traditional Inuit society was to help the wrongdoers accept responsibility for their actions and to reintegrate them back into the community. Elders play a central role in teaching and advising. Ukaliannuk gave us examples of this in his own classes and through his presence at the Law School. He was the real uncle of one of the students, but seemed like everyone else's adopted uncle or father. Sometimes it seemed he could read minds!

Indigenous and non-Indigenous education more generally needs the help of elders like him. The road forward for all of us must always have its roots in the past. Elders are living libraries of traditional teaching – about how to be human according to worldviews very different from those of us from the South. But elders are much more than this. Like Ukaliannuk they can be a centre of calm and wisdom, of respect and perspective. Many Inuit laws that we learned in his classes emphasize the connection between all things, both material and spiritual. At times these laws reminded me of Buddhist teachings about the "middle way." Ukaliannuk himself was not perfect – he was as human as we all are. But his humanity helped him to help us. Lucien passed away not long after the students graduated. I and they miss him sadly.

## Language

I tried to learn some Inuktitut while in Iqaluit and have learned a little more since. While I was working at Nunavut Arctic College my teacher was Mick Mallon – a veteran of Inuktitut language training in the North. Mick has a

2.3 Lucien Ukaliannuk with Akitsiraq students (from left to right) Susan Enuaraq, Aaju Peter, Lillian Aglukark, and Connie Merkosak after a visit with Governor General Adrienne Clarkson and John Ralston Saul at Rideau Hall, Ottawa

broad Northern Irish accent and would occasionally speak Inuktitut like an Inuk from Belfast! Inuktitut is very different from European languages. Filmmaker John Houston, who is also fluent in Inuktitut, has described it as like Lego. It consists of syllables that you put together to form words and phrases – what is known in linguistic theory as a polysynthetic language. I struggled in vain to learn much, although I did gain a love for the sound of the language and the few words or phrases I can recognize and speak. During the graduation ceremony I had the honour of introducing Professor Ukaliannuk and did my best to include some Inuktitut. I saw nodding heads among some of my students and members of the audience, so I think I managed to make myself understood!

Inuit (i.e., Inuktitut and Inuinnaqtun) is now one of the three official languages of Nunavut, along with English and French, under Nunavut's *Official Languages Act*.[18] Inuktitut is spoken by a majority of Inuit living in Nunavut. There is however a fear that the heavy influence of English media like television, radio, the Internet, and video games is undermining the survival of the language. Although 85 per cent of Nunavummiut ("people who live in Nunavut") are Inuit, only about 65 per cent speak Inuktitut at home. This is a 12 per cent decline over ten years and is mainly attributed to the very high number of young Inuit under age twenty-five.[19] Although children can go to school in Inuktitut up to grade 4, after that they must switch to an English or French curriculum. There is both radio and television programming available in Inuktitut, but this is often overwhelmed by the dominance of English-language media beamed in by satellite.

The sophistication of the language may also be declining. Elders may not want to teach words to younger Inuit that are more appropriate to a traditional culture, and young people who speak Inuktitut often use it in a more limited way than previous generations did. In addition some Anglicized phrases are creeping in. For example, Inuit have their own calendar of months, but they also now use our calendar. The names of our months in Inuktitut are based on English: *jaannuari* (January), *viivvuari* (February), *maatsi* (March), *iipuri* (April), and so on. Inuit also have their own numbers but often use numbers borrowed from English: *uan* (one), *tuu* (two), *talii* (three), and so on. The Inuktitut words are *atausiq* (one), *marruuk* (two), *pingasut* (three), and so on. The Inuktitut word for the Canadian Broadcasting Corporation is Siipiisiikkut ("the CBC thing")! Nevertheless, Inuit still have one of the strongest Indigenous languages in North America and are determined to protect it.

Ways of thinking are determined by language use. Once a language is lost, much of the cultural richness expressed by that language, as well as the perspective of its speakers, is also lost. Inuktitut words indicating thought, knowledge, wisdom, and mind reflect this. The name of the film and television company Isuma Productions comes from the Inuktitut word for "thought" or "wisdom," *isuma*. Hugh Brody, who was also taught Inuktitut by Mick Mallon, has talked about the wide meaning of this word in the context of the Inuit belief that children learn and develop at their own pace. Inuit believe that human development is innate, that each of us is hardwired to grow and learn in a particular way. Elders like Ukaliannuk teach patiently with an awareness of each individual's own ability to absorb and learn. This is very different from the more pressured way in which children and adults are expected to learn and think in *qallunaat* society. Ukaliannuk's presence at our Law School did much to mitigate the pressure-cooker demands of legal training in an environment that was highly visible to a sometimes critical outside world.

Hugh Brody says,

In Inuktitut, there is a linguistic indication of this faith in the extent to which human potential is hard-wired. When a person experiences extreme grief, he might say *"Isumaga asiujuq."* "My *isuma* is lost; I am out of my mind" ... And in many conversations I heard *"Isumatuin-narpunga,"* "I just thought," a caveat that conveys the sense of the English "It's only my opinion." The root *isuma* has many uses; they show it to be something that also has an independent existence. In Inuktitut, thought is tightly linked to the capacity to think.

... The place of thinking in Inuit ideas of psychological development, and the related ways in which the word *isuma* is used, offer many clues about Inuit society. Parents identify children with respected elders, trust children to know what they need, do not seek to manipulate who children are or what children say they want. This way of treating children tends to secure confidence and mental health. And Inuit child raising is inseparable from many aspects of interpersonal behaviour. Adults respect one another as separate but equal. This is the basis for cooperation – by respecting individual skills, judgments, and knowledge, the strengths of the economy and the social order are shared. *Isuma* is the notion that underlies and unites many of these features of Inuit life, for it affirms that in crucial ways the development of *isuma* is independent of social manipulation and control. Embedded in this use of the word for mind is a view of mind itself.[20]

There are other words in Inuktitut for "thinking," "thought," "wisdom," or "knowledge." The root word *qau* (knowledge) leads to *qauq* (forehead), *qaumajuq* ("it is light or illuminated"), *qaujijuq* ("he/she knows or is conscious of"), *qaujimaji* ("one who is in a state of knowing, a guide, a guru or pilot"),[21] and Inuit Qaujimajatuqangit ("what Inuit elders have always known and will always know"), or simply Inuit Traditional Knowledge. This last phrase forms the basis of Nunavut's philosophy – to keep the knowledge of the elders alive and to pass it on to others. Most people shorten the phrase to "IQ."

A final word for "wisdom" or "mind" is *sila*, which can also mean "air" or "atmosphere," "weather" or "the outdoors" – "the environment." Mind, knowledge, wisdom, and the capacity to think as well as light, air, and the environment are all connected through root words in Inuktitut. Inuit elders, land, environment, and relationships are all part of an intricate web of life and awareness. This interconnectedness is reflected in the structure of the language itself.

## Names

The connections in Inuit language and culture also extend over time. Not only are elders traditionally respected and their knowledge passed on from one generation to the next, but people's names are also passed on in a way unique to Inuit culture. The Inuit naming system depends on *sauniq*, the Inuktitut word for "bone." People who share the same *atiq* (name) are of the same "bone," the same spirit, and have a special relationship. As John Bennett and Susan Rowley discuss in their book *Uqalurait: An Oral History of Nunavut*, "Three essential parts made a human in the Inuit view; body, soul, and name. A nameless child was not fully human; giving it a name, whether before or after birth, made it whole. Inuit did not have family surnames. Instead, each person's name linked him or her to a deceased relative or family friend."[22]

Names are not gendered. Ukaliannuk, for example, was named after his grandmother. When a name is passed on to a child, the spirit of the namesake passes with it. It is something like reincarnation, but not quite. A person's soul is not passed on; rather it is the spirit or character of the person that passes with the name. Armand Tagoona says, "An Inuk believes that when you name your child after the dead one, then the dead one lives again in the name, and the spirit of the dead one has a body again."[23] Usually a name is passed from someone who is already deceased or close to death. A name may be shared among many people, all of whom also share a relationship with each other. When Inuit are close to death, they often ask that their name be passed to a newborn baby or to a child about to be born. Names need not be of relations but may also come from friends. The passing on of names has occurred over many generations for hundreds, perhaps thousands, of years. Each time a name is passed from one person to the next, the spirit belonging to the name passes with it.

In the 1940s the Government of Canada decided that Inuit names were too complicated for bureaucratic purposes. Inuit were given leather tags with numbers on them for identification – like dog tags. They were required to carry these with them wherever they went. Some elderly Inuit, especially carvers, still use their tag numbers as an informal identity. Name tags did not affect the traditional naming practices. When Inuit were forced to take a second or family name during Project Surname (after 1969) their long tradition of naming was in danger of being disturbed. Most Inuit during this time were given their father's name as their surname, and almost all Inuit today have at least two names – a given name and a patrilineal family name. This completely goes against Inuit culture, which does not automatically pass down fathers' or mothers' names.

The tradition of passing down names extends to the nature of the relationship between the deceased and others in the family or community. If a child is named after his grandmother he becomes in a way his own grandmother. Other Inuit will refer to him according to their own relationship with the deceased grandmother. Since Inuit often refer to each other by the relationship they have with each other (as calling someone by his or her given name can seem disrespectful or may even be forbidden), a baby boy may find himself being called *anaana* (mother) by his own parent, aunts, and uncles – everyone who was a child of his grandmother! Alexina Kublu explained this in more detail to Valerie Alia:

> I am my *paniq*'s *atatukulu* [daughter's stepfather]. My *paniq*'s my grandmother ... My grandmother is my *paniq*, which is "daughter." I'm her *atatukulu* because I'm named after her stepfather. Her biological father was lost out at sea when she was a baby, so she never knew her father. The only father she knew was Kublu and so, to her, he was her father. My younger daughter calls me *irniq* (son), and I in turn, call her *atatta* (father).
>
> Some people call me Apak and it's through Apak that she's my *atatta*. And through Apak that I'm her *irniq*. But first of all, I was always going to be Kublu because my *atiq* (namesake) died before I was born ... and so my family knew who I was going to be, I was born already about to be Kublu, so when I became born, so naturally I became Kublu.[24]

As Alexina's husband, Mick Mallon, says, "Kublu and I are fellow old men. I'm an old man because I've reached that stage all on my own. Kublu started life as an old man, because she is her own great-grandfather."[25]

Children who are named after someone of the opposite sex may find themselves treated as if they were of that sex, at least for a while. One of my Akitsiraq students told me she was raised as a boy until she was eight or nine years old. If a girl is named after someone who was a great hunter, she herself may become a hunter, as this is part of her *atiq*.

Naming helps with grief when someone has died – that person lives on in some sense in the child named after him or her. A name is sometimes revealed through dreams, and it often used to be the midwife (the first person to hold a child) who would name the baby. Although Inuit now have surnames their given names are still frequently passed on in the traditional way as the *atiq* of a deceased person. Inuit still believe that they take on the character or spirit of their namesake. So seriously do Inuit take naming that one man at least was willing to go to court to regain his name. Kiviaq was named Peter Ward after his family moved to Edmonton. He was given a birth certificate with that name on it. He successfully petitioned the Alberta government to restore his one true name in 2001. He was also Canada's first Inuit lawyer, a Golden Gloves champion boxer, and the first "real Eskimo" to play for the Edmonton Eskimos football team![26]

Names connect Inuit to others living today, to the dead, and to the unborn who are to come. They create a network of relationships through time that links all those who bear the same name and are of the same *sauniq*. In a sense each person is all the people who have ever borne their name. As was said by Maniilaq to Knud Rasmussen nearly a century ago, "I was held up solely by names. It is because of names that we breathe, and it is also because of them that we can walk on our legs … Through all these names I have grown old. I have withstood the attacks of shamans and all the dangers that would otherwise have uprooted me from the dwelling places of man."[27]

## The Mother of the Sea

When I began my job as northern director of the Akitsiraq Law School in January 2003, I came from Australia, where the temperature was +30° Celsius, to the cold of midwinter, where it was -30° with a wind chill 15 or 20°

colder. Walking from the plane to the terminal was an unnerving experience. The words "what am I doing here?" did float briefly through my mind. After moving into my apartment above a frozen Frobisher Bay, I remember looking out my window toward the horizon. A glimmer of sun was just disappearing behind the southern hills across the bay. It was still early afternoon. As when standing on the shores of Iglulik in January a few years later, I could see the sun's red breast blooming over a misty icebound sea. Land and ice merged into one frozen world of warm colour. But beneath that frozen stillness there was and is a living world of ocean – the sea that is central to the life of the region and all its inhabitants.

There is another great story known throughout the Arctic that I learned about soon after I arrived in Iqaluit. This is the story of the Inuit Mother of the Sea, known in South Baffin as Sedna or Talelayu. She has many other names. Perhaps the oldest and most beautiful is Nuliajuk ("she is a wife").[28] Her different names are really titles used in order to avoid saying her true name directly. This might be perceived as disrespectful or even dangerous. The elders tell different versions of her story. In some she is a disobedient young woman who refuses to marry, so her father curses her and she is married to a *qimmiq* (dog) who has transformed into a man. She runs away with him to an island where they have several children. Those who looked like dogs became *qallunaat* – white people. Those who looked more like humans became *allait* or *iqqiliit* – Indians.

> Our ancestors said she lived in Qikiqtaarjuk ["big island"]. This is at the point at Iglulik which used to be an island on its own. Her father's dog ended up as her husband. At night he would come in human form but he still had his fangs. Whenever he would come, it was always with a new white caribou skin. She became pregnant, and when she gave birth, some were dogs and some were humans. The ones that were in human form were *iqqiliit*. They started walking inland and they became the ancestors of the Indians. She put the ones that were more dog-like into an old *kamik* [boot] sole and she made it grow. The *kamik* sole floated away. When it got to a deep area – you can usually tell which is the deep area because it is dark water – it turned into a ship. You know the pictures of ships where the stern portion is higher; that is the kind of ship it became. After they had gone further and further out, you could hear the sound of metal and there were humans

walking around. They had become *qallunaat*. They went out past Iglulik through the strait. This is what I have heard of *Uinigumasuittuq* ["the one who didn't want a husband"]. I heard this story from my father who heard it from the people that lived before.[29]

Inuit were not surprised when they first met Europeans, assuming they had come home to their place of birth.

In other stories Nuliajuk falls in love with a man who has beautiful long black hair and turns out to be a raven. This is the version of the story that I heard in Iqaluit. She goes with him to an island where she becomes his wife. In some versions of this story her father comes in his boat to rescue her from the island; in others he forces her to leave her husband and family. While paddling away they are sometimes attacked by a fulmar, a sea bird, who creates a violent storm that threatens to overturn her father's boat. In other versions it is the raven who chases her and tries to bring her back by creating a powerful wind. In all stories the father is frightened by the storm and tries to save himself by throwing his daughter overboard. She clings desperately to the side of the boat, but her father cuts off her fingertips with his knife. She still hangs on, so he cuts off her fingers to the second joint. Then the third joint. Then her hands. And finally her arms to the elbows. Eventually she falls to the ocean floor. There she still lives in a house guarded by a dog, and her fingers, hands, and arms have transformed into all the creatures of the sea. She is their mother and their guardian. As the shaman Awa told Knud Rasmussen, "Should the hunting fail at any season, causing a dearth of meat, then it is the business of the *Angakoq* (shaman) to seek out the Mistress of the Sea and persuade her to release some of the creatures she is holding back ... He remains in meditation for a while, and then invokes his helping spirits ... to find a passage opening of itself for [his] journey down under the earth to the sea."[30]

The story of Nuliajuk reflects how important the animals of the sea are to Inuit. They are traditionally a people who hunt marine mammals, relying mainly on seals but also on walrus, polar bears, narwhal, belugas, and great bowhead whales. Without these marine mammals the Inuit could not have survived. Some Inuit, particularly those who hunt on the Barren Grounds of the mainland west of Hudson Bay, rely mainly on caribou. But for most Inuit the animals of the sea are their principal resource. These marine mammals form an integrated ecosystem centred on sea and ice. Ring seals give birth to their pups on the spring ice, where polar bears and humans hunt them. Walrus dig with their tusks for clams in the shallow seas of the Arctic, sunning themselves on floating ice in the spring and summer. Narwhal and belugas herd at the floe edge as the sea ice melts, and the great bowhead whales circle Baffin Island throughout the year. Without the annual advance and retreat of the ice, this ancient panorama of life may well come to an end.

In another sense the story of Nuliajuk is another great creation myth. Inuit recognize their interrelationship across the Arctic, and they have carried their creation stories with them in their travels. On one level they acknowledge their origins in Siberia and Alaska, but on another they embrace their ancient obligations to the Mother of the Sea, who (in one version) lived on an island near Iglulik. I learned to be careful about using that word "myth" to describe her. While I was discussing her resemblance to other goddesses and transformation myths of the northern hemisphere at dinner one night, an Inuk friend of mine interrupted me: "She is real, I have seen her!"

The world of the Arctic in winter still seems solid from horizon to horizon. Our tiny bubble of houses, roads, and cars – civilization – clings to the

2.4 Walrus mother and pup, Croker Bay

edge. But that winter stability is becoming deceptive. Those fragile signs of civilization are proving to be a destructive force. The ice is melting and we are all at risk. The creation story of the sun and moon tells a tale of betrayal, tragedy, loss, and renewal. Some elders believe that Earth itself has shifted and that this is what is causing the ice to melt. Some say Siqiniq is rising in a different place and that she is hotter than before. Nuliajuk is the great female power of Inuit religion. As the ice melts and the Arctic changes, she may withhold her gifts. The Inuit, who depend on her generosity for their livelihood, no longer have shamans who can travel to the bottom of the sea to plead with her. Most have given up the old ways for the one God of Christianity. But Inuit have a curious way of adapting, of blending old with new. Nuliajuk is making a comeback, and the vision of the world she represents has never really disappeared. Can she survive global warming? Or the political and economic demands made by outsiders? Not only her world, but also our world, may depend on the answers to these questions.

# 3

# The Northwest Passage

Ah, for just one time I would take the Northwest Passage
To find the hand of Franklin reaching for the Beaufort Sea;
Tracing one warm line through a land so wide and savage
And make a Northwest Passage to the sea.

Stan Rogers[1]

## Greenland Dreaming

When I was at the University of Alberta in the early 1970s, I had no real idea what the world had to offer or what I wanted. Like most middle-class North American kids of that era, I fell in love, avoided thinking about future career choices, and (this being the 1970s) experimented rather nervously with drugs, alcohol, sex, and politics (not necessarily in that order). I had no clear academic direction other than a love for language, literature, and history as well as a keen interest in avoiding the unemployment line for a while. I took courses in creative writing, the history of the English language, and Anglo-Saxon literature (learning *The Dream of the Rood* and parts of *Beowulf* by heart), as well as a class on the Old Norse sagas. These courses were partly inspired by J.R.R. Tolkien's *Lord of the Rings* – a book on everyone's reading list at that time. But perhaps it was also due to a longing for narrative roots, for the cultural heritage and language I might have acquired from the northern European countries where my ancestors had lived for generations, and that they had eventually left. I wrote poetry for Douglas Barbour's class and kept a literary journal for my other first-year creative writing teacher, W.O. Mitchell, who, on one magical never-to-be-forgotten day, read out my efforts in class (it was much funnier in his voice – something about God, evolution, and swimming pools). In my second creative writing course, taught by the wonderful teacher and writer Rudy Wiebe, I wrote a long fictional narrative about Vikings in Greenland. I remember it involved a fair amount of research. I don't recall much about the story, other than the ending. As the last Norse settler lies in his hut dying of starvation and cold, he looks toward the open door and sees the shadow of another human being – the round face and short silhouette of a *skraelling*, the Norse word for "savage." Then the image fades and the story ends. The mood I was aiming for was of fear and despair. From the Norse perspective, *skraellings* were rarely encountered, and the encounters were mostly bloody. But from the perspective of the Inuk peering into the hut, it might have been a story of help or rescue or perhaps just curiosity. My imagination did not yet see the Inuit as active participants in the story I was telling.

Perhaps that was because at the time I was still immersed in a mindset that identified human agency with European exploration and colonization, where Indigenous people were part of the background being "discovered." But human beings have been exploring, settling, adapting to, and altering Earth's diversity of geography and climate for tens of thousands of years. We are all descended from a very small group of humans living in southern Africa. From there, people moved outward to colonize the planet. What makes us most human – language, culture, art, sophisticated tool making, religion, domestication of other animals – only began about 80,000 to 50,000 years ago, when the last great glacial period was at its coldest and the exodus from Africa had begun. From a tiny pool of human survivors struggling with drought in Africa (perhaps descended from a single mother), our *Homo sapiens* ancestors populated Earth, driving earlier hominid relatives such as *Homo erectus and Homo neanderthalensis* out of Eurasia.[2] However, not all encounters were destructive. There is now DNA evidence pointing to interbreeding between humans and Neanderthals in the Middle East, where these two species coexisted for probably about 50,000 years.[3] Descendants of these hybrids then travelled to Europe, Asia, and beyond. It would appear that all non-African humans have inherited about 1 to 4 per cent of our genes from Neanderthals.[4] When the last glacial period began, there were at least three species of hominids sharing the planet with humans like us (*Homo erectus*, *Homo floresiensis*, and our near cousins *Homo neanderthalensis*). By the end we were alone.

## People of the Ice

For most of the history of human migration out of Africa, North America and Eurasia were locked under sheets of ice miles thick. The timing of the first migration of humans to North America is contentious, with proponents arguing for dates anywhere between 60,000 and 11,000 years ago – although many Indigenous peoples of America dispute a distant origin or migration altogether. The most widely accepted theory until recently was that humans first made their way south from the Beringia land bridge between Siberia and Alaska about 13,000 years ago as the ice melted. These people (known as the Clovis culture after the town in New Mexico where the first artifacts were found) are believed to have been fast-travelling and aggressive big-game hunters who quickly exterminated most of the large mammals of the western hemisphere and then, unaccountably, disappeared.[5]

This theory seems to me to be highly implausible given the behaviour of most contemporary hunting cultures, such as the Inuit, who have strict traditional rules about protection of animals. Ancient cultures could not have survived their travels through Eurasia to North America with such a "slash and burn" mentality. I think a better interpretation of the evidence suggests a series of migrations beginning sometime between 30,000 and 20,000 years ago. This view is based on the oldest archaeological sites in Siberia and North America – possibly including Yukon, dating to about 25,000 years ago; Meadowcroft Rockshelter, Pennsylvania, dating to about 14,250 years ago; and Monte Verde, southern Chile, dating to about 12,500 years ago – as well as more recent linguistic and DNA evidence.[6] Other theories suggest that some humans may have travelled by sea, skirting the coasts of Asia, North America, or even Europe while living off the rich marine life found on the ice floe edge. Beginning about 7,000 years ago, people certainly did travel this way across the Arctic, from Siberia to Greenland, hunting marine mammals such as seals, walrus, and whales as they went.

There have been significant changes to Earth's climate during these migrations, forcing humans to adapt or move on. Over the past 1,000 years or so, the most recent of these changes (before our own time) created more challenges for people over large parts of the globe. At first there was a warming of global temperatures in what is called the Medieval Warm Period (AD 900–1300).[7] This was followed by a drop in temperatures that began about AD 1300 and ended sometime around the middle of the nineteenth century.

This period of colder conditions is known as the Little Ice Age. Although not as severe as glacial conditions, cold temperatures and aridity again put human ingenuity and capacity for expansion to the test. In some parts of the world (principally Europe and Asia), temperatures rose between 1 and 2° Celsius during the Medieval Warm Period, creating conditions for rapid human development during the High Middle Ages in Europe, Asia, and elsewhere. This included expansion of agriculture, cities, and populations. Other parts of the world were swept by droughts that lasted for generations and destroyed whole civilizations, such as the Anasazi of southwestern America and the Mayan city-states of Central America. Beginning in about 1315, heavy rains and long periods of cold devastated Europe and other parts of the northern hemisphere. This was especially severe in the late seventeenth century, when the Thames in London regularly froze over. Alpine glaciers advanced and Arctic climatic conditions were very severe. The climate shifts between warm and cold over the past millennium propelled revolutions in agriculture, urban living, art, science, and exploration.[8]

## Tuniit, Thule, and Eric the Red

Between about AD 1000 and 1400, two new groups of migrants and one long-term resident met intermittently in the Eastern Arctic – the Thule people (ancestors of modern Inuit), the Vikings, and the Tuniit. Inuit oral history describes the Tuniit as shy and distrustful of strangers. They had lived in the Arctic for at least 2,000 years before the arrival of either Vikings or Thule people. The enigmatic Tuniit seem to have disappeared sometime after AD 1200, apparently unable to compete with the incoming Inuit or perhaps overcome by other causes. No one really knows. As Ivaluardjuk told Knud Rasmussen nearly a century ago, "The *Tuniit* were a strong people, and yet they were driven from their villages by others who were more numerous, by many people of great ancestors; but so greatly did they love their country, that when they were leaving Uglit [islands in the Foxe Basin], there was a man who, out of desperate love for his village, struck the rocks with his harpoon and made the stones fly about like bits of ice."[9] The Tuniit also play a role in stories as a "race of bestial or beast-like men who were said to have inhabited Inuit country before the Inuit came. These people were said to run down game on foot and kill by breaking the animal's neck and carrying it

home over their shoulders (immensely strong) and were also said to live in
whale-bone houses and to sleep with their feet up in the air so as to make
them light of foot or fleet (incredibly fast runners)."[10] Some Inuit today suggest that the Tuniit survived until very recently on Southampton Island in
northern Hudson Bay as a group called Sadlermiut. Others suggest that they
established trading relations with the Vikings for walrus ivory in return for
metal. The most widely accepted story suggests they were then wiped out
by incoming Inuit. Since the Inuit remember both pushing Tuniit out of settlements as well as living peacefully as distant neighbours, I suspect the history is more complicated. It is possible that Inuit and Tuniit intermarried or
adopted children from their different communities. Skills such as *igluvijaq*
(snow house) building may have been taught to the Inuit by Tuniit as the
climate began to cool around AD 1300. The "disappearance" of the Tuniit
may have been simply a matter of absorption into Inuit culture. It also appears from Inuit oral history that the Thule people took over many Tuniit
communities in a manner that leads to some uncomfortable questions about
the nature of colonization:

> Despite all of their complexity, though, Tuniit stories challenge con-
> temporary audiences with their unsettling resemblance to the very colo-
> nial rhetoric and mimetic strategies that have been inflicted upon
> contemporary Inuit. Yet to shy away from the problematic or "colo-
> nial" aspects of Tuniit stories is to play into the idea that pre-colonial
> Indigenous societies were peaceful utopias, without their own complex
> histories of political conflicts and alliances. And this, I would argue,
> amounts to yet another erasure of Indigenous politics. We should be
> cautious, however, about constructing an unproblematized comparison
> between Inuit and European colonizers … Unlike the Europeans, Inuit
> were not extracting resources from the new territory to support the
> economy of a distant motherland.[11]

I suggest that the introduction of European diseases by the Vikings may
have also played a role. If the Tuniit did trade with the Norse, they may well
have contracted diseases such as smallpox, measles, or other pathogens,
which then spread to Tuniit communities farther away. Given the role that
disease played in drastically reducing other Indigenous cultures that came

into contact with Europeans, it is possible that the Tuniit may well have at least partly succumbed to alien bacteria and viruses brought by Norse explorers and traders. Although there is no direct evidence for this theory, I suggest that it fits with other known European-Indigenous contact histories, including in the Arctic during the nineteenth and twentieth centuries.[12]

The Norse Vikings arrived by way of Iceland. Eric the Red ("the Red" likely referring more to his bloody reputation as a brawler and killer than to the colour of his hair) was banished from Iceland after being involved in a blood feud that led to murder. He sailed west and bumped into a large landmass – Greenland. Despite his banishment he returned to Iceland three years later to organize and lead a large expedition of Norse settlers to a land that he gave the attractive name "green," in contrast to the discouraging "ice" of his homeland. Public relations were important even then as more Norse arrived from Norway and Iceland. From AD 982 to 986, when Eric founded his new colony, the Medieval Warm Period was in full swing, and temperatures across the northern hemisphere were warmer than they are now, although not by much. Greenland really was partly green around the edges, as it is increasingly becoming today. It was warm enough to graze sheep and cattle, do some farming, and support two fairly extensive settlements of Norse, who survived for at least another 400 years: the Eastern Settlement, where Eric set up; and the Western Settlement, near the present-day capital, Nuuk. Eric's son Leif and other adventurous men and women went on to explore Baffin Island and Labrador. A small settlement was established at L'Anse aux Meadows in northern Newfoundland.[13] It is also possible that trading posts were set up elsewhere, such as on Baffin Island near what is now Kimmirut. Trade goods travelled as far south and west as New England and the Mississippi Valley as well as into the central Arctic, although it still remains unclear how deeply the Norse themselves penetrated the continent.

One of the earliest appearances that any North American Indigenous people make in European histories is contained in the *Historia Norvegiae*, a brief account of Norway's history that may have been written in the early thirteenth century. The only manuscript we have of it is dated to about AD 1500. There is only one cryptic reference to *skraellings*: "This country [Greenland], which was discovered, settled and confirmed in the universal faith by Icelanders, is the western boundary of Europe, almost touching the

African islands where the waters of ocean flood in. Beyond the Greenlanders some manikins have been found by hunters, who call them Skraellings. Weapon wounds inflicted on them from which they will survive grow white without bleeding, but if they are mortal the blood hardly ceases flowing. But they lack iron completely: they use whales' teeth [narwhal or walrus tusks] for missiles, sharp stones for knives."[14]

The earliest written record we have of any meeting between Greenland Vikings and Indigenous peoples is contained in the *Graenlendinga Saga* and *Eirik's Saga*, both from the late thirteenth century. These two sagas record violent confrontations between Viking settlers and Indigenous people in Labrador and Newfoundland at the time the Norse first colonized Greenland and then set out to explore neighbouring lands. It is very unclear which group of Indigenous people the *skraellings* were in these stories. The Indigenous peoples described as arriving in skin boats from farther along the coast may have been Inuit, although Thule people probably did not arrive as far south as Labrador and Newfoundland until 200 years after the time when these events are supposed to have occurred. Could they have been Tuniit? Others who appeared out of the forest may have been Beothuk, an Indigenous group in Newfoundland later wiped out by incoming Europeans between 1500 and 1850. The people arriving by skin boats (whoever they were) had driven the Vikings out of their settlement at L'Anse aux Meadows in Newfoundland by the middle of the eleventh century. Surviving accounts by the Inuit of western Greenland tell a similar story of violence and misunderstanding, but there are also hints of a friendlier relationship. Inuit arriving in the Nuuk region of Greenland were curious about these strangers. One of the most haunting of the old stories, as recorded by Henrik Rink in the mid-nineteenth century, has echoes of my own imagined tale:

A kayaker one day went to the bay of Iminguit to catch thong-seals [bearded seals]. Arriving there he observed a tent belonging to some *Kavdlunait* (Norse Greenlanders). He heard them jesting and prating inside, and was strongly minded to go and look in upon them. Accordingly he left his kayak, went up to the place, and began to strike on the sides of the tent. This made them apprehensive, and they now became quiet, which only encouraged him to continue all the more, until he succeeded in silencing them altogether. Then he took a peep in at them, and behold! they were all dead with fear.[15]

These brief tantalizing accounts leave much unsaid. But it is obvious that meetings between Inuit and Europeans were not usually peaceful, unless a less dramatic trading relationship may have developed in northwestern Greenland or on Baffin Island. Ivory from walrus tusks was a main source of export income for the Greenlanders in their trade with Europe and could have been most easily obtained in exchange for iron tools or weapons with either Tuniit or Inuit (although the *Graenlendinga Saga* makes it clear that the trade of weapons was discouraged).

By the mid to late fifteenth century, the Norse had disappeared from Greenland – or rather they had lost contact with Europe, and whatever happened to them is not recorded. They were likely the victims of a drop in temperature that resulted in shorter cooler summers, colder winters, and increased pack ice – the Little Ice Age. The Norse settlers may have been unable to adapt to the changing climate. Their reliance on cattle and sheep may also have been their undoing – even now during a warming period almost all sheep fodder in Greenland has to be imported.[16] Once the animals died, people were forced to live off whatever the land and sea could give them. Doing so would have become very difficult as summer seasons shortened and winter ice spread. Vikings, a farming people, simply did not have the knowledge or technology to survive as hunter-gatherers in such an extreme climate. Papal records of 1345 indicate that Greenlanders were excused from paying tithes because of poverty. But Greenlanders may also have died out from imported diseases. The plague, or Black Death, spread throughout Eurasia from the 1340s onward and may well have reached the remnants of Greenland society by one of the last European ships, although there is no record of this. An isolated and marginal population such as the Greenlanders would have had even less resistance to a new disease such as bubonic plague than did their cousins in Europe, one-third of whom died from this disease. Other pathogens such as those responsible for smallpox, influenza, typhus, and even venereal diseases could have killed many already vulnerable people, especially the very young and the very old.

It is also possible the settlers came under attack. In the past the theory was that Inuit were responsible for this aggression, but it may well have been North Atlantic pirates, mainly from England, who began to penetrate deep into the North at this time while looking for rich fishing grounds. They may have raided the most southerly Eastern Settlement after 1400, carrying off essential food and supplies, kidnapping or killing individuals, and terrorizing the local population (the more northerly Western Settlement was found abandoned around 1350 – again the reason is not known). Inuit oral history indicates that a few Norse were taken in and sheltered by Inuit, but there is no evidence through DNA sampling or other methods that indicates a large-scale migration of Norse into Inuit society through intermarriage.

The last clear record of the Greenlanders' existence is from a ship that left Greenland in 1410, bringing news back to Europe of a witch who had been burned at the stake for driving some poor victim mad through diabolical means. More happily, there was also news of a marriage. After that, there is nothing but silence. There is some archaeological indication that the Greenlanders in the southernmost colony may have continued on for nearly another century. Just as Christopher Columbus was sailing west in search of Asia – finding America instead – the last of the Greenlanders disappeared. When the Norwegian-Danish missionary Hans Egede arrived in Greenland in 1721, he was surprised to find no European survivors. He began a successful Christian missionary effort among the Inuit of Greenland, establishing both the Lutheran Church and Danish governmental authority there. The modern Danish presence in Greenland traces back to Egede's arrival and establishment of Christian Danish authority among the Kalaallit (Greenlandic Inuit) near what is now the capital, Nuuk. Norway attempted to re-establish claims to eastern Greenland in the 1930s but was not successful.[17]

There is a probably apocryphal story that when the English explorer Martin Frobisher landed on the rocky shore of Greenland in 1576, he discovered the body of a recently deceased European man. The remains of a stone hut stood nearby. Could the last Greenlander have died within days or even hours of the next wave of European exploration? We simply do not know. Their final days are a complete mystery.

# Martin Frobisher

Iqaluit, the modern-day capital of Nunavut, has been inhabited by a number of Inuit communities for at least the past 800 years. Up until the cooling of temperatures that began around AD 1300, the first Inuit lived in small villages and hunted marine mammals, including seals, walrus, and whales. Tuniit may also have lived in the area – they certainly did farther south near Cape Dorset and northwest near Iglulik. The region at the head of Frobisher

3.1 The first European map of the Arctic based on the travels of Martin Frobisher (1576-78) and John Davis (1585-87) by Gerard Mercator, *Septentrionalium terrarum descriptio*, 1613. People in Europe believed for centuries that the North Pole was a temperate region of open water – hence the abiding myth of a navigable Northwest Passage from Europe to Asia (and perhaps a self-fulfilling prophecy).

Bay is also a rich fishing ground – hence the name Iqaluit, meaning "many fish." But migration routes began to change as the Arctic cooled and the pack ice increased. The early Inuit again became more mobile. They began to live in portable skin houses or tents during the summer and in more permanent *qarmait* (sod houses) and *igluvijait* (snow houses) in the winter, facilitating easy movement over a wide territory. The area around what is now Frobisher Bay was and has remained rich in marine life as well as land resources such as caribou, birds, eggs, berries, and mosses – although the caribou have become very scarce in recent years.

In mid-July 1576 Inuit and Europeans again met. The people of South Baffin Island may or may not have had contact with Norse Greenlanders, but they may have been aware of the existence of the strangers and their disappearance a century earlier through contact with Tuniit or their Greenlandic cousins. The Inuit are great travellers and tellers of tales. Their oral histories stretch back over hundreds or even thousands of years. Stories about Inuit-European contact going back to the arrival of Martin Frobisher in that long-ago summer of 1576 still survive among elders in the Iqaluit area, just as there are stories related to first contact in other parts of the Arctic.

A single English ship sailed into Frobisher Bay near modern-day Iqaluit one summer day. A small party of strange men put a small boat over the side and rowed to a rocky island. They climbed to the top of the island to look around. A group of hunters approached cautiously to see what these strangers were up to. The appearance of the Europeans must have been surprising – they were bearded, fair-skinned, and fair-haired, almost like ghosts, wore clothes that were clearly unsuitable for the weather, and spoke an incomprehensible language. The hunters were spotted from the height above by the *qallunaat* ("big eyebrows") and were no doubt as much of a shock to the English as the latter were to the Inuit. The quiet approach of the hunters was interpreted by the strangers as an attempt at an ambush. A little convoy of kayaks then appeared, causing immediate concern to the English. Mutual misunderstanding characterized European and Inuit contact from the beginning. A meeting was however arranged, and some exchange of gifts took place.

But over the next two days a series of mishaps resulted in the disappearance of five English sailors and the kidnapping of one of the Inuit. As early as 25 August the weather began to worsen, with ice closing in. This was in the depths of the Little Ice Age, when long cold winters and short unpredictable summers were the norm. Captain Frobisher pulled up anchor and sailed back to England without recovering his missing men and without finding anything of value (although when he returned to England he claimed there was gold). He was also no closer to discovering the fabled Northwest Passage from the Atlantic to the Pacific and the riches of Asia. He did take his captive with him, but the Inuk died soon after being taken ashore in London. Frobisher returned the following summer and set up a mining operation on an island in Frobisher Bay in a futile endeavour to take what he called "black gold" back to his commercial sponsors in Elizabethan London. The "black gold" turned out to be useless rocks of no value. The tons of black rock Frobisher brought back went to build walls and roads in England. Some of it can still be seen. Meanwhile Sir Martin went from disgraced explorer to knighted champion of English freedom through his naval actions against the Spanish Armada in 1588.

Frobisher was one of many explorers who, over the next 400 years, would sail to the Arctic Archipelago in search of a passage through to the East Indies, or at least in hopes of finding the wealth that might come from whale oil, sealskins, fox and other furs, precious metals, and (more recently) gemstones, minerals, and oil and gas. Frobisher did not at first realize he was in a bay with no exit. Most subsequent explorers sailed up Davis Strait between Greenland and Baffin Island, approaching the main entrance to the various northwest passages through Lancaster Sound above Bylot Island. A few explorers would attempt the route through the Bering Sea from west to east over the top of Alaska. There were also attempts to find a northeast passage over Russia and Siberia. The most recent attempts, such as the voyages of nuclear submarines, have traversed the Arctic Ocean under the North Pole, avoiding the islands and the passages between them altogether.

The Inuit of the bay named after that first explorer, Martin Frobisher, can still retell stories passed on to them from previous generations about their ancestors' meeting with *qallunaat* more than 400 years ago:

During the first meeting, the Inuit were just in awe. The *qallunaat* came with their huge ship. The Inuit themselves had only sealskin boats ... They had never seen a ship. They had never heard a shot.

Right away, there were some conflicts. Because they weren't Inuit. When the ship was spotted, the Inuit took their kayaks and went to meet the ship ... The *qallunaat* fired two warning shots in the air ...

So when they met there was a lot of uncertainty. The Inuit were scared. They didn't want to give in to these people because they didn't know what they were. Because they weren't quite Inuit. And their clothes – how they dressed! The Inuit dressed in sealskin or caribou skins. The *qallunaat* looked so different. They were different beings. The Inuit had never seen clothes like that. Eventually we decided the first explorers basically were dressed in rags. This was partly because we knew their clothes would never protect them from the cold ... They were ghostly.[18]

## Rule Britannia

Over the next three centuries the British launched a prolonged search for the Northwest Passage. Their own stubborn arrogance in insisting on sailing in wooden ships with too many men and inadequate supplies remained a problem long after it should have been obvious that this was wrongheaded, if not suicidal. Another problem was the severely cold climatic conditions of the Little Ice Age, which created impossible barriers of ice, storms, freezing cold, and more ice. The Europeans were not aware that they had chosen the worst possible time to find the Northwest Passage and continued throwing men and ships into the Arctic until the latter half of the nineteenth century, when global warming was actually making such a transit feasible.

After the defeat of Napoleon and the end of war in Europe in 1815, thousands of ships, officers, and men of the British Navy were left idle. The second secretary to the Admiralty, John Barrow, came up with an ambitious plan to keep at least some of the best in active service through exploration. Barrow became obsessed with the possibility of finding and exploring a northwest passage that would connect Europe (specifically Great Britain) with China, Southeast Asia, and Britain's great Asian conquest, India. From 1818 to 1875 no fewer than twenty separate expeditions to the Arctic were sent out by the Admiralty. Other expeditions were also sent to other parts of the world, including West Africa and Antarctica, and there were several attempts by other nations and private adventurers to find a passage between the Atlantic and the Pacific. Whalers also explored these waters in the search for bowhead, sperm, finback, and blue whales. But the British Navy dominated until the end of the nineteenth century.

In 1818 Captain John Ross made an initial British attempt to find the Northwest Passage. Ross succeeded in reaching the far northwestern coast of Greenland. While anchored offshore, he and his officers were the first Europeans to encounter the Polar Eskimos, or Inughuit ("great people"), at least since the disappearance of the Norse Greenlanders. The Inughuit had split off from the Inuit who lived farther south sometime around 1450 and had become isolated from their cousins in Greenland and the Arctic Archipelago. As a result of their isolation, they had lost many Inuit skills such as how to use a kayak or fire a bow and arrow. Ross awkwardly named these people the "Arctic Highlanders." The meeting was a bizarre experience for both sides, each anxious to learn as much as possible about the other. The

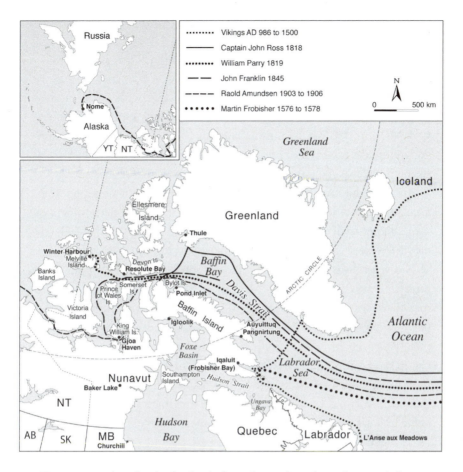

Legend:

- Vikings AD 986 to 1500
- Captain John Ross 1818
- William Parry 1819
- John Franklin 1845
- Raold Amundsen 1903 to 1906
- Martin Frobisher 1576 to 1578

0          500 km

N

Russia

Alaska

Nome

YT | NT

Greenland
Sea

Iceland

Ellesmere
Island

Greenland

Thule

Winter Harbour
Melville
Island

Devon Is.
Resolute Bay

Baffin
Bay

Banks
Island

Somerset
Is.

Bylot Is.

Pond Inlet

ARCTIC CIRCLE

Davis Strait

Atlantic
Ocean

Prince
of Wales
Is.

Victoria
Island

King
William Is.
Gjoa
Haven

Igloolik

Baffin Island

Auyuittuq
Pangnirtung

Foxe
Basin

Iqaluit
(Frobisher Bay)

Labrador
Sea

Nunavut

Southampton
Island

Hudson Strait

Baker Lake

NT

Ungava
Bay

AB

SK

MB

Churchill

Hudson
Bay

Quebec

Labrador

L'Anse aux Meadows

3.2 European exploration in the Arctic from the tenth to the early twentieth century.

Inughuit were astonished to discover they were not alone in the world, and the British explorers were equally astonished to find anyone living so far north. After several days of meetings and an exchange of gifts, the two British ships carried on but not very far.

On the morning of 1 September 1818, Ross sailed his ship, the *Isabella*, into Lancaster Sound. He then made a fatal error:

> The land which I then saw was a high ridge of mountains, extending directly across the bottom of the inlet. This chain appeared high in the centre, and those towards the north had, at times the appearance of islands, being insulated by fog at their bases. Although passage in this direction appeared hopeless, I was determined completely to explore it, as the wind was favourable; and, therefore, I continued all sail. At eight the wind fell a little and the *Alexander* being far astern I sounded

and found six hundred and seventy-four fathoms, with a soft muddy bottom ... [t]he weather now variable, being cloudy and clear at intervals. Mr. Beverley, who was most sanguine, went up to the crow's nest; and at twelve, reported to me, that before it became very thick, he had seen land across the bay, except for a very short space.

Although all hopes were given up, even by the most sanguine, that a passage existed, and the weather continued thick, I determined to stand higher up ... Here I felt the want of a consort, which I could employ to explore a coast, or discover a harbour; but the *Alexander* sailed so badly, and was so leewardly, that she could not be safely employed on such a service ... At three, the officer of the watch ... reported ... that there was some appearance of its clearing at the bottom of the bay; I immediately, therefore, went on deck, and soon after it completely cleared for about ten minutes, and I distinctly saw the land, round the bottom of the bay, forming a connected chain of mountains with those which extended along the north and south sides ... At a quarter past three, the weather again became thick and unsettled; and being now perfectly satisfied that there was no passage in this direction ... I tacked to join the *Alexander*, which was at a distance of eight miles; and having joined her a little after four, we stood to the south-eastward.[19]

Ross was dead wrong. Lancaster Sound is indeed the entrance to the Northwest Passage, as his second-in-command, William Edward Parry, would discover the following year. What did Ross and (apparently) his men see? It was most likely a combination of human error and light refraction creating a mirage-like effect called the Fata Morgana. What Ross saw was an illusion. He named what he thought he saw Croker Mountains after John Wilson Croker, first lord of the Admiralty. Parry later disputed Ross's findings, and Barrow was intensely critical of the indeterminate results of the voyage. Ross's reputation was permanently damaged. Parry's expedition the following year conclusively proved that Lancaster Sound was the gateway to the Northwest Passage, wherever that might ultimately lead. John Ross returned to the Arctic in subsequent years, especially in the search for the Franklin Expedition, but never with Admiralty support.

Perhaps the most successful of these early Admiralty voyages was William Edward Parry's attempt in 1819. He commanded an expedition of two ships,

HMS *Griper* and HMS *Hecla*, which succeeded in reaching as far west as Melville Island, a feat that would not be repeated for another thirty years. His success was due not just to good planning and seamanship (although Parry was undoubtedly one of the most competent and least deluded of the Arctic explorers) but also again to climate. Parry was lucky enough to hit a milder winter than most, with less ice and a longer sailing season. He was forced back after wintering off the coast of Melville Island in a place he called (prosaically enough) "Winter Harbour," but his success propelled even greater efforts to find and map one of the several routes now believed to lie through the Arctic islands.

Parry's success was also partly due to his care in looking after his officers and men, including providing for entertainment. As his two ships lay iced in over the winter, Parry encouraged theatrical events, celebrations, and even the distribution of a newspaper called the *North Georgia Gazette and Winter Chronicle*, edited by Parry's second-in-command, Edward Sabine, "a Weekly Newspaper, to be supported by original contributions from the Gentlemen of the Expedition … [which will] … under your [Sabine's] censorship, be productive of much amusement, and serve to relieve the tedium of our hundred days of darkness."[20] Not long before the winter ended and the ships broke free of the ice, allowing them to return home, Captain Parry wrote in the *Gazette* under the pseudonym of "Amicus,"

Let us look back for one year, and consider what our situation and prospects were. The greater part of us had just returned from a similar enterprise, vexed and mortified at the ill success which we had met with. Our own hopes, and those of our country disappointed, nothing appeared left for us but a long season of inactivity, and leisure to brood over the past!

How different is the prospect we have now before us! Selected once more for this interesting service – placed in a situation of credit and honour, which the sons of noblemen may reasonably envy – with the eyes of our country and of all Europe fixed upon us – how highly should we value these proud distinctions! … Could it have been predicted to us before we left England that we should winter comfortably in a secure harbor of our own finding, near the 111th degree of longitude? … We have succeeded in breaking the spell, which made the sea of Baffin a *bay*.[21]

## The Man Who Ate His Boots

The most ambitious attempt to conquer the Northwest Passage was led by Sir John Franklin in 1845. He got the job partly through very able lobbying on his behalf by his wife (among others). Lady Franklin (or Lady Jane as she is usually called) established herself as a major player in the Arctic saga without ever setting foot there. Her husband set sail from England in HMS *Erebus* and HMS *Terror*. Sir John's two previous missions overland through what is now the Northwest Territories in Canada were famous for being mostly disastrous – but still heroic by Victorian standards. Men under his command tended to die, but that only increased the sensational interest in his and others' exploits. On his return to England after his second overland adventure, he became known as "the man who ate his boots." He was a national celebrity.

Franklin, after an unfortunate time as governor of Van Diemen's Land (now Tasmania) in Australia, returned to England with his knighthood and reputation mostly intact. But in the years since his last northern adventure, he had become old and flabby. He was not fit enough for the ardours of another Arctic exploration. He probably knew this himself, but he was no match for his own celebrity and his indomitable wife. There is a story that, not long before the voyage began, he was laid up with a bad cold. He fell asleep in front of the drawing room fire while Lady Jane sat by sewing a Union Jack for him to take with him. When he awoke he found that she had draped it over him in an attempt to keep him warm. He was horrified – being covered with the flag was something that was done to naval officers who had died! It was a very bad omen of what was to come.

Nevertheless, Sir John left England with a large contingent of 133 officers and men (four of whom were left behind in Orkney as being unfit) and every hope of achieving success at last. The ships were specially reinforced to stand up to heavy ice, had modern steam engines to supplement sails, and were equipped with all the latest Victorian comforts and exploration gear. These included pipes throughout the ships to provide steam heat during the long winters, when they were expecting to be iced in. Everything had to be brought with them, including very large stocks of coal. There was no thought of living off the land. Canned food and other provisions were carried that should have been good for three years or longer with careful rationing. The plan was to sail as far north and west as possible. After that,

Franklin's orders directed him to choose a path through the labyrinth of the Arctic waters lying beyond Devon and Somerset Islands until he had transited the passage and sailed through to the Pacific. The two ships were last sighted by whalers in Baffin Bay tethered to an iceberg. They were waiting for the ice to clear sufficiently to allow them an entrance into Lancaster Sound. All seemed happy and hopeful. The date was 26 July 1845. Neither the ships nor any surviving men were ever seen again – at least not by Europeans.

By September 1847, more than two years after Sir John had left Great Britain, Lady Franklin was sufficiently concerned by the lack of news that she wrote to the first lord of the Admiralty, asking to see her husband's original orders. What followed were ten years of repeated Arctic voyages, both naval and privately funded by Lady Franklin and others, to find the missing expedition. This massive search effort, more than anything else, provided detailed cartographic and scientific information about the waters and ice of the various passages threading between the Arctic islands. No trace of the two ships has ever been found (although there is an ongoing effort by the Canadian Geographic Society and Coast Guard to locate one of them off the shore of King William Island), but a great deal of information about the fate of the Franklin Expedition was eventually uncovered. In addition the Arctic Archipelago was largely mapped by Europeans, and the unsuitability of the Northwest Passage for commercial navigation at that time was clearly shown. The Canadian claim to sovereignty in the Arctic has historically been based on this British effort. Great Britain lost interest in discovering the passage by the late nineteenth century, and it transferred what jurisdiction it had to the new Dominion of Canada in 1880.[22]

One of the first Franklin rescue missions was captained by James Clark Ross, John Ross's nephew, who had established himself as the premier polar explorer of the age. He had led an extraordinary expedition to Antarctica with the *Terror* and the *Erebus* just ten years earlier. He had successfully outmanoeuvred his ill-fated uncle, who had been lobbying for command of the mission. The nephew set out in 1848 but, beset by ill health and poor weather, never made it past Somerset Island and the head of Prince Regent Inlet.

By August 1850 fifteen ships were searching in various parts of the Arctic for traces of Franklin. Unfortunately they were all looking in the wrong place. Franklin had in fact sailed down Peel Sound and Victoria Strait to the west of King William Island. Although this wide stretch of water may have been ice-free when he entered it in 1846, it quickly returned to its usual state, becoming choked with ice from the great moving polar icepack that flowed down McClintock Channel past Victoria Island and jammed up against King William Island. This normally made navigation impossible in summer as well as in winter. The searchers simply did not believe he had sailed in this direction. They were also unaware until late in the search that there was a passage that was sometimes navigable to the east of King William Island – Rae Strait.

The first real traces of Franklin were found on Beechey Island – a tiny dot of land connected to the southwestern corner of Devon Island on Lancaster Sound by a thin bridge of pebbly land accessible at low tide. At the other end of this bleak island is a giant craggy tower of stratified rock. There, three of Franklin's men died and were buried. Remnants of his winter camp were discovered by the searchers in 1850, including a huge cairn of rusted empty cans and a single abandoned glove belonging to one of the officers. But there was no written record left behind to indicate in which direction Franklin had gone four years earlier. Leaving written notes in a cairn was common practice at this time. Franklin's failure to abide by this custom would probably not have saved his life, but it might have sent searchers in the right direction in time to find a solution to the mystery much sooner and perhaps to save the lives of some survivors who were still struggling as late as 1850. The lack of any written record, and even the one abandoned glove, has suggested to some historians that Franklin left Beechey Island in a hurry. But why?

In 1984 a thorough investigation, including an autopsy of the three dead Franklin Expedition men who are buried on Beechey Island, was conducted by a team led by Professor Owen Beattie of the University of Alberta and recounted in a book co-authored by John Geiger called *Frozen in Time: The Fate of the Franklin Expedition*. The photographs and written account of their discoveries are both disturbing and sensational. Owen and his team concluded that the two sailors and one marine were suffering from lead poisoning, probably from inadequate soldering of the cans of food on which they all depended to survive. Although this may not have been the cause of death, it certainly indicated that Franklin and his men were in serious trouble well before they sailed west and south on their final journey. Symptoms of lead poisoning include "[a]norexia, weakness and fatigue, irritability, stupor, paranoia, abdominal pain and anaemia,"[23] as well as disruptions to neurological activity that can lead to depression, erratic behaviour, and paralysis. Lead poisoning in combination with the perils of the journey, isolation, twenty-four hours of darkness in winter, the crippling cold, incipient scurvy, and increasing despair might explain the evidence subsequently discovered on King William Island. Members of the expedition seem to have gone insane before dying a collective death marked by starvation, piles of useless belongings, and misguided efforts to walk to safety after the ships were either sunk or abandoned. Astonishingly, the survivors had sufficient guns and ammunition to hunt but either failed to find any game or were not sufficiently skilled to kill much more than a few birds. Also, for the most part, they do not seem to have attempted to get any help from Inuit living or travelling in the vicinity, although it is possible there were simply too many men for any Inuit community to assist without endangering their own resources.

3.3 Grave of John Hartnell of HMS *Erebus*, Beechey Island

The physical evidence of the disaster on King William Island was not found until 1859, when one of many searches organized by Lady Franklin and led by Captain Francis Leopold M'Clintock finally found significant and convincing remains of the Franklin Expedition and the men's miserable attempts to save their lives. Other searches were conducted in subsequent years, but the mystery had at last been solved. A written note with somewhat cryptic information covering two years (1846–48) was found on the west coast of King William Island. Franklin had died in June 1847. An unusually high number of officers had also died, as well as some of the men – perhaps leading to a fatal lack of leadership in the final days. After that, the written record falls silent. Some of the men may have travelled north and east to find a large food cache left by one of John Ross's earlier expeditions. However, no trace of anyone actually reaching this place has ever been discovered. The last struggle for survival can be found in the remains of those who sledged and walked south toward the mainland of North America. It is assumed they were trying to get to a Hudson's Bay Company post. They died as they walked. A few died in camps set up on the mainland. Others simply vanished as if they had been swallowed up by land or sea. Skeletal remains are still sometimes found. A huge number of useless arti-facts were carried and then abandoned along the way, including china, silver plates, clocks, books, and furniture. Written records, if any ever existed, have long since disappeared.

# John Rae

However, Inuit testimony of the Franklin Expedition's desperate end had al-ready reached Lady Franklin and the British public five years earlier. On 29 July 1854 the British explorer Dr John Rae wrote a letter from Repulse Bay to the British Admiralty, which was published by the *Times* the day after he arrived back in London. It is worth quoting at some length:

> At a later date the same season, but previous to the disruption of the ice, the bodies of some thirty persons and some Graves were discovered on the continent, and five dead bodies on an Island near it, about a long day's journey to the north west of a large stream, which can be no other than Great Fish River (named by the Esquimaux Ool-koo-i-

hi-ca-lik), as its description and that of the low shore in the neighbor-
hood of Point Ogle and Montreal Island agree exactly with that of Sir
George Back. Some of the bodies had been buried (probably those of
the first victims of famine); some were in a tent or tents; others under
the boat, which had been turned over to form a shelter, and several lay
scattered about in different directions. Of those found on the Island
one was supposed to have been an Officer, as he had a telescope
strapped over his shoulders and his double-barrel gun lay beneath him.

From the mutilated state of many of the bodies and the contents of
the kettles, it is evident that our wretched Countrymen had been driven
to the last dread alternative – cannibalism – as a means of prolonging
existence. A few of the unfortunate Men must have survived until the
arrival of wildfowl, (say, until the end of May), as shots were heard,
and fresh bones and feathers of geese were noticed near the sad event.
There appears to have been an abundant stock of ammunition, as the
powder was emptied in a heap on the ground out of the case or cases
containing it; and a quantity of ball and shot was found below the
high-water mark, having probably been left on the ice close to the
beach. There must have been a number of watches, compasses, tele-
scopes, guns (several double-barreled), etc., all of which appear to have
been broken up, as I saw pieces of these different articles with the Esquimaux, and, together with some silver spoons & forks, purchased
as many as I could get.[24]

His letter was written as a result of discoveries and stories he had heard
from Inuit while on a surveying trip to the far northern mainland of British
North America for the Hudson's Bay Company. His letter also described
artifacts he had obtained from the Inuit that clearly belonged to members
of the Franklin Expedition, including Sir John himself. A detailed inventory
of these articles – which included silver forks and spoons, watches, coins, a
round silver plate and other objects clearly belonging to Franklin, and
perhaps saddest of all, "sundry other articles of little consequence"[25] – was
also added to a report that Rae made to the secretary of the Hudson's Bay
Company in London.

Rae was unusual for European explorers of the time in that he regularly
used Indigenous methods of survival in his travels, including wearing skin
and fur clothing, hunting for food, travelling by dogsled or snowshoes, and

living in temporary snow houses for overnight stops. As a result he and his parties rarely suffered from the scurvy, starvation, frostbite, internal feuding, and madness that plagued so many other European maritime explorers of the Arctic as they spent one, two, three, or even four years trapped in their fragile ships by weather and ice. He was also unusual in that he listened to what Indigenous people of the regions through which he travelled had to say, treating their testimony and stories seriously. Rae's mission of the time was primarily related to surveying and mapping on behalf of his employers, but like any other European who might have been travelling through the Arctic at this time, he had an eye out for any evidence of the ill-fated and mysterious Franklin Expedition. Indeed, Lady Franklin had specifically put her faith in Rae's skills as an explorer, which she believed would aid him in finding traces of the missing men. After nearly eight years of futile naval searches in the Arctic, Rae, travelling overland, finally found proof of Franklin's terrible fate. In his blunt Scottish way, he broke the news to a world transfixed by the martyrdom of the saintly Franklin and his band of heroic explorers. But his account, gained from Inuit witnesses, made it clear that the survivors had resorted to desperate measures to stay alive – including cannibalism.

For the British Admiralty the news was scandalous. Lady Franklin was utterly devastated. Rae received a very frosty reception from Lady Franklin when he visited her in London: "When the explorer paid her the obligatory courtesy call ... Jane [Lady Franklin] told him to his face that he never should have accepted the word of 'Esquimaux savages' ... Rae refused to recant. He insisted that he knew the truth when he heard it."[26] Rae's reputation as an explorer was destroyed, and to this day, his name is associated with a tale of ruin and devastation. But the findings of M'Clintock and other searchers mostly confirmed what Rae had learned from the Inuit. His reputation is now undergoing a posthumous revival.

While Europeans were wandering around the Arctic gradually mapping what to them was the unknown, encounters between Inuit and Europeans no doubt led to misunderstanding and anxiety on both sides. Lady Franklin's attitude that the "Natives" were savages who could not be trusted was typical of her time. After John Rae's damaging disclosures became public, outraged opinions were expressed by many English commentators, notably by Charles Dickens, who published a two-part hagiography of the explorers in his own weekly magazine, *Household Words*. In this article he virtually accuses "the Esquimaux" of murdering Franklin's men themselves: "Lastly, no man can, with any show of reason, undertake to affirm that this sad remnant of Franklin's gallant band were not set upon and slain by the Esquimaux themselves ... We believe every savage to be in his heart covetous, treacherous, and cruel; and we have yet to learn what knowledge the white men – lost, houseless, shipless; apparently forgotten by his race; plainly famine-stricken, weak, frozen, helpless, and dying – has of the gentleness of the Esquimaux nature."[27] Rae, to his credit, wrote a rejoinder (which Dickens also published in *Household Words*) exonerating the Inuit and demonstrating the high regard in which they were held by himself and other experienced Europeans, especially employees of the Hudson's Bay Company and Moravian missionaries and Danish residents of Greenland.[28]

Dickens was at this time somewhat obsessed with Arctic images and themes, assisting sensation writer Wilkie Collins in the authorship and production of the play *The Frozen Deep* in 1856. This was first performed at Dickens's house in Tavistock Square with Dickens, Collins, and members of Dickens's family in the various roles. The play (and Wilkie Collins's subsequent novel of the same name) was explicitly based on the lost Franklin expedition. The play went on to some success on the stage in both England and America. Dickens's strange involvement with the whole Franklin saga is an indication of how much Europe's and America's attention was captured by the loss of the sainted Franklin and his band of martyrs. Rae's stories of cannibalism were simply unacceptable to Lady Franklin and the British public more generally. It was not until further missions to the Arctic finally discovered the sad last remains of the expedition that Rae's stories from the Inuit were proven to be correct. To this day the question of cannibalism remains controversial, and many historians insist that Franklin did indeed find the Northwest Passage. Only recently, through the efforts of historian Ken McGoogan and others, has Rae's reputation been vindicated. McGoogan's book *The Fatal Passage*, along with John Walker's award-winning documentary *Passage*,[29] have gone a long way toward exonerating Rae and offering amends to the Inuit for the savagely critical stories propagated by Dickens and others.

The Inuit of Gjoa Haven on King William Island still recall stories told to them by their ancestors about the last ghastly struggle of the expedition:

At this time there were four or five families with four or five separate igloos on the west side of King William Island to the south side of Terror Bay. The men were out seal hunting, and the women and children, and one elder too old to keep up with the younger men, were left in camp. At that time eight or nine white people came to the camp ...

When the white men entered the camp, all the Inuit were inside one of the igloos; they started hearing people outside. One of the women says, "The hunters are here – they're back already." They didn't expect them back so soon. Then a woman went out to see them. She comes back very shaky and says, "They're not Inuit; they're not human." Everyone got scared, very, very scared and no one wanted to go outside. But the old man, when he hears something outside the igloo, he goes out to investigate – to see what's going on. When he sees what's outside, he says to himself, "No, I have never seen anything like this."

He'd seen a shaman but he wasn't a shaman himself. He says to himself, "I've never in all my life seen a devil or a spirit. These things are not human; so if they are not human I cannot see them. I have never in all my life seen any kind of spirit – I've heard the sounds they make, but I've never seen them with my own eyes; these are not spirits."

Then the old man goes over to touch one, to feel if it's cold or warm. He touched a cheek with his hand: cool but not as cold as a fish! They were beings but not Inuit. They were beings but he didn't know what they were ...

These beings seemed disoriented – not too interested in the Inuit, more aware of the igloo building, touching it. The Inuk invited them inside and the women tried to give them something to eat – seal meat that was cooked already, and they gave them water to drink. They drank the water. But when they tried to give them seal meat, they'd take a bite and some of them swallowed; some of them wouldn't swallow, they'd spit it out. They gave them soup. Some drank a little; some didn't want to take any.

... [After the hunters got back and the Inuit discussed whether to kill the strangers or leave] they got all their belongings together and took off towards the southwest. They never encountered those qallunaat again. But because they were in a hurry, they must have left a few of their belongings behind. Later that winter, two or three of them decided to go back to their old camp to gather up their possessions; they saw four dead bodies in that igloo. Originally there had been nine or ten white men. The seals were never touched; but two of the men were partly eaten; the other two must have been the last survivors.[30]

## The Inuit Way

It would not be until the twentieth century, with explorers such as Roald Amundsen, Knud Rasmussen (who was part Greenlandic Inuit), Vilhjalmur Stefansson, and others that Europeans would finally understand that Inuit knowledge and culture were uniquely successful in adapting to the Arctic climate. Amundsen, the brilliant Norwegian polar explorer, finally achieved the great dream of European efforts in the Arctic – sailing through the Northwest Passage from east to west between 1903 and 1906. He succeeded partly because he deliberately adopted an approach more like the Inuit method of travel, as Rae had done a half-century earlier. In addition he was also assisted by a climate already significantly affected by increased greenhouse gas emissions, which had resulted in some reduction in summer ice. Although the Arctic was still cold and the passage still frozen for much of the year (Amundsen spent nineteen months on King William Island before continuing westward through the narrow passage between the mainland and Victoria Island on his way to the Beaufort Sea), maritime travel was already becoming easier. Lessons Amundsen learned from the Inuit about using dogs and wearing caribou clothing were also put to good use when he successfully reached the South Pole five years later.

The Royal Canadian Mounted Police vessel *St. Roch* sailed through the Northwest Passage over the course of two years, leaving Vancouver on 21 June 1940 and arriving in Halifax on 11 October 1942. It was the first non-Inuit vessel to transit the passage from west to east, even though it spent much of that time trapped in the ice. But in 1944 the same vessel managed the east to west voyage through a more northerly route in just 86 days, again thanks to a longer sailing season and less ice. In 2000 the *St. Roch II* replicated the west to east voyage of the first *St. Roch* and succeeded in completing the voyage from Vancouver to Halifax in just 100 days. Again this was thanks to improved technology, less ice, and a significantly longer sailing season. Whereas Martin Frobisher, in the depths of the Little Ice Age during the sixteenth century, found he could not remain in Frobisher Bay past late

August, in the twenty-first century the seas around South Baffin Island are regularly open until late October.

To the Inuit, the Europeans' method of travel must have seemed foolish. European ships were generally too big and carried too many men. They relied on sails to catch often unfavourable winds or used coal-fuelled engines in a land where coal was scarce. The hulls could not withstand the pressures of ice during long winters when travel by sea was impossible. The sailors' heavy woolen clothing was not adapted to the cold. Also, there were no women. For Inuit survival, tasks are divided equally between men and women. The women's ability to sew and make warm waterproof clothing from skins and furs is as essential as the men's ability to hunt for seal, caribou, walrus, whales, bear, and other game. Men traditionally built the *igluit* (houses) for winter shelter, but women kept the houses light and warm with their *qulliit* (stone lamps). No Inuk man would have seriously considered going on a long journey, especially into unknown territory, without his wife (or wives) and other female family members. Knowledgeable elders and shamans also provided essential wisdom and foresight, and children would need to come in order to learn the necessary skills of travel and survival over long distances and extended periods of time.

Europeans, especially the British, were slow to recognize the value of any of these practices. They were very reluctant to eat "country food." The British Navy had learned that fresh vegetables, especially lime or lemon juice, were necessary to ward off scurvy on long voyages. But the supplies would often run out or lose their potency. The cause of scurvy, a lack of vitamin C, was not known until the twentieth century. How did Inuit manage to avoid this and other vitamin deficiency illnesses when their diet included almost no fruits or vegetables? Raw meat, particularly seal, is rich in vitamin C. The insistence of British explorers on bringing often inadequate or even dangerous preserved food, and on refusing to live off the land, meant the death of many. The British also remained stubbornly insistent on using man-hauled sledges for overland travel. Seamen were hitched to sledges like mules and expected to pull enormous loads under already difficult conditions over great distances. If this didn't kill them, it sapped their strength and aggravated the effects of scurvy. Officers of course were not expected to engage in such heavy labour. The Inuit had long adapted to travel in light skin boats during the summer and in *qamutiik* (dogsleds) during the winter. Dog teams pulling sleds allowed for relatively quick and easy travel over long distances.

3.4 Remains of a cross made with empty tin cans left by the Franklin Expedition, Beechey Island (which has since disappeared)

Dogs also assisted in hunting. By using sleds and dogs, the Inuit were able to use coastal routes by sea or across the straits throughout the Arctic Archipelago during winter and spring travel. To Inuit the ice-covered sea during winter is really an extension of the land. The British naval insistence on viewing such routes as maritime is still a difficult issue with regards to sovereignty in international law. From an Inuit perspective, the land and sea are one entity governed by the same laws. From a European perspective, which still dominates international law, land and sea are fundamentally different entities ruled by completely different legal regimes (see chapter 5).

At the same time as British explorers were groping their way through the Arctic, looking for the lost Franklin Expedition, a great Inuk shaman and explorer was also journeying from South Baffin Island thousands of miles north to the land of the Inughuit in Greenland. In one of history's great ironies, this Inuit explorer met several of his British counterparts along the way. But he is not remembered in general histories of exploration, whereas

Europeans like Franklin are. The travels of Qitdlarssuaq should be taken as seriously as those of Sir John Franklin, William Edward Parry, and Dr John Rae in deciding who really owns the Arctic. The tradition of great Inuit exploration is as ancient as the migrations from Siberia and Alaska across the Arctic hundreds and even thousands of years ago. At the beginning of this ancient history, another hero, the mysterious shaman Kiviuq, also travelled across the North and then south to the land of the *qallunaat*. Perhaps when he got there he discovered us.

# 4

# Inuit Odysseys

All true wisdom is only to be found far from the dwellings of men, in the great solitudes; and it can only be attained through suffering. Suffering and privation are the only things that can open the mind of man to that which is hidden from his fellows.

Igjugarjuk of the Padlermiut (Caribou Inuit)[1]

## Kiviuq

When European travellers returned to the Arctic in the nineteenth century, they were sometimes asked a strange question: "'Have you seen the great Kiviuq? Have you met him on your travels?' ... 'Who is Kiviuq,' they wondered, 'and why are you asking me about him?' They were told that this legendary Inuit hero had gone south into exile among the white people after a life of continuous journeying."[2]

Kiviuq's story is the epic of an Inuit shaman and hero known all over the Arctic. There are many versions of this narrative. Knud Rasmussen recorded different parts of the story in the early twentieth century as it was told to him by elders he met during his travels across the North.[3] Kira Van Deusen went to Nunavut in 2004 with the filmmaker John Houston and heard versions of the story from elders living eighty years after Rasmussen. This latest retelling resulted in Van Deusen's book *Kiviuq: An Inuit Hero and His Siberian Cousins*, the film *Kiviuq* by Houston, and a detailed website.[4] John Houston has described this story as the Inuit equivalent of Homer's *Odyssey*.[5] One interesting aspect of Kiviuq's tale that Van Deusen points out is the parallels between the version of the story told by Inuit and stories told by Indigenous peoples in Siberia.[6]

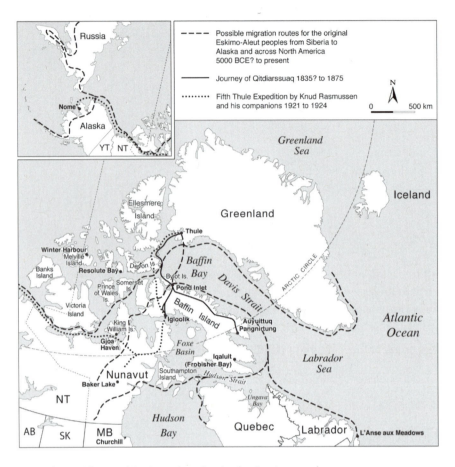

4.1 Eskimo-Aleut and Inuit exploration in the Arctic over the past 7,000 years (or more)

The epic is told in episodes that do not always follow the same order in the different versions across the Arctic. There is the story of the seal child who becomes an orphan. Kiviuq is saved from death because he is kind to the child. With a sandpiper as his helping spirit, Kiviuq begins his long journey. As Lucassie Nutaraaluk recounts,

He [Kiviuq] was not an orphan. He travelled to many places by *qajaq* [kayak]. He came upon various beings. He came upon worms that had become humans. He also encountered a mother and daughter who lived alone. When they found a piece of wood it became the daughter's husband. She had a piece of wood as a husband. Kiviuq also became the daughter's husband for a while. The other husband, who was a piece of wood, was very jealous. The way that the mother and daughter would get the piece of wood to go hunting for them was to set it afloat.

One day when Kiviuq was out hunting the mother became envious of her daughter having a human for a husband, so she killed her daughter and put on her daughter's face. She killed her daughter by telling her to put her head on her lap so she could take the lice out of her hair. Instead she stabbed her three times through the ear with a *pauktuut*, a drying peg. When Kiviuq returned and found out what the woman had done, he once again left in his *qajaq*.[7]

In some versions of the story, the strange husband is a penis. On his travels Kiviuq also meets a bee woman, an evil spirit surrounded by the skulls of dead men. He escapes but the bee woman throws her *ulu* (knife) after him. It skips on the water, which, for the first time, turns to sea ice. His adventures continue, during which animals transform into humans and other animals become his wives under mysterious circumstances. Jealousy causes him to kill two of his wives, but his favourite returns as a beautiful fox wife. An envious wolverine offends her and she leaves. Kiviuq follows her to meet the other animals of her family.

Many of these stories are highly sexual or scatological. Transformation from human to animal and back again is a constant theme. Kiviuq also meets grizzly bears (which are native to the Arctic in Siberia, Alaska, and western Canada) and finally his goose wife. She gives birth to several children, and they are all happy together, except for Kiviuq's mother. The goose wife flies away, taking her children with her. Kiviuq thinks his mother has offended her and heads south looking for his wife. One version of the story is told by Theresa Kimmaliadjuk of Igluligaarjuk (Chesterfield Inlet):

Yearning for his family, Kiviuq set off on foot towards the south. He came upon a man whose mouth had an opening all the way to his rear end. He could see the other side of the land through the hole.

The man was bent over, chipping pieces of hard and soft wood and throwing them into the lake. He would chip off a piece then rub it against his penis, giving it color, then place it in the water. Once in the water, the soft wood pieces turned into trout and the hard wood pieces turned into char.

Carefully, Kiviuq approached the man from his side. With a surprised look, the man asked; "From which direction did you arrive?"

"From your side."

"From which direction did you arrive?" he insisted.

"From your side."

This went on for a while, finally the man mellowed and Kiviuq explained that he wanted to reach his family who had flown beyond the big water.

The man motioned to what Kiviuq thought was an island in the water.

It began to move towards them, it was a large fish. The man told the fish that Kiviuq wanted to reach his family and instructed Kiviuq that when the fish notices shallow water it'll start jerking nervously, that's when you should leap for the shore.

Kiviuq sat on the fish and was taken on a long journey across the lake, when they reached the other side the fish began nervously jerking. As was instructed, Kiviuq leapt towards the shore and landed in the water up to his waist.

He walked to the land and soon found his children among many birds on the land. Recognizing their father, the children cried, "Our father has arrived." Their mother in disbelief answered, "My children, we left your father on the other side of this land, it's not possible for him to come."

The children replied happily, "He is here!"

The goose had remarried a Brant goose but when Kiviuq entered their tent, it ran away exclaiming, "I forgot my tool bag." His tool bag was his gut! I've never heard of Kiviuq's return from that area since.

I have never heard of his return from that land, but I've heard that Kiviuq grew old there and his cheeks turned into stone from old age.[8]

In other versions of the story, the goose wife has forgotten the song that will turn her back into a human. She flies north again in the spring with her children, as is the nature of geese, and Kiviuq remains behind.

Kiviuq's journey is not normally told as a single mythic story from beginning to end. It is very much as the *Odyssey* must have been before it was transformed into a written account from the earlier oral versions. Kiviuq's story is described as a sequence of encounters with people, animals, and spirits where he is both a man and an *angakkuq* (shaman). The stories have a strong moral element. Kimmaliadjuk comments on the story: "There's lots to use out of this story. Our parents tell us things that are good to hear and make sure the kids don't hear the bad things. Kids would even be sent away while those conversations were going on. Kids heard all of the Kiviuq story because we encounter good and bad in life and the story contains it all. Which other stories should be recorded and reenlivened? All of them!"⁹ Kiviuq himself is said to be immortal, falling asleep or disappearing until he returns again. However, in the modern retellings of the story, this aspect seems to have changed. No modern elder looks forward to Kiviuq's return to the North. "Most agree that he is still alive, but they are uncertain about where he is. They say that when he dies, there will be no more air to breathe and life on earth will end. But until then he lives on in story."¹⁰

Are there echoes here of the great Inuit migration from Siberia to Alaska and then eastward to Greenland and perhaps southward to the Barren Grounds west of Hudson Bay? Van Deusen and Houston tried to map the story onto modern Nunavut and felt that the strongest presence was in Netsilik territory west of Iglulik, but other versions take place elsewhere or are told in a different order or manner depending on the location of the storyteller. Is Kiviuq the embodiment of a great Inuk hero and shaman who led his people across the Arctic? Or is he more like an Inuit Odysseus travelling ancient Earth, only to return home to a world changed almost beyond recognition, before disappearing to the land of the *qallunaat* far to the south? The faithful Penelope (more than one) and the faithless Sirens are here, as are the gods and demons of an older time.

What are the elements of Inuit heroism? Are arctic heroes different from those of other cultures? We see [in Kiviuq's story] kindness to orphans, correct treatment of animals, courage, perseverance, control of emotions, getting things right the first time, walking away from trouble, clever dodges, creativity, hunting skill, willingness to give and receive help, and strict adherence to the rules of Inuit life. Most of these elements show up as the morals of the various parts of the story, and indeed the overriding moral can actually shape the story. It's no coincidence that today the story of the seal-child usually comes first, given that most elders consider the need to be kind to orphans the most important moral of the whole story. But in nineteenth-century Greenland the hero paddled away from home through a storm, surviving many obstacles after murdering his wife and her lover. He arrived at the home of the wolf-women and announced, "I left home because I was jealous" ... On the other hand, across the water in Chukotka [Siberia] the moral drawn from the fox-wife story involved the fact that the fox had been helpful and the people failed to recognize it.[11]

Echoes of Kiviuq's story can be heard from Siberia to Greenland. While listening to the stories told by elders and thinking about the meaning of what the hero learned from his many adventures, Van Deusen's interpreter Philip Paniaq kept saying, "there are no second chances in the Arctic."[12] In an unforgiving world, it is important to try to "get it right" the first time. This means keeping one's emotions under control, staying alert, and following the *malagait* (rules). As the late Mariano Aupilaarjuk, an elder from Rankin Inlet, is quoted as saying, "The story was and is alive for me. It helps Inuit to survive and live. All Inuit feel the story is real and that it has usefulness in life. If we were raised in only happy times we wouldn't learn. We have both good and bad in life. To survive is to do our best even in hard times, and grow mature, strong, and respected. As children we were taught to live well and to follow things through even if we didn't like it."[13]

## Inuit Qaujimajatuqangit

Akitsiraq elder-in-residence Lucien Ukaliannuk used to teach similar lessons in his class on Inuit traditional law. Inuit rules emphasize the life of the community, not the individual. An Inuit leader would have been respected as a good hunter or shaman as long as he was effective in protecting his people. He might be devious or harsh, even feared, but if his leadership protected those who followed him, he would be respected. The traditional knowledge of the Inuit – Inuit Qaujimajatuqangit – expresses the importance of kindness, consideration for others, helpfulness, humility, cooperation, and emotional maturity in the life of Inuit communities. The word for "the environment" or "the outdoors" in Inuktitut is *sila*, which also means "intelligence." The connection between land, mind, sea, and spirit is always close.

The Inuit were and still are great travellers over long distances, and their stories reverberate over vast tracts of space and centuries of time. The first European attempt at life in the Arctic (that of the Norse Greenlanders) ended in dismal failure, whereas the Inuit survived and thrived. Kiviuq's story also has echoes of the great Norse myths and sagas – Eric the Red, who founded the Greenland community around AD 1000, was a troublemaker and a murderer, but he was also a great leader who travelled with his people into unknown territory. We see these themes again in a more recent story that has been well documented in the history of the Arctic – the travels of Qitdlarssuaq. According to Jaypeetee Arnakak,

> The wonderful feature of all this is that these stories are adaptable to local places and landmarks. This is *Inuit Qaujimajatuqangit* in the flesh. The local lay of the land is encapsulated by and encoded into these stories ... The point, though, is the mnemonic value of the stories to local places and landmarks. Only a stable and mature civilization (about 5,000 years old for the Inuit culture) would have the subtlety and refinement to pull off something like this without the aid of written texts and physical maps.
>
> The Inuit are not unique in this respect. Most human cultures before the industrial revolution told stories this way. The sacred scriptures of major religions, the Norse Sagas, and the Dreamtime of the original Australians are fine examples.[14]

Not only did Inuit have the technological know-how to survive in the Arctic, but they also had, and still have, cultural traditions of law passed on from one generation to the next in which the physical, mental, emotional, and spiritual demands of the Arctic are recognized. Europeans simply do not have this ancient knowledge and (until recently) tended to dismiss or denigrate those who do. The British in particular stuck with suicidal obstinacy to the erroneous idea that the Northwest Passage is a sea lane to be treated as a maritime route. The prevalence of ice throughout the Arctic Archipelago for most of the year means that the physical realities are fundamentally different from sea lanes and maritime routes elsewhere. The Inuit have always recognized this and have adapted their methods of travel over the sea as a solid surface similar to land for much of the year.

The archaeological record discovered by Europeans, as well as Inuit oral history, indicates that the ancestors of the Inuit, perhaps including Kiviuq himself, moved into the eastern Arctic about 800 years ago. Previous to this, they lived for at least 7,000 years in Alaska and Siberia, where many Inuit still live. This necessarily means that individuals and family groups traversed

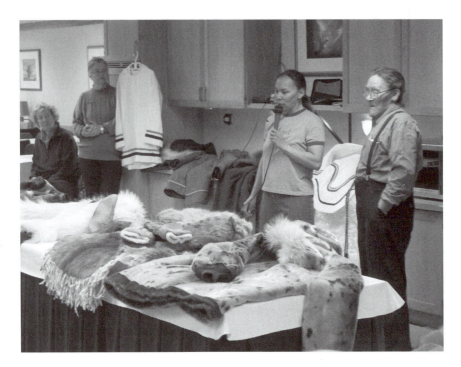

4.2  Meeka Mike and her father, Jamesie Mike, demonstrating Inuit clothing on board the *Akademik Ioffe* for Adventure Canada

a northwest passage or passages long before Europeans. Mostly we think of this travel as prehistoric and generic without focusing on actual events in which individual Inuit themselves were the explorers. But there are instances of long migrations in the Arctic preserved both in Inuit oral history and in the written records of European explorers.

## Qitdlarssuaq: A Modern Journey

Perhaps the most famous of these expeditions is a journey from Cumberland Sound on Baffin Island to far northwestern Greenland led by a powerful leader named Qillaq or Qitdlarssuaq, "the great Qillaq," in the mid-nineteenth century. Firsthand accounts of this journey told by Meqqusaaq and Pankippak (two of the original travellers) and a family narrative by Itussaarssuaq, the granddaughter of Qitdlarssuaq's brother-in-law, have been recorded by various explorers and historians, including Knud Rasmussen and the Green-landic historian Inuutersuaq Ulloriaq (as translated by Kenn Harper and Navarana Harper).[15] A valuable account was also written by Father Guy Mary-Rousselière of Pond Inlet in 1980.[16] The oral history and written nar-ratives are well-accepted historical descriptions of this Inuk explorer.

Qitdlarssuaq was reputed to have been a great *angakkuq* (shaman) capa-ble of foreseeing the future and changing his shape to that of a polar bear or other animal. He is said to have originally been an Uqqumiutaq, an Inuk of southeastern Baffin Island near Cumberland Sound and modern-day Qikiqtarjuaq (Broughton Island). Between 1830 and 1835 the young Qitd-larssuaq and another man named Uqi were involved in the attempted killing of a shaman and the murder of her brother. This seems to have occurred in the Auyuittuq area near modern-day Pangnirtung on South Baffin Island.

Qitdlarssuaq, Uqi, and their followers travelled from Cumberland Sound to North Baffin Island near Pond Inlet and Bylot Island. Here their travails are again recorded by Father Mary-Rousselière based on his own interview with the great-grandson of Qitdlarssuaq's sister Arnatsiaq, herself a famous shaman. Qitdlarssuaq, Uqi, and their families were living in the area of Bylot Island in about 1850 when they were attacked by a neighbouring camp. It was "the last straw." Qitdlarssuaq and about forty or fifty follow-ers (a large number for a journey in those days) set out for Iglulik over the mountains on the west coast of Baffin. These journeys around the island would have been by dogsled, following well-known trails used by hunters throughout the region. These trails and camping areas both on land and on ice have been used for centuries by the different peoples of the Baffin region. People used to carry all their belongings with them, hunting as they went. Families included wives, children, and elders. These routes and travel methods are well known and are still used, although modern travellers tend to use snowmobiles rather than dogsleds. After heading toward Iglulik, Qitdlarssuaq travelled around the North Baffin region for another one or two years before deciding that he and his followers would never be at peace until they had found a new home far from their enemies. They then turned north, crossing Lancaster Sound over the ice, and arrived on Devon Island at about the same time as the massive search for the lost Franklin Expedi-tion was reaching its height.

The party of Uqqumiut had spent nearly twenty years travelling around North Baffin Island while trying to avoid the vengeance of relatives of the

man Qitdlarssuaq and Uqi had murdered in Auyuittuq. They likely crossed
Lancaster Sound from Bylot Island in early spring (April) of 1853 when the
sea was frozen and the constant grinding of ice due to treacherous currents
ceased for a few weeks (although the movement of the ice never really stops).
Elders in North Baffin have known for many years the best times to cross
the ice, although it is known by the Inuit in the area always to be hazardous.
Hunters from Pond Inlet and Arctic Bay still patrol this area to hunt, fish,
and camp. The whole region, from Iglulik in the west, north to Admiralty
and Navy Board Inlets, and across Lancaster Sound to Devon Island, is part
of the wide territory traditionally hunted by the Inuit of North Baffin.

The mid-nineteenth century was a particularly cold period in the Arctic.
The ice must have been firmer then than it is now. Whereas the thicker ice
of the longer winters proved impassable by British explorers searching for
the Northwest Passage, it made travel for Qitdlarssuaq and other Inuit
easier. Although Inuit do travel and hunt by *umiaq* (boat) or kayak on the
open water, the preferred method of travel is by *qamutik* (dogsled) over the
ice. But it is not easy. Even though the ice may not be moving, great pressure
ridges create a trail full of jagged peaks and deep fissures that make travel
difficult and dangerous. Pulling a sled becomes extremely slow and arduous
as men and dogs try to manoeuvre heavy loads over or around daunting
barriers of ice. In addition the area of Lancaster Sound is a prime place for
polar bears, which can easily stay hidden in this world of jagged white only
to emerge with fearsome suddenness. Oral history, recorded by the Inughuit
historian Inuutersuaq Ulloriaq and repeated in Father Mary-Rousselière's
account, tells us that Qitdlarssuaq crossed over to Devon Island in these
conditions without losing anyone in his group. They would have navigated
by wind, snow, ice, and stars in the night sky. *Uqalurait* are arrow-shaped
patterns in the snow caused by the prevailing winds. These could be used
like compass needles pointing the way. Predicting weather reliably would
have been crucial. They must have all camped several times on the shifting
pack ice before reaching land. Even in early spring the temperature can be
-30 or -40° Celsius, with even colder wind chills. Ground blizzards can ob-
scure sight even when the sky is clear above the heads of the travellers.
Shelter meant building snow houses each night in which the women would
light their *qulliit* (stone lamps) to prepare a meal. Stops would have to be
made for the men to hunt and replenish supplies of meat, oil, animal skins,
and other necessities. This is no country for the arrogant or the unprepared.

In 1853 Captain Edward Augustus Inglefield of the British naval supply ship *Phoenix* encountered a group of Inuit on the southern coast of Devon Island in a place since named Dundas Harbour. Inglefield was in the area engaged in the wider search for the Franklin Expedition. Qitdlarssuaq himself recounted this first meeting with the British Navy five years later in 1858 to Captain Francis Leopold M'Clintock, also engaged in a search for the Franklin Expedition. Qitdlarssuaq exchanged news with Inglefield through a Greenlandic interpreter with whom Inglefield was travelling. It is possible that Inglefield (or his interpreter) told Qitdlarssuaq about a small community of Inuit living in far northern Greenland across from Ellesmere Island. The discussions with Captain Inglefield may have been the first time Qitdlarssuaq gained knowledge of a group of Inuit living so far to the north. Father Mary-Rousselière speculates that Inglefield may have shown Qitdlarssuaq his own map of the narrow passage between Ellesmere Island and Greenland, complete with Inuit and Inughuit encampments. But it is also possible that Qitdlarssuaq was already aware of Inuit living far to the north of Baffin Island.

The meeting with Captain M'Clintock occurred on 11 July 1858 while M'Clintock's ship, the *Fox*, was sailing south under a clear midnight sun and became becalmed on the east coast of Devon Island. A group of Inuit called out to the ship from pack ice near shore. The ship tied itself to the ice and greeted the dozen or so Inuit who approached. Qitdlarssuaq asked after Captain Inglefield. He also informed the naval rescue party that he had seen no other ships other than the *Phoenix* five years earlier.

One of the original travellers, Meqqusaaq (or Merqusaq), told Knud Rasmussen,

After Qitdlarssuaq had once heard that there were Inuit over on the other side of the sea, he could never settle down to anything again. He held great conjurations of spirits in the presence of all the people of the village. He made his soul take long journeys through the air, with his helping spirits, to look for the country of the strange Inuit. At last one day he informed his fellow-villagers that he had found the new country! And he told them, that he was going to journey to the strange people, and he exhorted them all to follow him.

"Do you know the desire for new countries? Do you know the desire to see new people?" he said to them.[17]

A year after his meeting with Qitdlarssuaq and Uqi, Inglefield discovered that a cache of supplies on North Baffin Island had been ransacked, with the meat and flour left behind, but the rum taken. This discovery agrees with a story about a man identified as Uqi who left Baffin Island about this time. It is probable, but not certain, that Qitdlarssuaq was also involved. These discoveries and the comparison with Inuit oral history provide compelling details about the journey of this group of Inuit either travelling together or in separate stages.

## The Journey Continues

By the time Qitdlarssuaq's party met up with M'Clintock in 1858, they had already travelled far to the north of Dundas Harbour. Qitdlarssuaq had been led on his journey by dreams and visions. His *tuurngait* (helping spirits) spoke to him of the road ahead, and it is said that he himself was able to fly through the air or under the water. If his band had not believed in his powers as a shaman, a leader, and a hunter, they would never have followed him so far. Whatever skepticism a non-Inuit observer may feel about these powers, they were essential to him and his people on their long journey. The ability of a leader to inspire people to follow him or her may differ from one culture to another, but if this power is not there in some form, journeys such as these quickly descend into catastrophe. This may well have been what happened to the Franklin Expedition. Either Sir John Franklin and his officers did not have the capacity to make others believe in them, or they died too early, leaving a critical lack of leadership.

> The story of Qillaqsuaq [Qitdlarssuaq] is about the last great Inuit epic journey ... it is said, he knew what to expect most of the way by stories that he had heard. There is little doubt that these were not just dry descriptions of the surroundings and its landmarks. It was more likely that all Qitdlarssuaq had to recall were the stories to anticipate what was around the corner.
>
> The underlying events of a story are perfect spots to encode advice, explanations, and landmarks: the medium is the message. Inuit legends and stories are not mere superstitious musings. What they contain is far richer and more profound than what a superficial glance can grasp.[18]

Up to the time of the meeting with M'Clintock in 1858, the Inuit were travelling in known territory. The Tununirmiut (Inuit of North Baffin Island) were and still are used to crossing Lancaster Sound and hunting around southern Devon Island. But the journey farther north would have been into unknown territory. Qitdlarssuaq needed to rely on his powers as a shaman to see the path ahead and also to convince his followers that he knew the way in order for the long journey to continue. Like many European explorers, from Eric the Red and Martin Frobisher to Franklin himself, Qitdlarssuaq headed out on his travels for less than noble reasons. However, he was unusual in that he was not only a powerful shaman but also a well-known hunter and leader. He was obviously a very charismatic individual who combined both spiritual and political power. His history includes accounts of his ability to see the path ahead by travelling through the air, by transforming himself into animals, and by changing objects and creatures into other things. His story has become partly what Europeans would call "mythical," like the stories of Siqiniq and Taqqiq, Nuliajuk and Kiviuq. The film *Atanarjuat: The Fast Runner* is based on a similar legendary story of a famous hero who overcomes obstacles and defeats his enemies.[19] But, like the history of Qitdlarssuaq, these stories contain many layers of truth, including what we in the South might call "fact." The stories are told and retold not only as history but also as moral lessons embedded with information about survival on the land and ice.

Even as a young man, Qitdlarssuaq evidently had great personal power; by the time he died in 1875, he was legendary. Once, for instance, while out hunting for polar bears far from land, Qitdlarssuaq and a young companion were caught in a severe storm. The sea ice was shattered, and the open sea raged around them. Qitdlarssuaq ordered the young man to lie face down on the sled and to keep his eyes shut. Soon, however, the young man felt the sled begin to move, and being frightened and curious, he opened one eye and saw that Qitdlarssuaq had turned himself into a polar bear and that his own dogs were chasing him. Wherever the bear trod, the sea turned to ice. He also saw, to his horror, that the runner on the same side of the sled as his open eye was sinking into the sea. He quickly closed his eye again and did not reopen it until the sled stopped and Qitdlarssuaq ordered him to rise. The shaman was again a man, and they were safely on land.[20]

The Tununirmiut of North Baffin call Devon Island "Tallurutit," meaning "red stripes" or "tattoos on the chin," because of its steep, deeply slashed, ruddy-coloured coastline. It is a vast and bleak landscape of gravel, rock, and mountains with a few patches of lichen. There are places where muskoxen and other wildlife can eke out a living, but it is a challenging as well as a beautiful place. Qitdlarssuaq and his party spent about five or six years hunting and camping around the island. Even after hearing of the existence of Inuit far to the north, Qitdlarssuaq does not appear to have been in a hurry to leave Devon Island. He is known to have been in the region between 1853 (when he met Captain Inglefield) and 1858 (when he met M'Clintock's ship, the *Fox*). It is clear that the party moved around the area for a considerable period of time before heading north. Since the party that met M'Clintock was also quite a bit smaller than the large group in Dundas Harbour, it is also likely that Qitdlarssuaq and Uqi split up for periods of time – a wise thing to do in order to better hunt and provide for their families.

But eventually they regrouped and, early in 1859, began the crossing of Jones Sound to Ellesmere Island. The meeting with M'Clintock may have been the final push. Meqqusaaq remembers, "We started on our journey in the winter, after the light came, and set up our permanent camp in the spring, when the ice broke. There were plenty of animals for food on the way, seals, white whales [belugas], walrus, and bears. Long stretches of the coast along which we had to drive [the dogsleds] were not covered with ice, and so we were often obliged to make our way over huge glaciers. On our way we also came to bird rocks, where auks built, and to some eider-duck islands."[21]

Again, the journey over a wide body of water would have been best tackled in the early spring, when the ice is still as solid as it will ever be and the daylight hours are long and bright. They would have still travelled by *qamutiik*, carrying all their possessions with them. Many side trips must have been made to hunt. Hunting and fishing would have sustained the group throughout the journey. Qitdlarssuaq continued as a strong and energetic leader, using his powers as a shaman to see the trail ahead. He is reported to have been seen at times with a white flame over his head. The Inughuit claim that he met with two of their own shamans during his spirit flights ahead of his followers, reporting back that there really were people like themselves ahead, although they spoke a dialect of Inuktitut that was not immediately understandable. Qitdlarssuaq's peculiar behaviour and powers as a shaman became legendary:

> They say that the old leader did not like anyone to follow him too closely. He travelled far ahead of the others, carrying his wife and children on his own sled. And it happened that, one day, they noticed on the pack ice ahead of them a group of naked people. At the sight of them, their dogs threw themselves forward, while the family was overcome with fear. But Qitdlarssuaq had more than one trick in his *angakkuq*'s bag. He began to cry out, "Seaweed! Seaweed! Nothing but seaweed could look like that!" And suddenly, the creatures were transformed into seaweed, as those who were following him confirmed.
>
> On another occasion, they saw a long-haired giant on the shore. Once again, the dogs rushed forward. Qitdlarssuaq used the same trick, crying out that it was baleen (whalebone). Sure enough, as they approached, they saw the whale's jawbone to which some baleen was still attached. Thus Qitdlarssuaq triumphed over the magic of his enemies, until he was finally able to stop and make camp for the summer.[22]

The group was not however uniformly enthusiastic about this journey to the "promised land." Uqi longed for the rich hunting grounds on North Baffin Island and was tired of his subordination to the old shaman. The group had reached a small island in Talbot Inlet on the east coast of Ellesmere Island when the dispute reached an impasse. The group was now somewhat south of where they would cross Smith Sound toward Etah in northwestern Greenland (near present-day Thule Air Base). Uqi and other members of the group were no longer willing to follow Qitdlarssuaq. According to Meqqusaaq,

> We had travelled thus for two winters, and neither year had we lacked food. Then it so happened that one of the oldest amongst us, old Oqé [Uqi] grew homesick. He had long been grave and without words, then all at once he began to talk about whale-beef. He was homesick for his own country, and he wanted to eat whale-beef again. In our old country at home we used to catch many whales.
>
> After he had once started talking, he began to accuse old Qitdlarssuaq, who had been the leader all through the journey, of cheating.

He said it was all lies that Qitdlarssuaq had told about the new country, and he invited them all to turn back.

... The quarrel ended by five sledges turning back, while five went
on. Twenty-four people turned back, and fourteen went on, and
amongst these latter was Oqé's own son, Minik.[23]

## The Death of Qitdlarssuaq

When Qitdlarssuaq reached land, he did indeed find a small group of re-
silient Inuit who had learned to survive in the most northern continuously
inhabited place on Earth. They had however in recent years been plagued
with diseases brought by visiting Europeans. They had also at some time
in their past lost the use of essential Inuit technology. These were reintro-
duced by Qitdlarssuaq's people. The newcomers brought new blood and
quickly taught the Inughuit old skills of kayak building and hunting with
bows, arrows, and harpoons. Life for the Inughuit improved, and the newcomers learned the Inughuit dialect and adopted their method of hitching
dogs to sleds. For several years the Inughuit and Qitdlarssuaq's party lived
and hunted together in peace. But this arrangement did not last. Meqqusaaq recalls,

We taught them to shoot with bow and arrows. Before our arrival they
did not hunt the many reindeer [caribou] that are in their country. If
by any chance they got an animal they did not even dare to eat it, being
afraid that they might die, but they fed their dogs with it.

We taught them to spear salmon [Arctic char] in the streams. There
were a great many salmon in the country, but they did not know the
implement that you spear them with.

And we taught them to build kayaks, and to hunt and catch from
kayaks. Before that they had only hunted on the ice, and had been
obliged during the spring to catch as many seals, walruses, and nar-
whals as they would want for the summer, when the ice had gone ...
They told us that their forefathers had known the use of the kayak,
but that an evil disease had once ravaged their land, and carried off
the old people. The young ones did not know how to build new kayaks,

4.3 Ice in Smith Sound near the place where Qitdlarssuaq and his followers crossed over to Greenland

and the old people's kayaks they had buried with their owners. This was how it had come about that kayak hunting had been forgotten.[24]

By 1875 Qitdlarssuaq was growing old and wanted to return to his original home to die. He had also become involved in another killing, this time of a Greenlandic shaman named Avatannguaq. The two shamans had become deadly rivals. Qitdlarssuaq appears to have been pressured by both his own people and some of the local Inughuit who were afraid of the strange events attributed to Avatannguaq. Qitdlarssuaq was reluctant to again begin the cycle of violence and revenge. Eventually he agreed to a plan of attack and succeeded in killing Avatannguaq. Soon afterward Qitdlarssuaq became extremely ill with stomach pains and a swollen belly. It is said that the spirit of his victim had entered his body and was slowly killing him. He gathered up a few of his followers and headed west toward Ellesmere Island. Meqqusaaq told Knud Rasmussen,

Qitdlarssuaq never saw his country again. He died during the first wintering. And after his death things went very ill with us all. During our second wintering we had not food supplies enough for the winter, and during the great darkness, famine broke out among us … Qitdlarssuaq's wife, Agpaq, and my father and mother … died of hunger. And those who were left, and who refused the salmon, began to eat the dead bodies. Minik and Mataq were the worst. I saw them eat my father and my mother. I was too young and could not stop them. Then one day Minik flung himself upon me from behind, to kill me and eat me. But fortunately my brother came up just then, and Minik only had time to thrust out my one eye, after which he rushed out of the house [iglu]. Then we saw him and Mataq break into a neighbouring house and each take a dead body over his shoulders and flee up into the mountains. Before they disappeared, we heard them call down snow and snowstorms. That was so that their footprints might be covered up. And we never saw anything more of them.[25]

The Greenlandic shaman's posthumous search for revenge had succeeded.

There are conflicting stories as to whether Qitdlarssuaq's body was left on the ice or was carried onto Ellesmere Island. His followers, no longer able to rely on their powerful *angakkuq* to lead them, attempted to travel south to where the group had separated from Uqi's band years earlier. Eventually they were stranded in Makinson Inlet, a place still known by the Inughuit as Perdlerarvigssuaq ("the place of great famine"). Only five survived. They returned to Greenland and did not attempt any further long journeys. The descendants of Qitdlarssuaq and his followers still live in Qaanaaq in northwestern Greenland. In the words of the Inughuit elder Navarana K'avigaq' Sørensen, "He was a leader, feared and respected. He went into trances, and his soul travelled to distant shores across the sea. He is in my blood … Our ancestors are not people who are lost in the past."[26]

## An Inuit Hero

The reasons for Qitdlarssuaq's journey were undoubtedly as mixed and perhaps ill-conceived as those of any European explorer. He was certainly motivated by a desire to escape vengeance for an attempted killing and for a murder. But he also seems to have had a genuine explorer's desire to see new places. He obviously had essential leadership skills and the ability to make his followers believe in him. He told them that their journey was guided by his visions and dreams, whereby he, as a shaman, could travel ahead and find the best route. The journey across Lancaster Sound and the long stay on Devon Island indicate that he and his people were immensely skilled travellers and hunters. It may be that Qitdlarssuaq would not have continued on to Greenland if he had not learned of the existence of an Inuit settlement there, but we don't know that. He succeeded in connecting Inuit from two areas of the Arctic separated by thousands of miles of difficult terrain on both land and sea and by hundreds of years of history. Most of the travelling, particularly the crossings of Lancaster Sound, Jones Sound, and Smith Sound, were accomplished in winter or spring over the ice by dogsled, not by boat.

Qitdlarssuaq's journey was recreated in 1987 by a group of Canadian explorers, half Inuit and half *qallunaat*, led by Renee Wissink.[27] The voyagers included descendants of Qitdlarssuaq's sister Arnatsiaq. They travelled by three teams of dogsleds from Iglulik to Pond Inlet and Arctic Bay, across Lancaster Sound to Devon Island, overland to Jones Sound and the settlement of Grise Fiord on Ellesmere Island, and then east across Smith Sound to Greenland. They used traditional dogsleds and purebred dogs, built *igluvijait* (snow houses) for shelter, and wore skin and fur clothing. They found the snow houses and traditional clothing considerably warmer and more comfortable than southern parkas, tents, and sleeping bags. They left Iglulik in early March and arrived in Qaanaaq, Greenland, two and a half months later.

Qitdlarssuaq's journey of discovery, particularly the years he spent travelling from North Baffin Island across Devon Island to Ellesmere and Greenland, is a remarkable example of the Inuit's ability to travel and survive in their own environment. The journey was made mostly over ice, not by water, and demonstrates the Inuit claim to sovereignty over both land and sea. The passages between the Arctic islands have been well travelled by Inuit for centuries. Like Qitdlarssuaq, some of these travellers must have been exploring new territory as well as moving through familiar hunting grounds. Travel between the islands was accomplished more by dogsled travel than by boat. Knowledge of ice conditions and ocean currents that might cause ice movement and upheaval, awareness of the prevalence of bears and other wildlife, and complete adaptation to the harsh climate meant the difference between survival and disaster. As Father Mary-Rousselière concludes in his fascinating account of Qitdlarssuaq's journey,

> When we study the prehistory of the Eskimos, we see that the peopling of the Arctic went through periods of expansion and contraction that usually coincided with cyclical rises and falls in the Arctic temperature.
>
> Some regions on the periphery of the area inhabited by the Eskimos had less abundant game, a fact that made them less attractive to settlement. When the climate grew colder, the season for hunting by kayak grew shorter, and winter hunting became more difficult. The ever-precarious ecology would be upset, and conditions for human existence would become intolerable. In a season of particularly severe conditions, a camp would be unable to make sufficient provisions of marine game for winter. Available caribou and musk-ox herds would be ever more distant, and the population would be reduced to famine. This cycle recurred several times ... In sparsely populated regions, where camps were few and too far apart to come to each other's aid, human life might disappear completely for several centuries at a time.
>
> More than 4,000 years ago, the first Paleoeskimos reached the eastern Arctic during a relatively temperate period. There have been several ebbs and flows of population since then, particularly in the islands north of Lancaster Sound, that have served as routes of passage towards Greenland. They seem to have remained uninhabited for long periods.
>
> Qitdlarssuaq's migration in the middle of the 19th century should be seen in this context. It seems to have been an extremely cold period ... Some glaciers on the west coast of Greenland reached their maximum westward extension around 1870 ...
>
> The migrants set out for the north along a trail that offered little comfort, and at a singularly unfavourable time. Theirs was a journey that had not been successfully completed in several centuries. The famine that afflicted them, when they tried to return, and the fate of others who tried to follow them, show the risks they knowingly faced, and make their accomplishments all the more significant.
>
> The saga of Qitdlarssuaq, which can be placed side by side with the

legend of Kiviuq as an Eskimo odyssey of the modern era, describes a great human adventure. It shows how a band of highly motivated persons, led by an exceptional chief, can triumph over the most arduous constraints and the most difficult physical circumstances.[28]

## The Fifth Thule Expedition

Another great explorer, the Danish-Greenlandic scientist Knud Rasmussen, provides another example of how well Inuit were able to live and journey through the vast distances of the Arctic. Rasmussen proved to the Western world that "Eskimos" indeed shared a single culture stretching over the largest expanse of geography of any group on Earth. Rasmussen's great journey, his Fifth Thule Expedition from 1921 to 1924 across the Arctic from Thule (Qaanaaq) in northwestern Greenland to the far edge of Alaska, was an incredible re-enactment (going in the opposite direction) of what an Inuit migration might have been like. He travelled as an Inuk would, with dogsleds, lived in tents or *igluvijait*, and hunted for food on the way. He and some of his companions covered 20,000 miles from east to west – one of the greatest exploration treks of modern times. Rasmussen had planned to travel on to the Chukchi Peninsula in order to meet the Russian Inuit, but the arrival of the Bolshevik Revolution in the Russian Far East meant that his stay there was cut short. He travelled with two Danish companions who went on separate excursions of their own during their travels: Peter Freuchen and Therkel Matthiassen. In March 1923 the three Danes separated for the last time, and Rasmussen set out westward with his two Greenlandic companions, Qavigarssuaq and Arnarulunguaq.

Peter Freuchen became almost as well known as Rasmussen himself. The two men established a trading post in Thule, where they met a young Inuk named Minik, who was

famous because he and his father had been kidnapped in 1897 by Robert Peary and taken by ship to New York. Soon after arriving the father died, leaving Minik an orphan in a strange land. The boy was put in the care of someone at the American Museum of Natural History. It was there that Minik found his father's skeleton on display. The shock was almost more than he could bear. Minik survived twelve more years in New England. He asked to be taken home in 1909, but Peary refused. By the time the young man returned home, he was destitute and cultureless, struggling to relearn his language and hunting skills.[29]

Minik and his wife moved in with Rasmussen and Freuchen in Thule. A young Greenlandic woman named Navarana moved in with them as a companion for Minik's wife. Freuchen and Navarana fell in love and married. Navarana accompanied her husband on many of his travels.

Rasmussen's first rule was to live, hunt, and travel as Inuit would in order to gain the trust of the different Inuit communities where they stayed along the way. He recorded many stories, cultural traditions, and details of life in Inuit society before most Inuit had had much contact with Europeans. By doing so, Rasmussen preserved much that might later have been lost. He himself spoke fluent Greenlandic (Kalaallit/Inuktitut) and discovered, to his own surprise, that he could understand and be understood by Inuit right across the Arctic.

He was born in Ilulissat and grew up in Greenland, where he learned to speak Greenlandic before learning Danish. His maternal grandmother was a Greenlandic Inuk, and his father was a Danish missionary who compiled a Danish-Greenlandic grammar and dictionary. From his grandmother and father, the young Kununguaq ("Little Knud") became immersed in his own Inuit heritage. Rasmussen's Greenlandic background and his acute sense of Inuit cultural life made him unique among polar explorers. He is remembered with great respect both in Greenland and in Arctic Canada, particularly Iglulik, where he spent considerable time with the shaman Awa. His journey demonstrated that Inuit travels across the Arctic 800 years ago may well have first been accomplished by a single Inuit group travelling for two or three years, perhaps headed by a charismatic and resourceful leader such as Kiviuq or Qitdlarssuaq. In Rasmussen's day Inuit were often on the move, covering hundreds and even thousands of miles in search of food or to visit friends and relatives. Rasmussen's detailed information about the Inuit he met revolutionized how the world saw Inuit culture. Rasmussen describes his first meeting with the shaman Awa:

The 27th of January was fine, but cold; it was bright starlight towards the close of the journey, but we had had a long and tiring day, and wished for nothing better than to find shelter without having to build it ourselves.

Suddenly out of the darkness ahead shot a long sledge with the wildest team I have ever seen. Fifteen white dogs racing down at full speed, with six men on the sledge. They came down on us at such a pace that we felt the wind of them as they drew alongside. A little man with a large beard, completely covered with ice, leapt out and came towards me, holding out his hand white man's fashion. Then halting, he pointed inland to some snow huts. His keen eyes were alight with vitality as he uttered the ringing question; "Qujangnamik" (thanks to the coming guests).

This was Aua, the angakoq ...

We explained that we had come down to hunt walrus, and the news was greeted with acclamation by our host and his party. They had been thinking of doing the same themselves ...

The winter ice extends some miles out from the shore, to all intents and purposes as firm as land. Then comes the water, with pack ice drifting this way and that according to wind and current. When the wind is blowing off shore, holes appear in the ice just at the edge, and the walrus follow these, diving down to the bottom to feed.

Aua and I had settled ourselves, like the others, in comparative shelter behind a hummock of ice, with a good view all round. The vigil was by no means monotonous; there was something going on all the time, calling up memories of past hunting.

... "Men and the beasts are much alike," said Aua sagely. "And so it was our fathers believed that men could be animals for a time, then men again."[30]

Rasmussen ended his journey on the Bering Strait with some last thoughts that are typical of the beliefs of non-Inuit of his time. He never quite escaped his European heritage even while revelling in his time with the Inuit:

One morning at the end of October, 1924, I awoke for the last time in the little wooden dwelling on the outskirts of Nome (Alaska), where I had been living for the past month. By noon that day I must be on board the big tourist steamer bound for Seattle, and these years of life among the Eskimos would be at an end.

As fate would have it, this very morning I received a visit from an *angakoq*; one of the few still remaining in these parts. And as he was the last of all I met, it seems fitting to conclude with him.

His name was Najagneq, and I met him for the first time in the streets of Nome, as a fugitive in a strange place …

"What does man consist of?"

"Of the body; that which you see; the name, which is inherited from one dead; and then of something more, a mysterious power that we call Yutir – the soul, which gives life, shape and appearance to all that lives."

… [Najagneq explains,] "I have searched in the darkness, being silent in the great lonely stillness of the dark. So I became an *angakoq*, through visions and dreams and encounters with flying spirits … The ancients devoted their lives to maintaining the balance of the universe; to great things, immense, unfathomable things."

"Do you believe in any of these powers yourself?"

"Yes; a power that we call *Sila*, which is not to be explained in simple words. A great spirit, supporting the world and the weather and all life on earth, a spirit so mighty that his utterance to mankind is not through common words, but by storm and snow and rain and the fury of the sea; all the forces of nature that men fear. But he has also another way of utterance, by sunlight, and calm of the sea, and little children innocently at play, themselves understanding nothing. Children hear a soft and gentle voice, almost like that of a woman. It comes to them in a mysterious way, but so gently that they are not afraid; they only hear that some danger threatens … When all is well, *Sila* sends no message to mankind, but withdraws into his own endless nothingness, apart. So he remains as long as men do not abuse life, but act with reverence towards their daily food."

… [Najagneq adds,] "No one has seen *Sila*; his place of being is a mystery, in that he is at once among us and unspeakably far away."

These mighty words form a fitting close to the sketch I have tried to give throughout this book of Eskimo life and thought. Before many years are past, their religion will be extinct, and the white man will have conquered all, the country and its people; their thoughts, their visions and their faith.

I am glad to have had the good fortune to visit these people while they were still unchanged; to have found, throughout the great expanse of territory from Greenland to the Pacific, a people not only one in race and language, but also in their form of culture; a witness in itself to the strength and endurance and wild beauty of human life.[31]

4.4 Dogsledding on Frobisher Bay – the temperature was around -40° Celsius. Shortly after taking this photo, I fell off the *qamutik* (dogsled) and had to run to catch up.

# Canada's Arctic Dominion

I remember camping in the winter season out on the frozen ice. [When I was] a child, during the winter, the people never stayed on the land. When winter came, the people moved out on the ice. For the winter, the people would build a large snowhouse with a big workspace in the centre. From the sides, they would build tunnels. And at the end of each tunnel, a family would build their living quarters. The centre was a workspace or a place to gather for games, drum dances, and stories. That was repeated each year.

Ruth Nigiyonak[1]

## The Largest Uninhabited Island on Earth

The myth of the "disappearing Eskimo" was common by the end of the nineteenth century and throughout the first half of the twentieth. In the words of the great Norwegian explorer Fridtjof Nansen, writing in 1928, "During ages they ["Eskimos"] have learnt to master the severe forces of nature, and no other people can take their place and develop the possibilities of those northern regions. But contact with our civilization, when not carefully guarded as in Greenland, will upset the whole system of their life and community, and they must sink."[2] Anthropologists generally predicted the ultimate extinction of all Indigenous peoples everywhere in the world, not just in the Canadian Arctic. This view was partly a reflection of European attitudes of racial superiority – a superiority that had led to a belief in the ultimate disappearance or assimilation of all cultures that could not or would not accept the European mission of "civilization." Observations of the massive destruction that colonialism and the introduction of modern

5.1 Iceberg near Ilulissat, Greenland

European values were bringing to Indigenous cultures everywhere also en-couraged this belief. Populations of Indigenous peoples in North and South America plummeted by at least 50 per cent and as much as 90 per cent as a result of European colonization between 1500 and 1900.[3] This mortality was often (but not solely) the result of introduced diseases, against which Indigenous people had no immunity. For the Inuit, these were primarily in-fluenza and tuberculosis. But the predictions of ultimate extinction proved in the end to be false. Inuit and other Indigenous peoples have survived. Today First Nations, Inuit, and Métis are the fastest-growing populations in Canada. But the threat of extinction is not just about numbers. It is also about language and culture – about a distinct way of life. Inuit were colo-nized more recently than most Indigenous peoples and still retain a grasp on their language and culture. But this may be changing.

Inuit sometimes ask what European Canadians are doing on their land in the first place. By what right does any non-Inuit nation claim sovereignty over the land or sea of the Arctic? As Lucassie Nutaraaluk remembers,

After England defeated Germany in the First World War, the *qallunaat* came up here and claimed our territory. Our ancestors were never compensated, never paid even though the *qallunaat* came up here and took over our land. I know our ancestors were very skilled people. They had very few tools but they survived. They were very strong and very capable. Thanks to their ability to survive we are here today. I know if we tried today to do what our ancestors did, we would die because we don't have the same skills.[4]

Any sovereignty that Canada can claim over the Arctic has been established very haphazardly over the past 150 years and is still tenuous as far as the Arctic Ocean, including the Northwest Passage, is concerned. The history of the interaction between Inuit and *qallunaat* Canadians, told here and in the next chapter, highlights how difficult this shared journey has been. One place in the High Arctic that seems to encapsulate this strange dance of sovereignty is Dundas Harbour, where Qitdlarssuaq met with the British Navy more than 160 years ago.

On the south coast of Devon Island, there is an inlet or harbour where a ship can anchor in the brief weeks of warmer weather and clear water. Behind the inlet is a massive glacier pouring down from central Devon Island. On the seaward side of the hills that overlook the inlet is a small curved bay. The place is some distance east of Beechey Island, not far from Croker Bay, where another glacier calves small icebergs (mostly "growlers" and "bergy bits") directly into Lancaster Sound.

The first time I visited this place, it was grey and cold. Near the zodiac landing spot is an old Thule site – the ancient ruins of a *qarmaq* (sod house). Little remains beyond a ring of stones and a circular depression in the tundra. Yellow Arctic poppies and striped white and purple bladder campion peep out between the stones. Lichen colours the rocks with vivid splashes of orange and yellow. There used to be a walrus skull nearby (the tusks removed), but it was no longer there the last time I visited. Small stones are still evenly sunk into the tundra to make a little pathway. The archaeological site appears to be very old – perhaps as old as the original Thule migration across the North from Alaska to Greenland. It may also have been a campsite used by Qitdlarssuaq or Uqi on their long stops around the island. They both certainly spent time here, and the campsite is an obvious place to stay. Hunters from Arctic Bay and Pond Inlet still camp here occasionally. Devon

Island is said to be the largest "uninhabited" island on Earth. But humans have lived and travelled around it for centuries, perhaps thousands of years.

Between the site and the bay is a small lake that, on a sunny day, reflects the grim mountains behind like a shield of steel. Beyond the camp site is a sudden sentinel peak of green shaped like a pyramid. Walking past this over several rolling hillsides of tundra and rock, a traveller finally (and in my case breathlessly) steps out onto a high shelf that overlooks the little curved bay below. Red-striped rock cliffs surround it to the north and east. Beyond, the blue shimmer of Lancaster Sound is dotted with quiet islands of ice. From here it is possible to see muskoxen. Armed lookouts have to be posted to watch for bears. They can easily hide behind boulders of white ice that have washed up onto the steep gravel beach, waiting there for a lunch of unwary visitor.

It was here in 1924 that the Canadian government established one of its first Royal Canadian Mounted Police (RCMP) posts in the High Arctic. Close to the beach, there are three or four small derelict buildings that housed the RCMP constables (all young and single) and the Inuit constables with their families. The two archaeological sites – one old and the other fairly recent – represent the bookends of Arctic history as it has been lived so far. In this quiet place, Inuit and Europeans met and lived briefly together. Dundas Harbour, which at first seems so barren of life, slowly begins to fill with long years of silent history.[5]

Viewed from the sea, the buildings are sad, blinkered little boxes perched on the edge of an unknown continent. In late summer a skim of snow already shrouds the land in a quiet shadow of white. The great darkness falls quickly here and lasts for more than three months. At the back of the main building, an old red door opens up to the hillside beyond. There is a path climbing past the outhouse (now a work of abstract art in black and white, as lichen has crept into the wood on the inside) and up the east flank of a massive rocky hill. Here on a small ridge overlooking the post below are two graves. Constable Victor Maisonneuve lies in one, and in the other is Constable William Stephens. The old wooden crosses are still here, but the graves are now headed by two large stone markers and are surrounded by a white picket fence. The site is carefully maintained by the RCMP detachment in Arctic Bay. There is another grave somewhere nearby of an Inuit child, but it is not marked as far as I have ever seen. Dundas Harbour is a vast and silent space, but it is not empty. I have visited this place several

5.2 Inuit family with (from left to right) Nukappiannguaq, unidentified boy, Inalunnguaq, and Tauttianguaq, Dundas Harbour, Devon Island, Northwest Territories, August 1925. They were from Greenland and worked for the RCMP.

5.3 Huts used by Native constables, Dundas Harbour

times, and each time the buildings and graves seem haunted with the past. There are ghosts here.

## A Neglected Dominion

When Britain transferred the Arctic islands to the Dominion of Canada in 1880, the newly created country hardly knew what to do with this vast new acquisition of territory. Some of the islands were contested by other countries, particularly Ellesmere Island far to the north next to Danish Greenland. Canada actually bought the Sverdrup Islands from Norway in the early twentieth century, but little else was done to establish sovereignty until Roald Amundsen completed his historic transit of the Northwest Passage in 1906. Canada was suddenly galvanized into a fit of anxiety over its jurisdiction in the North. Captain Joseph-Elzéar Bernier of the CGS *Arctic* was instructed by the Canadian government to conduct three years of "sovereignty patrols" into and through the Arctic Archipelago.

In the summer of 1908 Bernier sailed for the Arctic from Quebec City down the St Lawrence River. The beautiful old capital was festooned with banners and flags in celebration of the 300th year of the French presence there. Bernier and his little ship chugged down the river and out to sea, rounded Newfoundland and Labrador, and then went up Davis Strait and into the Northwest Passage. The CGS *Arctic* made it as far north and west as Captain William Edward Parry's old wintering place, Winter Harbour, on Melville Island in the High Arctic. There Bernier anchored the ship and waited out the ice for spring, just as Parry had done nearly 100 years before. As the light returned and Siqiniq circled the sky during the long days of summer, Bernier and his crew began preparations for Dominion Day – 1 July 1909 – the anniversary of Canada's union into a single federal nation forty-two years before:

> Dominion Day was celebrated by all on board; all our flags were flying, and the day itself was all that could be desired. At dinner we drank a toast to the Dominion and Premier of Canada; then all assembled around Parry's Rock to witness the unveiling of a tablet sculptured by J.V. Keonig, our first engineer, and placed on the Rock, commemorating the annexation of the whole of the Arctic archipelago. I briefly

referred to the important event in connection with the granting to Canada by the Imperial government on September 1st, 1880 all the British territory in the northern waters of the continent of America and the Arctic Ocean, from 60 degrees west longitude to 141 degrees west longitude, and as far north as 90 degrees, that is to say to the North Pole. Three cheers were given in honour of the Premier, and the Minister of Marine and Fisheries of Canada, and the men dispersed for the balance of the day to enjoy themselves. Most of them engaged in picking wild flowers which grew in abundance, and securing objects of interest.

We built a number of cairns and rebuilt Parry's cairn on Northeast Hill, putting up a copper plate on a piece of oak, abreast of the cairn, with the names of the ships Hecla and Griper 1819–1820 inscribed on it, to indicate where Parry left his records.[6]

Five years later Canada, along with the rest of the British Empire, went to war with Germany. The First World War changed everything. When Canada entered the Great War our foreign and defence policies were dictated by Great Britain. By the end of the war Canada wanted to play a more assertive and independent role. The Dominions (including Canada) insisted on separate delegations at the Versailles Peace talks in 1919.[7] Although still part of the British Empire, Canada (along with Australia, New Zealand, South Africa, and India) was determined to take control of its own destiny. The 1920s were a time of economic expansion, newly assertive nationalism, and cultural revolutions all over the world. Photography, railways, and the telegraph were being joined by moving pictures, wireless radio, the telephone, and the automobile, leading to the telecommunications and transport revolution that is still shrinking our planet. In North America and Europe, Charlie Chaplin, Greta Garbo, and Canadian Mary Pickford ruled silent movies. African American "jazz" music by the likes of Duke Ellington and Ella Fitzgerald began to break through into the mainstream. Women's haircuts and hemlines got shorter in imitation of the "It Girl" of the silver screen and mass-circulation magazines. Canada was beginning to express itself with a new global confidence, despite remaining resolutely a part of the British Empire. Canadian workers demanded political and economic rights.[8] Artists such as Tom Thomson, the Group of Seven, and Emily Carr were establishing a Canadian genre of landscape painting.[9] Authors, artists, filmmakers, and scholars in both French and English were making their mark.

5.4 Captain Joseph Bernier (centre behind the ship's dog) with his crew at Winter Harbour, 1 July 1909.

The population of the country was expanding and changing. The nation had accepted massive numbers of European as well as Chinese and South Asian immigrants in the preceding decades while consolidating its hold over a huge geography. However, Quebec was still in the iron grip of the Catholic Church and English business interests, and "the French" were routinely dismissed as second-class citizens. At this time "citizen" still meant a British subject. "Indians" had no citizenship at all – they were moved onto reserves and their children were sent to residential schools to be "civilized." Métis were generally thought of as "half-breeds" and either treated as Indians with no rights at all, assimilated into white society, or (in Alberta) settled in "colonies" that were administered in a manner similar to Indian reserves. The prevailing orthodoxy was that the "Natives" were dying out. Those who remained were treated as wards of the state in the hope that they would either assimilate or disappear. The deputy superintendent of Indian affairs, and one of the young Dominion's most prominent poets, Duncan Campbell Scott, summed up this philosophy: "I want to get rid of the Indian problem. I do not think as a matter of fact, that the country ought to continuously protect a class of people who are able to stand alone ... Our objective is to continue until there is not a single Indian in Canada that has not been

absorbed into the body politic and there is no Indian question, and no
Indian Department."[10]

"Eskimos" were largely ignored at this time, other than in Canadian concerns over Greenlandic hunters whose travels around Devon and Ellesmere
Islands were jeopardizing Canadian sovereignty claims. In the narrow vision
of international law at the time, travel by Inuit between Greenland and
Ellesmere Island, which had been going on for centuries, was never interpreted as establishing Inuit sovereignty over the High Arctic. Rather it was
always interpreted as a threat to Canadian (British) sovereignty by Danish
interests. There were also concerns about the growing number of exploration parties in the Arctic, particularly American, and about the killing of
game. Regulations were added to the Canadian *Northwest Game Act* of
1917 in order to outlaw the killing of muskoxen.[11] This prohibition was
mostly aimed at Greenlandic hunters on Ellesmere Island, but it would also
have a devastating impact on "Canadian Eskimos" during times of hardship.
An RCMP detachment was established in Craig Harbour on Ellesmere Island
(near modern-day Grise Fiord) and another on the Bache Peninsula to the
northeast. These were for the purpose of policing the new regulations in
order to control the entry of Greenlandic Inuit onto Canadian soil. Other
than contact with the Hudson's Bay Company, whalers, missionaries, and a
few RCMP constables, most Inuit had little to do with Canadian government
officials or other *qallunaat* at this time. But this was about to change.

## The Trial of Nuqallaq

Canada was determined to protect its interests in the High Arctic. The establishment of RCMP posts and the enforcement of game regulations were
only part of the story. Not quite fifty years after Qitdlarssuaq died on his
way back from Greenland, another death, this time on North Baffin Island,
made Arctic history. This case involved the killing of a Newfoundland fox
trapper, Robert S. Janes, by Nuqallaq, a hunter from the area. The killing
triggered a police investigation and the first criminal trial held in the High
Arctic. It was not the first criminal trial of an Inuk, but it was the first held
in an Inuit community, in this case Pond Inlet.

According to Inuit law, the survival of the group is more important than
an individual's well-being or rights. An individual, whether Inuk or not, can-

not survive in the Arctic without the support of a group or community. Hunters live in close relationship with the land, the ice, and the sea, as well as with the animals they kill. Shamans could transform themselves into other animals, and *tuurngait* (helping spirits) guided them on their travels. Both Kiviuq and Qitdlarssuaq were guided by animal spirits. When Awa reluctantly embraced Christianity, he sent his *tuurngait* to his shaman sister in North Baffin. Nuliajuk is the guardian of the animals of the sea, and if she is not respected, she will withdraw her bounty and the people will starve. Elders still teach the importance of respecting wildlife, the land, the environment, and spirits in order to survive. Humans are necessarily in relationship with all other living beings as well as with the powerful force of the environment and intelligence – Sila.

In his film *Diet of Souls*, John Houston explores the relationship between Inuit and animals. Inuit believe the animals that humans eat also have souls of their own. It is this fact as much as the size and ferocity of a polar bear or a walrus that makes the hunt dangerous. Inuit did not traditionally hunt for commercial gain or the accumulation of wealth but to support their families and communities. The obligations were not only physical and social but also spiritual. As David Pelly writes,

> For Inuit, traditionally, hunting was the basis of survival; theirs is a hunting culture. But the Inuit hunt is different from the typical western hunt, in which a more powerful, technically better equipped, or perhaps smarter being tracks down and kills an inferior being. The difference may lie in the notion of "soul." Whereas the European world-view is that only humans have a soul, the traditional Inuit belief is that all beings have a soul. For Inuit, success at the hunt was a result of respecting the soul of their quarry, of holding the proper attitude toward the seal.
>
> Traditionally, the hunt is a pact between Inuit and the seal. The Inuit hunter is not extracting from the environment but creating a bond between his people and their environment. When the seal gives itself to the hunter, it is an act of sharing in which the seal is transformed from animal to human. Being consumed is a form of rebirth or renewal for the seal.
>
> According to ancient Inuit philosophy, sharing among all beings makes survival in the Arctic possible. A real Inuk would never brag about his hunt, overhunt, or not hunt. Nor would he decline to share

the hunt's reward, for to do so would be to contravene the basic laws of respect among all creatures, who exist as equals. To be disrespectful in this way would offend the seals and encourage them to disappear. And for Inuit through the centuries, life depended on the seals and on this pervasive respect for them.[12]

This respect for wildlife is fading, however, as *qallunaat* and young Inuit adopt modern European attitudes toward animals. As Mariano Aupilaarjuk has said,

There are times you would come across bones. For instance, bones from a caribou that had been killed by wolves. We were told if we came across bones on the ground we were to turn them around and then leave them. I still follow this practice today. I'll explain the reason for turning the bones. If I am in bed sleeping, I would become very tired if I just slept on one side. I would feel better if I were to move. In the same way, we have to turn them the other way. That is the *maligaq* [law] concerning bones. I still follow this because I want to take away their tiredness.

We shouldn't be killing our wildlife without reason. We should only be killing them for food. There is no need to have new laws about wildlife for Inuit had their *maligait* about wildlife, even though they were not written. The present laws about wildlife are not our *maligait*. The *maligait* that we follow are not seen because the Inuit *piusiq* [way] is not visible. What I told you about the bones is a *maligaq* although it doesn't require a licence. It is a *maligaq* where respect is shown through wanting the bones of the caribou to feel rested. That way we show our gratitude to the animal. This is an Inuit *piusiq* that is not being practiced anymore. In the past, all bones were carefully gathered together for this was one of the great *tirigusuusiit* [ritual laws].[13]

During the nineteenth and twentieth centuries, some Inuit had become part of a wage economy, working with American and Scottish whalers or trapping for furs, especially fox, in return for goods at the nearest Hudson's Bay Company post. Even so, they still lived by their old laws. Although Inuit laws stress reconciliation and restoration of relations rather than punishment, if an individual demonstrated that he or she could not or would not stop causing harm, drastic measures could be taken. Tolerance for persistent and recurrent harmful behaviour, whether caused wilfully or through some form of mental illness, could not continue indefinitely. If the behaviour threatened to harm the survival of the group, including threatening to drive away the animals on which Inuit depended, banishment or killing could be seen as the only solution. Threats to kill dogs were also taken very seriously, as the dogs were crucial to hunting.

Nuqallaq and his family were travelling around North Baffin Island when they encountered a group of Inuit camped out on the ice of Admiralty Inlet. The fur trapper Janes also arrived in the little village of *igluvijait* (snow houses) after having travelled on his own for some time. The trapper was frostbitten, hungry, exhausted, and desperate. He began threatening to shoot dogs or possibly people when his demands for fox pelts were not immediately satisfied. His fury seemed uncontrolled and frightening. The Inuit thought he had gone mad. Eventually the group felt that the situation was getting out of hand. A meeting of the hunters, including Nuqallaq, agreed that killing Janes was the only way to ensure the safety of the people and their dogs. When Janes walked out of an *igluvijaq* (snow house) the evening of 15 March 1920, he was shot. This was done by Nuqallaq with the help of two or three others. After Janes's execution (for that was effectively what it was), the Inuit of the community carefully wrapped his body in caribou skins, putting mittens and boots on his hands and feet. They then placed the frozen body in a box and stowed it in the rocks above the ice of Admiralty Inlet out of respect for any possible relatives who might wish to claim his remains. The Inuit, including Nuqallaq, made no secret of their actions and believed they had done no wrong. It was their custom – harsh but effective – to kill anyone who posed such a serious threat to the community.

Nuqallaq then travelled to the Iglulik area along with his father, Umik, a shaman who began preaching the Christian Gospel. Nuqallaq acted as his assistant, and many families in the area joined the new church during the winter of 1921–22. Meanwhile a police investigation was launched. Janes's body was exhumed and transported to Pond Inlet on Eclipse Sound at the top of Baffin Island. He was eventually buried in a lonely grave above the beach well outside of the community. His body remained there, gradually disintegrating off a low cliff into the sea, until members of the local community removed it to a safer location in August 2004.[14]

The *angakkuq* (shaman) Awa tried to warn Nuqallaq that the *qallunaat* would not allow the killing of one of their own to go unavenged. Perhaps this is why Nuqallaq turned to Christianity. Perhaps he hoped that by adopting the Europeans' religion, he would escape vengeance. He was eventually arrested and tried for manslaughter along with two of his "co-conspirators" before a judge and jury in Pond Inlet. The trial was held at a specially established Stipendiary Magistrate's Court of the Northwest Territories the last week of September 1923. Nuqallaq and one of his co-defendants were convicted. Nuqallaq was sentenced to ten years penal servitude. He actually spent nearly two years in Stony Mountain Penitentiary near Winnipeg, Manitoba. There he contracted tuberculosis. He was given early release and shipped home to Pond Inlet in September 1925. The return of this shadow of a formerly strong and even feared hunter had a devastating effect on the Inuit communities in North Baffin. Tuberculosis spread like the plague. In addition hunting activities had been seriously curtailed by the numbers of Inuit who had been kept in and around the Eclipse Sound area throughout the investigation and trial. As a consequence of disease, disruption in hunting, and the inability to fill food caches for the winter, there was much suffering and death throughout North Baffin following these events. Nuqallaq himself died within months of his return to the North.

## Dundas Harbour

This case represents one of the earliest exercises of the Canadian criminal justice system in the Arctic. In the years following Janes's death and Nuqallaq's trial, RCMP posts were established in remote parts of the Arctic not normally inhabited by Canadian Inuit, although Greenlandic Inuit had been crossing the ice to hunt for muskox on Ellesmere Island for many years. The RCMP posts were part of a pattern of activity by the Canadian government to establish sovereignty over the northern third of the continent. Police detachments were established both at Craig Harbour on the southern end of Ellesmere Island and in Pond Inlet in 1922, at Dundas Harbour on Devon Island in 1924, and on the Bache Peninsula on the east coast of Ellesmere Island in 1926. Two or three constables were landed at these remote outposts, along with one or two Inuit families hired to assist them in building and maintaining the posts. Ironically many of the Inuit families drafted for this purpose were Greenlandic, as Canadian Inuit tended to be unwilling to leave their homes and work for the RCMP at this time. Devon Island, and its detachment at Dundas Harbour, was particularly isolated.

The RCMP detachment at Dundas Harbour existed from 1924 to 1933, was turned into a Hudson's Bay Company post during the 1930s, closed down during the Second World War, and then was briefly reopened by the RCMP again from 1945 to 1951. For the first season, three young constables had to manage on their own without the help of Inuit constables and their families to hunt and sew winter clothing. In 1925 a small group of Inughuit was stationed there, and the original three constables were reduced to two – Victor Maisonneuve and a newcomer named William Stephens. Once a year the supply ship from the South would drop off flour, tea, coffee, sugar, ammunition, and other essential items, but otherwise the young men (both *qallunaat* and Inuit) and one young Inuk woman with her child were on their own. By early September the freezing weather would begin and the ice would form. By December there was continuous darkness and the sea ice was solid from horizon to horizon. The reluctant sun did not return until February, after which many more months of snow and ice would keep the little detachment locked into its winter routine. The men could get out onto the ice to hunt for walrus and seal only in the spring. They would have learned to watch out warily for polar bears who would also be on the hunt. By mid-summer constant daylight could bring its own challenges, as sleep becomes extremely difficult. In fact the rhythms of darkness and light in the North are as challenging as the cold for *qallunaat*. Long hours of darkness in winter cause lethargy, depression, and a constant craving for simple carbohydrates – something not readily available in the Arctic until recently. The summer's constant light makes sleep impossible. Many months of winter and summer are passed in states of chronic fatigue, stress, and loneliness. Two young men locked up together in one small cabin can learn to hate each other.

In June 1926, for reasons and in circumstances that are still a mystery, Constable Victor Maisonneuve shot himself while on his own at a seal hunting camp in Croker Bay.[15] He had been one of the original three constables and was due to be transferred out on the CGS *Arctic* on its annual supply stopover in August. He had also accompanied the legendary RCMP explorer Sergeant A.H. Joy in his transit across Devon Island and back earlier that year.[16] The following August, Constable William Stephens appears to have accidentally shot himself while hunting for walrus not far from the detachment. There was no official investigation. The local Inuit had their suspicions. Says Sam Arnakallak of Pond Inlet,

> At Tallurutiit [Devon Island], they used to have Greenlanders. When we moved there, we were the first Canadian Inuit. They sent the Greenlanders out on a ship. After they left, there were two graves. We went there in 1928 and there were two RCMP graves, and I used to hear that they shot themselves. The first one shot himself and later on, the other one shot himself ... I think myself that they were shot because of jealousies. I think they were shot by Greenlandic husbands. I think they were just saying that they just shot themselves. I suspected this because they wanted to exhume them. They wanted to know where they shot themselves and where the bullet entered and left the bodies.[17]

As Shelagh D. Grant points out in her definitive book on Nuqallaq's trial, *Arctic Justice*, any hint that a Greenlandic Inuk might have shot an RCMP officer because of suspected sexual delinquencies with an Inuk woman would have created a storm of negative publicity domestically and a potentially embarrassing fallout on the diplomatic front (as the Inughuit were Danish subjects). Suspicions of suicide were almost as bad in those days, when the RCMP had inherited a reputation for indomitability from its British imperial past as a rugged tamer of the Canadian wilderness. Although very little information is publicly available, it appears the two constables reached a terrible impasse. They drew a line down the middle of their tiny cabin and refused to speak to each other for months. This would have made living in close quarters through the black, bitter winter almost impossible to endure. I also suspect (although I have no direct evidence) that the fact that the senior constable was French Canadian and a veteran of the First World War whereas the junior member was English may also have created tensions at a time when Quebecois were assumed by English Canadians to be their inferiors. It is difficult to portray in words how isolated this place is and how haunted. The death of the two young constables remains a mystery hidden by this daunting land.

# The Empire of Canada

The trial of Nuqallaq was one of a few early judicial proceedings and official actions whereby the Canadian government set out to achieve three aims. One was to demonstrate to "the Eskimo that Canadian law must be respected." Acting commissioner Cortlandt Starnes of the RCMP believed that holding a jury trial in the tiny remote settlement of Pond Inlet with all its judicial pomp and circumstance would not only be more economical (which was doubtful) but also "have a deterrent effect on the Eskimos." In his opinion, "some such steps appear to be necessary in order to impress upon the natives that their disregard for human life will not be tolerated."[18] That Janes was a British subject – a white man – undoubtedly played a role in the decision to hold a trial.

The second and more important aim was to reinforce Canada's claims of sovereignty over the Arctic Archipelago. The judicial party aboard the CGS *Arctic* sent to Pond Inlet for the trial took a leisurely tour of the Arctic on its way, partly it seems to impress upon the Danish government Canada's superior claims to Ellesmere Island. The party stopped briefly at Godhaven, Greenland (now Nuuk), where the ship's officers and the judicial party were entertained by Danish dignitaries. The visit was covered by the local press. A news story was wired to Copenhagen claiming that "neither scientific nor practical investigations form the objective of these visits, but first and foremost a demonstration of Canadian sovereignty over Arctic America is intended."[19]

A third aim, although perhaps less consciously pursued, was to justify a certain type of Canadian national identity typical of the late nineteenth and early twentieth centuries – white, British, northern, hardy, brave, resolute, masculine, quietly disciplined, law-abiding, and calm in the face of crisis. For Constable Stephens in Dundas Harbour the assignment in the Arctic may well have started out as a kind of "Boy's Own Adventure" – something from the pages of John Buchan or Arthur Conan Doyle. The early years of the North-West Mounted Police, later the Royal Canadian Mounted Police, typified the image that the young nation of Canada wanted to project to its citizens and to the world. It was (and remains) consciously non-American. Any flag-waving done at the time was directed toward "king and country," as represented by the Union Jack (later the Red Ensign with the British flag in one corner and the Canadian coat of arms in the other – the ubiquitous

Canadian Maple Leaf is a child of the 1960s). The RCMP's role in the North epitomized this romantic view of Canadians as the inheritors of British imperial history with its continuing civilizing mission among the "Natives." In the Arctic the Natives were the "Esquimaux" or "Eskimos." Although this type of Canadian national identity may seem anachronistic, it is still very much alive, particularly in the North. During its meandering travels toward Pond Inlet in 1923, the CGS *Arctic* anchored off the southwestern tip of Devon Island. Here the judicial party destined for Pond Inlet and Nuqallaq's trial paused: "The opportunity was seized to visit nearby Beechey Island, Franklin's last winter quarters, and acknowledge Canada's debt to the old explorers. Every man in the expedition able to do so went to the Franklin cenotaph, keystone of Canada's Arctic Dominion, and with all at attention, the Union Jack was slowly hoisted to the top of the flagpole above the cenotaph, and fluttered in the breeze amid complete silence for a minute. At the conclusion of the ceremony three hearty cheers and a tiger were given for His Majesty the King."[20]

The exotic appeal of the Arctic continues to have much to do with our image of ourselves as Canadians. Canadian national identity is partly built on our cultural and legal claims against other nation-states in the North. Canada's claim to sovereignty over the Arctic Archipelago, angling north between Greenland to the east and Alaska to the west and extending all the way to the North Pole, is the expression of this cultural identity in geographic, political, and (possibly) legal terms. In this sense it can be said that Canada's self-image as a nation-state becomes clearer the farther away we move from its southern boundary with the United States. But this northern trajectory is one that few Canadians ever travel in reality. For many Canadians, the Arctic remains the imaginary Great White North – a boundless expanse of snow and ice with the occasional polar bear in the background.

It is not possible to understand the relationship between legal definitions of sovereignty and the sociological, political, cultural, and economic roots underlying this concept in law without looking at the nature of Canada's status as a nation more generally. Although Canada's statehood in international law is not in doubt, its coherence as a nation has always been ambiguous. Quebec nationalism, western discontent, the gradual accretion of Canadian sovereignty over Newfoundland and other territory, and the continuing renegotiation of Canadian boundaries and regional relations (most recently in the creation of Nunavut) make Canadian nationality much more fluid than might be considered "normal" in other national entities. The historical trajectory has been for Canada's boundaries to expand externally (from east to west and then south to north) while being occasionally rearranged internally to meet new political requirements. What impact does an ambiguous Canadian nationalism have on questions of Canadian sovereignty? The presence of Indigenous peoples in northern Quebec should be crucial to resolving longstanding conflicts over the legal and political status of Quebec as part (or not) of Canada. However, in the Supreme Court of Canada's *Reference on Quebec Sovereignty* case, Aboriginal voices were acknowledged but then quickly set aside as irrelevant.[21]

In 1982 the Canadian Constitution was amended to include section 35 (1), which states, "The existing aboriginal and treaty rights of the aboriginal peoples of Canada are hereby recognized and affirmed."[22] Aboriginal people are specifically defined to include Indians, Métis, and Inuit. Treaty rights also specifically include not only treaties already in existence but also any such rights, treaties, or land claim agreements that may be concluded in the future.[23] Non-Indigenous Canadians generally see the recognition of Aboriginal rights under section 35 (when they have any awareness of them at all) as a very imperfect compromise between small, impoverished Aboriginal minorities who continue to make exorbitant demands and white or migrant majorities in southern Canada who believe they defeated and displaced Aboriginal peoples years ago. Most Canadians do not see the changes to the Constitution in 1982 as fundamentally affecting the status quo, which they also do not recognize as colonial. For Aboriginal peoples, who have always been acutely aware of Canadian colonialism, the constitutional recognition of Aboriginal and treaty rights was long overdue. Aboriginal peoples lobbied extensively for their inclusion in the new "repatriated" Constitution along with a Charter of Rights and a "made-in-Canada" amending formula.

During the Centennial celebrations of 1967, which I remember so well as a kind of "coming-of-age" for all of Canada, Chief Dan George of the Tsleil-Waututh Nation addressed 35,000 people in Vancouver's old Empire Stadium on Canada Day:

How long have I known you, Oh Canada? A hundred years? Yes, a hundred years. And many, many *seelanum* [lunar months] more. And today, when you celebrate your hundred years, Oh Canada, I am sad for all the Indian people throughout the land.

For I have known you when your forests were mine; when they gave me my meat and my clothing. I have known you in your streams and rivers where your fish flashed and danced in the sun, where the waters said 'come, come and eat of my abundance.' I have known you in the freedom of the winds. And my spirit, like the winds, once roamed your good lands.

But in the long hundred years since the white man came, I have seen my freedom disappear like the salmon going mysteriously out to sea. The white man's strange customs, which I could not understand, pressed down upon me until I could no longer breathe.

When I fought to protect my land and my home, I was called a savage. When I neither understood nor welcomed his way of life, I was called lazy. When I tried to rule my people, I was stripped of my authority.

My nation was ignored in your history textbooks – they were little more important in the history of Canada than the buffalo that ranged the plains. I was ridiculed in your plays and motion pictures, and when I drank your fire-water, I got drunk – very, very drunk. And I forgot.

Oh Canada, how can I celebrate with you this Centenary, this hundred years? Shall I thank you for the reserves that are left to me of my beautiful forests? For the canned fish of my rivers? For the loss of my pride and authority, even among my own people? For the lack of my will to fight back? No! I must forget what's past and gone.[24]

Most Canadians remember Chief Dan George as a movie star in films such as *Little Big Man* (for which he was nominated for an Academy Award) or *The Outlaw Josey Wales*. But he was much more than this. Alas his hopes of seeing the barriers of isolation shattered still seem very remote.

From the more recent perspective of John Borrows, an Indigenous constitutional law professor, hope for the future lies in "multi-jurisdictionality," which means the inclusion of European and Indigenous laws as equally authoritative under the Constitution:

If the broader legal system does not acknowledge Indigenous laws, the rule of law will be more severely constrained in the process. Unfortunately, the burden will be weightier for Indigenous peoples if this occurs ... In working to expand our traditions it must be remembered that Canadian law derives its authority from appeals to precedent, consensus, reason, and consistency. It should also be remembered that Canadian law also derives its authority from force. Its application can be hard to wrest from the biases of wealth, status, social convention, and established Western traditions ... [but] [l]egal cultures are fluid. Law is in the process of continual transformation, and Indigenous peoples must participate in its changes ... Our legal traditions have great wisdom, durability, and flexibility in their ability to generate stability and order across this land. Multi-jurisdictionalism must receive the support it needs to nourish these strengths. Indeed, our Constitution depends upon it.[25]

## The Meaning of Sovereignty in International Law

It is rarely remembered that, north of the 60th parallel, Inuit and other Indigenous peoples significantly outnumber incoming Europeans from the South in most circumpolar nation-states, including Canada. The population of Nunavut, for example, is 85 per cent Inuit. In the smaller communities outside of Iqaluit, the language spoken by most people most of the time is Inuktitut, not English or French. On an international level, the Arctic encircles the northern regions of nation-states in North America, Europe, and Asia, yet its population is predominantly Indigenous – neither clearly Canadian nor American, European nor Asian. The nationalisms of all Arctic states can be seen as contingent on this predominance of non-European populations in their northern regions. Almost all Arctic nations are settler states; their European populations have come from elsewhere. The Faroe Islands, Greenland, Lapland (territorial lands of the Saami in Norway, Sweden, Finland, and Russia), the autonomous regions of northern Siberia, as well as the Canadian territories of Yukon, the Northwest Territories, and Nunavut are each different attempts at autonomy, self-government, and (more recently) some recognition of the right to self-determination on the part of the Indigenous inhabitants of Denmark, Norway, Sweden, Finland, Russia, and Canada. Alaska also recognizes some autonomous political and legal status for Aleuts, Iñupiat, Yupiit, and other Indigenous peoples. However, their cultural status and their relationship to American sovereignty in the Arctic are not secure, nor are the status and sovereignty of their counterparts in other nation-states of the region.

What is clear is that Canada, Finno-Scandinavia, Russia, and the United States are all imperial powers in the Arctic. Canada, Russia, and the United States accumulated massive amounts of territory in the nineteenth century without consulting the Indigenous inhabitants. There are no historic treaties north of the treeline – the earliest agreement involving Indigenous peoples in the Arctic is the *Alaska Native Claims Settlement Act* of 1971.[26] Much of the land and sea in the Arctic were in fact obtained through huge real estate transactions. Alaska was purchased by the United States from Russia in 1867 and was known at the time as "Seward's Folly" after Secretary of State William H. Seward dared to spend US$7.2 million (two cents an acre) on what then seemed a worthless wilderness.[27] Most of what became the Canadian Arctic was transferred to Canada by Britain in 1880 following the breaking of the Hudson's Bay Company's monopoly over trade in the West and the transfer to Canada in 1870 of much of Rupert's Land, which had been held by the company since 1670.[28]

What does this mean for sovereignty in the Arctic? "Sovereignty" is a term that defies any clear definition. In international law it is inextricably tied to "the exclusive ability of a state to regulate activities occurring in its territory, subject only to the strictures of international law ... [This] is the ultimate hallmark of a state's independence and, hence, of its sovereign status in international law. Thus, exclusive possession of territory is not only required of a state as a matter of legal definition, it is also one of the principal methods by which it exhibits its sovereignty."[29] "Territory" includes land, inland waters (lakes and rivers), and coastal waters as well as columns of air and subterranean areas above and below the geographic extent of the nation-state. It can include straits or passages between islands. Here are the usual methods whereby sovereignty over territory is recognized in international law, with descriptions by John Currie:

1  Effective occupation: "an effective and continuous display of state authority over territory, coupled with a demonstrated intent by that state to establish and maintain its sovereignty ... What constitutes a sufficient display of state authority or sovereign intent for purposes of establishing title

based on effective occupation will vary from case to case. Relevant state activities may take such obvious forms as the establishment and maintenance of settlements or industry, but may also extend to other less direct manifestations of sovereign authority such as the enactment of legislation or the conclusion of treaties that apply to the territory in question."[30]

2  Conquest: military invasion and takeover of territory from someone else. This is no longer a valid way of establishing sovereignty, but "a valid root of title may still be traced to acts of conquest occurring prior to the early twentieth century, at a time when such a mode of acquisition was legally permissible ... The clear basis of title so acquired was the effective and actual exercise of control ... over the conquered territory ... [with] an intent to establish ... sovereignty."[31]

3  Other methods include prescription (long-term effective occupation of a territory that belongs to another sovereign state), cession (giving up territory through a treaty), renunciation, and abandonment, as well as natural accretion or erosion of land (such as is currently happening because of climate change).

Sovereignty in the Arctic is frequently compared and contrasted with the international regime regarding territorial sovereignty and control of the Antarctic. However, there are significant differences. European incursions into Antarctica are much more recent than in the Arctic. Initial exploration of Antarctica occurred in the early nineteenth century, including the voyages of the *Terror* and the *Erebus* under the command of Captain James Clark Ross from 1839 to 1843. Sustained efforts to explore and study the continent did not begin until the turn of the twentieth century when British and Norwegian explorers vied with each other to reach the South Pole. National claims by Britain, France, Australia, New Zealand, Norway, Argentina, and Chile to slices of Antarctica have been suspended or frozen under the Antarctic Treaty System, which first came into force in 1961.[32] The continent is preserved for scientific research and environmental protection. Mining, oil and gas exploration, and other industrial activities are forbidden. The only continuing commercial activity is marine harvesting, including fishing and whaling (both of which are controversial) as well as bioprospecting for potentially valuable microbial life, such as krill. Antarctica's status under international law is more like the high seas or outer space. The closest parallels are to international treaty rights in relation to the moon.[33] Nevertheless, Antarctic circumpolar states as well as Europeans and Americans do have control over parts of Antarctica through arrangements created under international treaty law. Although these arrangements do not establish formal sovereignty, they do allow for the construction and maintenance of research bases, airfields, and more or less permanent camps – including one at the South Pole.

The major difference between the Arctic and the Antarctic is the lack of any Indigenous population on the Antarctic continent or nearby islands. Although there are Indigenous populations in the southernmost regions of circumpolar nations such as Australia, New Zealand, South Africa, Chile, and Argentina, none of these people ever travelled south, other than a few who obtained knowledge of the southern seas sailing out of Patagonia with whaling ships. None of these populations have settled near or across the Antarctic Circle. The only human presence in the Antarctic is limited to scientific research stations, weather stations, tourist destinations, historic sites of explorers such as Robert Falcon Scott, Roald Amundsen, and Sir Ernest Henry Shackleton, and the remains of massive seal and whaling operations from the early twentieth century. Unlike nearly everywhere else where Europeans have staked out claims of sovereignty, Antarctica truly is *terra nullius*, or "empty land." But the Arctic is not, nor ever was, *terra nullius*. It has been inhabited by humans for thousands of years.

Canada's sovereignty over the Arctic region is based on a patchwork of three legal theories, not all of them recognized by other nation-states: the sector theory, the straight baselines theory, and historical occupation.

The *sector theory* is what most Canadians are used to seeing on their maps. The polar region can be divided along longitudinal lines running north of the land borders of nation-states immediately contiguous to the region like a giant frozen pie. For Canada, this means extending the boundary between Alaska and Yukon to the North Pole and the not-so-straight line between Greenland and Ellesmere Island in the same direction, creating an irregular triangle that encompasses all the Arctic islands and the waterways in between. This is what Bernier claimed for Canada in 1909. Not all Arctic states accept the sector theory. Russia supports it, not surprisingly since this gives it by far the biggest piece of the pie. Canada first proposed this theory in support of its claims in 1907 when Senator Pascal Poirier proposed a resolution in the Canadian Senate claiming "all lands that are to be found in the waters between a line extending from the eastern extremity north, and another line extending from the western extremity north."[34] Canada maintained this very inconsistently as a basis for its claims with greater or lesser enthusiasm until the 1980s.[35]

Under international customary law, as established by the *North Sea Continental Shelf Cases* in the International Court of Justice, an international legal rule or custom (not contained in an agreement or treaty) must be supported both by the general practice of nation-states and by a belief on their part that their actions are as a result of a legal obligation.[36] This somewhat circular logic does not give Canada much ground for relying on the sector theory, as it is not supported by the United States or Europe (except Russia). In addition simple proclamations of discovery (symbolized by cairns, plaques, flags, and little notes) must now be accompanied by "effective occupation." You cannot claim what you do not use. Canada has been slow to recognize that its Inuit citizens and their forebears have been effectively occupying much of this region for hundreds or even thousands of years and that effective occupation should take this into account.

There is more support for the *straight baselines theory*. International law as laid down by the International Court of Justice in the *Fisheries Case* of 1951 (and now codified in the *United Nations Convention on the Law of the Sea*) supports the practice of states drawing straight lines from each of the outermost extensions of land bordering on the sea around a heavily indented coastline (as exists in the Arctic).[37] Instead of hugging the low-tide mark at a distance of 12 nautical miles, straight baselines allow states to claim all the water within the lines as part of their internal waters. Canada relies on this theory to claim the routes between the Arctic islands, including the Northwest Passage. There are points at the various entrances and exits into and out of the passages through the Arctic Archipelago that are clearly covered by overlapping baselines that enclose Canada's internal waters. Therefore, ships transiting the Northwest Passage must pass through Canadian waters regardless of the legal status of the passage itself. Unfortunately the United States and Europe insist that the Northwest Passage is an international strait connecting two areas of the high seas – the North Atlantic and the western Arctic Ocean, which extends around Alaska to the Pacific. There is an argument that nations cannot draw straight baselines across such a strait, meaning that Canada's claim to the passage (or passages) is not supported by most states. The United States in particular has consistently insisted that the passage is indeed an international strait.

However, as the eminent Canadian international lawyer Donat Pharand points out, the establishment of an international strait depends not only on geographic criteria (whether the Northwest Passage connects two areas of the high seas – which it appears to do) but also on a functional requirement as outlined in the *Corfu Channel Case*[38] (whether a strait or passage of water has "been a useful route for international maritime traffic, as evidenced mainly by the number of ships using the strait and the number of flags [ships' nationalities] represented").[39] In 1988, when Pharand's book on the subject was written, only forty-five ships had made a complete transit of the Northwest Passage since Amundsen's journey, and of these over half were Canadian.[40] In the twenty-five years since then, there has been a significant increase in traffic through the Arctic Archipelago but hardly enough to warrant the assertion that the Northwest Passage is a functional strait between areas of the high seas. And again, most of these transits have been made by Canadian ships. "Those who maintain that the Passage may be so classified [as an international strait] obviously confuse *actual use* with *potential use*."[41] In 2013 a Danish-owned cargo vessel became the first large commercial vessel to successfully transit the Northwest Passage from Vancouver to Europe. As Michael Byers pointed out in the *Globe and Mail*,

> Stephen Harper should lose sleep this week, as the Danish-owned *Nordic Orion* becomes the first cargo vessel to use the Northwest Passage as an international shipping route – at no little risk to Canada's environment and sovereignty. Last week, the crash of a Coast Guard helicopter in the Northwest Passage underlined how very dangerous Arctic waters can be. The three men on board were wearing survival suits. They escaped the aircraft before it sank but froze to death in the hour it took for the icebreaker *Amundsen* to reach them ... The *Nordic Orion* will not undermine Canada's legal position that the Northwest Passage constitutes internal waters, since the ship has registered its voyage with the Canadian Coast Guard – thereby seeking and receiving permission from Canada. But other ships will follow, and their compliance with Canada's domestic laws – and therefore our ability to ensure safety and environmental protection – cannot be assumed.[42]

As commercial traffic in the Canadian Arctic increases through the transit of cruise and cargo ships, the line between actual and potential use is beginning to blur.

## The Law of the Sea

There is no longer any dispute over sovereignty in relation to the islands of the Arctic (including Ellesmere), with the exception of a residual and largely friendly dispute between Canada and Denmark over a lonely bit of rock called Hans Island between Greenland and Ellesmere Island.[43] There is much more dispute in relation to the continental shelf underlying the Arctic Ocean. This shelf is governed by the *United Nations Convention on the Law of the Sea*, which Canada ratified in 2003.[44] Russia, Norway, and Denmark (Greenland) are also parties to this convention, but the United States is not. The convention probably has the force of international customary law, by which the United States would be bound, but its failure to ratify the convention leaves an unfortunate lack of clarity in negotiations among Arctic nations. Under American constitutional law, a treaty must be ratified by a two-thirds majority of the Senate. The United States signed the *Convention on the Law of the Sea* in 1994 but will not be bound by it until such ratification takes place. All American presidents, both Republican and Democrat, have supported ratification of the convention, but continuing resistance among conservative Republicans in the US Senate makes ratification impossible.[45] Nevertheless, all the Arctic circumpolar nations recognize the principles of law set out in the convention. However, Inuit are again left out in the cold, as they are not recognized in international law as having the status of a nation-state. Therefore, Inuit must rely on their home states to negotiate sovereignty issues on their behalf. The Inuit Circumpolar Council, along with other Indigenous organizations, has questioned this requirement as a continuation of colonialism in the Arctic.

The *Convention on the Law of the Sea* now governs almost all international law related to maritime issues in the Arctic. Under this treaty, Canada can claim the continental shelf (a natural extension of land from the shore outward under the sea) for up to 350 nautical miles beyond its baselines. Any country claiming its continental shelf had ten years from the date it joined the convention to prove its claims. Canada therefore had until 2013 to establish whatever claims it could make to the continental shelf lying under Arctic waters. These claims appear to be extensive. Russia, Norway, Denmark, the United States, and Canada engaged in major operations to collect data from the polar seabed in order to determine where their continental shelves end. The most interesting area is the Lomonosov Ridge, a range of mountains extending under the North Pole for hundreds of miles from Greenland and Ellesmere Island to the waters claimed by Russia.

In 2008 the five circumpolar nations – Canada, Russia, the United States, Denmark, and Norway – signed the *Ilulissat Declaration*, in which they agreed to cooperate "in the overseeing of polar oil and mineral exploitation, maritime security, transportation and environmental regulations."[46] During the summers of 2008 and subsequent years, all claimant countries had ships in the High Arctic, with Canada, the United States, and Denmark cooperating on gathering data. Although the right-of-passage for ships in the waters above the continental shelf would still be allowed, the shelf itself could be exploited by whoever owns it for oil and gas, fishing, or other economic endeavours (with certain environmental limitations). This is in addition to an Exclusive Economic Zone of 200 nautical miles that Canada already claims. The laws related to all this are complicated. Arctic nations are however determined to control as much of the Arctic maritime area as possible, or at least to prevent others from making claims. It is a question not only of jurisdiction over maritime transport through the region but also of economic exploitation and national security.

In addition to these major claims, Canada also successfully negotiated article 234 in the *Convention on the Law of the Sea* when the agreement was developed in the 1970s. This article says,

> Coastal States have the right to adopt and enforce non-discriminatory laws and regulations for the prevention, reduction and control of marine pollution from vessels in ice-covered areas within the limits of the exclusive economic zone, where particularly severe climatic conditions and the presence of ice covering such areas for most of the year create obstructions or exceptional hazards to navigation, and pollution of the marine environment could cause major harm to or irreversible disturbance of the ecological balance. Such laws and regulations shall have due regard to navigation and the protection and preservation of the marine environment based on the best available scientific evidence.[47]

The "Arctic clause" in the *Convention on the Law of the Sea* was an attempt to buttress Canada's claims to authority in the Arctic. The Canadian Parliament also passed the *Arctic Waters Pollution Prevention Act* in 1970.[48] This act was in direct response to the sailing of the American oil tanker the ss *Manhattan* into the Northwest Passage in 1969 after refusing to seek or gain Canadian permission. Under this parliamentary act, Canada has the authority to monitor the Arctic environment. Ships are prohibited from dumping waste into Arctic waters. The act now covers up to 200 nautical miles around Canada's Arctic shoreline. Canada has also recently made compulsory the reporting and clearance of ships passing through Arctic waters that are part of the Northern Canada Vessel Traffic Services Zone.[49] Unfortunately none of these actions are sufficient to establish Canadian sovereignty over the waterways of the Arctic, although they are evidence of an intent to do so.

This situation leads to the third possible basis for Canada's claims to sovereignty in the Arctic – *historical occupation*. Although this occupation is perhaps the strongest basis for its claims, Canada has mostly ignored or waffled about the historical basis for its right to the waters of the Arctic. No one disputes Canada's rights in relation to Hudson Bay, which is universally recognized as part of Canada's internal waters based on a long-standing historical presence in the area by the Hudson's Bay Company, whose holdings were transferred to Canada by Britain in 1870. Britain subsequently transferred most of the Arctic islands to Canada in 1880, basing its own sovereign right to do so on British naval explorations that had looked for the Northwest Passage (and the lost Franklin Expedition). Canada, perhaps recognizing that this is a rather weak historical basis for making claims, has tried to find stronger grounds.

## Inuit Sovereignty in the Arctic

For Inuit, this international legal logic is very disturbing. *A Circumpolar Inuit Declaration on Sovereignty in the Arctic*, tabled by the Inuit Circumpolar Council in 2009 on behalf of the Inuit of Nunaat (the entire Arctic region), makes it clear that claims of sovereignty must depend on the human dimension in the Arctic.[50] Inuit were here first. The Arctic land, water, and ice originally belonged to them. Although willing to concede sovereignty

5.5 Canadian flag in front of the RCMP post, Grise Fiord, Ellesmere Island

claims to their own nation-states, Inuit insist that their own views on who owns the Arctic must be listened to. John Amagoalik, one of the principal negotiators of the *Nunavut Land Claims Agreement* of 1993,[51] tells a story about the SS *Manhattan*: "after the Canadian government failed to persuade Exxon and the U.S. government to request permission for the Northwest Passage voyage of the SS *Manhattan*, two Inuit hunters took matters into their own hands. As the super-tanker ploughed through the ice of Lancaster Sound, the two drove their dogsleds into its path. The vessel stopped, a short discussion ensued, and then the hunters – having made their point – moved aside."[52] In the end the *Manhattan* had to accept help from a Canadian Coast Guard icebreaker to make it through the ice, so both Inuit and the Government of Canada succeeded in making their point.

As Byers has said in *Who Owns the Arctic?*,

[T]he strongest element in Canada's claim [to Arctic waters] is the historical occupation by the Inuit, who have hunted, fished, travelled and lived on the Northwest Passage for millennia. Alice Ayalik, who lives in Kugluktuk, is a powerful manifestation of this dimension of Canada's legal position. The seventy-two-year-old artisan spent most of the first thirteen years of her life on the frozen surface of Coronation Gulf, where her family lived in igloos, fished through the ice, and hunted seals. All along the Northwest Passage, there are hundreds of Inuit elders who, in their youth, called the frozen waterway home ...

And the Inuit are, of course, Canadian citizens. Their longstanding use and occupancy is the most compelling component in Canada's historical internal waters argument. What stronger claim could anyone make to the Northwest Passage than by living on it for thousands of years?[53]

In 2008 Inuit Tapiriit Kanatami, Canadian Inuit's principal national organization, released a policy statement on *An Integrated Arctic Strategy*. In this document, it outlined Inuit views on issues of sovereignty:

Critical Considerations:
- reinforcing Canadian sovereignty and security in the Arctic should entail building up healthy regions and communities as well; healthy regions and communities require a significant level of economic productivity and self-sufficiency and acceptable levels and trend-lines of basic social well-being; as Inuit say, "sovereignty begins at home"
- issues of use, occupation, monitoring of lands and waters have special dimensions in the Arctic given its history, demographics and cultural make-up
- high costs of "doing business" in the Arctic argue for achieving efficiencies wherever possible
- possibilities exist for efficiencies in areas such as infrastructure, transportation and navigation, surveillance and environmental monitoring, and security and emergency preparedness

Priority Policy Initiatives:
- ensuring that new investments in military infrastructure serve civilian as well as military functions as much as possible
- a re-conceptualization and expansion of the Arctic Rangers program so that, in addition to serving as a resident militia, it is able to serve the

following functions effectively: (a) environmental monitoring; (b) supply of country food to communities; (c) work for those unqualified or unable to work in wage employment, particularly in small communities; and, (d) sustaining of land based skills and cultural/linguistic continuity

- acknowledging, particularly in the face of climate change, that the renewable resource economy is the patrimony of the aboriginal peoples of the Arctic, and investing in both the creation of a major Arctic-based commercial fishing fleet and industry, and the completion of a national parks and protected areas system

- major investment in a geological surveying/mapping project that, according to scheduled increments, will supply essential information, and fill in large base-line information holes, for the resource development industry

- commitment to finding techniques, using whatever tax and other tools are available in the public sector, to smooth out, as much as practicable, the boom-bust dimensions of mining and oil and gas activity as a consequence of the volatility of international prices.[54]

The Canadian Arctic Rangers are a volunteer force of Inuit who perform many functions as an adjunct to the military. They are not paid, they carry sixty-year-old rifles, and their uniform consists of a red hoody and a baseball cap or tuque. Yet they regularly patrol the Arctic, including long "sovereignty patrols" every spring from Qausuittuq (Resolute) to Alert Bay in the far north of Ellesmere Island.[55]

Inuit have lived in the Arctic region for at least the past 7,000 years. They established their presence in the eastern Arctic about 800 years ago, preceded by others, such as the Tuniit, more than 3,000 years before that. They have had camps there that have been more or less permanently settled for most of that time. They travel over both land and ice throughout the Arctic Archipelago and have done so for centuries. Travels and extended stays by Inuit such as Qitdlarssuaq indicate a long history of occupation by the Inuit of the North. Thule sites are scattered all over the Arctic, and new such sites are being discovered by archaeologists every summer. Oral histories of travel by Kiviuq and other Inuit heroes of the past need to be taken much more seriously in establishing who really owns the Arctic. Modern occupation of land and ice still maintains similar patterns. The Nunavut Planning Commission extensively consults with elders, hunters, and other Inuit on the use of land and seas:

The Nunavut Planning Commission (NPC) is required to pay special attention to Inuit values and Inuit Owned Lands as it carries out its mandate for land-use planning. One way of achieving this is through the collection and analysis of use-and-occupancy data from large numbers of residents. Despite the fact that more use-and-occupancy mapping has been done for Nunavut than anywhere else in the world, the NPC recently initiated an ambitious round of new mapping to obtain datasets that meet current best practices. The resulting information is allowing the NPC to analyze possible impacts of proposed developments, identify potential opportunities as well as constraints, determine Inuit and non-Inuit shared-use areas and to identify zones that may require special management terms. The Commission is finding that having high-quality use-and-occupancy maps greatly enhances the decision-making process for land-use planning.[56]

Mapping done by the NPC clearly indicates seasonal occupation of the ice. Although today this occupation is mostly in relation to short hunting trips, in the not-too-distant past Inuit lived in villages on the ice for months at a time, returning to these same sites every year after the ice was thick enough. Nuqallaq's encounter with the fox trapper Janes occurred in such a village. Qitdlarssuaq's and Uqi's parties camped on the ice for extended periods of time on their travels, including on Lancaster Sound (the eastern entrance to the Northwest Passage). As Byers indicates, Inuit of the central Arctic regularly lived on the ice of Coronation Gulf (near the western end of the Northwest Passage) for many months each year. All Inuit, with the exception of the inland caribou-hunting peoples of the Barren Grounds, used the ice as a base to hunt, fish, camp, and even store caches of food during the winter and spring. This ancient history of occupation of the ice by Inuit shows that it was as natural a part of their territory as the land.

But when international lawyers talk about historical occupation, they almost inevitably mean European occupation. Pharand doubts that Canada could substantiate a claim that all of the waters in the Arctic Archipelago are Canadian by historic title: "On the positive side, it may be stated that virtually all of those waters were discovered by British explorers before the transfer of 1880 and most of them were explored and patrolled by Canada after that date. However, not only were the takings of possession by Great Britain and Canada limited to lands and islands, but Canada has not always demonstrated the exclusive control required for the acquisition and maintenance of sovereignty over maritime areas."[57] No mention at all is made of Inuit occupation or use of the Arctic.

This relates to the problem of sovereignty. Does Indigenous occupation of territory establish any claim to sovereignty? Or is this concept limited to nation-states? Even though Inuit may have formally surrendered sovereignty to Canada at the conclusion of the *Nunavut Land Claims Agreement*, this does not necessarily mean that issues of sovereignty have been completely extinguished. Inuit support Canadian sovereignty in the Arctic, but sovereignty depends on Canada's own ability to keep and maintain strong claims to both land and sea. A weakening of Canadian sovereignty over maritime waters or recognition of the Northwest Passage as an international strait would have a major impact on Inuit use of the sea ice and water for subsistence and development purposes. In addition other Indigenous peoples of the Arctic have not surrendered sovereignty. Canadian sovereignty also depends on what was actually surrendered. In international law, nation-states no longer have unfettered rights of sovereignty over lands owned by Indigenous peoples. The international law of the sea and issues of sovereignty must now stand alongside rights to self-determination, human rights, environmental rights, and Indigenous rights.

Prior to the Second World War, Indigenous interests were ignored in most cases regarding questions about sovereignty. In the only case where an international court has adjudicated issues of sovereignty in the Arctic, the rights of Greenlandic "Eskimos" were dismissed despite the assumption that "Greenlanders" had retaken their land from the Norse sometime in the fifteenth century:

> The word "conquest" is not an appropriate phrase, even if it is assumed that it was fighting with the Eskimos which led to the downfall of the settlements. Conquest only operates as a cause of loss of sovereignty when there is war between two States and by reason of the defeat of one of them sovereignty over territory passes from the loser to the victorious State. The principle does not apply in a case where a settlement has been established in a distant country and its inhabitants are massacred by the aboriginal population. Nor is the fact of "conquest" established. It is known now that the settlements must have disappeared at an early date, but at the time there seems to have been a

belief that despite the loss of contact and the loss of knowledge of the whereabouts of the settlements one or both of them would again be discovered and found to contain the descendants of the early settlers.[58]

Since the 1970s the International Court of Justice and other international institutions have gradually developed a different view.[59] In the *Advisory Opinion on the Western Sahara*, the UN General Assembly had requested the court's legal opinion on the nature of the right of self-determination as it affected nomadic peoples living in the Western Sahara region of Africa. Spain had been the colonizing power, but relinquished its colonial claims after the fall of its fascist government in the mid-1970s. Both Morocco and Mauritania claimed that the region should revert to them on the grounds that it had been part of their sovereign territories before Spain's acquisition in the nineteenth century. The court discussed the claims of Morocco at length and then went on to look at the position of Mauritania:

The migration routes of almost all the nomadic tribes of Western Sahara, the Court was informed, crossed what were to become the colonial frontiers and traversed, inter alia, substantial areas of what is today the territory of the Islamic Republic of Mauritania. The tribes, in their migrations, had grazing pastures, cultivated lands, and wells or water-holes in both territories, and their burial grounds in one or other territory. These basic elements of the nomads' way of life, as stated earlier in this Opinion, were in some measure the subject of tribal rights, and their use was in general regulated by customs. Furthermore, the relations between all the tribes of the region in such matters as inter-tribal clashes and the settlement of disputes were also governed by a body of inter-tribal custom. Before the time of Western Sahara's colonization by Spain, those legal ties neither had nor could have any other source than the usages of the tribes themselves or Koranic law. Accordingly, although the Bilad Shinguitti has not been shown to have existed as a legal entity, the nomadic peoples of the Shinguitti country should, in the view of the Court, be considered as having in the relevant period possessed rights, including some rights relating to the lands through which they migrated. These rights, the Court concludes, constituted legal ties between the territory of Western Sahara and the "Mauritanian entity," this expression being taken to denote the various tribes living in the territories of the Bilad Shinguitti which are now comprised within the Islamic Republic of Mauritania. They were ties which knew no frontier between the territories and were vital to the very maintenance of life in the region.

... The materials and information presented to the Court show the existence, at the time of Spanish colonization, of legal ties of allegiance between the Sultan of Morocco and some of the tribes living in the territory of Western Sahara. They equally show the existence of rights, including some rights relating to the land, which constituted legal ties between the Mauritanian entity, as understood by the Court, and the territory of Western Sahara. On the other hand, the Court's conclusion is that the materials and information presented to it do not establish any tie of territorial sovereignty between the territory of Western Sahara and the Kingdom of Morocco or the Mauritanian entity. Thus the Court has not found legal ties of such a nature as might affect ... the principle of self-determination through the free and genuine expression of the will of the peoples of the Territory.[60]

This was a very qualified assessment of the rights of nomadic peoples and did not amount to support for the principle of sovereignty as it might apply to Indigenous peoples more generally. But it did open the door to a serious legal discussion both internationally and in national courts (including in Canada and Australia) of the meaning of self-determination as it relates to Indigenous peoples, including nomadic peoples such as Inuit. Canada's assertion of sovereignty over the Arctic must therefore include an acknowledgment that Inuit had and still have rights as a "people" or a "nation." It took a very long time for this concept to crystallize into clear international law, but there can now be little doubt that the fundamental human right of self-determination does give significant rights over territory to Indigenous peoples, including Inuit.

The concepts of self-determination and human rights clearly apply to Canada and the citizens of Canada. Article 1 of both the *United Nations International Covenant on Civil and Political Rights* and the *United Nations International Covenant on Economic, Social and Cultural Rights* states, "All peoples have the right to self-determination. By virtue of that right they freely determine their political status and freely pursue their economic, social and cultural development."[61] This right is recognized as having the highest authority in international law. This right is also stated in nearly identical language in article 3 of the *United Nations Declaration on the Rights of Indigenous Peoples*.[62] In addition, the human rights contained in these two UN covenants and recognized in this UN declaration bind Canada under international law to ensure that all Canadian Indigenous peoples, including Inuit, "have the right to the full enjoyment, as a collective or as individuals, of all human rights and fundamental freedoms as recognized in the Charter of the United Nations, the Universal Declaration of Human Rights and international human rights law."[63] Whatever controversy may exist in relation to the legal status of the declaration on Indigenous rights as a whole, or to other rights stated within it, self-determination and human rights in general clearly do apply to Inuit. Discussions of sovereignty must therefore include recognition of these rights. A transfer of sovereignty either within Canada or between nation-states that ignores long-term Inuit interests is no longer acceptable as a matter of either international or Canadian constitutional law.

Effective occupation is the surest way of establishing sovereignty in international law. Canada's best case in relation to national control of the Arctic lies in supporting its Inuit citizens and putting them at the centre of all discussions on sovereignty claims. Because we are now so intent on pursuing sovereignty issues as part of the law of the sea, we have forgotten, or never bothered to pay attention to, the fact of Inuit occupation of the ice as self-determining people with longstanding rights. The irony is that, as the ice melts, this "best evidence" of effective occupancy is also disappearing. In addition Canada has a duty under international human rights law to respect and provide for all its citizens as equals – including Inuit. At the moment this is not the case. Inuit lag significantly behind other Canadians in their enjoyment of many human rights. International human rights law is as compelling as the law of the sea in governing relations between states in the Arctic. It is definitely in Canada's long-term best interests not only to listen to and respect Inuit rights and needs but also to do all in its power to mitigate the acceleration of global warming. Otherwise our claims to the ice of the Arctic Archipelago will literally disappear from under our feet.

## The Myth of Dominion

Although Canada's vision of itself has changed over the past 100 years from a willing subject of the British Empire to a modern independent nation-state, many attitudes toward Arctic sovereignty still seem to be caught in a colonial time warp. This may have something to do with our continuing insecurity as a nation. We are a vast geographic entity of disparate peoples who have never fully integrated into a single national unit. In many ways this is a good thing – it contributes to our sense of freedom and social diversity. But it also makes it hard to set large national agendas and see them through. Achieving such goals sometimes means harking back to "truths" created during a seemingly simpler era. There is also an element of buried history. Canadians have never come to terms with the debt we owe to the Indigenous peoples of the land we now occupy. It is as if our country was created out of nothing by migrants who thought they had discovered a blank slate empty of human history. The great vistas of white snow and ice in most of Canada for most of the year help to reinforce this feeling of strangeness and discovery for Europeans and other migrants who come here from greener pastures. Perhaps I glimpsed a little of this myself when I first arrived in Iqaluit. On a superficial level, we now acknowledge that this rendering invisible of thousands of years of human history is false. But at a deeper level, recognizing how much of Canada is in fact Indigenous means also facing up to what we have done, and are still doing, to our fellow citizens. To see Canada as Aboriginal or Métis or Inuit, as well as French or English or migrant, means recognizing the need to share a land we mistakenly think we conquered.[64]

Much of the land we think of as ours was taken or purchased in circumstances of very dubious legality. All of what we think of as ours is still claimed by Indigenous peoples as part of their pre-existing Aboriginal title. But there are also vast tracts of Canada that are still owned outright by Indigenous peoples. As John Ralston Saul has written, "Two thirds of our country lies in what is normally categorized as North lands. One third of our gross domestic product comes out of the three territories and the equally isolated northern parts of our provinces. And that one third is what makes us a rich, not a poor, country. Our cities, our high-tech service-based lives are built upon the foundation provided by that one third of riches. And now the South believes that the percentage of the GDP coming from the Arctic section of the North will grow."[65]

This North is the land of Indigenous peoples. The creation of Nunavut itself was and remains the largest transfer of authority over land from white to Indigenous control in global, not just Canadian, history. It is rivalled only by Greenland. The peoples of the North, particularly the Inuit of Nunavut, are the owners and guardians of our sovereignty claims. Saul continues:

> Most of the sovereignty debate has been framed in old-fashioned western empire terms. *We have a distant frontier that must be defended. This frontier is ours, not theirs,* whoever they may be. It is only in this context that the people of the North are mentioned, as if the reason for their existence were to serve Canadian sovereignty. There is little sense in all this that the well-being and success of the people of the North is a purpose in and of itself. And they do not need to be the guarantors of our sovereignty – even though they are – in order to deserve well-being and success. They deserve these exactly as any other Canadian citizen deserves them.[66]

Stephen Harper stated during a visit to Victoria, British Columbia, in 2007 not long after he became prime minister, "Canada has a choice when it comes to defending our sovereignty in the Arctic; either we use it or we lose it ... And make no mistake this government intends to use it. Because Canada's Arctic is central to our identity as a northern nation. It is part of our history and it represents the tremendous potential of our future."[67]

How strange and insulting this must sound to Inuit ears! What does he think Inuit have been doing for the past thousand years? But Harper's statement is characteristic of a colonial attitude toward sovereignty that cannot let go of some innate sense of European superiority – the same attitude that led to suicidal British naval expeditions in search of the Northwest Passage, to the establishment of High Arctic RCMP stations and patrols, and to the introduction of criminal law to the Inuit of North Baffin Island in the 1920s. If "we" (*qallunaat*) are not "there," then "there" somehow doesn't exist. When we exclude Inuit from the collective "we" a big chunk of our geography, of our history, and of any international claims "we" might have to "there" simply disappears. The "Boys' Own" school of Canadian nationalism is not dead; it has just taken on a more modern suit of clothes and a marginally more sophisticated public relations strategy.

## Nanook of the North

Between Nuqallaq's execution of Robert S. Janes and his trial for manslaughter and not long before the RCMP constables of Dundas Harbour began their struggle with isolation and hatred, another strange encounter between *qallunaat* and Inuit occurred in what is now Nunavik, or northern Quebec. *Nanook of the North: A Story of Life and Love in the Actual Arctic* was released to the world in New York City in June 1922.[68] This famous movie is credited with being the first documentary feature film and is an amazing example of silent cinematic art. It was filmed entirely in northern Quebec by Robert Joseph Flaherty and purports to depict the life of the great Eskimo hunter Nanook, his family, and his community. It follows Nanook on a walrus-hunting trip and on a journey to the Hudson's Bay Company post to sell furs, and it shows scenes of family life, including building an *igluvijaq* (snow house) and travel by *qajaq* (kayak). Flaherty filmed and developed his scenes "on location" near Port Harrison (now Inukjuak) on the east coast of Hudson Bay. Much of the film was actually shown to the Inuit before he took it south for general release. The film was a phenomenal success, giving rise to Nanook fever all over the world. Eskimo merchandise (like ice cream Eskimo Pie) became hot commodities, and Flaherty was honoured widely for his pioneering effort.

What was not generally acknowledged until relatively recently is that the film is almost entirely fictional. The Inuk who played Nanook and the others who portrayed his wife and children were not actually a single family, and the life shown in the film was entirely staged for the camera.

Nanook was played by an Inuk hunter named Allakariallak. Walrus-hunting scenes were filmed using spears at Flaherty's insistence, whereas Allakariallak would normally have used a rifle. The filmmaker was searching for a reality that was already anachronistic. On the other hand, Flaherty often exaggerated the peril of life in the Arctic. Upon the death of the actor two years after the film was released, Flaherty claimed that "Nanook" had died of starvation. In fact it is likely that Allakariallak died at home of tuberculosis. Another example of how the film was staged is the scene "inside the igloo." Because there was not enough light or space for Flaherty's bulky camera with its primitive film, the top half of the *igluvijaq* was left off. It looks like Nanook and his family are warm and cozy inside their snow house. In fact they were pretending to cook and go to sleep in temperatures

5.6 Original movie poster for *Nanook of the North*

that were around -40° Celsius. The filming of the movie involved close relations between Flaherty and the Inuit families with whom he was living and working. Although these relations seem to have been generally cordial, there is no doubt that Flaherty fathered a child with the female star of his movie, Maggie Nujarluktuk, who portrayed Nanook's wife, Nyla. The boy was named Josephie Flaherty after his father, and the descendants of that child are now prominent citizens of Nunavut. But Flaherty never saw his Inuk son – once he left the North, he never returned.

White Canadian encounters with the Inuit were at this time entirely determined by the agenda of a newly assertive country – the Dominion of

5.7 Maggie Nujarluktuk as Nyla (Nanook's wife in the film *Nanook of the North*) and child, Cape Dufferin, Quebec, 1920–21

Canada – that had just proven its mettle during the First World War. Although Canada's sovereignty over the Arctic had been transferred to it by Great Britain in 1880, significant areas of the Canadian Arctic islands were still in dispute, particularly Ellesmere Island. Canada itself was finding its feet as a young nation. The "Eskimos" had a role to play in the southern Canadian image of itself as the "True North strong and free" but only as subsidiary players. In many ways, it seems that nothing has changed. As Saul has said,

In 1985, following an earlier sovereignty scare [the passage of the US Coast Guard vessel *Polar Sea* through the Northwest Passage without Canada's consent], our elites had announced a solid and clear six-part program to solidify our arctic position. We then forgot about most of it. Indeed, today we can be proud that our rigorous economic policies have been so successful that we may have set the stage for losing a good part of our Northern sovereignty. When faced with choices between economic theory and poverty, economic theory and housing, economic theory and citizen health, economic theory and taking responsibility for your country, which includes the North, the choice is obvious. Far better to have children at food banks and lose control of a large part of your country than to risk upsetting the Department of Finance economists. But perhaps it is not too late for the Arctic.

The curious thing about these new Northern policies is that they have an almost-charming retro air about them. It is as if some old-style imperial government huddled in the temperate South were cranking itself up to send ships and soldiers off to a distant, mysterious, threatened frontier of the empire.[69]

The process of establishing Canadian sovereignty in the Arctic paused during the Great Depression and the Second World War. Dundas Harbour briefly became a Hudson's Bay Company post and then was reopened as an RCMP station after the war only to be shut down again less than five years later. The derelict post remains a haunting reminder of our attempts to establish a presence in the Arctic. But these efforts were also often simply "experiments" hatched by southern "experts" with little regard for those who were already there, or indeed for the young men we sent up there to work in an environment for which they were naively ill-prepared. In the 1950s Canada again began to reassert its claims to the Arctic, but this time the focus was not only on land but also on the sea routes through the islands. Canada was changing from an outpost of the British Empire to a modern social welfare state where government would play an increasingly important role in the lives of its population. Inuit themselves fell more and more under southern Canadian rules of governance. Citizenship came to mean "citizen of Canada" rather than of Britain. This privilege was gradually expanded as a right open to all, including Indians and Inuit as late as 1960. But the repercussions for Inuit were often catastrophic, as their traditional life was finally deeply penetrated by southern agendas. Inuit became the human symbols of Canada's sovereignty and identity in the North. The cost for many was immense suffering and death.

# 6

# Human Flagpoles

"Sovereignty" is a term that has often been used to refer to the absolute and independent authority of a community or nation both internally and externally. Sovereignty is a contested concept, however, and does not have a fixed meaning. Old ideas of sovereignty are breaking down as different governance models, such as the European Union, evolve. Sovereignties overlap and are frequently divided within federations in creative ways to recognize the right of peoples. For Inuit living within the states of Russia, Canada, the USA and Denmark/Greenland, issues of sovereignty and sovereign rights must be examined and assessed in the context of our long history of struggle to gain recognition and respect as an Arctic indigenous people having the right to exercise self-determination over our lives, territories, cultures and languages.

Inuit Circumpolar Council[1]

## Kikkik's Choice

The deepest cold of an Arctic winter is a living force. Its teeth bite into bare skin. The very air cuts and burns. The simplest movement becomes a struggle. A short walk is like climbing a mountain, the cold becoming heavier with every step – fierce, relentless, unforgiving. On the open tundra, ground blizzards that may be no higher than a man's or woman's head can blind and confuse the most seasoned traveller. Wind knifes through everything but the warmest caribou clothing. It steals the breath out of your mouth. It is as if Earth's atmosphere has become thinner and you gasp for breath as exhaustion settles in. Cold seeps into you, clutching your fingers and toes until they are without feeling, stiff and numb. It wraps around your body, claiming possession down to your very bones. At -40° the temperature scales of Celsius and Fahrenheit converge. A small breeze can create wind chills 15 to 20° colder. Even the smallest exertion saps the strength and will. Exposed skin quickly freezes, burning into patches of white and brown. Repeated freezing and thawing of human flesh leads to gangrene. Eyes water in the cold, and you soon become blinded by the brilliance of frozen sunlight glaring off snow and ice. The fur around your hood freezes into sharp icy needles from the moisture of your breathing. You become blind, breathless, numb. The world narrows to a tiny frame of light through your hood and the deafening squeaky crunch of your boots through the hard snow. Except for that and the whisper of the wind, everything is silent.

On the Barren Grounds west of Hudson Bay, a mother and her children walked in such weather, pushing through to the nearest trading post in Padlei. It was February 1958. The woman had not eaten in five or six days. Beside her walked two young children, a boy and a girl. In her *amautiq* (hood) she carried her youngest child. She had nothing else with her. She struggled forward a few yards at a time before she and her children collapsed into the snow. Then they got back to their feet and moved on, foot by foot. This happened over and over, and still their destination was miles ahead. She may not at first have heard the drone of the plane above her, but finally she must have looked up. Did she wave her arms to get its attention? The Otter's pilot saw the little family and landed on the flat snow-packed ice of a small lake not far from them. Constable J.-L. Laliberté of the Royal Canadian Mounted Police (RCMP) jumped out and walked up to the mother. He was puzzled. He had been told there was a woman and five children walking from Henik Lake to Padlei. He knew of the woman. Her name was Kikkik. Others of her people, the Ahiarmiut, had already reached the Padlei trading post and had told the story of her struggle. After many delays the plane had finally been sent to find her. But where were the other children? She said they were dead, that she had buried them in the snow back up the trail.

Kikkik and her children were loaded onto the plane and flown to Eskimo Point (now Arviat). But the mystery of the other children needed to be solved. Constable Laliberté went back to Padlei and, with an Inuk guide, took a dog team and backtracked from where the mother and her surviving children had been picked up. They crossed a small frozen lake and approached a large rock. The dogs pricked up their ears. There was a faint sound, eerie and soft, as if it was coming out of the earth beneath their feet. Or perhaps it was a trick of the wind. But the dogs were insistent – there was something there. They explored around the rock and found, beneath the packed snow-cake, a caribou skin. Inside were two little girls. One looked up and smiled. "There were no tears," the constable would later recall. The other one was dead. They had been wrapped in the skin and left there. It was a day and a half before they were found.

Why would a loving mother leave her children behind? The week before, Kikkik had been in her *igluvijak* (snow house) with her children making tea. Her husband, Hallauk, was out jigging for fish on Henik Lake. He was usually able to catch one or two. This meant that his family was in better shape than other families in the area. Their camp was next to that of Kikkik's half-brother Ootek. As Kikkik was about to send her eldest daughter out to fetch her father for tea, Ootek came in and sat down near the door. He seemed morose and strange. He ordered the children to go outside, but they wouldn't leave. Finally he picked up Hallauk's rifle and left. He said he was going to shoot a few ptarmigans before walking to Padlei for food. Kikkik knew this was impossible since Ootek and his family had nothing. Even his caribou clothing was gone. He would have starved or died of cold long before he got more than a few steps from the camp. As time went by Kikkik became more and more disturbed. She went outside and saw Ootek approaching her.

The two families were very close. Ootek was small and had never been a good hunter. Kikkik's husband, Hallauk, was tall and resourceful, a skilled hunter, and a practical man of action. He had managed to keep his family alive and reasonably healthy through the worst of times. He was also Ootek's closest friend and supporter. It is possible Ootek was a shaman – he certainly believed he could see the future, and at that moment the future looked utterly dark. Famine, bitter cold, and the madness of despair closed around him. He could see that the end was near. Hallauk had already told him that he, Kikkik, and their children were leaving. Ootek knew that for him this was a death sentence. In the end it is impossible to know what was going through his mind. His baby son had died of starvation only a day or two before. His wife, Howmik, was crippled from an earlier bout of polio. She could barely walk and could use only one hand. His two little girls were almost dead, the older one permanently deaf from the starvation years of the late 1940s. They had nothing – not even clothing, for they had long since eaten anything made of skin in order to stay alive.

Ootek raised the barrel of the rifle and pointed it at Kikkik. She grabbed it and pushed it to one side. It went off with a dull pop over her shoulder. They struggled and Kikkik managed to pin the weaker man to the ground. She told her eldest daughter to run and get Hallauk. The girl fled to the lake in terror. She saw her father leaning over the fish hole with his head down on the ice. As she approached she could see the blood and brains scattered around him. She began to cry and scream. What had happened? Her father was dead. Ootek had taken the rifle and walked up behind him, shooting Hallauk in the back of the head at point-blank range.

Kikkik took a knife and tried to stab Ootek, but the blade glanced off his chest. She told her daughter to grab another smaller knife, and with this she succeeded in cutting his forehead. He was blinded by the blood and began to plead with her, "Let me go, I won't hurt you anymore." But she knew if she did, he would kill her and all her children. So she buried the knife in her half-brother's chest and held it there until he was still.

Kikkik knew she had to make a decision. With her husband dead, she and her children would also die unless they went for help. So she and the two older children pulled Hallauk's body into the *igluvijaq* and covered him with some fox traps to protect him from animals. Then she gathered together a few supplies on a small sled and, with her children, began to walk to the Padlei trading post 45 long cold miles away. The two middle girls were wrapped in skins on the sled. They had no clothes left. She passed Ootek's *igluvijaq* and called inside, but she could not bring herself to tell his wife and daughters what had happened. She knew she was leaving them to die.

Kikkik walked northeast into a stiff, bitter wind that flung snow into her face like needles. The blizzard must have wailed around her like the voice of a woman keening in grief. But neither she nor her children had time to mourn. If they didn't reach the trading post, they would die. As she walked, she saw straggling ahead of her in the hazy white a line of tiny black figures. These were almost the last of the Ahiarmiut trying to get away from Henik Lake. They had also left their camps and were struggling slowly toward Padlei. They stopped and waited for her, but they had nothing to offer her, for they themselves had nothing. Eventually Kikkik had to stop, sheltering in a makeshift *iglu* (house) with her five children while the others went on ahead. If they reached Padlei, they would tell the people there to come back and look for her. Perhaps the plane would come up from Churchill or Rankin

Inlet. Kikkik waited. Twice she heard a plane overhead but it didn't land. She knew she had to try to make it by herself.

She huddled the two middle girls into a caribou skin that she pulled behind her. The oldest girl and boy walked with her, and the baby was still on her back. The weight of the girls in the caribou skin became heavier and heavier as Kikkik became weaker. That night she came across a large boulder. On the leeward side, she dug a hole in the snow to protect the children and herself from the cruel wind. She did not have the strength to build an *igluvijaq*. As the morning sun finally crept over the horizon to the southeast, Kikkik realized she could not go on as she was. She had to make a terrible choice. She knew that some of them might survive, but she did not have the strength to walk and pull the two little girls as well. It was already five days since they had left Henik Lake and they had eaten nothing. She wrapped Anacatha and Nesha in the caribou skin and told them to remember that she loved them. Then she turned and walked away.

After Kikkik was picked up and taken to Eskimo Point, she was questioned about what had happened. After further interrogation in Baker Lake, she was charged with the murder of Ootek and with criminal negligence in Nesha's death. She was not told that Anacatha had survived until long after her arrest. She was tried in Rankin Inlet in April 1958. Judge Sissons flew in from Yellowknife, and Sterling Lyon, Kikkik's defence lawyer, travelled north from Winnipeg. Officials from the Department of Indian Affairs flew in as well. Her case was unusual in that a jury was sworn – six men from the nearby nickel mine. The story was covered by the southern newspapers. "The Trials of Kikkik, an Eskimo of the Barren Grounds" made the mother suddenly famous.

Then, just as suddenly, the incomprehensible ordeal was over. Judge Sissons understood the great gulf that existed between Inuit life and the life of Canadians to the South. He appreciated the incongruity of establishing guilt by the standards of British/Canadian criminal law. His instructions to the jury left them with little choice but to acquit her of both charges. And they did. Kikkik was told she was "not guilty" – that she hadn't killed anyone. This made no sense to her. Finally she was told that she was not to blame for what had happened, that it was all over and that she should put it behind her. At last she was allowed to see her children again. She knew that Anacatha had lived. She went down to Eskimo Point, where the other Ahiarmiut were and tried to pick up the pieces of her life again. Miraculously, Ootek's

6.1 Keenaq and her son Keepseeyuk rubbing noses, 1950. On assignment shooting photos of the Arctic for *Life* magazine, Richard Harrington came across the village of Padlei and discovered that the people were starving

widow, Howmik, and her two children had also survived, picked up by the RCMP Otter airplane sent up from Churchill. But what the constables found around the lake was horrifying – not only the bodies of Hallauk and Ootek, and Ootek's tiny son, but also many other bodies starved and frozen in that bitter tundra winter.

## The Barren Grounds

The Ahiarmiut and the Padleimiut were, and are, the peoples of the Barren Grounds – that vast expanse of tundra west of Hudson Bay. These people were unlike the Inuit of the coastal regions in that they depended almost exclusively on *tuktu* (caribou) for their needs. Most of them had never seen a seal or a walrus. They were the "people of the deer." They also fished and gathered berries and moss, but the Barren Grounds caribou provided them with meat, warm clothes, antler and bone to make tools, skins to sleep in and cover their tents, sinew, and hide – even the contents of a caribou's stomach were eaten for the vitamin-rich vegetable material. When the caribou failed to come, the people starved. This happened in the late 1940s and again in the 1950s, recounted in detail by Farley Mowat in his books *People of the Deer* and *The Desperate People*, where the story of Kikkik was first told. Mowat has described the public reaction to his writings: "[T]he book [*People of the Deer*] came under furious assault from the established orders. Some claimed it was no more than a tissue of malicious falsehoods. Others, including the federal cabinet minister responsible for northern natives, insisted that the people I wrote about did not exist – had not *ever* existed, except in my imagination. So ferocious was the counter-attack from commerce, church, and state that echoes of it still reverberate and attempts are still being made to stigmatize me as a liar."[2]

The baby in Kikkik's *amautiq* was a little girl, Nurrahaq. After Kikkik and her children moved to Eskimo Point, the baby was baptized as Elizabeth – or Elisapee. Elisapee grew up knowing nothing of her family's tragedy until she was in her late teens and came across a copy of Farley Mowat's book *The Desperate People*. Kikkik died soon after this. The mother and daughter were never able to talk about what had happened.

I got to know Elisapee after I went up to Iqaluit as the northern director of the Akitsiraq Law School, where she was one of our students. She eventually decided that the law program was not what she wanted, although she continued to play a valuable role as our Inuit cultural advisor. She has since moved back to Arviat. She became a close friend – one of the best friends I made while I was in the North. After I learned her story, I often wondered – how is it possible for two women of about the same age and both raised in the same country to have led such radically different lives? Where was I in the winter and spring of 1958? While Elisapee's mother, father, and the rest of her people were struggling to survive a famine on a scale almost unimaginable to most Canadians, I was living the life of a middle-class white girl in the South. My Dad was in the Royal Canadian Air Force, so we travelled around a lot. In 1958 we were living in Edmonton, where my father was stationed. While the Ahiarmiut were dying, I was in kindergarten. My brother and I played together. Our little sister was born not long after Elisapee's sister died. I remember our first black and white television. We watched the *Howdy Doody Show, The Lone Ranger*, and *Pecos Bill.* Percy Saltzman of the CBC told us about the weather on a squiggly black and white map. At the end he always threw his chalk in the air, catching it without fail. I don't remember him talking about deadly cold and famine in the Arctic. No one explained to us that the caribou migrations had failed. No one told us about Inuit being moved around like pawns on a giant chessboard. But if ordinary middle-class Canadians like my family knew nothing then, there is no excuse now. Perhaps even then it was wilful ignorance – a matter of closing one's eyes so as not to see what was there in front of us. My father had been in the North in the early 1950s and must have had some knowledge of relocations of Inuit around the Arctic.

The famine that struck Elisapee and her family was not an unfortunate "act of God." White fox fur was immensely fashionable during the first half of the twentieth century. During the 1920s the Hudson's Bay Company moved into the Barren Grounds and elsewhere in the Arctic, encouraging Inuit to abandon their old ways and set up traplines. The killing of not only fox for their beautiful white pelts but also other game turned into a slaughter. Caribou, on which Ahiarmiut depended for survival, were hunted ruthlessly. Inuit all over the Canadian Arctic came to rely on the fox fur trade for goods from the Hudson's Bay Company, including tea, lard, flour, rifles, and ammunition. When the Depression of the 1930s hit, the fox fur trade collapsed. Ahiarmiut could no longer trade for white goods at the company store. The inability to purchase ammunition was particularly hard. They were able to hunt caribou with spears again, as they had done in the past, but then the caribou migrations failed. During the 1940s caribou numbers dwindled radically, and the migration patterns of these animals shifted. By the late 1940s the Ahiarmiut had already suffered repeated famines in which something like half of their already dwindling numbers had died. A few families, like Hallauk's and Ootek's, clung to their traditional ways.

Then in 1948 and 1949 more changes came.[3] The Ahiarmiut traditionally camped around Ennadai Lake some distance inland from what is now Arviat. The lake is large and rich with Arctic char, and the caribou hunting had been good until recent years. The people had lived there travelling around the Barren Grounds in search of game for centuries. But after the Second World War, Canada and its allies were increasingly concerned about Soviet aggression over the polar region and were building communications, transport, and military stations across the Arctic. The Cold War arrived at Ennadai Lake in the form of a military communications station. Between 1949 and 1954 the Ahiarmiut and the *kabloona* (*qallunaat* in the dialect of the Keewatin region of the Northwest Territories) established a cordial relationship. The soldiers tried to help the Inuit as they continued to struggle with hunger, and the Inuit made the white men warm clothing and helped with work around the station. The chief cause of the Inuit's problems was the thin trickle of caribou and their own lack of ammunition. Despite pleas from the station, it was not until 1954 that adequate supplies were delivered to the Ahiarmiut.

Meanwhile the station had been transferred to the authority of the Department of Transport and was staffed by civilians. These newcomers immediately began to complain about the Inuit as "a filthy, stinking bunch who don't want to work for a living ... bums who foul up the place."[4] This did not prevent some of the men from sexually abusing the women for their own amusement. Meanwhile the lack of caribou and the Inuit inability to obtain adequate ammunition to hunt, along with the hostility of the Department of Transport employees at the Ennadai station, convinced Ottawa that something must be done. The people were in dire straits. It was decided that they would be moved to Henik Lake, where they would be under the care of Henry Voisey, manager of the Padlei trading post, and Bill Kerr, the Northern Service officer. The Ahiarmiut had been moved from Ennadai Lake once before. In 1950 they had been taken to Nueltin Lake in northern Manitoba, where they were supposed to learn how to become fishermen. The scrubby trees had seemed dark and claustrophobic, and they were afraid of the Indians who lived nearby. So they packed up and walked home more than 150 miles, taking five weeks to make the journey. At no time were the Ahiarmiut themselves consulted about any of this. The second removal was meant to be permanent.

In May 1957, without warning, the people's tents with all their belongings were bulldozed. Families were loaded onto airplanes with what they had managed to save from the wreckage and were flown about 200 miles north-east to North Henik Lake. There they were dropped off and left to fend for themselves. They were about 45 miles from the Padlei trading post and 150 miles from Eskimo Point. They were essentially on their own without adequate supplies – only three dogs, no kayaks, no big sleds, few rifles, and little ammunition – and they were in an area they did not know. The caribou did not come, and the fishing in the lake was poor. They managed to survive through the summer and fall, but as winter approached, it became clear to most of the Ahiarmiut, and even to the powers-that-be in Eskimo Point and Ottawa, that Henik Lake had been a poor choice for relocation. Plans were laid to move the Ahiarmiut again, but meanwhile they were stuck. Slowly they walked to the Padlei trading post, and from there they were airlifted to Eskimo Point. Others remained behind and tried to survive. Many did not make it.

The Padleimiut, cousins of the Ahiarmiut to the northeast, also suffered devastating losses as the caribou failed to show up year after year. Throughout the Barren Grounds, a way of life was swallowed up by famine. Richard Harrington's haunting photographs of the people of the Barren Grounds taken between 1948 and 1953 were described at the time as pictures of the most "primitive of Eskimos." In fact the "primitiveness" was a direct result of extreme privation and starvation. This was caused by the repeated failure of the caribou to appear for reasons that are still controversial. The Ahiarmiut were finally moved to Arviat, where they were strangers to the Inuit who already lived there. A way of life that had existed for centuries simply vanished, except among those people who were settled in Baker Lake, the only inland Inuit community in the Canadian Arctic.

## The Experiment of Relocation

During the middle years of the twentieth century, the Canadian government authorized repeated relocations of Inuit all over the Arctic. In the 1930s after the RCMP temporarily abandoned its remote detachment in Dundas Harbour, the Hudson's Bay Company set up a post there. In one of the first relocations of Canadian Inuit, a small group of families from Cape Dorset and Pangnirtung in South Baffin Island as well as from Pond Inlet were shipped north to Dundas Harbour in the summer of 1934. The company

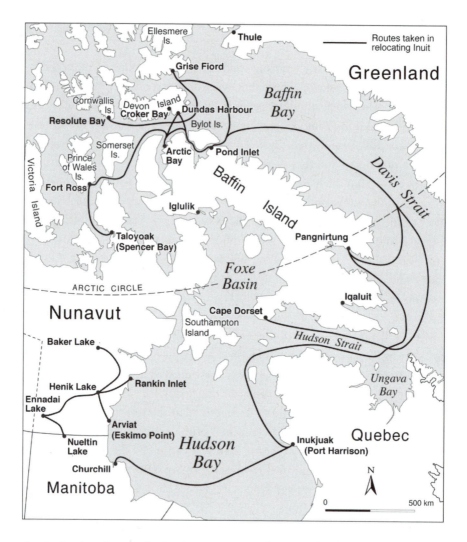

6.2 Inuit relocations in the Arctic, 1934–58. In the 1930s families from Cape
Dorset and Pangnirtung were relocated to Dundas Harbour and Fort Ross. In the
1950s families from Port Harrison (Inukjuak) were relocated to the High Arctic.
The Ahiarmiut were moved from Ennadai Lake several times.

thought that Inuit would be useful in trapping fox in the neighbourhood.
The Inuit were persuaded to go after years of hunger and privation in South
Baffin Island, where the fur trade had collapsed and their access to white
goods had come to a halt. They had been weaned away from the old ways by
the company – now they were taken north to a land they knew nothing about.
Cape Dorset is below the Arctic Circle, so the people had never experienced

the total darkness of a High Arctic winter. The ice around Devon Island was treacherous, and although there was game, it was hard for the hunters to find it or get to it. They tried travelling westward in search of a crossing back to Baffin Island and eventually ended up wintering in Croker Bay. They returned to Dundas Harbour to spend another miserable year waiting to go home. They were trapped as surely as any fox.

Finally, in 1936 the company ship *Nascopie* returned, and they were taken on board. The Inuit thought they were going home at last. What they did not realize was that the company was intent on setting up another trading post in Netsilik country far to the west. Because of bad ice conditions, the ship dropped everyone off in Arctic Bay, promising to return the next summer. The families from Pangnirtung refused to leave the ship, insisting they be taken home. Eventually their wish was granted. The Cape Dorset people reluctantly disembarked. They were still hundreds of miles from home among Inuit they did not know and whose dialect of Inuktitut was unfamiliar to them. They were afraid to hunt in the territory of the Tununirmiut, the people of North Baffin Island, so they became utterly dependent on the company post. The families from Pond Inlet quietly left, returning to their home, which was relatively close by. The families from Cape Dorset were picked up by the *Nascopie* the next summer, but they were not taken home as they thought. Instead they were shipped farther west to Fort Ross. They were finally resettled permanently in Spence Bay (Taloyoak) on the western side of the Boothia Peninsula. Here the descendants of the Cape Dorset settlers still live.

What began as a commercial experiment turned, twenty years later, into a full-blown attempt to solve two problems at once: first, by establishing Canadian sovereignty in the Arctic and, second, by providing for Inuit after the fur trade collapsed and caribou hunting was threatened by recurring lack of game. In 1952 Prime Minister Louis St Laurent told Parliament that the Canadian government had "administered the North in an almost continuous state of absence of mind"[5] since it had been transferred to Canada from Great Britain in 1880. A conference was held in Ottawa to decide what to do about the "Eskimo problem." Should they be taught how to herd reindeer? Should they be pushed farther toward assimilation? Should they be weaned from their "dependence" on the Hudson's Bay Company and made to return to their traditional life on the land? The conference included representatives of the company, the churches, the government, the

6.3 Derelict Hudson's Bay post, Fort Ross

RCMP, northern "experts" – everyone except Inuit themselves. It was felt that "few had reached the stage where they could contribute to the talk," so their voices were not heard.[6]

In Canadian government eyes, the situation regarding sovereignty was even more serious. Inughuit were crossing over from Greenland to Ellesmere Island to hunt for polar bear and muskox, as they had been doing for hundreds of years. This continual penetration of Canadian boundaries by Greenlanders meant (to Canadian government officials) that control over "our" territory was threatened. The Americans were building a huge airbase in Thule just across Smith Sound (with Canadian cooperation), but there was a concern that American military interests would begin to overtake the ability of Canada to control incursions into the territory. During the 1950s there were more American military personnel in the High Arctic then there were Canadians. As for the Inuit in Canada, many had become dependent on the fur trade and found the old ways increasingly difficult. It was not only the Barren Grounds people who suffered from repeated failures of the caribou migration – the people of what is now Nunavik, or northern Quebec, were also suffering, although not to the same degree. Many still lived independently in camps strung along eastern Hudson Bay, whereas others were seen as "hangers on" in Port Harrison (Inukjuak), not far from where the first major feature documentary, *Nanook of the North*, had been filmed thirty years earlier. Robert Joseph Flaherty's hugely popular silent film *Nanook of the North* had created an image of the "smiling Eskimo," self-sufficient and resourceful, that became known all over the world. That image now seemed to have disintegrated into the reality of people whose lives had fallen apart. In the eyes of *qallunaat*, the Arctic version of the "noble savage" had turned into a needy indigent. It was decided to try relocation from Port Harrison northward as an "experiment."

It is hard for those of us who are not Aboriginal to recall or acknowledge the intensity of racism and how casually it was (and sometimes still is) expressed. Walter Rudnicki was a reform-minded member of the Department of Northern Affairs and National Development appointed in 1953. He carried out an analysis of the situation of the Ennadai Lake Inuit after they were taken to Eskimo Point in 1958. Included in his report was a survey of the opinions of whites living in the community: "Although some concern and anxiety seemed evident about the well-being and future of the Eskimos, most references to them were couched in such terms as 'those lazy bums,' 'those heroes (in a sarcastic sense),' 'the sun-burnt Irishmen,' etc. Other generalizations were made about the Eskimos to the effect that they are 'unfeeling and unemotional,' that they live 'like dogs,' etc. Although these expressions suggest a generally uninformed and perhaps, an undesirable outlook on the problems of the Eskimo people, these probably reflect also a sense of resignation that anything positive will ever be done for them."[7]

In Port Harrison the department and the RCMP were determined to solve the "Eskimo problem" and the issue of sovereignty at one stroke. Although the earlier Hudson's Bay Company relocations to Dundas Harbour, Fort Ross, and Spence Bay were remembered, the problems tended to be forgotten. The hope was that Inuit could be relocated to the RCMP post at Craig Harbour or close by on southern Ellesmere Island, to the north in Alexandra Fiord facing east toward Greenland, or to the west at Resolute Bay on Cornwallis Island. Constable Ross Gibson was given the task of choosing families to go:

> I went out to the camps [near Port Harrison] and chose the people ...
> I called the school teacher and the Hudson Bay and so on, and I said
> that I had received this thing and that I was going to be the one to bear
> the brunt of this thing and I asked for their cooperation. Marjorie

[Hinds, the teacher] wasn't too happy about that one, but I guess maybe it was the way I expressed myself ...

I took the message – I took the wire right along with me and I just read the thing out. And I said this is it and they're going to move further up into the North and in fact they were going up into Twin Glaciers and Alexandra Fiord [on Ellesmere Island] – which is where they were all going to go ... But little did I know that I was going to be the one who was going to take them.[8]

The Inuit tell a different story of how they were chosen. John Amagoalik remembers,

[T]he first vivid memories I have are when the policemen from the RCMP came to our small hunting camp with a request, a proposal, for my parents. I remember them coming back more than once. When a policeman visited your camp it was something you remembered in those days. I was five years old. It was a big event, so I remember it very clearly. My parents talked about the RCMP officers' request after they had left. The proposal was basically for our families to be relocated to another place away from Inukjuak.

The initial reaction of my parents was, no, they didn't want to move. This was their ancestral homeland, this was what they knew, and this was where their families were from ... They weren't told exactly where they would be going, but they were told it would be a better place than where they were living then. My parents didn't want to move. The RCMP officers came back again and again ...

The RCMP officers described this new place in very glowing terms. They told my parents that there would be a lot more animals, that we would have the opportunity to catch a lot of foxes and seals and to make money. They even said that there would be opportunities for employment if we desired. Reluctantly, my father finally agreed to the relocation, but only if two conditions were met. One was that we could return to Inukjuak if we decided that we didn't like the new place, and that the whole group would stay together, that we would not be separated. The RCMP officers readily agreed to those conditions and promised that we could return after two years if we didn't like the place, and that we would all stay together.[9]

Many of those who were chosen seem to have been among the poorest people in the region. One was an elderly lady in her eighties, and another was a child partially crippled from polio. Gibson himself said that "these people were all welfare cases and were perhaps some of the poorest Eskimos in the Arctic."[10] Marjorie Hinds, whose job included not only teaching Inuit children *Fun with Dick and Jane* but also reporting to the department on the health and welfare of the Inuit, "suggested that those who have proved themselves capable of living far from the trading post, and who get along without much help from the government or the H.B.C. are more likely to prove successful folk to go north."[11] Gibson, representing the RCMP, was of the opinion that he did not have to take anyone else's views into account in making the selection. In the end he got some help from the local Hudson's Bay Company manager but otherwise made his own decisions: "When we went out on that patrol, we travelled to all the camps between Port Harrison and Povungnituk and as far as Sugluk. But it was too late in the season to go any further. It was my decision. We had records and we knew who the good, bad, and indifferent hunters were, and you could see it in how they handled their camps. In the end, they all wanted to go."[12] Amagoalik explains why the Inuit finally agreed to go: "I think it's also important for people to understand that when the RCMP made a request to you in those days, it was seen as something like an order. You are ordered to do this. The RCMP officers had a lot of power. They could put you in jail. That's the way they were viewed in those days. A request from the police was taken very, very seriously."[13]

On 28 July 1953 the CGS *C.D. Howe* picked up seven Inuit families from Port Harrison and ferried them north to Pond Inlet. On the way they were supposed to rendezvous with the icebreaker *d'Iberville*, but bad ice conditions prevented this. On 28 August the *C.D. Howe* picked up three more families in Pond Inlet. The Tununirmiut families were selected to assist the more southerly group in the adjustment to a High Arctic life, including total winter darkness, which the Inukjuak families had never experienced. It was decided by department officials and the RCMP to drop off half the families in Craig Harbour on southern Ellesmere Island and then try to take the others farther north to Alexandra Fiord before ferrying the rest to Resolute Bay on Cornwallis Island. Some Inuit were already stationed at Craig Harbour. They had been persuaded to move farther north by way of Dundas Harbour from Pond Inlet or Arctic Bay. After landing at Craig Harbour, the remaining families were loaded onto the *d'Iberville* for the trip north up the east coast of Ellesmere Island. But ice conditions were not suitable for a landing at Alexandria Fiord, so the ship turned around. It was then decided that the families would be taken to Resolute Bay. Meanwhile the first group was moved to a location about 50 miles southwest of the Craig Harbour RCMP post near the site of the present-day hamlet of Grise Fiord.

The decision to split the group up came as a distressing surprise to the families. Not only was one of the conditions for leaving Inukjuak completely disregarded, but the decision about which families would go where seems to have been made at the last minute. It came as an unpleasant shock to Constable Gibson, who had to communicate the decision to the Inuit. John Amagoalik remembers,

> We had been promised that our whole group would stay together, that we would not be separated. But when we got near Craig Harbour on Ellesmere Island, the RCMP said to us, half of you have to get off here. We just went into a panic because they had promised that they would not separate us. That was the first broken promise. And when we realized it, I remember we were all on the deck of the *C.D. Howe*. All the women started to cry. And when women start to cry, the dogs join in. It was eerie. I was six years old then, standing on the deck of the ship. The children were crying, the dogs were howling, and the men had to huddle to decide who is going to go where.[14]

The conditions for the two groups were extremely difficult. By early September, winter in the High Arctic was already settling in, although there would be no ice safe for dog team travel for another month or more. The Inuit had no boats. The country around Grise Fiord is ruggedly mountainous and forbidding, and Resolute Bay is a flat windswept gravel plain. Both were completely strange to the Inukjuak families. Even the Tununirmiut from Pond Inlet found adjusting to three months of winter darkness difficult. Because of the lack of supplies, hunters had to go out constantly to find game, even in total darkness. They had no flashlights and only a limited supply of lanterns. It is bitterly cold in the High Arctic during the long black winter night. It is also much drier than it is in the Hudson Bay area. Finding fresh water quickly became a problem. The people lived in canvas tents. In Grise Fiord the RCMP supplied them with buffalo skins to line their tents for warmth, but it made the inside even darker. They were not given adequate clothing. Fuel for warmth in Resolute consisted of broken-up wooden packing crates burned in makeshift stoves. In Port Harrison the families had had access to the trading post for supplies, a school, a birthing clinic, medical help, and a varied diet of sea and land food. They had already begun the transition from a traditional life to life in a town. The government was deliberately experimenting with the idea of making Inuit return to their traditional ways. There was no thought given to how difficult this would be, whether there really was adequate game where they were going, or how much hardship it might cost. The first years were a nightmare.

One individual was described by Constable Gibson as follows: "We were looking for – well – I guess the word I'd use would be 'resourceful' trappers ... Fatty wanted to go. He was always pulling fast ones and he was a real 'bum' in some ways and we thought that all he needed was a good environment and he would do well."[15] The Inuk named "Fatty" by Constable Gibson was Paddy Aqiatusuk, who was left in Grise Fiord with his wife, Mary, and their children. Aqiatusuk was a talented and internationally known carver. No one had bothered to find out whether there was any soapstone to work with in the High Arctic. He became despondent as his family's difficulties increased. The isolation of the Grise Fiord families was a serious problem. The RCMP detachment would not relocate from Craig Harbour to Grise Fiord until 1956, three years later. Grise Fiord is extremely difficult to fly in and out of due to its steep terrain and bad weather. Ice conditions can make it impossible for ships to get in even in July or August. Aqiatusuk's son Larry Audlaluk remembers how troubled his father was by the relocation. In early July of the next summer, he climbed the 2,400-foot mountain behind the settlement, searching in vain for a way home. He died of a heart attack (or perhaps a broken heart) a week later. He had been a leader of the Inukjuak families, and his death was a serious blow to the tiny community. In 1954 his fame as a carver merited an obituary notice in *Time Magazine*, which reads (inaccurately), "Death Revealed. Akeeaktashuk, 56, one of the leaders of the small group of Eskimo primitive sculpturists whose work came to the attention of the outside world in recent years because of its fluent, uncluttered simplicity; of drowning July 31, when he slipped from an ice floe while hunting walrus off Ellesmere Island."[16]

If the conditions in Grise Fiord were grim, on Cornwallis Island they could be described as dire. In Resolute Bay, Nellie Amagoalik also did not

6.4 Mountain behind Grise Fiord, Ellesmere Island

survive that first winter. John Amagoalik's older brother Markoosie Patsauq was spitting up blood from tuberculosis before he left Inukjuak. No x-ray machine was available on the ship, and there were no health services available for the Inuit in either Grise Fiord or Resolute Bay. Markoosie became so sick that he finally had to be sent south to Manitoba in the summer of 1954 on the *C.D. Howe*. This delay in getting him medical treatment occurred despite the fact that the Royal Canadian Air Force (RCAF) base at Resolute was nearby with both medical facilities and air transport. There was even less game on Cornwallis Island than there was on Ellesmere, and hunters in both places were restricted in what they could kill. Regulations under the *Northwest Game Act*, first passed in 1917 to prevent Inughuit from hunting on Ellesmere Island, were still in existence. In addition both settlements were in the Arctic Islands Preserve, created in 1926, another example of Canadian sovereignty and game management. Inuit in both Grise Fiord and Resolute Bay were forbidden to hunt for muskox, the most numerous large land mammal in the area. Doing so would result in a $500 fine or jail time. Their take of caribou was also severely limited to one caribou per family per year. Their diet therefore consisted mainly of fish, birds, seal, and walrus. Grise Fiord was relatively rich in marine mammals, but Resolute Bay was not.

Relations between personnel of the air force base at Resolute and the relocated Inuit were difficult from the beginning. Air Commodore Ripley voiced his objections to the relocation even as the *C.D. Howe* and the *d'Iberville* were on their way. He was rightly concerned that resources in the area were not sufficient to support several families of Inuit. Ben Sivertz, administrative officer with the Arctic division of the department, noted these problems: "I think there is danger these people will become camp fringe dwellers, combing refuse dumps and looking for handouts. If they are to be hunters, they should live away from the base. If they are to live near the base they should be made part of it."[17] John Amagoalik remembers that there simply was not enough to eat. Everyone was hungry: "The first couple of years we did not have a store of any sort, so we depended heavily on the garbage dump to supplement our diet, for clothing, and of course for our shelter ... Also, after a military flight arrived, we all rushed to the dump because we knew that the people who came on the plane would have box lunches and they never finished them. There would be sandwich leftovers, so we would rush to the dump and get those sandwiches, those pieces of

6.5 Inuit houses, Resolute Bay, March 1956

food."[18] If an RCMP officer discovered they were raiding the dump, he would search every tent until the food was found and confiscated.

As a result of these difficulties, Inuit in both settlements asked to be sent home. Their requests were either refused outright or were actively discouraged by the RCMP. Instead people were encouraged to invite their relatives to join them. Samwillie Eliasialuk remembers, "When we were still in the High Arctic and our parents attempted to make the case for returning, they were told outright that there's no possible way for them to ever go back and in fact some government official said, 'If you want to return, you are going to have to find other people to take your place before we allow you to go back.' This was said by people where no appeal was available to a higher authority."[19] The second promise had been broken.

In 1955 four more families from Inukjuak were shipped north on the C.D. Howe for Grise Fiord and Resolute Bay. Among these newcomers was the family of Josephie Flaherty, the son born to Maggie Nujarluktuk (Nanook's wife, Nyla, in Nanook of the North) and the film's director, Robert Flaherty, on Christmas Day 1921. Flaherty had never revisited the Arctic after his film was made and refused to speak about or make any contact with his son. The filmmaker died in July 1951 just four years before his son and grandchildren would leave Inukjuak for Grise Fiord. Paddy Aqia-tusuk had been Josephie's stepfather. In March 1954 he wrote a letter to Josephie asking him to come up to Grise Fiord in order to provide some comfort to his relatives there. Josephie did not receive the letter until three months later, when it was delivered in the mail sack on the C.D. Howe. By this time Aqiatusuk was dead. Josephie also learned of the death of his qal-lunaq father during a short and no doubt uncomfortable first meeting with his uncle David Flaherty, who had come up on the C.D. Howe that same July. Josephie decided to go north shortly after this. He and his family boarded the C.D. Howe in July 1955. Josephie would never see his mother's homeland again.

During the voyage it was discovered that one of Josephie's daughters and another little girl had tuberculosis. The parents were told the children would have to be removed south for treatment. The news left the families distraught, but they were given no choice. The children were removed and taken to Churchill, Manitoba. The ship continued its journey north. On the way another baby girl died of pneumonia despite the best efforts of the ship's doctor to save her. Martha Flaherty, who was five years old at the time, remembers the stormy weather and how terrified everyone was as they headed into the August gales of Davis Strait.[20]

The conditions in the two settlements remained bad for years. Martha Flaherty also remembers that her father "used to go hunting in -40° to -60° weather in the dark for days at times without eating ... I don't think I even had a childhood between the ages of 5 to 12 because I had to hunt with my father for food, in very cold weather, with absolutely no daylight ... Sometimes I used to cry knowing how cold it was going to be, but then my father would just say, 'Do you want us to starve?'"[21] In addition to hunger, people endured tragic accidents and repeated sickness. In 1958 two young boys fell into the water. One body was found, but the other was never recovered. Martha recalls that the dogs used to bark mysteriously at something or someone for about a year after this incident. People thought the boy was still alive, but afraid to come home. He has never been found.[22] In 1960 Grise Fiord went through a serious whooping cough epidemic in which many children were very sick. Medical facilities were still primitive or nonexistent. Perhaps the worst problem that many suffered from was depression. The long hours of winter darkness and the poor diet would have inevitably led to serious deficiencies of vitamin D, in addition to the homesickness and isolation everyone felt. At this time Inuit in both settlements lived in tents on the beach in both winter and summer. As Anna Nungaq remembers, "I hardly slept for years, cried, wanting to go home. I was extremely depressed. Practically for a year I slept very little, because I was so scared, threatened. I did not think there would ever be a day of light again. It is also very, very cold. Because I had never been in a place where there is no daylight at all, I was so scared and thought there would never be light again."[23]

During the 1960s the RCAF base in Resolute Bay opened a bar for the officers and men. Alcohol became a problem. Liquor was taken to the Inuit camp by base personnel. Sexual exploitation of girls and women, including assault, became common. Families, already stressed by the poor conditions and long periods of time when there was nothing to do, fell apart from drink. Children were left to fend for themselves, sometimes going without food or living together in unheated dwellings without adult supervision. Suicide, domestic violence, fights, and killings turned the community in on itself. Tommy Iqaluk and Elisapee Allakariallak grew up in Resolute during this time and remember it as extremely tough. They had no remembrance of the old life in Inukjuak and could not believe that there was anything better; it was "just the way it was." Elisapee described Resolute Bay as a "fake community."[24] In Ottawa the experiment was seen as an unqualified success.

## Truth and Restitution

In the 1970s the bar in Resolute Bay was finally shut down. In time the communities managed to make the best of their situation and created two small hamlets that now have many of the amenities of modern living – schools from kindergarten to grade 12, medical clinics, community centres, and government services such as a post office and an air strip. People now live in houses and have access to satellite television, Internet, and radio. At least in Grise Fiord, the Inuit and local RCMP seem to have good relations. There is a concerted effort to retrieve the traditional knowledge necessary to survive in the High Arctic, where the Inuit have learned how to hunt under forbidding conditions. Both communities are now serviced by the local store with southern goods. As in many communities throughout Nunavut, the price of grocery store food is so expensive that hunting and sharing "country food" is still an important source of nutrition. Inuit artists are again able to work and market their carvings through the local co-op, thus providing a needed source of cash income. Tourism is becoming an important part of the local economy, as cruise ships put in several times each summer. I was fortunate enough to be on the first one ever to stop at Grise Fiord in 2004. There are still many challenges, but life is better.

The hamlet of Grise Fiord on Ellesmere Island is the northernmost Inuit community in Canada and one of the most northerly communities in the world. There are research stations at the top of Ellesmere in Alert and Eureka, but these are staffed by southerners and Inuit who do not live there fulltime. The people of Grise Fiord are proud of what they have built in the face of terrible odds and point to their community as one of the best in Nunavut. Resolute Bay has become a staging area for sovereignty patrols and polar exploration. The infrastructure of the old RCAF base remains, although the Canadian military is no longer permanently stationed there. There has been discussion of reopening the base as a means of securing Canadian sovereignty claims over the Northwest Passage.

The Inuit who had been relocated were determined to achieve acknowledgment, including an apology and compensation, from the federal government for what had been done to them. Beginning in 1978, Makivik (the Inuit organization of northern Quebec) and Inuit Tapirisat of Canada (ITC, now Inuit Tapiriit Kanatami) lobbied Ottawa persistently to investigate their concerns. John Amagoalik became the president of ITC and was involved in both the relocation issue and negotiating Inuit land claims. In 1988 the government offered to pay to move some families back to Inukjuak but remained very reluctant to provide any further compensation. On 19 March 1990 Makivik and ITC testified before the House of Commons Standing Committee on Aboriginal Affairs, which recommended that the Inuit role in establishing sovereignty in the High Arctic be recognized and that compensation be paid to those who had been relocated. The Department of Indian Affairs and Northern Development was asked to submit a report on the issue to Parliament. The report was prepared by the Hickling Corporation and was presented to Parliament by the minister of the department in November of that year. The Hickling Report indicated that there had been no wrongdoing on the part of the government and that no compensation should be paid. Undaunted by this set back, ITC petitioned the Canadian Human Rights Commission. The commission recommended that the Inuit role in establishing sovereignty in the High Arctic be acknowledged and that they be thanked, that the government acknowledge the mistakes that were made in planning the relocation, and that the failure to live up to the promise to return Inuit to Inukjuak be admitted.

The *Nunavut Land Claims Agreement* of 1993 contains in its preamble this clause: "And in recognition of the contributions of Inuit to Canada's history, identity and sovereignty in the Arctic,"[25] thus recognizing the role played by all Inuit in support of Canadian sovereignty. In July 1994 the Royal Commission on Aboriginal Peoples prepared and published *The High Arctic Relocation: A Report on the 1953–55 Relocation*. The royal commission recommended that the contribution of the "relocatees" to Canadian sovereignty in the High Arctic be acknowledged, that there should be an apology, and that compensation should be paid after negotiations between the federal government and representatives of the "relocatees" of both Inukjuak and Pond Inlet.[26] In 1995 a $10-million "relocation trust fund" was set up to provide compensation, including housing, travel, and pensions to the survivors. The federal government finally issued an apology for the relocations in 2010 when the minister of Indian and northern affairs issued the following statement: "The Government of Canada apologizes for having relocated Inuit families and recognizes that the High Arctic Relocation resulted in extreme hardship and suffering for Inuit who were relocated ... We deeply regret the mistakes and broken promises of this dark chapter of our history."[27]

To my knowledge there has been no recognition, apology, or compensation of any kind given to Elisapee Karetak's family or the other Ahiarmiut for what happened to them on the Barren Grounds in the 1940s and 1950s, although a claim against the federal government was filed in court in June 2013. It is hoped that this will result in an apology and possibly compensation by 2014.[28] Perhaps John Amagoalik summed it up best when he described himself and others like him as "human flagpoles."[29]

## Residential Schools

The relocations were not the only disruptions to Inuit life in the postwar era. Many Inuit were also shipped south for tuberculosis treatment that could keep them away from their families and communities for years.[30] Not long after Kikkik settled in Eskimo Point, her youngest daughter Elisapee was sent south to a sanitarium for four years.[31] Inuit were moved off the land and into settlements, sometimes through the brutal expediency of RCMP shooting their dogs.[32] Perhaps the most traumatic assault on Inuit family life was through the education system. Many children were sent thousands of miles away to residential schools in Chesterfield Inlet (Igluligaarjuk), Frobisher Bay (Iqaluit), Inuvik, and Churchill until at least the 1970s. Other kids were sent to foster homes and white schools as far away as Ottawa.

From before Canadian Confederation in 1867 until as recently as 1996, when the last residential school closed, Aboriginal children all over Canada were sent to day schools or boarding (residential) schools, where they were taught English or French, a smattering of reading and writing, industrial or domestic trades such as farming or housework, and the Christian religion. They were punished for speaking their own language or practising their own culture. Many were abused or neglected, and an unknown number (in the thousands) died of tuberculosis, other illness, neglect, abuse, and violence.[33] Those who survived returned home to communities where they had become strangers. Children raised in institutions do not know how to be loving parents, either Aboriginal or European, and so find themselves unable to love or nurture their own children. The loss of culture, love, and security gets passed down from one generation to the next. Alcohol and drugs dull the pain, and reinstitutionalization in detention or prison takes them back to the only security they have been raised to understand. This policy of assimilation continued for more than 150 years, and its effects are still resonating:

> The impacts began to cascade through generations, as former students – damaged by emotional neglect and often by abuse in the schools – themselves became parents. Family and individual dysfunction grew, until eventually the legacy of the schools became joblessness poverty, family violence, drug and alcohol abuse, family breakdown, sexual abuse, prostitution, homelessness, high rates of imprisonment, and early death.
>
> Aboriginal observers were aware of the problems from the outset … Marius Tungilik felt he had been taught "to hate our own people, basically, our own kind" while at school in Chesterfield Inlet. When he returned to Repulse Bay he saw his community differently: "you begin to think and see your own people in a different light. You see them eating with their hands. You think, 'Okay, primitive.'"[34]

Generations of Aboriginal children became lost, swallowed up by European-Canadian national and colonial agendas. Prime Minister Stephen Harper finally apologized to Aboriginal people on behalf of all Canadians in 2008 for the years of residential schools.[35] A financial settlement has been devised and a commitment to healing begun through a Truth and Reconciliation Commission process, but it will be many years before the pain and loss created by these policies can be overcome.

Beginning in the 1950s, Inuit children were taken to schools hundreds of miles away from home. There they were discouraged, sometimes forcibly, from speaking Inuktitut or maintaining their identities as Inuit. They were taught to be little Christian Canadians. As with First Nations children in the South, there were also instances of physical, sexual, and emotional abuse and neglect.[36] The worst problems in the Arctic seem to have occurred in the Chesterfield Inlet Residential School (Turquetil Hall) and in Sir Joseph Bernier Federal Day School, as well as in these schools in Inuvik. Turquetil Hall was opened by the Oblate priests of the Catholic Church in 1929 and was closed in 1970. The worst abuses occurred in the 1950s and 1960s. Piita Irniq remembers his own experiences as a boy sent to Chesterfield Inlet:

Some *Naujaarmiut* (people from Naujaat – Repulse Bay) were sent off to school around 1953, 54 and 55. In those days, they were being sent to school in Igluligaarjuk (Chesterfield Inlet). As for me, I knew I was never going to school. I knew this because, I grew up as a true *Inummarik*, and knew that I would live an adult life as a true Inuk, a hunter, fisher, and trapper. Ones that are older than I am, they started going to school around 1954-55-57 to Chesterfield Inlet. It was around that time. For me, going to school was something that I was not prepared for as we never lived in a community with other people. My father used to say that living in a community, all you get is welfare from the *Qablunaat*. He didn't want to be like that. He always wanted to be close to animals for food and clothing …

Well, that summer of 1958, we could see a boat coming, with an engine. We could see it very clearly, as it was a very beautiful day. As our custom goes, my mother started to make tea by burning heather, as this was the summer time. We only used heather and other moss to boil tea in those days. It was such a wonderful feeling that we are having some visitors, so she decided to make tea to welcome the visitors. Then they beached the boat. As they beached, we walked down to the beach to greet the visitors, and all of us walked down behind my father. But that father, a priest, the late Father Dedier, came off the boat, first. He came off the boat, and said to my father, "Peter Irniq is going to school in Igluligaarjuk so we came to pick him up." He didn't even greet my father by shaking hands! I have never seen my father panicked but at that point, he was panicky. So he ordered me by saying, "they came to get you, go put on some nicer clothes." My mother and I quickly went back to our tent and she made me put on *niururiak*, seal skin boots, with the fur outside. I got all dressed up in my best, and off we went to Naujaat [Repulse Bay]. The visitors didn't have tea. As Inuit, they would have stopped to have tea, if they were regular visitors, then leave after they had tea. I don't have any idea why this happened the way it did. I wondered, if the priest had told them earlier that, before anything happens, we should leave immediately. I don't know. When we were traveling towards *Naujaat*, my goodness, it was lonely.

It was the loneliest time of my life! ... My parents, my sister and brother-in-law, and my little brother, who died in later years, my niece, I watched them, as we are traveling farther and farther away from them. They were all standing by the shore, seeing me off, until I was no longer visible by eye. [Inniq, who was eleven years old at the time, was then flown from Repulse Bay to Chesterfield Inlet.]

We beached on a beautiful rocky beach with the plane. When we beached, we all got off. I saw some Inuit there but then, I saw the Sisters, the Grey Nuns, for the first time in my life. They wore long dresses, and their hoods had little "furs," but with lots of little holes, just like window screens. Some of the nuns were extremely beautiful! ... The Grey Nuns that I noticed so much being different than most people, were to be our care takers, supervisors. They came to meet us ... We were led by a Sister to the hostel. I walked along with my good friend Paul Maniittuq. Both of us walked in behind a Sister, as we were told to follow her. We were apparently going to the big house, the Turquetil Hall. It was a huge building, green in color. I turned to one side and noticed another big building. These buildings looked really big. I also noticed the Church Rectory, it was beautifully built. When I looked to the west, there was a Statue of the Virgin Mary, surrounded by rocks, it was beautiful. From there, we saw another large building, two-storey, this was a hospital as well as being a home for the Nuns. This one was not to be our home, at that point. The one we were going to was a two-storey hostel, it was to be our home for the entire winter or during all the time that we were going to be in Igluligaarjuk ... When we got there, we were told to take our clothes off. We were to have a bath. We were deliced. We got our haircuts. We got our haircuts with those old fashioned manual hair cutters. I had very short hair. In fact, all of us young boys had very short hair at that point. I also noticed that day that the young girls also got a haircut, by cutting their hair, right across their forehead. They looked so different. It was the first time I ever saw a bath tub, as we didn't have bath tubs in Naujaat. It was the first time I ever saw and wore shoes. I put on a short sleeve shirt for the first time. That was the first time, I ever put on foreign clothing like that.

Then when the night time came, we were told to go into our large, huge bedroom. There were many beds. I was given my bed, complete with sleepers or pajamas. I didn't know a darn thing about these items, as we did not use them in Naujaat. As an Inuk, I slept completely naked, at home. Just before we went to bed, we were told "to kneel down" and pray. I guess, this was the beginning of praying. We prayed a lot. That evening was just the beginning of our praying. When we woke up the next morning, we prayed first thing, then just before our breakfast, when we got to the school, we prayed first thing, we used to go to school at 9 in the morning. Right after we said the Lord's Prayer, "our father who art in heaven ..." then we sang, what is apparently an "Oh Canada" song, Canadian National Anthem. I didn't know what I was singing about but just trying to follow along and copied everybody. I was completely unaware of what these songs meant.[37]

Piita Irniq went on to be a member of the Nunavut Legislative Assembly and commissioner of Nunavut (the equivalent of governor general of Canada or lieutenant governor of a province). He is now a highly respected elder who works with Inuit in prisons in the South and travels as an Inuit ambassador all over the Arctic, keeping his language and culture alive.

John Amagoalik's memories of residential school in Churchill, Manitoba, are relatively happy:

The government tested all the school children; they gave us all an IQ test. Those of us who got a certain score qualified to go to Churchill. The brightest students from each community in the Eastern Arctic and Northern Quebec went there. It was a residential school, but our experience in Churchill was not typical of the residential school experience of other aboriginal groups. It was a great experience for us; it really opened up the world for me. I learned how to live on my own. It gave me a good basic education. Many of today's leaders are from that school, I was there for two years ... [I]t still had negative effects when students returned home to their communities and family. In many ways, we had changed. We dressed differently. We now had long hair and rebellious attitudes. Many became alienated from their parents. Many were less able to communicate with their elders. And, of course, many could not obtain the skills and knowledge needed for Inuit to survive in the Arctic. We had been further removed from our

6.6  Piita Irniq beside an *inuksuk* he built at Acadia University, Nova Scotia

culture, history and our natural environment. We got better educated in the white man's world, but it was at the expense of our culture.[38]

Unlike the schools in Chesterfield Inlet, the Churchill school was run directly by the federal government and seems to have provided a better education and less bitter experience for the students.

## Aftermath

The impact of both the relocations and residential schools is still being felt in Inuit communities across the Arctic. Inuit will tell you that in many ways their lives are easier now than in their parents' or grandparents' day. A wonderful evocation of the transition from living on the land to the modern world is told in Nancy Wachowich's book *Saqiyuq: Stories from the Lives of Three Inuit Women*. Apphia Agalakti Awa was born and raised on the land in the traditional way. Her daughter Rhoda Kaukjak Katsak had to make the difficult transition to life in the settlements of Frobisher Bay (Iqaluit) and Pond Inlet. Apphia's granddaughter Sandra Pikujak Katsak Omik graduated from the Akitsiraq Law School in 2005, is now a member of the Nunavut Bar, and is legal advisor to Nunavut Tunngavik Incorporated, the organization that administers the *Nunavut Land Claims Agreement*. The Iglulik shaman Awa is Sandra's great-great-grandfather. Elisapee Karetak became the first Inuk principal of her school in Arviat before going on to write and narrate a film about her mother's experiences called *Kikkik E1-472*.[39] John Amagoalik is now remembered as the "Father" of Nunavut and continues in his role as advisor to government and the Qikiqtani Inuit Association. Martha Flaherty became the president of the Pauktuutit Inuit Women's Association and was also an executive member of Inuit Tapiriit Kanatami. She has lobbied extensively for the rights of Inuit women, children, and youth. She has also rediscovered and reunited with some of her "white" relatives who now live in Burnaby, British Columbia.

Canadian government activity in the Arctic did not really become a major factor until the 1950s. This activity was associated mainly with the militarization of the Arctic during the Cold War and the continued establishment of Canadian sovereignty. The mistreatment of Inuit Canadian citizens during the postwar era does not bode well for the outcome of present and future discussions on security and sovereignty issues. As climate change creates the conditions for a more open maritime Arctic, the Canadian government seems to be slow to realize its responsibilities toward the best evidence of any sovereignty they may have there – Canadian citizens who actually live in the Arctic, the majority of whom are Inuit. Inuit have explicitly recognized Canadian sovereignty, and most describe themselves as Canadian, often with pride. Greenlandic Inuit demanded and got home rule in 1979 and gained a major increase in powers over all domestic issues in 2009. The hope is that independence from Denmark can be achieved by 2021. There is no similar push for independence in Canada, but legal and political requirements for cooperation do exist and need to be observed.

While my father was flying observation missions over Davis Strait and Baffin Bay in the early 1950s the situation of the people who lived in the Arctic was steadily worsening. The lives of southern Canadians, like myself, were following what we thought of as a normal trajectory during the economic boom times of the postwar era. Meanwhile Elisapee and her family

6.7 Elisapee Karetak (on left) with Sandra Omik during a roundtable discussion with the Honourable Irwin Cotler, then minister of justice, Ottawa

were struggling with relocation, starvation, tuberculosis, and a difficult transformation from a traditional to a modern lifestyle. From the 1970s onward, Inuit began to form political organizations in order both to hang onto what remained of their traditional lives and to resist the efforts of outsiders to take away what was left. For Inuit, this meant claiming their land, their sea, and their ice. Now, as the ice melts and the land and sea are exposed, all our lives are becoming increasingly interwoven.

# Nunavut: Our Land

The land is so beautiful with its high rivers and lakes waiting
to be fished. It has great mountains and images form as if you
could be caribou among them.

Rosa Paulia[1]

## Food

9 July 2003, was one of those perfect summer days in Iqaluit. The sun
was glimmering off Frobisher Bay in a thousand shades of diamond blue.
The mountains across the bay were pale misty white, still covered in snow.
The tundra was a deep soft green carpeted with the yellow, purple, pink,
and white of Arctic poppy, river beauty (or dwarf fireweed) (*paunnat*),
mouse-ear chickweed, moss-campion, Arctic cotton (*kangoyak*), mountain
avens, cloudberry flowers (*aqpiit*), purple saxifrage (*aupilaktunnguat* – now
the territorial flower of Nunavut), white Arctic heather, Labrador tea, and
woolly lousewort. Perhaps they weren't all blooming on that particular day,
but that is how I remember it. It was Nunavut Day and the town was cele-
brating. At the new hockey rink on the road to Apex a big summer fair and
market were in full swing with booths and tables of women's sewing, sealskins, caribou skin and antlers, carvings, prints, and jewelry. Children were
being entertained with games and stories, and people were wandering in
and out, happily eating ice cream and sipping soft drinks. At one end of the
rink there was something else to remind me that I was in the Arctic. A huge
pile of raw meat – Arctic char, caribou, seal, walrus, and *mattaaq* (whale

skin) – was spread out on cardboard on the floor. Anyone could pick some up in a plastic bag and either eat it there or take it home. This was Nuliajuk's bounty, the rich wealth of food from land and sea. I hesitantly helped myself to a bit of char.

In June of the following year, a few of the students of the Akitsiraq Law School, their professors, and I took ourselves up the Sylvia Grinnell River for an early spring picnic. The weather was abysmal – windy, cold – and soon it was snowing. But we persevered. The students put up a tent for the children and began cooking over an open fire (fuelled with heather and a few sticks of stray wood brought specially for the purpose). The main course was Arctic char cooked in butter. This was preceded by an appetizer of grilled baby seal. The seal was delicious! I find adult seal to be too oily and rich, but it is a great source of nutrients, and the oil helps to keep you warm on a cold day. Caribou meat, whether made into a stew or soup, is also nutritious and very tasty. Within a few weeks of my arrival in the North, I had already mastered the art of caribou chili.

Picnics, potluck meals, feasts, the Saturday morning women's breakfast club at the "Frobe" (Frobisher Inn), lunches, and dinner parties are a big part of socializing in the North. This has always been true. Catching, harvesting, preparing, and sharing food form one of the essential foundations of human social life. When the Inuit travel in the South, they crave "country food." The land and the sea provide what Inuit need to survive, although this is becoming more difficult as game dwindles or moves away. Caribou can now be very hard to find in much of the Arctic – their numbers seem to be again plummeting. New species are threatening the established chain of life that has existed in the Arctic for hundreds of thousands of years. Humans are only the latest creature to invade the North, but now we are bringing more strangers with us.

The Nunavut economy is mixed, still relying partly on traditional hunting and foraging skills developed over thousands of years, as well as on commercial hunting and fishing, mining and resource development, the service industry, government, and tourism. Most Inuit now live in settled communities on the fringes of Hudson Bay and the Arctic Ocean (except those in Baker Lake, which is the only inland community) and participate in a wage or welfare economy. This mixed economy can itself lead to stress as Inuit try to blend the old with the new. In traditional Inuit culture food was never purchased and rarely hoarded, although it might be cached to provide for the lean times. Even after the arrival of the Hudson's Bay Company enabled Inuit to trade fox furs for flour, tea, sugar, and other basics, the food was always shared. The rules in relation to sharing food were extensive. Elders, widows, children, and those who could not hunt for themselves were always given meat to ensure that no one went hungry. During starvation times these rules might be bent or broken, but doing so always caused cultural as well as physical distress. Inuit still do not like to see seal, caribou, char, or other meat sold in the marketplace. As Pilitsi Kingwatsiaq of Cape Dorset wrote in a letter to *Nunatsiaq News*:

> I have been noticing some things changing in Inuit culture over these last couple of years.
>
> I keep hearing on the radio that there is country food for sale. It doesn't happen much here in my home community – there is the occasional sale of fish to the co-op, but I rarely see the sale of a seal from one person to another person.
>
> People in my home community still share their country food, and it is part of Inuit culture. I think the sale of country food should not be allowed and should be stopped.
>
> Sharing is part of Inuit culture, and it should remain that way.[2]

Sharing food isn't the only thing that has changed. Modern conveniences such as CBC Radio, CKIQ "Raven Rock," regular flights between the South and all northern communities, satellite television, grocery stores, modern housing, snowmobiles and cars, as well as schools, offices, and businesses are now a familiar part of life in the North. But these southern imports have also brought alien problems – geographic and cultural dislocation, high unemployment, disparities in wealth, poverty, substance abuse, violence, suicide, and the increasing loss of traditional language and hunting skills. Food imported from southern Canada can be three to five times the cost in Montreal or Vancouver. A half-gallon of milk can be twelve or thirteen dollars; a small handful of grapes carefully wrapped in plastic can cost eight to ten dollars.

This imported food has led to nutritional problems. Inuit love to eat "country food" but are more and more resorting to store-bought items. These products include especially processed and "junk food" like pop, chips, pizzas, and hamburgers because they are cheaper than imported fruits and vegetables

| Subsidy (with tax dollars) | Food item | Southern prices (Gateway city: Ottawa) | Northern prices | |
|---|---|---|---|---|
| | | | (Arctic hub: Iqaluit) | (Remote communities) |
| High | Head of cabbage (2.1 kg) | $2.20 | $5.79 | $28.54 (Arctic Bay) |
| | Milk (4 litres) | $4.40 | $10.30 | $12.00 (Pond Inlet) |
| | Regular ground beef, frozen (2 lb) | $1.99 | $16.39 | $17.29 (Arctic Bay) |
| | Fried chicken, higher quality, frozen (2 kg) | $18.98 | $45.99 | $64.99 (Arctic Bay) |
| | Pineapple, whole | $1.88 | $8.59 | $11.59 (Iglulik) |
| | Watermelon, whole | $3.97 | $14.99 (and up) | $68.00, or $17.00 per quarter (Grise Fiord) |
| | Apples (5 lb) | $3.28 | $8.79 | $15.18 (Clyde River) |
| | Strawberries (1.36 kg or 3 pints) | $4.32 | $16.47 | $26.97 (Iglulik) |
| | Juice from concentrate, frozen (8 cans X 295 ml) | $5.99 | $34.99 | $51.89 (Iglulik) |
| | (1 can X 295 ml) | $0.88 | $ 4.99 | $11.29 (Arctic Bay) |
| | Cheddar cheese, Black Diamond (300 g) | $1.99 | $8.29 | $11.00 (Grise Fiord) |
| Lower | Chicken noodle soup, canned (540 ml) | $1.49 | $5.59 | $11.39 (Pangnirtung) |
| | Flour, all purpose (5 kg) | $9.49 | $25.78 | $33.29 (Iglulik) |
| | Sugar, granulated (4 kg) | $3.76 | $16.39 | $19.99 (Pond Inlet) |
| None (as of October 2012) | Spring water, 1 case (24 bottles X 500 ml) | $2.97 | $42.99 | $104.99 (Clyde River) |
| | Pogoes, frozen corndogs (20 pieces, 1.5 kg) | $11.99 | $24.99 | $44.80 (Pond Inlet) |
| | NutriGrain Bars (8 bars, 295 g) | $2.49 | $6.99 | $16.19 (Arctic Bay) |
| | Ice Pops, unfrozen (100 X 20 ml) | $2.49 | $16.99 | $42.79 (Pond Inlet) |
| | Vanilla Wafers, cookies (400 g) | $1.29 | $6.39 | $11.39 (Pangnirtung) |
| | Soda pop (24 cans X 355 ml) | $5.97 | $35.98 | $160.00 (Grise Fiord) |
| Totals | | $91.82 | $356.86 | $764.56 |
| | Possible added expense: IAMS dog food, dried (7-8 kg) | $21.98 | $39.99 | $140.00 (Iglulik) |

7.1 A comparison of food costs in southern Canada and Arctic Canada as of January 2014

(which are often of poor quality anyway, particularly in the smaller communities) and are easier to obtain than "country food." Processed food can be shipped in on the "sealift," the small cargo ships that deliver supplies every summer, but fresh produce has to be flown in. There are as yet no roads between the South and any of the communities in Nunavut. Those who eat "country food" are in danger from the high levels of persistent organic, metallic, and chemical pollutants that congregate in the Arctic food chain. Seals in particular eat fish that have eaten other small animals and plants laced with pollutants. The higher up the food chain we go, the more concentrated the toxicity becomes. Humans and polar bears are at the top of this food chain. Mother's breast milk in many Arctic communities is now heavy with chemicals and metallic poisons. These toxic elements can lead to higher rates of cancer, neurological disorders, and allergic reactions.[3]

The change in lifestyle has been exacerbated in recent years by climate change as traditional game, such as caribou, alter their migration routes or die out. The famous hole in the ozone layer exists in the Arctic as well as the Antarctic. The international community succeeded in minimizing the effects of human-made chlorofluorocarbons (used in air conditioners and spray cans) in time to slow the destruction of the thin layer of ozone in the stratosphere that protects us from toxic ultraviolet radiation. Still, the hole has not yet disappeared and is at its worst in the spring, when seals birth their pups on the ice and then are hunted by polar bears and humans. In the Arctic spring sun reflects off the snow and ice for long hours until the twenty-four-hour daylight of summer arrives. The ultraviolet radiation causes damage to the skin and eyes that can lead to skin cancer, cataracts, and blindness. Not only humans but also wildlife exposed to the unfiltered sun suffer from these afflictions. Elders have noticed deterioration in the quality of sealskin as the effects of toxicity, sun exposure, and other pollutants damage seals' hides. In October 2011 a large hole in the ozone layer again appeared over the Arctic for reasons not yet understood.[4]

Too many people in the North smoke and too many more live in cramped, rickety housing with inadequate heating. Alcohol and illegal drugs have become a scourge in many communities, even those that are technically "dry." The black market is alive and flourishing. Problems related to diet and lifestyle, such as obesity, diabetes, and heart disease, are on the rise. Nunavut has some of the highest rates of respiratory diseases in the world, especially among children. Family violence (child abuse and neglect, spousal abuse, and elder abuse) is a serious problem. Young girls often do not finish school because they become pregnant – although many schools now have daycare centres to help with this circumstance. Young boys drop out of school because of language and literacy problems, substance abuse, or simply a feeling that they have no future no matter what they do. One or two generations of young men have been essentially lost due to the huge transition from a traditional to a modern society. Violence and murders are now much more frequent than they were in traditional Inuit society. The suicide rate is at least ten times the Canadian national average, especially affecting young men and boys. Mental illness, including depression, is another serious problem.

Inuit learned over many generations how to live north of the treeline, finding ways to survive and even thrive in the most extreme and formidable environment on Earth. Southerners moving into the North have been much slower to understand the limits of human interaction with this severe and fragile environment. As Inuit have adopted a modern Canadian lifestyle, and as a modern industrial economy has invaded the Arctic, reciprocal interaction between humans and the environment has begun to melt away – quite literally. As the Arctic ice melts the shape of Canada and the world is changing, perhaps permanently. To the peoples who are native to the North the Arctic is not a barren wasteland of snow and ice, nor is it a potential mother lode of rich resources to be dug up and shipped out. Instead it is a home of abundance and great beauty. Sovereignty and national boundaries seem more artificial in the Arctic than anywhere else on Earth – and are becoming more and more intensely guarded as these frontiers melt under our feet. As temperatures increase and the ice disappears, this balance of habitat and sovereignty is becoming increasingly unpredictable.

## Empire in the North

One part of North American history that most of us forget, are unaware of, or would like to ignore is how those of us of European or Asian descent got here and what happened afterward. As Stephen Mercer explains,

> The development of North America is a colonial story ... the Dominion
> of Canada was first settled (or passively invaded) by both the French

and the English in the 200 years predating Confederation [1867] ...
The history of the creation of Nunavut can be adequately dissected
into the major components and themes of colonialism. The story of
every country and every region's struggle with colonialism is vastly different in context but markedly similar in theme. How does the concept
fit with the development of the Nunavut Land Claims Agreement and
eventual establishment of the Nunavut Territory?

Colonialism can be described as governance or forced change in
which one culture or society dominates another. It is authority over
people by a group who are not representative, not endorsed by the
population whom they govern. Not until the passing of the NCLA were
the Inuit released from colonialism.[5]

I am not sure I agree with the final sentence – and there are Inuit who certainly do not agree that the completion of the land claim in Nunavut ended
their experience of colonialism. Mercer, in this history of the creation of
Nunavut, quotes at length a passage from "On Our Own Terms: The State
of Inuit Culture and Society," published by the Nunavut Social Development
Council in 2000. It is worth quoting again:

When whalers first came to the Arctic our ancestors did not object to
them because our way was to share. We believed that the wildlife did
not belong to us but that it existed for our benefit. It was there for the
taking for those who pursued it for sustenance. Some of our elders
have described the Inuit attitude to wildlife as a moral relationship. As
one elder has said, they "let themselves be killed." We shared our
wildlife willingly with these visitors and welcomed them because they
brought trade, excitement and more security. But along with the benefits, there were terrible consequences. They brought diseases for which
we had no resistance or remedy. Many Inuit died. As more whaling
fleets arrived, the whalers hunted the animals we depended on for
clothing and shelter until they were on the verge of extinction. Consequently many Inuit starved.

When the whalers left the traders and missionaries quickly established themselves in our land. The traders promoted a barter system
using tokens which Inuit hunters could exchange for food supplies.

This system was foreign to us as our economy traditionally depended on sharing and exchanging meat, skins and other necessities. Inuit did not know how to manage the new token system and quickly fell afoul of it, incurring debts, making up late payments and leaving themselves short of tokens to buy food and new equipment. So, while Inuit enjoyed new goods they had never had before, they became indebted to a system that eventually controlled them.

The coming of missionaries was a mixed blessing. They were confident of the superiority of their beliefs, but their actions often brought confusion and sorrow. In some part of the Arctic they forbade drum dancing and other spiritual activities, so these traditions stopped. They christened us with foreign names. As they diminished or proscribed our traditional spiritual values, the missionaries unwittingly destroyed our independence and pride little by little. It hardly occurred to them that the ideas about hygiene, sex, and God, which were well accepted in their European homes, could be alien and perverse in the Arctic. The Anglican Church in particular frowned upon Inuit cultural and spiritual practices considering them a 'way against God.' Little wonder we were confused as to what was right and wrong, true or false.

In retrospect, we can see clearly how the first visitors to the Arctic began to erode our culture with terrible consequences for our family lives, economy and self-esteem. The struggle for converts between the Anglican and Roman Catholic missionaries caused division in our groups and families that had depended on cohesion and cooperation to survive. Faced with the powerful influences driving the commercial and religious activities of these strangers to our land, we were inevitably led to see our culture as second class.

Of course, these strangers to our land did bring some benefits. These were the days before the Government of Canada was concerned to help us. Some whalers and traders did provide support in difficult times, and the missionaries, working with few people and limited money, tried to give education and medical help across our vast country. And in recent years, they have become defenders of our language and customs. But what the early visitors to our land did not recognize was the irreversible process they had started, a process that for us Inuit was the beginning of a long slide toward disaster. In retrospect we can see this. From a European perspective, it was simply an exploration of this last frontier. But for Inuit, it was the beginning of the greatest crisis we had faced since we first learned to live and prosper in the Arctic many generations ago.[6]

Canada became a self-governing dominion in 1867 (it would not gain full independence from British constitutional oversight until 1982 when the Canadian Constitution was finally redrafted to allow amendments to be passed by Canada itself, not the British Parliament).[7] British ideas about colonial expansion and governance were transferred to the new federal government in Ottawa. Canadian political leaders, like the first prime minister, Sir John A. MacDonald, adopted a policy of European settlement across the West and into the North that was essentially a continuation of British imperialism. This expansion of the British Empire, whether in semi-independent "dominions" such as Canada and Australia or through direct conquest in Asia, Africa, and the Pacific, was at its height from the mid-nineteenth century until the beginning of the Second World War.

For Indigenous peoples, including Inuit, this period of global history has not really ended. In southern Canada during the nineteenth century Aboriginal peoples were persuaded to sign treaties that ostensibly indicated their agreement to share their land with the federal government, which then leased it to railways, commercial interests, farmers, and European settlers, who now claim the land was irrevocably surrendered. That is not how First Nations or Métis see it. Where the people were reluctant or unwilling to agree, force was sometimes used. Canadians like to imagine that the settlement of our western and northern frontiers was peaceful, at least compared to the violence south of the Medicine Line – the border between British Canada and the American West running along the 49th parallel. But in 1869–70 in Manitoba, and again in 1885 in Saskatchewan, military power was used to confront Métis and Cree who objected to the Canadian push west.[8] The slaughter of the buffalo in the nineteenth century created conditions in which the Indigenous peoples of the Prairies could no longer survive without government assistance.[9] They were moved onto reserves and, in 1876, became subject to government control under the *Indian Act*.[10] Métis were settled in what were then called "colonies" in Alberta and elsewhere on small strips of farmland. The opening-up of British Columbia during the Gold Rush years of the 1850s and 1860s was anything but peaceful, as First

Nations rose up along the Fraser River and later in Tsilhqot'in country to prevent their land from being taken over by miners and settlers.[11] Other incidents of violence continued into the twentieth century. Blockades and standoffs between Natives and non-Native officials in Haida Gwaii (British Columbia), Ipperwash (Ontario), Burnt Church (New Brunswick), Caledonia (Ontario again), Oka (Quebec), and elsewhere represent continuing militant protests against Canadian federal and provincial agendas by Aboriginal peoples. The Oka crisis of 1990 near Montreal was a forceful reminder that violent rejection of Canadian expansion is still possible.[12]

Inuit did not feel the full brunt of Canadian government control until after the Second World War. People were then pushed into coastal settlements, where a system of small hamlets was created. Although these settlements were not reserves, the effect for many Inuit was similar. A kind of urban ghetto life at a village level was created where welfare and minimal services were provided but chances for meaningful employment or a good future were lacking. Traditional life still hung on at the edges but became more and more difficult to maintain. Inuit are not subject to the *Indian Act*, but policies developed for First Nations in the South were replicated in the Arctic, and many of the same problems have been the result. Too many Inuit live in poverty in places where housing is inadequate or nonexistent. The homelessness rate for Inuit means that for many "couch surfing" from one friend's or relative's house to the next is not uncommon. There are not enough shelters or food banks. There is not enough physical or emotional support. There is not enough of anything.

I found the seriousness of social problems in the North a terrible shock when I arrived in Iqaluit, and I still feel a deep sense of anger and shame about the conditions in which so many Inuit live. Of course, like so many southern Canadians, I knew something about the terrible conditions in which many Aboriginals lived, especially in remote communities, from their portrayal in the media and in academic studies. I had seen something of Aboriginal deprivation when I lived on the Prairies and in Australia, where similar problems exist. But I had never really had any of this brought home to me. In Iqaluit I lived just up from the beach close to many of the older and poorer houses in the town. I remember driving home one afternoon on a chilly grey day in late October to find a young Inuk man staggering down the middle of the road toward my house. He had nothing on except a pair of jeans – no shirt, no shoes, no jacket, no socks. He was wavering from

7.2 Sled dogs on the beach, Pond Inlet

side to side, obviously drunk or stoned. I could not get past him so I slowed down, wondering what to do. I was about to stop and get out of my vehicle to try to help when the RCMP pulled up. They quickly took control of the situation and waved me on.

On occasion I would go and visit Lucien Ukaliannuk, the elder-in-residence at the Akitsiraq Law School. He lived in White Row, at the time a dismal housing estate located down the hill from the Frobisher Inn and Nunavut Arctic College. For a time he and his family were able to live in housing provided by the college, but that came to an end when his wife graduated from her jewelry-making course. I then had to negotiate a continuation of his housing so that he and his family would have a roof over their heads while Lucien was working for the Law School. The college eventually agreed to let them stay on, moving them to another apartment in White Row. He had many of his own children and grandchildren living with him, as well as frequent visitors from Iglulik and elsewhere. The house was tiny, poorly furnished, always crowded, and in bad repair, but at least there were beds or a couch to sleep on, electricity and heating, a kitchen, and a living area. I tried, as northern director, to make sure he received enough of a paycheque to live on and occasionally assisted with income tax and other financial issues. But I remain ashamed to this day that I could not help with better housing. There was simply none available that the Law School's elder-in-residence budget could afford. I still remember sitting on his front step and looking out toward Frobisher Bay on a sunny spring day while he tried to teach me to say "It's a nice day" in Inuktitut – *silattiavak*.

## The Creation of Nunavut

Nunavut was created in April 1999 as a result of the long-negotiated *Nunavut Land Claims Agreement* of 1993.[13] The boundary basically follows the treeline as it extends from the Manitoba-Saskatchewan border north to the High Arctic Archipelago. Thirty years before Nunavut was created, the newly elected government under Prime Minister Pierre Trudeau and Minister of Indian and Northern Affairs Jean Chretien issued the 1969 "White Paper" – a document outlining the government's "new" policies for Indians.[14] These policies were in fact a continuation of the old assimilation practices under a different name. First Nations, Inuit, and Métis took one look at this document and decided they had had enough. Two years later, while Aboriginal writers and leaders around the country were protesting the "White Paper,"[15] Premier Robert Bourassa of Quebec announced the building of a massive hydroelectric project in northern Quebec. The James Bay Cree and Inuit in the region were not told about this. They heard about it on CBC Radio like the rest of the province. They immediately objected, demanding a genuine agreement between themselves and government, and began the process of negotiating a comprehensive land claims agreement to secure their traditional territory, which covered most of northern Quebec. The *James Bay and Northern Quebec Agreement* of 1975 was the first modern treaty between the federal government and Aboriginal peoples since the early twentieth century.[16]

Inuit Tapirisat of Canada (ITC) was formed in 1971 by a group of young men and women determined to create an effective political organization for Inuit. It was based in Ottawa and took the lead in supporting Inuit organizations in negotiating land claims across the North. The only model anyone had at the time was the *Alaska Native Claims Settlement Act* of 1971.[17] John Amagoalik, who joined the ITC in 1974, remembers,

The Inuit Tapirisat of Canada in those early days was a real hive of activity. There were a lot of things going on. The Northern Quebec land claims settlement was being negotiated, and the Inuvialuit were moving toward negotiations. The Inuit Tapirisat of Canada was seen as the organization to push the land claims issue, right across the country, with the Government of Canada. ITC was busy preparing the Nunavut Land Claims Agreement, drafting it. They were having discussions on it, and debating what should be in it, and what kind of strategy Inuit should have when they came to the negotiating table with Canada.[18]

In 1975 a meeting was hosted by ITC in Pond Inlet to which all thirty-two Inuit communities across the Canadian Arctic sent delegates. Their task was to try to agree on a proposal and strategy for an Inuit land claims settlement. A proposed land claims agreement was presented to the Canadian government by ITC in 1976. This was followed by more than fifteen years of protracted and difficult negotiations. In the early days Inuit did not understand why they needed to claim their own land. It already belonged to them; no one else used it in the way they did; why did they need to claim what was already theirs? There was no deep commitment to Canada. Elders were used to white traders, missionaries, and explorers talking about the British king or queen. The Canadian government's control over the Inuit of the North was beginning to take hold. Project Surname had begun just a few years earlier, and the move into settlements was taking Inuit off the land. Once in town, dogs became vulnerable to being shot either for safety, disease control, or other reasons. Hunters without dog teams could not get out on the land. Snowmobiles were expensive, although Inuit began increasingly buying and using snow machines imported from the South. Life was changing more rapidly than anyone could remember.

ITC began a significant program of community outreach to try to understand Inuit's concerns and to explain its position on negotiating with the federal government. It insisted on a number of key issues on which it would not compromise:

1  ITC wished for Inuit to have their own territory over which they would have political control. At that time Inuit of what is now Nunavut lived in

the Northwest Territories, where they never formed more than about 30 per cent of the total population. Governance, controlled by the federal government in Ottawa, was gradually transferred to a legislature, executive, and judiciary based in Yellowknife. But the Inuit and Inuvialuit did not have majority control. The Inuvialuit of the western Arctic eventually decided to negotiate their own land claim with the federal and territorial governments, choosing to remain within the Northwest Territories. Nellie Cournoyea, an Iñupiat woman from the western Arctic, became the first female and the first Aboriginal premier in Canada, serving as leader in the Northwest Territories from 1991 to 1995. Inuit of the eastern Arctic pushed for their own homeland and government, where they would be the majority.

2 ITC wanted a public government similar to territorial government in Yellowknife and Yukon farther west. They were able to persuade Ottawa that they were not asking for "Aboriginal self-government" but rather for a parliamentary-style government with a legislative assembly, government offices, a civil service, and a separate court system. This request was in addition to the settlement of land claims and guarantees of government support in training, finance, wildlife management, national parks, and control of waterways.

3 ITC insisted that the Inuit role in establishing Canadian sovereignty in the Arctic be recognized.

4 Inuit joined with other Aboriginal organizations in supporting the protection of Aboriginal rights in the Canadian Constitution, resulting in section 35, where Aboriginal and treaty rights are recognized, future land claims agreements are protected, and Inuit are included in the definition of "Aboriginal peoples."

By the 1980s a great deal had been achieved, but treaty negotiations seemed to be stalled. John Amagoalik became the president of ITC in 1981 and pushed forward with negotiations. There had been ongoing opposition from the Canadian government, which was unwilling to agree that Inuit had any claim to their land. There was also disagreement over the creation of the Territory of Nunavut and a government controlled by Inuit. The federal government would have preferred to create a limited agreement that dealt with hunting and fishing rights and the quarrying of soapstone for Inuit carvers – more like a nineteenth-century imperial treaty. The Inuit would have none of this. There were also difficult negotiations with the territorial government of the Northwest Territories and opposition from some provincial governments. Even other Inuit were opposed, particularly the Inuvialuit of the western Arctic and the Inuit of Quebec and Labrador, who felt they were being ignored. Inuit within the eastern Arctic were not always convinced that their leaders were going in the right direction. The extinguishment of Inuit ownership of 80 per cent of the land once the agreement came into effect was bitterly opposed by some Inuit both then and since. Partly to defray these concerns, negotiation of the agreement was shifted from the national organization to the Tunngavik Federation of Nunavut (later Nunavut Tunngavik Incorporated, the umbrella organization administering the agreement), created by ITC for this purpose. John Amagoalik left his position as the president of ITC and became the constitutional advisor for the new Tunngavik Federation from 1991 to 1993.

By the early 1990s a Conservative government in Ottawa, led by Brian Mulroney, was facing a massive backlash from Aboriginal people across the country over the slowness of land claims negotiations and the continuing terrible conditions in Aboriginal communities. In July 1990 this backlash turned into a storm of protest centred on the village of Oka west of Montreal. The Mohawks of Kanehsatake held out for several months in a community centre while protesting against the expansion of a golf course onto a Mohawk burial ground and sacred territory. Their cousins in nearby Kahnawake barricaded the Mercier Bridge across the St Laurence River, blocking traffic into Montreal. The Canadian army was called in, and a full military occupation was established while government and Aboriginal leaders tried to negotiate a settlement. Eventually the Mohawk walked out from behind the barricades. They had not surrendered. One person had been killed and another badly beaten. Several were arrested. Aboriginals from across Canada either went to the two communities to support the Mohawk or protested in sympathy across the country. I was in Australia at the time and watched the events unfold as global headline news. This extremely tense experience, perhaps more than anything else, convinced Prime Minister Mulroney and the federal government that some sort of movement on Aboriginal issues had to be achieved. Amagoalik and other Inuit leaders were highly critical of the more militant actions of the Mohawk and have themselves been criticized by First Nations commentators for those views.[19] But it is clear that, although militant tactics have never been the Inuit way of doing things, the crisis in Oka as well as other pressures on the federal government did help to fast-track the final stages of the *Nunavut Land Claims Agreement*.

## Politics

In 1993 the *Nunavut Land Claims Agreement* became the first and (so far) only Aboriginal settlement in Canada to include parliamentary governmental structures and the only one to involve a division of territory into a new political entity. The Territory of Nunavut came into existence in 1999. The people of the eastern Arctic voted for the agreement, and the Canadian Parliament passed legislation enshrining it in Canadian law. The agreement is protected under section 35 of the Constitution, so Nunavut has the unique distinction of being both a political territorial unit and a constitutionally protected Aboriginal land claim. It was the largest rearrangement of Canadian territorial and political control since the creation of the province of Newfoundland and Labrador in 1949 – and the territory covered is much larger. About 20 per cent of Canada's land mass was transferred to the oversight of the people living in what became known as Nunavut, Inuit and non-Inuit alike. Of the people who now live in Nunavut, 85 per cent are Inuit, with the rest being a mixture of southern English- or French-speaking European Canadians. The capital of Iqaluit is about half Inuit and half non-Inuit. The Legislative Assembly sits in a beautiful building; the new courthouse is there, as are many government offices. Nunavut Tunngavik Incorporated continues to administer the land claim through its main office and branch organizations for the three main regions of Nunavut – Qikiqtani (Baffin Island and the High Arctic), Kivilliq (the mainland west of Hudson Bay), and Kitikmeot (the western mainland and islands).

When I first visited Iqaluit in 2001, the euphoria of the creation of Nunavut was just shading into the reality of governing this giant and unwieldy territory. The small town of Iqaluit had about 5,000 people and has continued to grow extremely rapidly, reaching about 7,500 by 2013. Inuktitut, English, and French can all be heard there on a daily basis, although the three linguistic and cultural communities do not interact much at a social level. Nunavut is, in one sense, a land of not just two solitudes but many – linguistic, geographic, cultural, communal, political, and economic. In another sense the 35,000 Nunavummiut, both Inuit and non-Inuit, who reside in the territory are like a small town scattered over vast distances. Everyone knows everyone else, nothing is private, and almost everything is personal. Inuit families are large and extended. I quickly learned that my life as northern director of the Akitsiraq Law School was basically public, and the students often felt oppressed by their sense of living in a fishbowl. On the other hand, *qallunaat* usually live isolated lives in "expat" enclaves of other southerners like themselves and have little interaction with the local community, very similar to what I experienced while living and working in Singapore in the 1980s. Sometimes it feels as if the sun really never did set on the British Empire! While in Iqaluit, I was very fortunate to work with Inuit and long-term northern residents all the time. I had to learn, not always successfully, how to adjust to a very different reality.

Political processes are quite different in Nunavut from what they are in Ottawa or the provinces. The Legislative Assembly represents all of Nunavut's nineteen territorial constituencies. But no political parties are officially allowed. After an election the speaker, premier, and Cabinet ministers are all elected by the members of the assembly. The half of the assembly that does not form the government acts as the Official Opposition, although consensus rather than confrontational debates and votes is preferred. Laws are enforced in a court system unique in Canada where federal and territorial courts are combined into one Nunavut Court of Justice. Much legal business is in fact administered by territorial justices of the peace who are not trained lawyers but are drawn from respected members of the community throughout Nunavut, a majority of them Inuit. Prior to the Akitsiraq Law School, there was only one Inuk lawyer in the territory – then premier Paul Okalik. The Akitsiraq graduates have nearly doubled the local Bar and increased the Inuit representation in the Nunavut legal system – something that will no doubt lead to significant changes in the future. Judge Beverley Browne was instrumental in creating the Law School, as she was in creating the justice of the peace program, training for interpreter services, the Inuit court worker program, the participation of elders in court cases, and the unified court system itself. She worked in an honourable tradition of enlightened northern judges like Judge Sissons (of Kikkik's case). She was vice chair of the Akitsiraq Law School Society Board of Directors and was therefore one of my bosses. She has since been appointed to the Alberta

Court of Queen's Bench but will no doubt sit on Nunavut appeals as part of her jurisdictional duties.

## Religion

One factor of major importance in the establishment of a non-Inuit presence in the North, and one that is still playing an important role today, is the influence of Christian missionaries. Missionaries of both the Catholic and Anglican Churches began converting Inuit from the early twentieth century onward, and the trend continues with the rapid growth of Pentecostal and Evangelical Protestant churches. The old shamanistic religion has either disappeared or been submerged by overarching Christian practice. The Isuma feature film *The Journals of Knud Rasmussen* shows just such an abandonment of shamanism and adoption of Christianity in Iglulik. The great *angakkuq* (shaman) Awa travelled around the North Baffin region in the early twentieth century. His meeting in 1921 with Knud Rasmussen resulted in the preservation of much information about the role of shamans in traditional Inuit culture, but not long afterward, he gave way to pressure from some of his own people to abandon his helping spirits.

Both men and women could be shamans, and they could be more or less powerful. Some shamans were feared because they used their powers for evil, whereas others were loved and respected healers and leaders. Shamans healed the sick, repaired injuries, protected the souls of people from evil shamans, visited the Mother of the Sea to release seals and other animals for hunting, and generally ensured that traditional customs were observed and passed on. They relied on *tuurngait* (helping spirits) to guide them. These spirits might be animals, the souls of the dead, or other supernatural entities. As Awa told Rasmussen,

A young man wishing to become an angakoq must first hand over some of his possessions to his instructor. At Igdlulik [Iglulik] it was customary to give a tent pole, wood being scarce in those regions. A gull's wing was attached to the pole, as a sign that the novice wished to learn to fly. He had further to confess any breach of tabu which he might have committed, and then, retiring behind a curtain with his instructor submitted to the extraction of the "soul" from his eyes, heart and vitals, which would then be brought by magic means into contact with those beings destined to become his helping spirits, to the end that he might later meet them without fear ... At last, without knowing how, he perceived that a change had come over him, a great glow as of intense light pervaded all his being ... and a feeling of inexpressible joy came over him, and he burst into song. "But now," he [Awa] went on, "I am a Christian, and so I have sent away all my helping spirits; sent them up to my sister in Baffin Land."[20]

The encounter between the old religion and Christianity is described in detail in Frédéric Laugrand and Jarich Oosten's book *Inuit Shamanism and Christianity: Transitions and Transformations in the Twentieth Century.* Anglican and Roman Catholic missions were often in direct competition with one another in communities, demanding that their converts not consort with families of the other church. This created divisions within communities that are still troubling today. Shamanism was condemned as an act of Satan and helping spirits as emissaries of the Devil. Nuliajuk was dismissed as a demon, and the old stories were suppressed. Songs, drum dancing, and other traditional activities were forbidden. Residential schools were mostly run by the church.

The influence of Christian missionaries was not always malign. The Inuktitut-speaking people of Nunavut use a written syllabic script introduced by Christian missionaries in the early twentieth century. Even elders with little or no "formal schooling" are fluently literate using syllabics. The syllabic script was introduced by missionaries from earlier work with Cree, Ojibwa, and Naskapi First Nations farther south. The literacy rate for an ostensibly "oral" culture is extremely high. Retention of literacy in Inuktitut syllabics is considered crucial to the survival of the language by most Inuit in Nunavut (unlike Greenlandic, which never adopted syllabics).[21]

The first work translated into Inuktitut syllabics was the Old Testament. Many Inuit adopted the new religion with real conviction, especially women who saw it as a way of escaping old taboos and restrictions within traditional culture (particularly around marriage, menstruation, and childbirth). Most elders today are devoutly Christian or practice a syncretic religion that contains elements of both Christianity and the old ways. I attended the Good

| "i" or "ee" | "u" or "oo" | "a" or "ah" | "ay" | Finals |
|---|---|---|---|---|
| ᐃ i | ᐅ u | ᐊ a | ᐁ ai | – |
| ᐱ pi | ᐳ pu | ᐸ pa | ᐯ pai | ᑉ p |
| ᑎ ti | ᑐ tu | ᑕ ta | ᑌ tai | ᑦ t |
| ᑭ ki | ᑯ ku | ᑲ ka | ᑫ kai | ᒃ k |
| ᒋ gi | ᒍ gu | ᒐ ga | ᒉ gai | ᒡ g |
| ᒥ mi | ᒧ mu | ᒪ ma | ᒣ mai | ᒻ m |
| ᓂ ni | ᓄ nu | ᓇ na | ᓀ nai | ᓐ n |
| ᓕ li | ᓗ lu | ᓚ la | ᓓ lai | ᓪ l |
| ᓯ si | ᓱ su | ᓴ sa | ᓭ sai | ᔅ s |
| ᔨ ji | ᔪ ju | ᔭ ja | ᔦ jai | ᔾ j |
| ᕆ ri | ᕈ ru | ᕋ ra | ᕃ rai | ᕐ r |
| ᕕ vi | ᕗ vu | ᕙ va | ᕓ vai | ᕝ v |
| ᕿ qi | ᖁ qu | ᖃ qa | ᙯ qai | ᖅ q |
| ᖏ ngi | ᖑ ngu | ᖓ nga | ᙰ ngai | ᖕ ng |
| ᙱ nngi | ᙳ nngu | ᙵ nnga | ᖏ nngai | ᖖ nng |
| sila = ᓯᓚ | siku = ᓯᑯ | Nunavut = ᓄᓇᕗᑦ | sikuvut nungaliqtuq = ᓯᑯᕗᑦ ᓄᖓᓕᖅᑐᖅ | |
| To create a long vowel sound in a syllable, add a dot over the syllabic (e.g., pii = ᐲ; tii = ᑏ). | | | | |

7.3 Inuktitut syllabics

Friday service in Inuktitut at St Jude's Anglican Cathedral in Iqaluit one Easter and was surprised at the level of emotion that was displayed by both men and women. People lined up the length of the church so that each could hammer a nail into a large wooden cross laid on the floor before the altar. There was audible sobbing as the people mourned the crucified Christ.

Almost all Inuit have been affected by the Christianization of the Arctic. The religious framework is important in tracing the development of the Canadian presence in the Arctic and how this influences both contemporary interpretations of traditional culture and modern political debates. The debate over the adoption of Nunavut's own territorial human rights legislation in November 2003 is an example of how profound this influence is. Many Inuit were very disturbed at the connotations some human rights provisions might have for traditional Inuit customs. A particularly contentious issue was the protection of gay rights contained in the bill debated in the Nunavut Legislative Assembly. Many older Inuit, including many members of the Legislative Assembly, maintained that homosexuality was not recognized or tolerated in traditional Inuit societies. Other elders insisted that homosexuality did exist and had been accepted. Lucien Ukaliannuk, who was by this time elder for the Nunavut Department of Justice as well as the Akitsiraq Law School, testified before the assembly that homosexuality had at least been tolerated in traditional Inuit society. The objections to recognition of gay rights seemed to have had more to do with the concerns of Christian churches (especially the Anglican Church) over the recognition of same-sex marriage. As a consequence, Christian leaders in the North led a crusade against passage of the bill. The "Inuit traditions" cited were largely Christian – or allegedly Christian. An underlying current in the debate was long-term memories of serious sexual abuse of children by teachers in many northern communities, especially the abuse by male teachers of young boys. One community that has been deeply damaged by the actions of one male teacher is Cape Dorset. Memories of abuse in both the residential and day schools in Chesterfield Inlet and Inuvik were also on people's minds. The nature of Inuit culture, the influence of a certain type of "fundamentalist" Christianity, the lasting influence of the introduction of formal schooling, and an attempt to bring Nunavut into the modern circle of law and justice was played out on many different levels during this debate. The bill was eventually passed but only with the tie-breaking vote of the speaker of the assembly.

The issue came up again in April 2005 when the Liberal Party introduced *Bill C-38* in the federal Parliament in Ottawa, amending the federal *Civil Marriage Act* to allow for gay marriages.[22] Nunavut's member of Parliament, Nancy Karetak-Lindell, was under enormous pressure by Christians in Nunavut to vote against the bill. "I am supporting the legislation, as I do not see how I can support discrimination of any kind against another human being on this earth," she said in a long letter to her constituents. "My Inuit, aboriginal and minority rights are protected in Canada by the charter and by the constitution of this country. Individual liberty and religious freedom are protected by the charter. If I decide not to defend this right by gay couples to marry, how will I defend other rights that are threatened, like our aboriginal rights?"[23] Karla Williamson Jensen, a Greenlandic Inuk who has lived in Canada for many years, wrote in the local newspaper,

> When I was growing up as a little girl in Kalaallit Nunaat, or Greenland, my maternal grandmother lived in a smaller community – Kangaamiut – north of where I was growing up in Maniitsoq. She was the person from whom I was introduced to Inuit *silarsuangat*, the Inuit world view ... Her best friend was Aada, a male, and even though he

was broad and hefty, his movements were always effeminate. He and my grandmother could talk for hours when they met and much of it full of good laughter. At one time my grandmother told me that Aada was *"arnaasiaq"* – a man who should have been a woman.

There was no drama involved in this statement, no rejection, no condemnation – just a fact. I loved him as he provided much love and assurance to my grandmother when she needed good company. Now, Aada in his state of *"arnaasiaq"* would, in the present-day context, be considered a homosexual, a person who, according to the present-day social unrest, is to be hated and condemned ...

To me, this is against the grain of Inuit thinking. *"Arnaasiaq"* and for that matter *"angutaasiaq"* (women who should have been men) talk about their roles in Inuit society with no reference to sexual behaviour ... Inuit across the Arctic have been very good at adopting various kinds of Christianity. In Greenland where I grew up, the Lutheran religion has held the Inuit imagination since the 1720s. In Canada, Inuit are either Catholics or Anglicans. In Alaska and Russia, our Inuit cousins have adopted different kinds of Russian religions ... Our new lives teach us to be judgmental and to reject certain people – but our true Inuktitut teaching teaches us differently. Directives on terms such as "homosexual" and *"arnaasiaq/angutaasiaq"* are very clear on that, and sometimes it is hard to make sense of changes since Inuit cultures have evolved so rapidly.[24]

The debate over sexuality is one example of how Inuit are struggling with the transition from a traditional to a modern life. There are strong and continuing efforts to preserve the old ways. The prevailing philosophy of Nunavut is Inuit Qaujimajatuqangit, or "IQ." This worldview encourages a continuation of the old values of sharing, humility, kindness, and cooperation in government and nongovernmental activities. But often these values collide with Western ideas of independence, competitiveness, and hierarchy, with a narrow view of "professionalism," and with strict adherence to a legalistic construction of agreements. This often means that the Inuit way of doing things does not measure up to southern standards applied in the workplace or schools. This conflict will remain until Inuit who are able to cross this divide are in full control of their own political, legal, and economic structures.

7.4 Stop sign in Inuktitut, Gjoa Haven

## Land and Resource Development

Does the self-determination of Inuit in Nunavut depend on resource development? Or does it depend on keeping true to Inuit cultural values and environmental wisdom? Is it possible to do both? These are the difficult questions facing Nunavummiut today. Development of mineral resources is rapidly expanding across the Arctic, with exploratory licences being granted under both Canadian and Nunavut authority in several places. Seismic testing in the Beaufort Sea by Chevron and Statoil of Norway began in the summer of 2012. Restrictions on offshore oil and gas exploration in Canada have been lightened: "To drill in the Arctic waters, companies must be able to complete a so-called relief well in the same season that they drill the exploration well, in order to cap any potential leak before it spews all through the long winter when ice conditions make such well shutdown operations impossible. Faced with industry complaints that the same-season relief well requirement is virtually impossible to meet, the [National Energy Board] said companies can proceed if they have an alternative that is clearly as effective."[25] On 27 September 2013 it was announced that "Imperial Oil Canada, Exxon Mobil and BP have jointly filed an application to drill at least one well in the Beaufort Sea 175 kilometres northwest of Tuktoyaktuk, NWT ... Imperial estimates ice conditions are manageable for only four months of the year, but that can vary dramatically from year to year ... the soonest the drilling can happen is in about six and a half years but it's by no means certain that this project is going to move ahead even if it is approved by regulators."[26] As much as "20% of Canada's potential oil and gas reserves are thought to lie in Canadian waters off the east and north coasts of Baffin Island, according to Bernie MacIsaac, the director of lands and re-sources for QIA [Qikiqtani Inuit Association],"[27] but the Canadian govern-ment and corporate interests should not assume that Inuit in the area support the development of this huge resource. Exploratory drilling for petroleum started off the west coast of Greenland in Disko Bay in 2010, al-though the current government says that it will not issue any new licences.[28] Oil and gas exploitation on the Alaska North Slope has been a big part of the American economy for many years, with new interest in offshore drilling in the Beaufort and Chukchi Seas. Russia is rapidly developing its fossil fuel and minerals industries in Siberia, and China is now a hugely important market for minerals, oil and gas, and coal.

The North is rich in fossil fuels and minerals as well as uranium, precious metals such as gold, and gemstones such as diamonds and sapphires. Ura-nium mining is also a possible industry that has been discussed in both Greenland and Nunavut, giving rise to fierce opposition by Inuit communi-ties and environmental groups in both countries. The pressures to develop these resources in the Arctic will only increase as sources elsewhere become more and more depleted and the Arctic warms up, becoming more accessi-ble. Inuit are working with the Department of Aboriginal Affairs and North-ern Development in Ottawa, their own Government of Nunavut, and private corporations to try to develop mining and transport options on their land that are both productive and sustainable.

The body responsible for reviewing both the biophysical and socio-economic impact of proposed developments in Nunavut is the Nunavut Impact Review Board (NIRB), a public body set up under the *Nunavut Land Claims Agreement*.[29] The board consists of nine appointed members who review development proposals in accordance with both natural justice and Inuit knowledge.[30] For large projects, the board also conducts community hearings where all can appear before the board and express their views.[31] The primary functions of the NIRB are

(a) to screen project proposals in order to determine whether or not a review is required;
(b) to gauge and define the extent of the regional impacts of a project, such definition to be taken into account by the Minister in making his or her determination as to the regional interest;
(c) to review the ecosystemic and socio-economic impacts of project proposals;
(d) to determine, on the basis of its review, whether project proposals should proceed, and if so, under what terms and conditions, and then report its determination to the Minister; in addition, NIRB's determination with respect to socio-economic impacts unrelated to ecosystemic impacts shall be treated as recommendations to the Minister; and
(e) to monitor projects in accordance with the provisions of Part 7.[32]

But "The mandate of NIRB shall not include the establishment of requirements for socio-economic benefits."[33] These are negotiated separately in an Inuit impact and benefit agreement between the relevant Inuit organization (such as the Qikiqtani Inuit Association for the Baffin region) and the corporate entity wishing to develop the project. The minister responsible for making a final determination on whether development should go ahead is the Canadian minister of Aboriginal affairs and northern development.[34] The NIRB must also work in cooperation with the Nunavut Planning Commission in relation to issues of land use planning.[35] Proposals may further require a review by a federal environmental assessment panel.[36] Two major resource development projects have come before the NIRB in recent years: the Bathurst Inlet Port and Road Project and the Mary River Iron Ore Mining Project.

*The Bathurst Inlet Port and Road Project*
One particularly sensitive area in Nunavut is Bathurst Inlet on the North American mainland in the western Kitikmeot region. It is a unique ecosystem of great beauty where Arctic and northern mainland animals (such as polar

and grizzly bears) come together. Inuit have lived on this land for centuries. Walking over the tundra in late summer is like walking through a scented garden of deep green moss, golden willow, and reddening Labrador tea. Caribou and even grizzly bears can be spotted at a distance. At the head of the inlet, swans gather before flying south for the winter. Mineral resources, including gold, have already been identified near the inlet on Coronation Gulf between Cambridge Bay on Victoria Island and Kugluktuk at the mouth of the Coppermine River. The Bathurst Inlet Port and Road Joint Venture was originally promoted by the Kitikmeot Corporation (a development body wholly owned by Inuit through the Kitikmeot Regional Organization in Nunavut) and the resource development firm Nuna Logistics (a Canadian company with regional offices in Yellowknife and Rankin Inlet). The financial interest of these two corporate entities was bought out by Sabina Gold and Silver Corporation (based in Vancouver) in January 2012.[37] Sabina is now working in partnership with GlencoreXstrata (based in Switzerland) to gain approval from the NIRB to go ahead with a deep-sea port and road construction. The building of transport facilities is essential to building, maintaining, and provisioning mines in the area, as well as shipping out the material once it is dug out of the ground and (in the case of gold) chemically refined on-site.

The project has been in the planning stage since 2003, during which the various partners have worked with the community of Cambridge Bay and a revolving cast of international mining interests to gain approval to build a deep-sea port at the head of Bathurst Inlet.[38] The project would also include all-weather roads running south and west to join up with other transport routes in the Northwest Territories. The port and roads could service mines in the Slave geological area of the territories, including the existing diamond mines Diavik and Ekati, as well as future projects in Nunavut. There are several proposed gold mines to the east and southwest of Bathurst Inlet that are being explored. It is hoped the project, when complete, would greatly decrease the cost of supplies and fuel to areas of the western Arctic, including the Kitikmeot hamlets of Cambridge Bay and Kugluktuk. Trucking in and out of the Slave geological area by ice roads is currently threatened by winter seasons that are getting shorter, resulting in unsafe ice conditions. Winter ice roads may in fact be reaching the end of their usefulness, creating even more pressure to open up all-weather roads. Upheaval of tundra caused by permafrost thawing in the summer is however a potential problem for any road construction or infrastructure. A *Draft Environmental Impact Statement* was put before the Nunavut Impact Review Board in 2007.[39] However, the approval process was put on hold because of the acquisition of the original Canadian mining company involved in the project by major international player China MinMetals Corporation and subsequent corporate takeovers (including the Kitikmeot and Nuna Logistics buyout by the Sabina Gold and Silver Corporation). It was announced in October 2012 that the review process was going ahead with long-term cooperation between the Kitikmeot Regional Organization and corporate interests. However, a geotechnical review of the area where the port would be located found that the site is unsuitable without extensive and expensive dredging. The project has again been put on hold until a new port site can be found.[40]

A deep-sea port in Bathurst Inlet would not be possible without the retreat of summer ice in the Coronation Gulf due to climate change. The communities of Cambridge Bay, Kugluktuk, and other Indigenous settlements in Nunavut and the Northwest Territories need economic development, jobs, financial resources, and a future for their people. Elders are however deeply concerned about the effects of this project on what is currently a unique and highly sensitive ecosystem. There are concerns about caribou migration routes,[41] pollution of watersheds and groundwater, damage to marine life, and disturbance of land-fast ice and pack ice by commercial vessels with icebreaking or ice-strengthened capabilities. There is also concern about the destruction of important archaeological and cultural heritage sites (including at the head of Bathurst Inlet, where the port was originally to be sited) and about the costs of reclamation of the land after mines close. In addition, although economic development is essential, traditional hunting skills and practices may well be lost. The choices are extremely difficult.

## The Mary River Iron Ore Mining Project

A major series of environmental reviews, community consultations, and public hearings was concluded in the summer of 2012 on the most ambitious resource development project ever contemplated in the Canadian High Arctic, the Mary River Iron Ore Mining Project. The corporate plan was for a gigantic open-pit mine in north-central Baffin Island to be serviced by a new railway from the mine south to Steensby Inlet, where a deep-sea port would be built to service ships carrying ore all year. The ships would also have to be newly built with significant icebreaking capacity. This would be the first time in Canadian Arctic history that a railway will be built north of the tree-line. It would also be the first time icebreaking cargo vessels will be used all year in Arctic waters between Canada and Europe. The project is massive, and the potential impact on the environment is steep. The socio-economic impact is also a matter of concern. Although the project promises employment, training, use of local businesses, and economic benefits to all the surrounding communities as well as to Nunavut as a whole, more negative social and environmental problems may also result.

Public hearings on the project were conducted in Iqaluit and the two communities of Iglulik and Pond Inlet during July 2012. On 14 September 2012 the NIRB presented its final report, approving the project and making 184 recommendations.[42] The minister of Aboriginal affairs and northern development in Ottawa has given approval for the project to go ahead subject to the NIRB's recommendations.[43] The board commented in its report,

> During the Final Hearing, the Board heard concerns expressed that when facing development many Nunavummiut feel caught between two worlds: their hopes for development to yield lasting and sustainable benefits to individuals, communities, their region, Nunavut and Canada in general; and their concerns regarding potential negative impacts on the air, land, water, fish, wildlife, marine mammals, traditional areas, traditional ways and communities. The Board understands these hopes and concerns and sees thorough impact assessment as a way to bridge the gap between these worlds by ensuring that only development which will ensure the future well-being of Nunavut residents and that protects our land, water and resources be allowed to proceed.[44]

I attended the week-long public hearing in Iqaluit, Nunavut, from 16 to 20 July 2012.[45] There were six board members in attendance, all of whom were Inuit. Baffinland Iron Mines Corporation (a Toronto-based subsidiary of the multinational mining giant ArcelorMittal of Indian ownership based in Germany) gave a detailed and professional presentation on the nature of the project and the benefits to the community. It appeared the corporation had done significant work in preparing environmental impact statements and setting up baseline data on the environment, and it promised to continue monitoring and communicating with communities. It outlined the socio-economic benefits that Inuit could expect from the project, including training, education, jobs, transport, individual and family counselling, medical assistance, emergency preparedness, time off for hunting, and significant royalties to Nunavut.[46]

But many community and government representatives, elders, and private citizens remained extremely concerned. I had a number of private conversations with several people who echoed the views of many that the amount of information was overwhelming and that the technical language used by the southerners was difficult to understand. Translation from English into Inuktitut and vice versa left much confusion and misunderstanding. Repeated attempts to get Baffinland personnel to change their minds on key issues were met with resistance. Many details remain to be determined or have been delegated to working groups whose mandates are unclear. No information was provided on the impact of icebreaking on sea ice and polar bear habitat in Foxe Basin and Hudson Strait. No detailed marine mammal plan is yet in place. Baffinland maintained that the North Baffin caribou population was in a cyclical low period, but there seemed to be little data about the future of the herd, and there was no mention at all of the impact of climate change and melting tundra on the herd's regrowth. Some hamlets, such as Arctic Bay, felt they had not been properly consulted. The then mayor of Iqaluit, Madeleine Redfern, pointed out that no real consultations had been conducted with the city until this final review process. Her comments to the review board were the first opportunity she had had to make concerns involving the capital known. Makivik Corporation and the Nunavik Marine Region Impact Review Board (from northern Quebec) expressed major concerns about not having been properly included in the review process.

A number of individuals both at the table and in the audience spoke up about their concerns. Lloyd Lipsett, legal counsel representing Zacharias Kunuk of Isuma Productions, emphasized the need for a "human rights impact assessment" based on existing obligations of both government and the company under United Nations instruments, the Canadian Constitution, and the *Nunavut Land Claims Agreement*. He particularly mentioned vulnerable groups such as women. Continuing consultation was essential. The news media, such as that represented by Isuma Productions based in Iglulik, could help with this. Kunuk himself emphasized this again during the hearings in Iglulik on 23 July. Susan Enuaraq asked about compensation for loss of wildlife. She indicated that there was a requirement of absolute liability under the *Nunavut Land Claims Agreement*.[47] This question was deferred until the creation of *The Mary River Project Inuit Impact and Benefit Agreement*, which was completed on 6 September 2013. A draft summary is now available, but the complete agreement has not been released to the public.[48] Mary Wilman of the Iqaluit Municipal Council expressed concerns about the lack of notice and knowledge about the hearings among people in her city or in other communities. She also commented on how overwhelming the information and decision-making process was. "Give us the real picture," she insisted. Martin von Mirbach, director of the World Wildlife Federation's Canadian Arctic Program, echoed the concerns about a lack of baseline studies, particularly in the Hudson Strait. He was also the first to point out potential interference with the Lancaster Sound Marine Protected Area, currently under negotiation, and the first to stress that this project would have cumulative effects, including the creation of more projects like it. Peter Ivalu of Iglulik was also one of the few speakers to comment on the amount of greenhouse gas emissions the project would release through its use of diesel fuel. Leesee Papatsie (creator of the Feeding My Family website, highlighting the extremely high food prices in the North) suggested that empty ore carriers or other mine ships might help communities by bringing in reasonably priced food. In a posthearing conversation, Mukshowya Niviaqsi of Cape Dorset expressed frustration about the limited response from representatives of Baffinland to repeated demands that shipping should keep to the south of Mill Island near Cape Dorset in order to protect marine mammal breeding groups, especially groups of walrus.[49]

Two of the most powerful presentations at the hearing were by Madeleine Redfern and by Chief Superintendent Steven McVarnock, commanding officer of the Royal Canadian Mounted Police's Nunavut branch. Redfern, although generally supportive of the project, was concerned about the lack of consultation over its probable impact on her city. Iqaluit is the government centre and transportation hub of Nunavut. The project would inevitably result in more people moving to Iqaluit or transiting through it. This would put pressure on housing (already in short supply), infrastructure (such as water), airport facilities, temporary accommodation, and services for travellers. She stressed that "people should be provided with services before major socio-economic impacts occur" and that "there needs to be family planning counselling for families who are thinking of moving to Iqaluit, education partnerships and recreational facilities and specific programs for substance abuse, family support and child neglect." She emphasized the vulnerability of women who may end up being sexually exploited by transient workers. The "fly in–fly out" shift schedule proposed by Baffinland would be very hard on families and needed to be rethought. Yellowknife, capital of the Northwest Territories, had received substantial support during the diamond and gold mining boom in that territory, so why not Iqaluit? "Don't forget about us," she reminded the board.

Chief Superintendent McVarnock described the social impacts of the Meadowbank Mine on the community of Baker Lake as seen from the perspective of the local police. Out of 1,500 people living in Baker Lake, 133 were employed in the mine. The period 2008–11 (covering the time when the mine first opened in 2010) saw a 22.5 per cent increase in calls to police, a 33 per cent increase in prisoners held in detention, and a 36.5 per cent increase in criminal activities in Baker Lake. In a comparable community (Pond Inlet), crime statistics had remained static over this period. The difference would appear to be from the mine. Increased policing activities have a ripple effect on other social services. Madeleine Redfern referred to a social worker from Baker Lake who lamented that "a mine means child neglect."

Zacharias Kunuk intervened during the hearings in Iglulik the following week. He had helped to organize Inuit into a group in order to insist on the inclusion of human rights impacts resulting from the project. In perhaps one of the more poignant reminders of what a significant change this project would be for the Inuit and how quickly the modern world has affected them, Kunuk stated,.

> I am a filmmaker as well as a hunter … I was born at Steensby Inlet and went for schooling in that area as well … In the springtime the caribou would migrate this way, and then in the fall time they would migrate towards the south. We would live in *qarmait* (sod houses) when I was a child. I took part of my schooling starting in 1962. And then I began to know about the world, and that world was not from my culture. We never knew any English, and that's the way we lived. We just began to know how the world ran at the time. For many of us we haven't completed our education and there are many people today

who haven't completed their education as well. We lived the traditional way, and today we've kind of started letting go of our culture, slowly.[50]

Steensby Inlet is the site of the proposed deep-sea port where icebreaking vessels would load iron ore for shipment to Europe during both the open-water and ice seasons. To put this in some perspective, Kunuk is a little younger than I am (late fifties). Like many older adults and elders, he has vivid memories of living on the land and the rapid change to a modern way of life.

In January 2013 Baffinland announced that it was substantially cutting back on the Mary River Project as a result of falling commodity prices and an uncertain economic future: "In a letter to Nunavut authorities, operator Baffinland Iron Mines Corp. said it is replacing a mine plan to produce 18 million tonnes a year of iron ore with one that will produce just 3.5 million tonnes. A planned railway for the project will be deferred, and the iron ore will instead be trucked to an existing small port instead of building a new one."[51] This decision raises a whole new set of issues. First, it is not clear that the smaller port at the northern end of Baffin Island can handle this increased activity. Second, although the construction of the railway and deep-sea port would have had a much greater impact on the environment, even a smaller mine will still generate many of the same problems, with fewer benefits for Inuit. And third, this underscores how vulnerable Inuit are to decisions made outside the North that do not include or require consultation. Hopes for economic development, jobs, training, and other benefits from the mine must now also be scaled back. Baffinland has also made it clear that shipping through the Northwest Passage is not practical even without ice. The waters are simply too shallow for large cargo ships carrying iron or coal. It is not practicable for cargo ships to be accompanied by coast guard vessels for the entire route, and insurance rates are likely to be too high because of the treacherous conditions.[52] A new review process before the NIRB has now begun. Public hearings were scheduled to begin in January 2014.

Inuit throughout the circumpolar region in the Arctic have taken on the issue of resource development as a matter of critical importance. In *A Circumpolar Inuit Declaration on Resource Development Principles in Inuit Nunaat*, the Inuit Circumpolar Council, representing Inuit from Siberia, Alaska, Canada, and Greenland, declares,

- Healthy communities and households require both a healthy environment and a healthy economy.
- Economic development and social and cultural development must go hand in hand.
- Greater Inuit economic, social and cultural self-sufficiency is an essential part of greater Inuit political self-determination.
- Renewable resources have sustained Inuit from the time preceding recorded history to the present. Future generations of Inuit will continue to rely on Arctic foods for nutritional, social, cultural and economic purposes.
- Responsible non-renewable resource development can also make an important and durable contribution to the well-being of current and future generations of Inuit. Managed under Inuit Nunaat governance structures, non-renewable resource development can contribute to Inuit economic and social development through both private sector channels (employment, incomes, businesses) and public sector channels (revenues from publicly owned lands, tax revenues, infrastructure).
- The pace of resource development has profound implications for Inuit. A proper balance must be struck. Inuit desire resource development at a rate sufficient to provide durable and diversified economic growth, but constrained enough to forestall environmental degradation and an overwhelming influx of outside labour.
- Resource development results in environmental and social impacts as well as opportunities for economic benefits. In the weighing of impacts and benefits, those who face the greatest and longest-lasting impacts must have the greatest opportunities, and a primary place in the decision-making. This principle applies between Inuit Nunaat and the rest of the world, and within Inuit Nunaat.
- All resource development must contribute actively and significantly to improving Inuit living standards and social conditions, and non-renewable resource development, in particular, must promote economic diversification through contributions to education and other forms of social development, physical infrastructure, and non-extractive industries.
- Inuit welcome the opportunity to work in full partnership with resource developers, governments and local communities in the sustainable development of resources of Inuit Nunaat, including related policy-making, to

the long-lasting benefit of Inuit and with respect for baseline environmental and social responsibilities.[53]

As the story of Kiviuq tells us, in the Arctic there are no second chances. You have to get it right the first time. Engaging in major resource development projects may well be the future for Inuit, but the land and sea will not be forgiving if too much damage is done. As Mariano Aupilaarjuk has said, "The living person and the land are actually tied up together, because without one the other doesn't survive and vice versa. You have to protect the land in order to receive from the land. If you start mistreating the land, then it won't support you ... [I]n order to survive from the land, you have to protect it. The land is so important for us to survive and live on; that's why we treat it as part of ourselves."[54]

## Law

Lancaster Sound and the east coast of Baffin Island lie in an area of the Arctic known to have large reserves of oil and natural gas. It is also sometimes called the "Serengeti of the Arctic," as it is one of the richest marine wildlife areas in the world. Inuit have lived and travelled here for hundreds of years harvesting the riches of land and sea. I have also travelled through the sound several times and have never failed to see a wealth of animals and birds, including narwhal, belugas, bowhead whales, polar bears, walrus, ring seals, bearded seals, muskoxen and falcons (on Devon Island), guillemots, gulls, thick-billed murres, snow geese, and much more.

During the spring of 2010 the NIRB screened a proposal by the Geological Survey of Canada to conduct seismic testing in Lancaster Sound. This was opposed by local communities in the High Arctic as potentially very damaging to local marine wildlife. At the same time as one branch of the Canadian government was (apparently) looking for oil and gas, Parks Canada was proposing the creation of a protected marine conservation area in the same location.[55] The NIRB eventually approved the seismic testing, and plans went ahead to begin in August of that year.

On 3 August 2010 the Qikiqtani Inuit Association (QIA), representing the communities of Pond Inlet, Grise Fiord, Arctic Bay, Clyde River, and

Resolute Bay, asked the Nunavut Court of Justice for an order to stop the testing. Three days later Judge Susan Cooper granted an interim injunction that halted all seismic testing activity in Lancaster Sound.[56] There were two legal issues at stake. The court concluded that a duty to consult and accommodate Aboriginal people wherever a project is proposed that may have a negative impact on their Aboriginal rights to traditional land was a serious constitutional issue that needed to be fully argued at trial.[57] The court further held that Inuit in the area would suffer irreparable harm if seismic testing went ahead in advance of a final ruling on this issue. The seismic testing was stopped. On 6 December 2010 the then federal environment minister, John Baird, announced that most of the eastern entrance to Lancaster Sound will be protected as a marine conservation area, including the area around Pond Inlet and Bylot Island. The boundaries of the area will be established in consultation with Inuit in the area and the QIA.[58] This means that further oil and gas exploration will not go ahead.[59]

This is an extremely important precedent for Inuit. It is a strong reminder to the Canadian and Nunavut governments of the need to fully consult with local Inuit about any proposed development or exploratory searches in relation to resource extraction that may have an adverse impact on Inuit rights. The case recognized existing rights of Inuit to land use, preservation of cultural heritage, environmental protection, and controls on resource development. It is also an indication that the creation of a self-governing territory such as Nunavut does not end the requirement for the Canadian federal government to consult with and accommodate Inuit rights under section 35 of the Constitution, which states,

1 The existing aboriginal and treaty rights of the aboriginal peoples of Canada are hereby recognized and affirmed.
2 In this Act, "Aboriginal Peoples of Canada" includes the Indian, Inuit and Métis peoples of Canada.
3 For greater certainty, in subsection (1) "treaty rights" includes rights that now exist by way of land claims agreements or may be so acquired.
4 Notwithstanding any other provision of this Act, the aboriginal and treaty rights referred to in subsection (1) are guaranteed equally to male and female persons.[60]

According to the Supreme Court of Canada, the Crown (meaning government at the federal, provincial, or territorial level) has a duty to consult with Aboriginals and, where appropriate, to accommodate their interests. Dwight Newman outlines five aspects of the duty to consult that determine its application:

1  the duty to consult arises prior to proof of an Aboriginal rights or title claim or in the context of uncertain effects on a treaty right;
2  the duty to consult is triggered relatively easily, based on a minimal level of knowledge on the part of the Crown concerning a possible claim with which government action potentially interferes;
3  the strength or scope of the duty to consult in particular circumstances lies along a spectrum of possibilities, with a rich consultation requirement arising from a stronger *prima facie* Aboriginal claim and/or a more serious impact on the underlying Aboriginal right or treaty right;
4  within this spectrum, the duty ranges from a minimal notice requirement to a duty to carry out some degree of accommodation of the Aboriginal interests ...; and
5  failure to meet a duty to consult can lead to a range of remedies, from an injunction against a particular government action altogether (or, in some instances, damages) but more commonly an order to carry out the consultation prior to proceedings.[61]

This does not give Inuit a veto on development, but it does mean that consultation must be genuine, going beyond an administrative review. Since Inuit land and water are already covered by an existing treaty, the *Nunavut Land Claims Agreement*, it is important that this duty to consult also exists where there is already a treaty.[62]

The duty depends on some government action that might adversely affect a potential claim of Aboriginal title to land, an existing Aboriginal right, or an existing treaty right. This requirement would seem to be a fairly easy trigger, as an Aboriginal claim does not even have to be proved for the duty to exist. However, lower courts are still struggling with the extent of the obligation. Where the adverse effect would be relatively minor, the duty may not arise. It also may not arise where government action has been delegated to another branch of government. Municipal governments are not bound by the duty, nor are private entities such as corporate bodies. The duty to consult is, however, a very important requirement imposed on government to protect Aboriginal, including Inuit, rights. Most cases brought by Indigenous groups in Canada that are related to the duty to consult and accommodate have in fact gone against governments. Bill Gallagher, author of *Resource Rulers: Fortune and Folly on Canada's Road to Resources*, "calls aboriginal entitlement 'the biggest under-reported business story in Canada of the last decade.'"[63]

A more stringent test is developing under international law. This is the duty of "free, prior and informed consent" in relation to a range of issues affecting Indigenous rights. This requirement is contained in the *United Nations Declaration on the Rights of Indigenous Peoples*.[64] It is particularly important in relation to any contemplated relocation of Indigenous people (article 10), adoption or implementation of legislative or administrative measures that may affect Indigenous people (article 19), or use of traditional lands (article 32). In addition, where traditional lands have been "confiscated, taken, occupied, used or damaged without their free, prior and informed consent," Indigenous people have a right of redress, compensation, or restitution, ideally in the form of land or territory equal to what was taken (article 28). It is arguable that the foundational philosophy of the declaration is based on consent, consultation, cooperation, and redress where this standard has not been met. For the first time in global history Indigenous rights are clearly expressed in an international document of persuasive and increasingly legal importance.

In voting against the declaration in both the UN Human Rights Council and the UN General Assembly, Canada expressed concerns about the "free, prior and informed consent" provisions as well as about other rights in relation to land use and natural resources. Although Canada has since relented and accepted the declaration, it continues to have reservations about these provisions. In addition Canada stated in its acceptance that "the declaration does not reflect customary international law nor change Canadian laws."[65] It is therefore not clear what effect the declaration might have in Canadian courts. The Supreme Court of Canada has recognized customary international law as part of Canadian common law in previous cases, as well as using international law to interpret legislation and the Constitution.[66] Whether the declaration amounts to customary law more generally is still a matter for debate. However, the more the declaration is relied on at all levels of legal action, the more likely it is to become customary or common law. The Canadian government's current position is likely to have a weakening impact on the application of the declaration as the requirement of consent becomes stronger in law. And of course, the federal government's position could change.

## Nunavut Dreaming

A year or two before I knew that the Akitsiraq Law School was envisioned by people like Alexina Kublu and Beverley Browne, or that it actually was going to happen, I saw an advertisement in the *Canadian Geographic Magazine* that caught my eye. It was for a cruise through the Arctic offered by Adventure Canada, a company founded by Matthew Swan. Margaret Atwood was to be one of the travellers on board, along with experts on the Arctic, including Inuit. My mother and I were both intrigued but eventually decided against going because we felt we couldn't afford it. At that point in our lives the Arctic was a distant exotic location on the edge of the known world. Like many Canadians we felt attached to the Arctic as an idea but felt the barriers of cost and effort were too steep to actually get there. However, like many people around the world, I saw the creation of Nunavut as a model of self-determination for Indigenous peoples everywhere. I felt some regret that I couldn't see it for myself.

Around the same time, I had a vivid dream – one of those dreams that stay with you. In the dream I am standing on a steep gravel beach. Behind me loom high grey-brown cliffs and before me is a wide grey sea. There are dark clouds barring the sky above me. The mood is sombre, chilling, even frightening. I feel a presence here – perhaps wolves, perhaps ghosts. There are people behind me walking around, but I am alone. In the dream I watch myself watching as if I am also a gull or falcon hovering some distance away. It is cold but I can't remember seeing any snow or ice. I knew it was somewhere in the Arctic, but I didn't know where or why I was there.

The odd thing about this dream is that a few years later I really did stand on that gravel shore. It was Beechey Island and I was travelling with my mother on the Russian-built research vessel the *Academic Ioffe* with Adventure Canada. My mother, Betty, discovered her ambitions for exploration and travel with Adventure Canada in 2004 – two years shy of her eightieth birthday. Together and separately we made many trips all over Nunavut and Greenland. Not long after my strange dream, I did get the opportunity to see the Arctic for myself.

But I learned there is more than one Arctic. There is the strange and beautiful land that I saw on my travels with Adventure Canada – the one that a few lucky tourists see. And there is the reality of life in the North – a life I shared briefly. Even this reality is fragmented. I lived as *qallunaat* live, in a comfortable apartment with a good salary and many opportunities to travel, including escapes down south when the going got a little too tough. But the students of the Akitsiraq Law School and their families, our elder-in-residence, Lucien Ukaliannuk, and his family, and my Inuit neighbours who lived down by the beach in Iqaluit – they lived very different lives. I saw some of this disparity for myself, but I was always to some extent a stranger and always will be. I love the land, the people, the communities, and the animals – but not as Inuit do.

Although the creation of Nunavut was a major step forward for Inuit, the new government and other organizations established under the *Nunavut Land Claims Agreement* have not solved the major socio-economic problems that leave many Inuit in a constant state of crisis. Inuit die on average ten to fifteen years younger than other Canadians. The overall suicide rate is eleven times the national average. For Inuit boys and young men, the suicide rate is as high as thirty times the national average.[67] Rates for respiratory illnesses and unintentional injury or accidents are also many times the average in the rest of the country.[68] Family violence, including child abuse and neglect, spousal abuse, and abuse of elders, is at epidemic levels. Substance abuse, including abuse of alcohol and illegal drugs, is rampant in many communities. Although a mental health training program was introduced in Nunavut Arctic College in 2006, it has since been discontinued. There are few mental health professionals working in the territory, leaving many residents, both Inuit and non-Inuit, without any care other than prescribed antidepressants or self-medication with illegal drugs and alcohol. Rates of homicide and violent crime are much higher than in the South, and many young Inuit, especially boys and young men, spend their lives rotating in and out of the criminal justice system and correctional facilities.

Every community now has schools from kindergarten to grade 12, but the educational standards are low and graduation rates are also extremely low. Children get primary school education in Inuktitut up to grade 4, but after that they must switch into an English or French stream. As a result many children struggle with both Inuktitut and a second language and fall behind because of problems with oral fluency and literacy. Fewer than one-third of young Inuit graduate from high school, let alone go onto college or university.[69] Poverty rates are very high, as the cost of living is three to five times higher than in southern Canada. The cost of healthy food from the South and the toxicity of "country food" as a result of an accumulation of persistent organic pollutants in the food chain from southern industries mean that nutritional needs are not being met. This deficiency has led to increasing levels of obesity, diabetes, cardiovascular illnesses, respiratory problems, cancer, and neurological disorders. A new study conducted in 2011 and released in 2013 reports that Nunavut has by far the highest rates of food insecurity in Canada, with 36.4 per cent of households unable to provide food for their families on a secure basis. In addition 56.5 per cent of children in Nunavut live in households where they don't know if they're going to eat every day.[70]

Inuit also suffer disproportionately from preventable diseases related to poverty, such as respiratory ailments and mental illness. Tuberculosis is still a problem in many communities, and shockingly Nunavut has the highest rate of lung cancer in the world, at twenty-three times the Canadian average.[71] Half of all health costs are spent on transporting patients by air to Iqaluit or down South for treatment not available in the communities, yet health care in the North is funded by the federal government at the same rate per person as in southern cities. The birthrate is higher than in any other province or territory, but the infant mortality rate is also three times the national average.[72] Removal of children to residential schools and relocation of families from one part of the Arctic to another after the Second World War left scars that have been passed on from one generation to the next.

The state of housing is in crisis, with far fewer homes than there are people who need them. What is available is often well below standards most Canadians take for granted. Nunavut has the highest average number of people per household in the country.[73] Homelessness is a serious problem in communities where sleeping on the streets during winter means freezing to death. Inuit do not often have the option of leaving the North and travelling to southern cities where more jobs, housing, and services are available.

7.5 Glacier on Baffin Island with ship's derrick in the foreground

The cost of air travel is prohibitively high, and those who do leave may experience incredible alienation in a southern urban environment where little education and few skills mean their employment prospects are bleak. Too many Inuit spend their lives lurching from one crisis to the next, leaving them little time to recover or to plan a healthy future for themselves and their children.

Nunavut is a dream about "our land" – the land the Inuit have known for many generations. The creation of the new territory did not, could not, solve the many problems generated by modernization and Canadian intrusion into the Arctic. Some people have expressed the view that Inuit were not ready for self-government – even some Inuit themselves have expressed this view. But my own experience suggests this outlook is too bleak. You do not fix colonialism by continuing colonialism. Inuit were masters of their domain long before Britain or Canada claimed dominion over the Arctic. Nunavut represents a unique response to the challenges of a changing world. What are the practical, political, economic, cultural, and spiritual answers to the continuing debate about sustainable development, self-determination, and environmental transformation in the Arctic? Perhaps Cornelius Nutaraq says it best:

> To my way of thinking, people never know everything about something immediately. When we are young and growing up, we experience things. We never know everything about anything immediately. This is especially true for things that are going to affect our lives. Knowing the characteristics of the land is not that easy, especially in our land. It is very cold in deep winter. You have to know about surviving on the land and you have to know how to live on it, for example how to hunt for food to survive. In order to do this, there are many things you have to know. You have to follow what you are taught about living here, especially outside of the community if you are alone in the winter when it is cold. You have to know how to survive on the land. When you are accustomed to a warm place, you will feel the cold much more deeply.[74]

8

# Silaup Aulaninga: Climate Change

In the North, climate change is not something that may happen
in the future; it's something that is happening now … There is a
connection between climate change and human rights. It's not just
about polar bears; it is about people and a way of life.
Siila Watt-Cloutier[1]

## Arctic Choices

If the future of Nunavummiut (and the rest of us) must depend on resource
development, climate change needs to be taken into account. Without the
melting of annual ice and the thinning of pack ice during the summer
months, resources such as petroleum, minerals, and precious metals would
remain locked in the ground or under the sea. The irony is not lost on citizens of the North. The more energy that is expended extracting minerals,
oil and gas, and other material from under the tundra or the ocean floor,
the greater the contribution to the greenhouse gases that are fuelling global
warming. In particular, as oil is extracted and shipped to markets elsewhere,
Canada is simply exporting its climate change footprint offshore (as it is
currently doing with the tar sands of Alberta). The biggest market at the
moment is China, followed by Europe, the United States, India, and Brazil.
Rapid economic development in Asia and sustained industrial activity in the
"developed" world underlie much of the human-made global warming that
is currently changing our weather, atmosphere, and oceans. One thing is
clear: as global temperatures rise, Arctic temperatures rise faster. We may

well have pushed polar ecosystems into a "positive feedback loop" that could be unstoppable.

The people of Nunavut need education, training, jobs, and resources in order to lift themselves out of poverty. The only route forward appears to be through resource development. But mines and oil wells are a double-edged sword. They may provide employment and royalties in the short term, but what about the long term? The operational life of a mine such as the Mary River Project is usually only about twenty years. Oil extraction can be measured in a few decades. Once the resources are gone, what will young Inuit do? Will they still be able to hunt? Will there still be elders who can teach them about the land? Will women's skills still be respected? And what will the land and sea look like? Will there be any summer ice left? Will seals and polar bears still be around? These are all questions that Inuit ask themselves as they face a Hobson's choice that will have generational impacts.

In November 2004 the Arctic Council (a group of representatives of eight circumpolar nations, including Canada, and various Indigenous groups) and the International Arctic Science Committee released their exhaustive analysis of all existing data on climate change in the North up to that date – the Arctic Climate Impact Assessment's report on *Impacts of a Warming Arctic.*[2] They took over four years to compile the scientific evidence and traditional knowledge related to climate change in the Arctic. The report presents their findings in a format that allows for the scientific evidence and the knowledge of Arctic Indigenous peoples to be readily accessible to policymakers and the public. Ten years ago this is what they found:

> Ice cores and other evidence of climate conditions in the distant past provide evidence that rising atmospheric carbon dioxide levels are associated with rising global temperatures. Human activities, primarily the burning of fossil fuels (coal, oil, and natural gas), and secondarily the clearing of land, have increased the concentration of carbon dioxide, methane, and other heat-trapping ("greenhouse") gases in the atmosphere. Since the start of the industrial revolution, the atmospheric carbon dioxide concentration has increased by about 35% and the global average temperature has risen by about 0.6 °C. There is an international scientific consensus that most of the warming observed over the last fifty years is attributable to human activities.

Continuing to add carbon dioxide and other greenhouse gases to the atmosphere is projected to lead to significant and persistent changes in climate, including an increase in average global temperatures of 1.4 to 5.8 °C ... over the course of this century. Climatic changes are projected to include shifts in atmospheric and oceanic circulation patterns, an accelerating rate of sea-level rise, and wider variations in precipitation. Together, these changes are projected to lead to wide-ranging consequences including significant impacts on coastal communities, animal and plant species, water resources, and human health and well-being.

About 80% of the world's energy is currently derived from burning fossil fuels, and carbon dioxide emissions from these sources are growing rapidly. Because excess carbon dioxide persists in the atmosphere for centuries, it will take at least a few decades for concentrations to peak and then begin to decline even if concerted efforts to reduce emissions are begun immediately. Altering the warming trend will thus be a long-term process and the world will face some degree of climate change and its impacts for centuries.[3]

The report does not discuss either how to mitigate such impacts or what adaptations to them will be necessary. It focuses on the scientific and Indigenous knowledge about climate change in the Arctic region. The report identifies ten key findings related to the disproportionate effect of climate change on the Arctic, paraphrased as follows:

1  Arctic climate is now warming rapidly, and much larger changes are projected. The report predicts that climate change could result in Arctic warming of up to 7° Celsius by the end of the century.
2  Arctic warming and its consequences have worldwide implications, including rising sea levels, increased uptake of greenhouse gases from open tundra, and global effects on biodiversity.
3  Arctic vegetation zones are very likely to shift, causing wide-ranging impacts. The treeline will move northward, bringing with it increased risk of invasive species, forest fires, and agricultural development.
4  Animal species' diversity ranges and distribution will change. Seal and polar bear habitats may be severely affected. Caribou and other land

animals may find their grazing and migration grounds severely stressed. Invasive parasites and the diseases they carry will move north.

5 Many coastal communities and facilities face increasing exposure to storms. Rising seas and more extreme weather events will lead to coastal flooding and erosion. Melting tundra will also weaken coastlines. Communities are already threatened and will have to be relocated.

6 Reduced sea ice is likely to increase marine transport and access to resources.

7 Thawing ground will disrupt transportation, buildings, and other infrastructure.

8 Indigenous communities are facing major economic and cultural impacts.

9 Elevated ultraviolet radiation levels will affect people, plants, and animals. The hole in the ozone layer has not disappeared but in fact seems to be increasing on a seasonal basis. The increases in ultraviolet radiation can lead to skin cancers, cataracts, and other health effects.

10 Multiple influences interact to cause impacts on people and ecosystems.[4]

The last finding is particularly important. Multiple climate change effects will not only interact but will also do so in a way that may amplify their impact on all the other factors. "Positive feedback loops" are part of this process. As the atmosphere and ocean warms, the release of greenhouse gases will increase, further accelerating the warming trend. As dark blue oceans and brown landscapes absorb more of the sun's rays as heat, less energy is bounced harmlessly out of the atmosphere. The albedo, or reflective, effect of white ice and snow decreases, and more heat is trapped in the lower atmosphere. Methane (natural gas) that has been trapped in the tundra or on the Arctic seabed for hundreds of millions of years is already beginning to seep into the air and ocean. It has ten to twenty times the greenhouse effect of carbon dioxide. It is actually quite simple – the more heat, the more melting; the more melting, the more heat. As all these different multipliers interact, there is the possibility of a runaway warming effect that will impact the entire planet. Inuit have faced major changes in the past, but this will likely prove the most challenging of all.

## What Is Climate Change?

Although the argument about human-made global warming seems to have been settled, there are still voices out there with an interest in causing confusion and skepticism among many people who don't really know what all this is about. In addition we have been told so many times that the sky is falling that, like Chicken Little's audience, we have become dismissive and tired of the "debate" such as it is. After repeated droughts, hot summers, floods, and unusually fierce storms like "Superstorm Sandy," which devastated parts of the northeastern United States in 2012, denying that climate change is really happening is no longer tenable. Most people now seem to accept that it is largely human-made. But it might still be important to pause and ask what the science and history of climate change actually tell us.

Climate change is not about the weather that occurs on a day-to-day basis, although obviously weather is influenced by changes in climate. Rather it is about changing patterns in air temperature, air pressure, sea temperature, sea levels, and seasonal variations measured over long periods of time (from decades to millennia). Much of our knowledge of how climate change works and how it will affect global ecosystems is based on *palaeoclimatology* – the study of ancient climates. Recent years have seen the development of an amazingly precise body of knowledge about previous changes to global climate that is useful in helping us to forecast future probabilities.

Climate change is also not about pollution, at least not directly. Pollutants in the atmosphere come from a variety of sources in the form of particulate matter released as smoke, ash, dust, soot, and exhaust fumes. These particles are sometimes referred to as *aerosols*. This is obviously a problem and does affect climate. However, the primary culprit in climate change is the release of invisible greenhouse gases – particularly carbon dioxide, methane (natural gas), nitrous oxide, and water vapour – which change atmospheric chemistry at a molecular level. These gases increase the capacity of Earth's atmosphere to convert solar energy (light) into heat, similar to the effect that glass or clear plastic has on the air in a greenhouse or in a car left in the hot sun. Another way of looking at it is that these gases, like glass or clear plastic, block short-wavelength energy like ultraviolet or visible light from escaping through the atmosphere back out into space. Instead they bounce back to Earth's surface as long-wavelength energy (heat).

The pattern that is clearly emerging is an overall global rise in average annual temperatures over the past 150 years of about 0.65 to 1.6° Celsius based on a correlation and charting of temperatures measured in the United Kingdom by the Met Office (in collaboration with the Climatic Research Unit at the University of East Anglia) and in the United States by the Goddard Institute for Space Studies, which is part of the National Aeronautics and Space Administration (NASA), and by the National Climatic Data Center, which is part of the National Oceanic and Atmospheric Administration (NOAA).[5]

NOAA also reported in 2013 that "[i]n the last 2 years, the United States experienced 25 climate and weather-related disasters exceeding $1 billion ($115 billion total) in damages and claiming 1,019 lives. The public, businesses, resource managers, and policy leaders are increasingly asking for information to help them understand how and why climate conditions are changing and how they can prepare."[6] James Hansen and other scientists at the Goddard Institute for Space Studies have been predicting serious changes to climate since the 1980s.[7] Despite cold snowy winters in northern Europe and northeastern North America in recent years, which have fuelled doubts about climate change in the media, the world as a whole is getting hotter. This appears to be associated with rising sea levels, greater weather variability and severity, longer summers and shorter winters, devastating variations in patterns of rainfall, glacier melt, and changes in both biological and human habitats. These alterations are occurring globally with regional and local differences. Nowhere is this more visible than in the Arctic, where average temperatures have increased by between 2 and 4° Celsius since 1900. Again according to NOAA,

The average Arctic sea ice extent during August [2011] was 28 percent below average, ranking as the second smallest August extent since satellite records began in 1979. The extent was 830,000 square miles (2.15 million square kilometers) below average and 61,800 square miles (160,000 square kilometers) above the record low August extent set in 2007 ...

... According to model analysis by the University of Washington's Polar Science Center, Arctic sea ice volume, which depends on both ice thickness and extent, reached a record low of 1,026 cubic miles (4,275 cubic kilometers) on August 31, 2011, breaking the previous lowest volume set on September 15, 2010. The average August 2011 volume was 1,200 cubic miles (5,000 cubic kilometers). This value is 62 percent lower than the 1979–2010 average and 72 percent lower than the maximum in 1979.[8]

The record was broken again in 2012, when ice melting exceeded the previous levels recorded in 2007:

The *Arctic Report Card* ... considers a wide range of environmental observations throughout the Arctic, and is updated annually. A major finding of the Report Card 2012 is that numerous record-setting melting events occurred, even though, Arctic-wide, it was an unremarkable year, relative to the previous decade, for a primary driver of melting – surface air temperatures. The exception was Greenland where record-breaking air temperatures and near-ice sheet-wide surface melting occurred in summer 2012. From October 2011 through August 2012, positive (warm) temperature anomalies were relatively small over the central Arctic compared to conditions in recent years (2003–2010). Yet, in spite of these moderate conditions, new records were set for sea ice extent, terrestrial snow extent and permafrost temperature.

Large changes in multiple indicators are affecting climate and ecosystems, and, combined, these changes provide strong evidence of the momentum that has developed in the Arctic environmental system due to the impacts of a persistent warming trend that began over 30 years ago. A major source of this momentum is the fact that changes in the sea ice cover, snow cover, glaciers and Greenland ice sheet all conspire to reduce the overall surface reflectivity of the region in the summer, when the sun is ever-present. In other words, bright, white surfaces that reflect summer sunlight are being replaced by darker surfaces, e.g., ocean and land, which absorb sunlight. These conditions increase the capacity to store heat within the Arctic system, which enables more melting – a positive feedback. Thus, we arrive at the conclusion that it is very likely that major changes will continue to occur in the Arctic in years to come, particularly in the face of projections that indicate continued global warming.

A second key point in Report Card 2012 is that changes in the Arctic marine environment are affecting the foundation of the food web in both the terrestrial and marine ecosystems. While more difficult to dis-

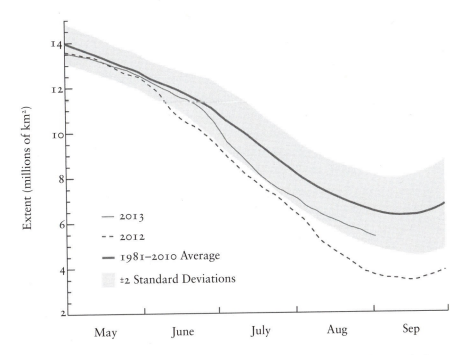

8.1 Arctic sea ice summer extent as of 2 September 2013, along with the daily extent for summer 2012

cern, there are also observations that confirm the inevitable impacts these changes have on a wide range of higher-trophic Arctic and migratory species.[9]

The record-breaking high temperatures and pervasive drought in the North American summer of 2012 seem to have convinced a majority of Americans and Canadians that climate change is indeed a reality.

*How do we know the Earth's climate is warming?*
Thousands of land and ocean temperature measurements are recorded each day around the globe. This includes measurements from climate reference stations, weather stations, ships, buoys and autonomous gliders in the oceans. These surface measurements are also supplemented with satellite measurements. These measurements are processed, examined for random and systematic errors, and then finally combined to

produce a time series of global average temperature change. A number of agencies around the world have produced datasets of global-scale changes in surface temperature using different techniques to process the data and remove measurement errors that could lead to false interpretations of temperature trends. The warming trend that is apparent in all of the independent methods of calculating global temperature change is also confirmed by other independent observations, such as the melting of mountain glaciers on every continent, reductions in the extent of snow cover, earlier blooming of plants in spring, a shorter ice season on lakes and rivers, ocean heat content, reduced arctic sea ice, and rising sea levels.

*How do we know humans are the primary cause of the warming?*
A large body of evidence supports the conclusion that human activity is the primary driver of recent warming. This evidence has accumulated over several decades, and from hundreds of studies. The first line of evidence is our basic physical understanding of how greenhouse gases trap heat, how the climate system responds to increases in greenhouse gases, and how other human and natural factors influence climate. The second line of evidence is from indirect estimates of climate changes over the last 1,000 to 2,000 years. These estimates are often obtained from living things and their remains (like tree rings and corals) which provide a natural archive of climate variations. These indicators show that the recent temperature rise is clearly unusual in at least the last 1,000 years. The third line of evidence is based on comparisons of actual climate with computer models of how we expect climate to behave under certain human influences. For example, when climate models are run with historical increases in greenhouse gases, they show gradual warming of the Earth and ocean surface, increases in ocean heat content, a rise in global sea levels, and general retreat of sea ice and snow cover. These and other aspects of modeled climate change are in agreement with observations.[10]

On 27 September 2013 the United Nations Intergovernmental Panel on Climate Change (IPCC) released its *Fifth Assessment Report*, which provides the latest in climate change analysis and synthesis. This report unleashed a barrage of climate skepticism similar to the reaction to earlier assessments and climate change conferences. For example, Canada's *Global News* released its own analysis ahead of the report and pointed out the following as criticisms:

1 The Earth has not warmed at all in the past 15–20 years.
2 Global climate models are severely flawed and have not predicted the pause in warming over the past 15–20 years.
3 Several of the same scientists that are claiming the planet will be free of ice by the summer of 2020, claimed we would be ice-free right now as recently as 2007.
4 The Arctic ice sheet is healthier than it's been in the past five years and is over 50 per cent above last year's ice total.
5 The Antarctic ice sheet has actually grown over the past 33 years and is now near an all-time record high.
6 The sun is in its quietest cycle since the early 1900s and there are increasing signs we are entering a prolonged quiet period similar to the Maunder Minimum that froze Europe and was the coldest period of the past millennium.
7 The Pacific Ocean has recently entered its cool cycle which will last for at least the next couple decades. The Atlantic will follow in a few years time. The last time the two oceans were cool was in the 70s where fears of a "mini ice age" made the cover of *Time* magazine among other major publications.
8 Floods, hurricanes, tornadoes, winter storms, droughts and other extremes are part of nature. Ballooning populations in major disaster zones are much more likely the cause for the billion-dollar disasters of the past couple decades.
9 Tornado numbers are at a record low this year and the hurricane season is practically non-existent with the ACE [Accumulated Cyclone Energy] value as low as we've seen since the late 70s.[11]

Since this analysis conveniently lists most of the climate skeptics' arguments, it is worth going through it if only to point out some obvious facts *Global News*'s chief meteorologist and other climate skeptics have overlooked:

1 Although atmospheric and surface warming has slowed over the past fifteen years, it has not stopped. Earth's temperature did indeed increase

over this period by about 0.05° Celsius. This slower increase is at least partly due to natural variability, which always has to be taken into account. The IPCC found that the overall global atmospheric temperature rise between 1880 and 2012 was between 0.65 and 1.06° Celsius. This increase may not seem like much to ordinary folks (or meteorologists, who are not generally experts in anything beyond daily weather forecasting), but it is in fact significant.[12]

2  Climate change models are not perfect, as the IPCC itself points out in its *Fifth Assessment Report* on the scientific basis for climate change: "There is *very high confidence* [virtual certainty] that models reproduce the general features of the global-scale annual mean surface temperature increase over the historical period, including the more rapid warming in the second half of the 20th century, and the cooling immediately following large volcanic eruptions. Most simulations of the historical period do not reproduce the observed reduction in global-mean surface warming trend over the last 10–15 years. There is *medium confidence* that the trend difference between models and observations during 1998–2012 is to a substantial degree caused by internal variability, with possible contributions from forcing error and some models overestimating the response to increasing greenhouse-gas forcing. Most, though not all, models overestimate the observed warming trend in the tropical troposphere over the last 30 years, and tend to underestimate the long-term lower stratospheric cooling trend."[13] In other words, some models may have overestimated the atmosphere's response to global warming as a result of the release of greenhouse gases. However, the models are improving all the time (as the IPCC describes in great detail), and it is clear that "[w]arming of the climate system is unequivocal, and since the 1950s, many of the observed changes are unprecedented over decades to millennia. The atmosphere and ocean have warmed, the amounts of snow and ice have diminished, sea level has risen, and the concentrations of greenhouse gases have increased ... Each of the last three decades has been successively warmer at the Earth's surface than any preceding decade since 1850 ... In the Northern Hemisphere, 1983–2012 was *likely* [better than 50 per cent] the warmest 30-year period of the last 1400 years."[14]

3  No reputable climate scientist seriously suggested that the Arctic would be ice-free by 2007. That year saw a significant reduction in summer ice. This loss of ice was even more extensive in 2012. Most climate scientists

have been overly conservative in predicting an ice-free summer by the end of this century. It is now possible that this may occur much sooner.

4 Although ice melting was less in 2013 than in previous years, since 2007 the ice extent has still been significantly less than it was in 1979, when satellite observations were first recorded. Ironically, as I was about to begin the final revision of this chapter, pictures taken by the North Pole Environmental Observatory's webcam showing a large pool of water sitting on top of the North Pole were beamed all around the world through satellite, the Internet, and social media. The date was 22 July 2013.[15] In May 2013 the White House and US government officials were being warned that the Arctic may have an ice-free summer by 2015. Although the summer ice extent in 2013 has been closer to normal, the trend is still downward both in the extent of ice over the Arctic Ocean and in the depth of the ice below the surface. We know that when American national security agencies become concerned, we're talking about something big. An article in the *Guardian* describes how "the IARPC [Interagency Arctic Research Policy Committee], charged with coordinating federal research on the Arctic Ocean, is chaired by the National Science Foundation, and includes among its members NASA, the US Department of Homeland Security and the Pentagon ... [In the Pentagon's own analysis of climate change, the military worries that a warming climate and melting Arctic ice may] act as accelerants of instability or conflict in parts of the world ... [and] may also lead to increased demands for defense support to civil authorities for humanitarian assistance or disaster response, both within the United States and overseas ... DoD [the US Department of Defense] will need to adjust to the impacts of climate change on its facilities, infrastructure, training and testing activities, and military capabilities."[16]

5 The Antarctic ice sheet is not growing, as *Global News*'s chief meteorologist reports; it is rapidly shrinking due to a warming ocean, as reported by NASA in September 2013.[17]

6 The sun is actually now in one of the most active phases of its eleven-year cycle. Whether active or not, solar radiation has been remarkably stable for billions of years. It does not appear to be having much impact on contemporary climate change.

7 The Pacific and Atlantic Oceans do not have "warm" or "cool" periods, other than regional effects such as El Niño and La Niña. All observers

agree that ocean temperatures are rising, not falling, and that this is having a measurable impact on sea levels and extreme weather events.

8 Extreme weather events such as hurricanes and tornados are notoriously difficult to predict, and the news media are often too quick to jump to the conclusion that a particular storm is due to climate change. Nevertheless, increased heat energy in Earth's system will (as a matter of basic physics and chemistry) necessarily lead to greater climate variability and instability. This outcome in turn will lead to more frequent and more severe weather events.

9 Both individual storms and an absence of storms from one season to the next may not be traceable directly to climate change. But extreme weather events are increasing, and this trend appears to be related to a warming atmosphere and oceans.

Regardless of what we might think about climate change,

uncertainty doesn't justify inaction. Among other things, uncertainly means that outcomes could turn out worse than predicted, not just better. Also, modern societies rely all the time on a balance of scientific evidence – in the face of uncertainty – to make important decisions. They began regulating tobacco even when scientists were still very uncertain about the exact link between smoking and cancer ... People who argue for inaction on climate change are betting that the vast majority of climate scientists are wrong. The balance of evidence is decisively against them.[18]

One aspect of climate change that is something of a mystery, and has been leapt upon by climate skeptics, is why Earth's lower atmospheric temperatures are not actually rising more rapidly. There are two possible reasons. The global average temperature between 2000 and 2009 was nearly flat. At the same time, "the observed energy imbalance at the top-of-atmosphere during this time indicates that warming should be occurring somewhere in the Earth's system."[19] Heat is simply a form of energy. Regardless of whether energy accumulating in the system is stored in the oceans or in the atmosphere, climate will be affected. Heat stored in the oceans can cause water to expand, leading to oceans rising. Or it can cause more frequent and severe storms, surging tides, and major weather events such as hurricanes. Or it can cause ice to melt, which is happening in the Arctic and the Antarctic despite little difference in surface air temperatures everywhere, except over inland Greenland, which is rapidly warming every summer. In Greenland warmer temperatures are causing a major melting of the glaciated plateau that covers most of its land mass. Arctic sea ice melting does not itself raise sea levels (ice and water are simply different forms of the same stuff), but the large-scale melting of inland glaciers does contribute to rising sea levels as fresh water stored on land for thousands or even millions of years cascades into the ocean.

One reason that air temperatures have been stable in recent years is that the world's oceans down to very deep levels are storing heat much more substantially than originally thought.[20] The IPCC's *Fifth Assessment Report* makes the same observation: "Ocean warming dominates the increase in energy stored in the climate system, accounting for more than 90% of the energy accumulated between 1971 and 2010 (*high confidence*). It is *virtually certain* that the upper ocean (0–700 m) warmed from 1971 to 2010 and it *likely* warmed between the 1870s and 1971."[21]

Another reason for the smaller rise in air temperatures might be that pollution in the form of dust, ash, and other particles from both natural and industrial sources is spreading through the lower atmosphere, creating a layer of smog that blocks the sun's rays. This may be counteracting the heating trend. Although pollution levels in Europe and North America have fallen, the amount of polluting aerosols has risen substantially in China, India, Russia, and other developing nations over the past ten to twenty years – to the point where smog over Beijing contributes to smog over Los Angeles! Even though greenhouse gases are also rising, layers of pollution act as a shield, reducing the amount of solar energy that reaches the lower atmosphere. Climate change is also increasing the amount of water vapour in the atmosphere through evaporation and condensation. An increase in aerosols provides more nuclei around which water vapour can cling, creating water droplets. This leads to more cloud cover, which can also act as a shield. Regardless of whether climate change is detectable in the lower atmosphere for periods of time (called "hiatuses"), it is occurring. Even *The Australian*, a well-known supporter of climate skepticism, does not try to claim that a pause in atmospheric global warming means that climate change is not happening; rather it quotes James Hansen in support of the theory that increased coal burning in China is causing sufficient pollution to block the sun's rays.[22]

The past twenty years have been the hottest on record, and the upward trend is continuing. The amount of carbon dioxide in the atmosphere measured at the Mauna Loa Observatory in Hawaii (far from any sources of pollution) approached or exceeded 400 parts per million during 2012 and 2013 for the first time since the beginning of the last ice age 2.5 million years ago. This level was reached in the Arctic some time ago, again showing that climate change indicators are more concentrated in the polar regions. These changes are also detectable in Antarctica, but the huge continental land mass buried under old, thick ice is slowing the changes in the southern hemisphere, although a large amount of melting of shelf ice around the continent is also happening. Earth (as far as can be measured) has never before seen such a rapid build-up of carbon dioxide in its atmosphere in the 4.5 billion years of its history. During the Pleistocene Era, beginning 2.5 million years ago, carbon levels were as high as they are today (for reasons not fully understood). Global temperatures 2.5 million years ago rose as much as 10° Celsius over thousands of years.[23] We are unlikely to see so dramatic a change in the near future. The trouble is that we are in uncharted waters and cannot accurately predict what is going to happen.

A few climate change skeptics continue to argue that whatever global warming is occurring is the result of natural cycles, not human intervention. From this point of view, there is nothing much we can do – so it remains "business as usual." Many scientists are disturbed by the politicization of the science surrounding this issue, as evidenced by the "Climategate" release of hacked e-mails from the University of East Anglia in late 2009 immediately before the Copenhagen Climate Change Conference (and again right before the Durban Conference in 2011). Concerns about the veracity and integrity of the science collected by the IPCC would also appear to be part of an orchestrated campaign to discredit climate science. The intensity of the debate means that reaching consensus and making decisions become that much more difficult, although incontrovertible evidence of climate change and the problems it is causing continues to mount. Skepticism is an essential ingredient in good science – but throwing reasonable scientific evidence into a quagmire of politically and economically motivated controversy is not. Even if climate change is occurring naturally, this does not preclude political,

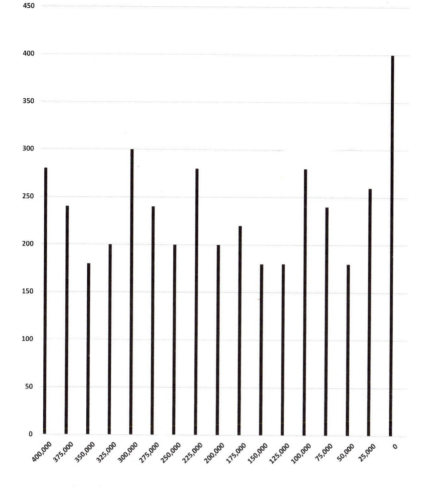

8.2 Carbon dioxide levels, 400,000 years ago to the present. Columns show CO² levels in parts per million (p/m). Over the past 400,000 years, CO² levels had not risen above 300 p/m until very recently. As of July 2013 they had reached 400 p/m and are still rising.

economic, and social measures to protect our environment and those vulnerable to its variability.

I too used to be a climate change skeptic until I went to the Arctic and saw firsthand the effects of melting ice and warming temperatures. I listened to what both scientific experts and Inuit elders were saying. There is no doubt now in my mind that the rise in global temperatures in both the atmosphere and oceans is occurring at a much more rapid rate than was predicted even ten years ago and that most of this warming is directly related to human use of fossil fuels (coal, oil, and gas) as well as to other chemical changes to Earth's atmosphere caused by human activity. Indeed, it now appears that the predictions of both the IPCC in 2007 and Arctic Climate Impact Assessment in 2004 were much too conservative. It seems to me to make little difference how much climate change is human-made or how much is natural. Human beings are part of the natural environment – to separate ourselves from nature is a mistake, and the dichotomy between human and nature is an illusion. Our industrial, urbanized world and its massively growing human population are not sustainable. The choices are now political, economic, social, and cultural. Do we try to preserve our world as a healthy, beautiful place for our children, grandchildren, and all other life on this planet? Or do we continue to pillage what is left for the short-term gain of a small minority.

## Twelve Thousand Years of Climate Change

Over the past 1,000 years, there has been a change in the global temperature of about 2° Celsius. From about AD 850 to 1350, Earth got warmer. Then, for reasons still not clearly understood, temperatures dropped. We have already seen how this decrease affected migration into the Arctic by Vikings and Inuit. Climate skeptics point to these fluctuations as evidence that climate change does not depend on human activities. What caused the Medieval Warm Period and the Little Ice Age that followed? After all, as Brian Fagan says in his popular book *The Great Warming: Climate Change and the Rise and Fall of Civilizations*, "'we've been through this before.'"[24]

One extremely interesting hypothesis has been proposed by William F. Ruddiman in his book *Plows, Plagues, and Petroleum*. He suggests that humans have been contributing to global warming not for just one or two centuries but for at least 8,000 years through the gradual expansion of agriculture, particularly rice cultivation in China and Southeast Asia. As a result the 12,000-year-old Holocene (our current period) has actually been longer and warmer than it otherwise would have been. According to Ruddiman, we might have already entered into a new glacial period if humans had not begun influencing climate from about 8,000 years ago. In graphs of temperatures over thousands of years, the Holocene actually appears to be remarkably stable. There are some rises and falls in overall temperature, but there has been nothing all that dramatic since the sudden cooling that occurred just as Earth was warming up again after the last glacial period ended 12,500 years ago. This drop in temperatures of as much as 7° Celsius is called the Younger Dryas period (named after a small flower that grows in tundra), and it ended about 11,500 years ago – a severe "cold snap" that lasted for 1,000 years. It appears to have been caused by a giant cold lake of continental glacial melt water that flooded into the North Atlantic, shutting down the warm conveyor belt known as the Gulf Stream. However, through data collected from ice-core samples, Ruddiman demonstrates that the stability in global temperatures since the Younger Dryas ended has mostly been the result of increased levels of both carbon dioxide and methane caused by human activity. This has protected Earth from a steep drop in temperatures that should have created the conditions for another glacial period thousands of years ago. The good news is that we seem to have unwittingly prevented another Ice Age!

Ruddiman also suggests that drops in global temperatures in the past 1,000 years seem to correspond to large-scale epidemics and famines, which led to significant decreases in human populations and, by extension, in human activity. Increased temperatures seem to accompany rebounds in population because of agricultural and industrial expansion. He suggests that the spread of the Black Plague through Eurasia during the fourteenth century may have actually precipitated the Little Ice Age. As a result of a drop in populations of 30 per cent or more in Europe, China, and South and Southeast Asia, farmers' fields were left fallow. As forests rebounded, replacing the abandoned farms, more carbon dioxide was absorbed by the expansion of leafy carbon "sinks." Temperatures dropped along with the drop in carbon dioxide. The coldest period of the Little Ice Age began about 250 years later, soon after the huge collapse of populations in the "New World." This massive depopulation of North, Central, and South America from 1500 to 1750 (and beyond in some places) was due primarily to the introduction of European diseases to Indigenous peoples:

> [U]p to 90 percent of the native populations died. Entire villages that once lined the valleys of the lower Mississippi River system were abandoned, along with endless cornfields in between ... Many decades later, so little evidence remained of the former occupation of North America that scientists and historians in the 1800s and early 1900s assumed that populations had been relatively small ... Today, the best estimate

is that some 50 million people died just from having come into contact with Europeans. This was the greatest pandemic in all of pre-industrial history, and, in proportion to the size of the global population, the worst pandemic of all time. Out of roughly 500 million humans then alive on Earth, 50 million (10%) died in the Americas.[25]

Ruddiman's hypothesis has not yet been supported by other scientific research, but it does raise intriguing questions. Have humans had an impact on Earth's climate for much longer than is currently supposed? Could massive increases and drops in human population have such a dramatic effect on climate? Or do periods of global warming and cooling have more to do with natural cycles? It is obviously extremely important to ask and investigate these questions, as we are seeing another period of warming that began about 150 years ago with the expansion of industrialization and commercial agriculture in Europe and elsewhere. This latest period of warming has not been continuous. As in earlier periods of climate change, there has been significant variation from one year to the next. But the overall trend is for warmer average land and sea temperatures of about 1° Celsius globally since 1850.

## Population

During this time, there has been an unprecedented growth in human population and resource utilization, which has radically increased the human impact on global systems. In 1800, after the pandemics and famines of the Little Ice Age, human populations had rebounded to a total of about 1 billion. In late 2011 Earth's human population reached 7 billion – a massive increase in just 200 years. It is possible that there are more people alive right now than there were in all the tens of thousands of years before 1800. The biggest jump has been since 1950, from about 2 billion to more than three times that number. This massive increase in human occupation of the planet, and the technological reasons for it, have not been emphasized enough in the climate change literature. Those who doubt the existence of human-caused, or anthropogenic, warming need to look at these population statistics, as well as the industrial and agricultural infrastructures that support such numbers. The seven-fold rise in human numbers over the past 200 years is unprecedented in all of human history.

It is becoming increasingly clear that the energy infrastructure that supports such a large number of humans is not sustainable. Petroleum in particular is a finite resource that may have already "peaked." Exhaustion of easily accessible supplies of carbon-based energy results in price rises and exploitation of more and more difficult sources – such as the Alberta tar sands or "fracking" natural gas from deposits of shale – or it means a return to coal or other power sources that are even more environmentally damaging. In addition all fossil fuels release greenhouse gases into the atmosphere and will do so no matter how "clean" they are. Increases in greenhouse gases cause global temperatures eventually to rise. The conclusion seems to me to be inescapable. In 2007 the IPCC stated in its *Fifth Assessment Report* that anthropogenic warming is the most likely cause of the global warming we are currently experiencing. This international body of global climate experts puts the percentage of likelihood at 95 per cent. The world's climate scientists are, with very few exceptions, convinced that global warming is now being caused largely by humans.[26] Although it is true that good science is not done by consensus, but rather through ongoing debate and the challenging of ideas, the currently prevalent view of most of the world's experts on the importance of anthropogenic contributions to climate change must be taken to be significant. Mike Hulme, one of the professors at East Anglia University whose e-mails were hacked and publicly distributed right before the Copenhagen Conference in November 2009, has written a fascinating account of *Why We Disagree about Climate Change*. The scientists can tell us only what they think is happening. It is up to us to decide what to do.

The key is the ice. The ice itself is telling the story of global warming, both through the extent of the melting that we are now experiencing and through the layers in long thin ice cores taken by scientists from the glaciers of Greenland and Antarctica. By examining the annual layers in these cores, it is possible to measure greenhouse gases, air-borne pollutants, and temperatures over hundreds of thousands of years. These ice cores, like similar cores taken from the deep seabed, act like tree rings, giving amazingly precise information about the chemistry, pollution, and temperature of the atmosphere year by year for up to half a million years in Greenland and nearly a million years in Antarctica. The information about past climates is not speculation – it is based on close observation of ancient atmospheric chemistry preserved in the ice itself. This detailed record goes back well before *Homo sapiens* had evolved in Africa or populated the globe. As James Hansen of NASA's Goddard Institute for Space Studies has repeatedly warned,

> Business-as-usual greenhouse gas emissions, without any doubt, will commit the planet to global warming of a magnitude that will lead eventually to an ice-free planet. An ice-free planet means a sea level rise of about 75 meters (almost 250 feet).
>
> Ice sheet disintegration will not occur overnight. But concepts about the response time of ice sheets that paleoclimate scientists have developed based on Earth's history are misleading. Those ice sheet changes were in response to forcings that changed slowly, over millennia. Ice sheet responses in the past often occurred in fairly rapid pulses, but disintegration of an entire continental-scale ice sheet required more than a thousand years.
>
> Humans are beginning to hammer the climate system with a forcing more than an order of magnitude [ten times] more powerful than the forcings that nature employed. It will not require millennia for the ice sheets to respond to the human forcing.[27]

## Inuit Knowledge of Climate Change

Inuit elders and hunters have noticed significant changes in their environment over the past two decades or more. For them the weather has become *uggianaqtuq* – "mixed up," "to behave in an unpredictable or unexpected way." According to Cornelius Nutaraq of Pond Inlet,

> I feel the weather is different now from back then ... The wind seems to blow more frequently and the duration of calm water seems to be shorter. Because I'm more aware, the direction of the wind seems to shift more frequently also. Maybe this is not so, but that is how I perceive it. I have also heard this from other people, older than I am. They too, have commented that the wind seems to blow more frequently ... As I see it now, I think that changes in the weather are more rapid. Sometimes the wind will even come before you see the clouds.

8.3 High winds and heavy seas prevent our ship from getting into Pond Inlet

… There is less snow now … When I was a child, there would be much more snow … to build *igluit* [houses] down at Sannirut, at the point closest to Mittimatalik [Pond Inlet]. There was enough snow for a slope to form from the top of the hills on downwards. There would be snow all the way up. You could go all the way to the top by dogteam. You could also go upwards from the point. You could build *igluit* anywhere it sloped downwards. There is not that much snow any more. We use snowmobiles now. I tried to ride a snow machine to the top the same way I used to go with my dogs, but I failed, as there was not enough snow to get to the top of the hill. There isn't enough snow that forms there to build *igluit*. The area around Mittimatalik also does not have as much snow now … Even though lots of snow falls; perhaps it hardens faster now. There is not a thick layer of snow anymore.[28]

Nutaraq, like most elders, was modest about his knowledge, never claiming to know more than what he himself had seen or heard. Other elders say similar things. In the Arctic Climate Impact Assessment's report on *Impacts of a Warming Arctic*, Indigenous peoples from around the Arctic region were asked about changes to the climate. Indigenous peoples ranging from those of the Aleutian and Pribilof Islands in Alaska to the Saami of northern Finland described how the climate has changed.

One of the more extensive studies that has been done in Nunavut was carried out between 1995 and 2004 by Shari Fox, who conducted interviews with elders from four communities: Iqaluit, Iglulik, Baker Lake, and Clyde River.[29] One of the most frequently observed occurrences has been an increase in weather variability similar to Nutaraq's observations about the wind:

> The weather has changed. For instance, elders will predict that it might be windy, but then it doesn't become windy. And then it often seems like it's going to be very calm and then it suddenly becomes windy. So their predictions are never correct anymore, the predictions according to what they see haven't been true. (P. Kunuliusie, Clyde River, 2000)

> The weather when I was young and vulnerable to the weather, according to my parents, was more predictable, in that we were able to tell where the wind was going to be that day by looking at the cloud formations ... Contrary to our beliefs and ability to predict [by] looking at the sky, especially the cloud formations, looking at the stars, everything seems to be contrary to our training from the hunting days with our fathers. The winds could pick up pretty fast now. Very unpredictable. [The winds] could change directions, from south [to] southeast in no time. Whereas before, before 1960s when I was growing up to be a hunter, we were able to predict. (L. Nutaraaluk, Iqaluit, 2000)

> When I lived out on the land I would always know when the weather would be bad from the clouds but nowadays when you look at the clouds and they say there is going to be bad weather that evening it doesn't always happen. You could wake up and it would be nice and through the whole evening it would still be nice. The indicators that

we would use before don't always happen. (J. Nukik, Baker Lake, 2001)[30]

The results of this variability are disturbing. Because the weather is no longer as predictable as it was in the past, conditions can quickly become treacherous. Ice melts earlier and freezes up later, so where the ice used to be thick enough to hunt and travel on in the spring and fall, it is now dangerous. Every year hunters die because of thin ice. Shifting winds and changing patterns in the snow can also create dangerous conditions for travellers on land:

> There used to be different layers of snow back then. The wind would not blow as hard, not make the snow as hard as it is now ... But nowadays, the snow gets really hard and it's really hard to tell [the layers] and it's really hard to make shelters with that kind of snow because it's usually way too hard right to the ground. (T. Qaqimat, Baker Lake, 2001)[31]

Hunters and travellers need to take more equipment to ensure they have shelter, food, and water in case of difficulties. Satellite phones have become essential equipment, as being able to make contact with search and rescue may mean the difference between life and death. Because elders can no longer predict the weather based on clouds, wind direction, sky, the northern lights, and even stars, their knowledge is no longer as relevant and is not always treated with the same respect. This has an impact on the cultural role of elders. It also creates a sense of loss and psychological distress to the individuals affected. Another problem, particularly around Baker Lake (the only inland community in Nunavut), is the impact that the drying-up of lakes and streams and lower water levels has had on fishing and other wildlife:

> The lakes and the rivers are getting less water and a lot of them are getting more shallow and some places don't have any water left. They're not as healthy anymore. Things are not as healthy because there is not as much water and there were a lot of places that probably in the '50s there was a lot of good water around [and] you could travel all over the place. [There used to be] a lot of water in the lakes and

rivers and anything that had water was a lot cleaner, but now some of the waters have things that cause illnesses and that has really affected the food in the water and also things that eat things that are in the water. That is quite dangerous, the level of the water going down, because of the effect on the things in the water and the things that use them. Like we eat fish or anything that gets things out of the water because the water is not as healthy as it used to be and there is less water. (N. Attungala, Baker Lake, 2001)[32]

Serious problems are also reported by the Inughuit of Qaanaaq in northwest Greenland:

Change has been so dramatic that during the coldest month of the year, the month of December 2001, torrential rains have fallen in the Thule region so much that there appeared a thick layer of solid ice on top of the sea ice and the surface of the land. The impact on the sea ice can be described in this manner: the snow that normally covers the sea ice became *nilak* (freshwater ice), and the lower layer became *pukak* (crystallized ice), which was very bad for the paws of our sled dogs.

In January 2002, our outermost hunting grounds were not covered by sea ice because of shifting wind conditions and sea currents. We used to go hunting to these areas in October only four or five years ago. It is hard to tell what impact such conditions will have to the land animals. Since I haven't been out to see the feeding grounds of the arctic hares (*Lepus arcticus*), musk ox (*Ovibos moschatus*), and reindeer this year, I can't tell how it is, but I can guess that it will be difficult for the animals to find anything to feed on because of the layer of ice that covers everything. It is hard to say what can be done about these conditions.

Sea-ice conditions have changed over the last five to six years. The ice is generally thinner and is slower to form off the smaller forelands. The appearance of *aakkarneq* (ice thinned by sea currents) happens earlier in the year than normal. Also, sea ice, which previously broke up gradually from the floe-edge towards land, now breaks off all at once. Glaciers are very notably receding and the place names are no longer consistent with the appearance of the land. For example, *Sermiarsussuaq* ("the smaller large glacier"), which previously stretched

8.4 Water and ice on the tundra in early summer, near Iqaluit

out to the sea, no longer exists. (Uusaqqak Qujaukitsoq, Qaanaaq, North Greenland, 2004)[33]

One of the most controversial claims that some elders make is that the sun is literally rising in a different location than in the past and that it returns earlier in the year. Similar claims are made about sunset.[34] What is going on here? The only apparent explanation is that Earth has moved rather dramatically on its axis, which seems impossible. After the Toronto premiere on 23 October 2010 of Isuma Productions' documentary film *Qapirangajuk: Inuit Knowledge and Climate Change*, the filmmakers, Zacharias Kunuk and Ian Mauro, made themselves available for questions from the audience. This claim about the sun was raised and questioned with skepticism by an audience member who wanted to know why such an obviously wrong-headed statement was included in the documentary, undercutting the credibility of what the elders had to say. The filmmakers responded by saying Inuit elders do not have to apologize for or adjust their knowledge to fit Western scientific beliefs.[35] In preparing the film for release, research had been done on why the elders were observing this strange behaviour of the sun. It was discovered that increased humidity in the atmosphere as a result of oceanic warming was causing the sun to appear to rise and set in different places at different times. The observance of this phenomenon by many elders from different communities across Nunavut was the first time that evidence of widespread warming of the Arctic Ocean had been discovered. The elders are right – the seemingly strange solar behaviour is indeed directly related to climate change.

The Arctic Climate Impact Assessment's report on *Impacts of a Warming Arctic*, released in November 2004, although thorough, is now becoming out-of-date. More recent analyses of climate change in the Arctic are finding that changes are occurring much more quickly and more drastically than this relatively conservative assessment records. For example, global temperature increases are already reported as being greater than the report gives – from 0.6 to nearly 1° Celsius. In the Arctic annual temperatures are climbing rapidly, from 2 to as much as 5° Celsius. It now seems possible that these increases may double by mid-century – something no one had predicted ten years ago. Melting of the polar ice pack is occurring at a much faster rate than originally predicted, and the passages through the Arctic Archipelago have already experienced ice-free summers (2007, 2011, and 2012). As I was reviewing this chapter in August 2011, I was on board a ship that was sailing through the southernmost Northwest Passage – the route Franklin died in and Amundsen sailed through in the *Gjoa*. We entered through Lancaster Sound and stopped in Gjoa Haven on King William Island. We emerged at the mouth of the Coppermine River in the hamlet of Kugluktuk on the edge of the Beaufort Sea. There was no ice.

# Global Warming and Inuit Rights

Challenges presented by climate change include serious questions about national authority, or sovereignty, environmental protection, security, military uses of the Arctic, commercial activity, maritime traffic, and human rights. Canada is slowly waking up to the importance of the North to its own sovereignty and security. Since 2006 the Canadian government has begun to at least promise greater attention to northern issues in the interest of protecting Canadian sovereignty, but many of these promises seem to focus on military activity and commercial development that may not benefit Inuit. The federal government is talking about icebreakers, an increased military presence, satellite surveillance, and other measures to ensure that Canada's claims to Arctic waterways are maintained and recognized by the international community. None of this would matter to Canada or the international community if the Arctic were not melting – a connection Canada's political and business leaders seem unwilling to make publicly. Indeed, government officials and the petroleum and mining industries seem to welcome a melting Arctic, as it opens up new fields of oil and gas as well as other resources, while providing the means to ship such resources to markets elsewhere. Efforts to map the continental shelf are ongoing, with the hope that massive reserves of oil and gas will be of economic benefit to Canada and other nations. The problem is that the burning of fossil fuels and the release of carbon emissions are the cause of the melting. The situation goes well beyond the ironic. The logic of government and business leaders is circular and frustrating, and Inuit are insisting on a greater say in these decisions.

The Inuit of Nunavut, the Northwest Territories, and Alaska were so concerned about the extent of climate change in the Arctic that they launched an international petition against the United States before the Inter-American Commission on Human Rights (IACHR) in 2005 (when the administration of President George W. Bush was still in power). The IACHR is a human rights body under the jurisdiction of the Organization of American States, of which the United States and Canada are members. The petition was brought by Siila Watt-Cloutier, former chair of the Inuit Circumpolar Conference (now Council), and by a long list of other Inuit from Canada and Alaska. Watt-Cloutier said at the announcement of the petition,

Inuit are an ancient people. Our way of life is dependent on the natural
environment and animals. Climate change is destroying our environment and eroding our culture. But we refuse to disappear. We will not
become a footnote to globalization.

Climate change is amplified in the Arctic. What is happening to us
now will happen soon in the rest of the world. Our region is the globe's
climate change "barometer." If you want to protect the planet, look
to the Arctic and listen to what Inuit are saying.[36]

A human rights petition or communication could well have been brought
in another forum against European or other nations, including Canada, that
contribute to global warming. China and India are rapidly increasing their
carbon dioxide emissions as industrialization in these countries escalates
and their use of fossil fuels increases. Deforestation and land clearing in
other countries such as Brazil and Indonesia and in parts of Africa are also
having a serious impact. The United States was selected as the target of the
Arctic petition because it remains one of the biggest emitters of greenhouse
gases (China has now achieved the dubious distinction of being the largest)
and because, under Bush's administration, it refused to join in international
efforts to reduce those emissions. The political realities seem to have changed
since the election of a Democratic administration more concerned about the
dangers of climate change and energy security, although hopes of significant
efforts by the United States are always clouded by local and regional politics
in that country. The IACHR was selected as the body best capable of hearing
the petition because of its significant record on Indigenous claims in other
cases.[37] In addition both the commission and the Inter-American Court of
Human Rights, under the umbrella of the Organization of American States,
have taken a broad approach to human rights more generally.[38]

The petition to the IACHR was eventually dismissed without any decision
on either jurisdictional grounds or the merits of the case. In November 2006
the commission stated in a letter to Watt-Cloutier and the other petitioners,
"the information provided does not enable us to determine whether the al-
leged facts would tend to characterize a violation of the rights protected by
the American Declaration [of the Rights and Duties of Man]."[39] Nevertheless, the petition created much greater awareness of how seriously Inuit take
this issue. The Inuit asked that the commission hold hearings in which testimony could be heard to assist in the investigation and understanding of

the relationship between climate change and Inuit rights. Very unusually (since the petition had already been effectively dismissed), a hearing was held in Washington, DC, on 5 March 2007. Inuit and Arctic climate scientists were able to express their concerns in a public forum. Although the commission promised to provide a report on human rights and climate change stemming from this testimony, nothing has yet appeared. Watt-Cloutier herself was nominated for the Nobel Peace Prize in 2007, which was eventually won by former US vice president Al Gore and the IPCC for their work on climate change.

The human rights violations complained of in the petition include the right of Inuit to enjoy

- the benefits of their culture;
- the use and enjoyment of their lands;
- the use and enjoyment of their personal property;
- preservation of health;
- preservation of life, physical integrity, and security;
- protection of their own means of subsistence; and
- protection of residence, mobility, and inviolability of their home.[40]

Inuit brought their application under the *American Declaration of the Rights and Duties of Man* of 1948,[41] as the United States is not a party to the *American Convention on Human Rights* of 1969.[42] Nevertheless, the IACHR will hear arguments based on rights contained in other human rights instruments on the grounds that all members of the Organization of American States are bound by human rights law as contained in the declaration regardless of whether they have ratified the convention.

The ability of Inuit to enjoy and practise their culture, as well as to gain protection of other human rights such as the right to personal property, health, life, subsistence, residence, and mobility, depends fundamentally on their right to use and enjoy both the land and the ice:

For millennia, the Inuit have occupied and used land in the arctic and sub-arctic areas of the United States, Canada, Russia, and Greenland. Included in the "land" that the Inuit have traditionally occupied and used are the landfast winter sea ice, pack ice, and multi-year ice. The Inuit have traditionally spent much of the winter traveling, camping and hunting on the landfast ice. They have used the summer pack ice and multi-year ice to hunt seals, one of their primary sources of protein. Because the international human right to property is interpreted in the context of indigenous culture and history, the Inuit have a human right to use and enjoyment of land and ice that they have traditionally used and occupied in the arctic and sub-arctic regions of the United States, Canada, Russia, and Greenland.[43]

Cultural rights for Indigenous peoples in different parts of the world have been well recognized by several international committees and tribunals.[44] The United Nations Human Rights Committee, in interpreting article 27 of the *United Nations International Covenant on Civil and Political Rights* on behalf of Canadian Indigenous applicants, has recognized the importance of protecting culture, including its close connection to land and natural resources.[45] Article 27 says, "In those States in which ethnic, religious or linguistic minorities exist, persons belonging to such minorities shall not be denied the right, in community with the other members of their group, to enjoy their own culture, to profess and practice their own religion, or to use their own language."[46]

The connection between protection of culture and use of land was also explicitly recognized in the *Awas Tingni* case, where both the IACHR and the Inter-American Court of Human Rights emphasized the close connection between Indigenous peoples, their culture, and their land.[47] The commission reiterated this in two additional cases involving the Maya of Belize and the Yanomami of Brazil.[48] In addition in its *Report on the Situation of Human Rights of a Segment of the Nicaraguan Population of Miskito Origin*, the commission reiterated, "[S]pecial legal protection is recognized for the use of their [the Miskito's] language, the observance of their religion, and in general, all those aspects related to the preservation of their cultural identity. To this should be added the aspects linked to productive organization, which includes, among other things, the issue of the ancestral and communal lands. Non-observance of those rights and cultural values leads to a forced assimilation with results that can be disastrous."[49]

Inuit's rights to their culture and land, including the ice, are part of the broader search for self-determination. These rights are protected in several human rights instruments. Canada is a party to the *United Nations Interna-*

*tional Covenant on Civil and Political Rights* of 1966 and the *United Nations International Covenant on Economic, Social and Cultural Rights* of 1966, both of which protect the right of self-determination under article 1.[50] This right is also specifically protected for Indigenous peoples, including Inuit, in the *United Nations Declaration on the Rights of Indigenous Peoples*.[51]

Canada was one of four nations that voted against the declaration in the UN General Assembly on 13 September 2007 (along with Australia, New Zealand, and the United States). Canada has since relented (as have the other three dissenters):

> On November 12, 2010, Canada issued a Statement of Support endorsing the United Nations Declaration on the Rights of Indigenous Peoples. This endorsement offers an opportunity to strengthen relations with Aboriginal peoples in Canada, and to support our ongoing work on Indigenous issues internationally.
>
> … On September 13, 2007, the United Nations General Assembly held a vote on the Declaration on the Rights of Indigenous Peoples. Canada, New Zealand, Australia and the United States voted against adopting the Declaration. Many States, including some who voted in favour of the Declaration, delivered statements to explain their votes, emphasizing that the Declaration is non-binding and that its provisions are subject to varying interpretations.
>
> In Canada's Explanation of Vote, Canada's Permanent Representative to the United Nations stated Canada's concerns with the wording of some of the Declaration's provisions, noting that these provisions failed to give clear, practical guidance to States. In particular, Canada made reference to the issues of:
>
> - lands, territories and resources;
> - free, prior and informed consent when used as a veto;
> - self-government without recognition of the importance of negotiations;
> - intellectual property;
> - military issues; and,
> - the need to achieve an appropriate balance between the rights and obligations of Indigenous peoples, member States and third parties.[52]

This very qualified statement of support also says that Canada does not recognize the declaration as reflecting customary international law or as creating any change to Canadian law.[53] However, many of the rights contained in the declaration are already well recognized and were legally binding principles in both national and international law prior to the vote on the declaration in the UN General Assembly in September 2007. It is no longer open to the Government of Canada to escape these legal obligations, wherever they are expressed. If the Canadian government is suggesting that international human rights law does not protect Indigenous peoples, it is clearly wrong. It would be truer to say that Canada does not accept the declaration as legally binding, except in relation to those rights already recognized in international and Canadian law.

The right of self-determination has frequently been described as having the highest normative value in international law as a peremptory norm, or *jus cogens*.[54] This means that it is a right that takes precedence over all other international laws and cannot be done away with or ignored. This is similar to laws against genocide, torture, and racial discrimination. The Supreme Court of Canada in *Reference re Secession of Quebec* specifically referred to self-determination as a "general principle of international law."[55] Land rights, Aboriginal rights, self-government, and treaty rights are either protected under the Canadian Constitution or have been accepted by the Canadian government.[56] For Inuit, a right of self-determination includes use, possession, and enjoyment of land and ice as well as rights to consultation, accommodation, and self-government. Many of these rights are also protected under the *Nunavut Land Claims Agreement* of 1993[57] as well as other land claims agreements that protect the rights of Inuvialuit of the Northwest Territories, Nunavimmiut of Nunavik (northern Quebec), and Inuit of Nunatsiavut in Labrador. The Canadian government is fully bound to protect Inuit rights, including the right of self-determination, under constitutional as well as international laws.[58]

## Global Indigenous Perspectives

Inuit frame the issue of climate change not only as an environmental challenge or a problem of sovereignty in international law but also as a matter of human rights. They are likely the first of a long list of people, both Indigenous and non-Indigenous, who may be able to make this type of claim. We do not usually think of climate change as a human rights issue. Indigenous organizations are beginning to deal with climate change from this perspective. The UN Permanent Forum on Indigenous Issues focuses on global warming as an Indigenous rights issue, emphasizing both challenges and opportunities:

- Indigenous peoples in Africa's Kalahari Desert are forced to live around government drilled bores for water and depend on government support for their survival due to rising temperatures, dune expansion and increased wind speeds which have resulted in a loss of vegetation, and negatively impacted traditional cattle and goat farming practices.
- In the high altitude regions of the Himalayas, glacial melts affecting hundreds of millions of rural dwellers who depend on the seasonal flow of water is resulting in more water in the short term, but less in the long run as glaciers and snow cover shrink.
- In the Amazon, the effects of climate change include deforestation and forest fragmentation and consequently, more carbon is released into the atmosphere exacerbating and creating further changes. Droughts in 2005 resulted in fires in the western Amazon region and this is likely to occur again as rainforest is replaced by savannas thus, having a huge effect on the livelihoods of the indigenous peoples in the region.
- Indigenous peoples in the Arctic region depend on hunting for polar bears, walrus, seals and caribou, herding reindeer, fishing and gathering not only for food to support the local economy, but also as the basis for their cultural and social identity. Some of the concerns facing indigenous peoples in the region include the change in species and availability of traditional food sources, perceived reduction in weather predictions and the safety of traveling in changing ice and weather conditions, posing serious challenges to human health and food security.
- In Finland, Norway and Sweden, rain and mild weather during the winter season often prevents reindeer from accessing lichen, which is a vital food source. This has caused massive loss of reindeers, which are vital to the culture, subsistence and economy of Saami communities. Reindeer herders are being forced to feed their herds with fodder, which is expensive and not economically viable in the long term.
- In Bangladesh, villagers are creating floating vegetable gardens to protect

their livelihoods from flooding, while in Vietnam, communities are helping to plant dense mangroves along the coast to diffuse tropical-storm
waves.

- Indigenous peoples in the Central, South American and Caribbean regions
  are shifting their agricultural activities and their settlements to new locations which are less susceptible to adverse climate conditions. For example, indigenous peoples in Guyana are moving from their savannah homes
  to forest areas during droughts and have started planting cassava, their
  main staple crop, on moist floodplains which are normally too wet for
  other crops.

- In North America, some indigenous groups are striving to cope with climate change by focusing on the economic opportunities that it may
  create. For example, the increased demand for renewable energy using
  wind and solar power could make tribal lands an important resource for
  such energy, replacing fossil fuel–derived energy and limiting greenhouse gas emissions. The Great Plains could provide a tremendous wind
  resource and its development could help to reduce greenhouse gas emissions as well as alleviate the management problem of the Missouri River
  hydropower, helping to maintain water levels for power generation,
  navigation, and recreation. In addition, there may be opportunities for
  carbon sequestration.[59]

During the Medieval Warm Period (AD 900–1300), large areas of southwestern North America, Central America, Africa, and Australia were devastated by severe droughts that went on for decades. A recurrence of shifting
rainfall patterns is having a major impact on agricultural production in our
own time. The problem of severe drought in northeastern Africa (Somalia,
Ethiopia, Eritrea, and Sudan) came to the world's attention in the last two
decades of the twentieth century and continues to be a major issue today.
This drought appears to be directly caused by a shift in the monsoonal rains
in the Indian Ocean. The famines of recent years in this part of the world
seem to be a result of changes to the climate. The war and refugee crises in
both South Sudan and Darfur are two extreme examples of the havoc and
suffering severe climate change can bring. Persistent drought in Sudan means
that nomadic pastoralists no longer have sufficient water for their flocks and
herds. They have started raiding farming communities to the south and west,
competing with small agriculturalists for control of water. The issue has

been compounded by oil and gas interests in southern Sudan, which have enlisted the aid of both governmental and paramilitary forces to control security. The people of northern Sudan (including the nomadic pastoralists) tend to be Muslims, whereas southern farmers tend to follow Native animist religions or have converted to Christianity. Although politics, resource development, religion, and land use have been important, climate change seems to be the catalyst that has created misery in southwestern Sudan (which has now achieved a tenuous independence as the Republic of South Sudan).

The Government of Australia was averse to controls on greenhouse gas emissions both nationally and internationally until the "Millennium Drought" of the first decade of the twenty-first century (and a change of government in 2007) created a complete turnaround in attitude. Aboriginals and Torres Strait Islanders in Australia, especially those who live in remote communities, are at greater risk from "cyclones, storms, bush fires, and droughts. In particular, much coastal infrastructure is likely to be at high risk of damage from storms and flooding. This is of serious and immediate concern for Torres Strait Islander communities because of rising sea levels and the inundation of freshwater systems by salt water."[60] Torres Strait Islanders live off Australia's northeastern coast on islands that are particularly vulnerable to rises in sea levels. Other risks include health and food security. Aboriginal people in coastal regions and the central deserts, where communities still practise subsistence hunting and gathering within their own "country" (land), face challenges similar to Inuit. Unfortunately, with a change of government in 2013, it looks like Australia will henceforth be under the influence of climate skeptics and deniers.

It is forecast that global warming will increase the frequency and severity of extreme weather events, such as hurricanes and typhoons. The victims of events like Hurricane Katrina may well have an international human rights case against their own governments. Heavier and more frequent cyclones in tropical Australia and Southeast Asia may also be partly caused by a warming ocean. Flooding in low-lying countries due to rising sea levels and increased storm surges is already causing problems in countries such as Bangladesh and the Maldives. The combination of severe weather and rising oceans will very likely result in towns like Tuktoyaktuk in the Northwest Territories or Shishmaref in Alaska having to be relocated. The village of Kivilina, Alaska, is suing twenty-four energy companies for greenhouse gas emissions related to climate changes that are threatening the 400 Iñupiat who live there with relocation or inundation. The village lies on a shrinking island now facing heavy storms and disappearing sea ice in the Chukchi Sea. The suit was filed in the US District Court of San Francisco against Exxon Mobil, British Petroleum, Conoco Phillips, Chevron, Duke Energy, a coal company, and fourteen power companies. They are being asked to pay the relocation costs of US$400 million to move the village to safer ground.[61] Larger urban areas may also be threatened as sea levels make it necessary to seek higher ground. Even entire nation-states may have to be abandoned, such as small low-lying nations in the Pacific. New Zealand has created a Pacific Access Category for resettlement of citizens of several small Pacific nations, including Kiribati, Tuvalu, and Tonga. Applicants are chosen by ballot and must meet fairly strict requirements as to age, education, employ-ability, and so on.[62] Both Australia and New Zealand can expect a big in-crease in regional asylum seekers as people flee from rising sea levels and increased storm activity.[63]

The consequences for major urban centres in Europe, North America, Asia, and Europe may also be profound. In September 2011 the Canadian National Round Table on the Environment and the Economy put out a study of the projected impact of climate change on the Canadian economy, infrastructure, and urban life.[64] The cost of climate change was predicted to be anywhere from about $5 billion dollars per year beginning in 2020 to as much as $43 billion by mid-century, depending on how quickly greenhouse gas emissions increase and how much effort Canada puts into mitigation and adaptation to climate change. The effect on coastal regions could be ex-treme, especially in British Columbia, as well as in the Atlantic provinces of Nova Scotia, Newfoundland and Labrador, Prince Edward Island, and New Brunswick. The highest per capita impact would be in Nunavut, where all but one community is on the coast. Iqaluit, for example, is low-lying and now has some of the highest tides in the world. An increase in ocean levels and tidal surges may result in serious flooding. The beach, causeway, and surrounding area in Iqaluit were coincidentally flooded during a high tide a few days before the results of the study came out.

The large urban centre in Canada most at risk is Vancouver:

The majority of dwellings at risk are in British Columbia – about 8,900 to 18,700 by the 2050s. Above we saw that the area of land at risk of

8.5 Causeway and beach area flooded during a very high tide, Iqaluit.

ocean flooding in British Columbia is small relative to the other provinces and territories. However, this small piece of land is much more densely populated than coastal areas in other jurisdictions ...

Our results for British Columbia require careful interpretation. First, we did not account for the role of dikes and other coastal defences in protecting land and dwellings from the risks of flooding. In the case of Metro Vancouver, an area that has many kilometres of protective dikes in place, much of the land (and dwellings on it) at risk of flooding in the baseline case is protected by dikes. However, dikes were not designed with climate change in mind, so additional risk from climate change remains a concern. Second, given that we did not include dikes, our modelling likely underestimates the number of dwellings at risk of flooding under baseline assumptions for the province – possibly by an order of magnitude – according to expert advice from British Columbia. Judging by maps of Metro Vancouver's floodplain, tens of thousands of homes would face a flooding risk were it not for the extensive diking system. Our analysis may be understating exposure for the following reasons: (1) our conservative approach to how we modelled flooding required land be adjacent to flooded areas in order to flood and (2) the resolution of data used to establish the elevation of coastal land was limited. Our methods were necessarily simplified to allow for a national assessment, but our findings emphasize the importance of a more detailed local assessment of Metro Vancouver.[65]

There is another alarming possibility – the Gulf Stream may shut down, resulting in a rapid and massive global cooling, particularly in Europe. This huge current of warm water from the Caribbean to the North Atlantic is part of a global network of oceanic currents. The Gulf Stream keeps temperatures in northern Europe considerably warmer than they ought to be considering how far north Great Britain and the Scandinavian countries are. Without the Gulf Stream, the climate of England could well resemble that of northern Canada as it exists today, destroying English agriculture and severely stressing English infrastructure and energy needs. About 12,000 years ago, a period of warming was interrupted by the Younger Dryas period. The most common theory is that a surge of cold fresh water from a huge lake, posthumously dubbed Lake Agassiz, flowed into the North Atlantic at this time. The lake (many times larger than the residual Great Lakes) was blocked by sheets of ice in central North America. This ice slowly eroded until the lake finally burst through its dam, allowing for a relatively sudden release of water into the North Atlantic, possibly by way of either Hudson Bay or the St Lawrence River or both. This massive flood of cold fresh water began interfering with the thermohaline effects of warm salty water flowing up from the South. This interference may have caused serious disruption of the Gulf Stream, returning the northern hemisphere to a thousand-year period of frigid temperatures. It was only after the Gulf Stream and oceanic currents resumed their more normal patterns about 10,000 years ago that the "long summer" of human transformation began, with hunter-gatherer societies becoming agricultural, urban, and eventually industrial.

These shifts can happen in a decade or less. Climate change, especially with the rapid forcings created by humans, is not necessarily gradual. Warming is already causing rapid and massive melting of glaciers in Greenland, creating large amounts of fresh water that pours into the North Atlantic every summer. Scientists are not in agreement on the likelihood of the Gulf

Stream slowing down or stopping, and this has not been factored into projections of climate change in current models. Even a slowing of the North Atlantic current could massively affect temperatures, weather patterns, snow and ice coverage, fishing, oil and gas extraction in the North Atlantic, shipping, agriculture, and human life. It is possible this slowing is already occurring given the severity of recent winters in Europe. Between about 1300 and 1850 a cooling of no more than 2° Celsius caused massive disruptions to European economies and political structures. It was only the advent of global warming during the Industrial and Agricultural Revolutions of the nineteenth and twentieth centuries that temperatures began to rise again. Studies of prehistoric environments suggest that, if past patterns are any indication, our interglacial "summer" should be coming to an end, or perhaps should have done so long ago. But there is no sign that this is happening – quite the opposite.

## Human Choices

Global warming or global cooling? Increased frequency and severity of weather events, including hurricanes, storms, tornados, droughts, very hot summers, and mild winters? Or a sudden drop in global temperatures resulting in the return of colder conditions to the northern hemisphere? More likely it will be a combination of the two, with environmental changes that create global warming also causing severe cold spells and winter storms in the northern hemisphere (due to alterations in the jetstream influenced by summer melting of Arctic ice) while the southern hemisphere experiences recording-breaking heat (as occurred during January 2014). The extent of the increasing human release of greenhouse gases means that another glacial period is extremely unlikely. Keeping global temperatures below the 2° Celsius upper limit set by the nations of the world in 2009 is going to be very difficult. Greenhouse gases remain in the environment for a long time. On the basis of cumulative impact, Europe and the United States are by far the biggest contributors, even though China and India are catching up. One of the highest per capita emitters of greenhouse gases is Canada. Although its overall impact is relatively small, its heavy reliance on oil, gas, and coal, with a particular attachment to tar sands, means that Canada is playing a very big role in the export of climate change around the world. On 12 December 2011 the Government of Canada emphasized its failure to take responsibility for this contribution to climate change by withdrawing from the Kyoto Protocol – the first and only member state to do so.[66]

The Arctic is where the impact of climate change is most visible, although it is not hard to find other heavily affected areas in Africa and the Asia-Pacific region. A significant difference with the extent of global warming in the Arctic is that it is occurring in developed, not developing, countries. Canada, the United States, northern Europe, and even Russia have ample resources to help slow down this process of change. Unfortunately, extracting and exploiting fossil fuels is a major source of economic wealth in all the circumpolar nation-states, creating an intense push to discover more in the Arctic itself.

The effect of climatic conditions on natural and human habitats is becoming increasingly important to Canada both as a sovereign nation making claims to the sea and ice of the High Arctic and as the protector of its citizens living in the North – principally Inuit. Therefore, these issues cannot simply be looked at as environmental, political, or economic but must also be understood from a human perspective. Canada periodically goes through a fit of interest in the Arctic, generally as a reaction to external events that raise questions about its sovereign control over land and sea. In 2008 and 2010 Canada called for high-level meetings of the five major circumpolar nations – Russia, Norway, the United States, Denmark (Greenland), and itself. This infuriated Inuit, who insisted all negotiations to do with sovereignty claims and climate change should be made through the Arctic Council and other bodies where they are represented and have a voice. The secretary of state for the United States, Hillary Clinton, supported the demands of Inuit, and Canada was left somewhat embarrassed. This, in light of Canada's history in relation to the Inuit, does not instil confidence for the future.

The opening of formerly ice-choked sea channels in August, in September, and even into the normally freezing months of October and November means that economic issues to do with resource development are becoming increasingly important. It also means that political claims to sovereignty over these waterways are a serious issue for all circumpolar nations, especially Canada. But for the Inuit and the environment on which they depend, melting ice is dangerous. Ice is the basis of the Arctic habitat. Climate change accelerates as the Arctic ice melts. For those who are still skeptical about climate change, the Arctic and its ice are where the big picture can be found.

# 9

## Is the Arctic Safe for Polar Bears?

Let me recall the great white
Polar bear,
High up its white body,
Black snout in the snow, it came!
He really believed
He alone was a male
And ran toward me.
Unaya – unaya.
He threw me down
Again and again,
Then breathless departed
And lay down to rest,
Hid by a mound on a floe.
Heedless he was, and unknowing
That I was to be his fate.

"My Breath" by Orpingalik[1]

## Is Nunavut Part of Canada?

Winter in the Arctic is not only a time of grim survival but also a time of brilliant short days with long beautiful sunrises and sunsets in those places where Siqiniq makes an appearance. During the long black nights, the sky sometimes bristles with hanging curtains of *aqsarniit* (northern lights). In Inuit legend the lights are the souls of the dead playing a game of football across the sky with a walrus head. Inuit believe that the lights make a swishing sound and can be brought closer to Earth by whistling. Children are warned not to play outside when the lights are rustling across the sky for fear the curtains will sweep down and cut off their heads. In Iqaluit my little balcony window faced south toward Frobisher Bay, the direction in which you can see the sun in winter as well as the northern lights. I would sometimes get up in the middle of the night to see if the *aqsarniit* were there. If they were, I would warm up the SUV and drive down to the graveyard. The graves are on the shore of Frobisher Bay below the cliffs of the Tundra Valley housing development not far from where I lived. Because there are no streetlamps or houselights past the gate, it is a good place to get away from light pollution. It was an eerie feeling to turn the car engine and headlights off and then stand in the dark looking up at sweeping curtains of gossamer light flickering across the black sky. During my stay in Iqaluit, the lights were especially brilliant. Usually they were white, more rarely pale green. On one occasion there were curtains of pink and violet bending in front of a brilliant full moon. I never did hear them make any sound, and I never tried whistling them down to Earth. They were just there, silently twisting and glimmering in ghostly sheens, behind them the sky black and brilliant with the Milky Way. Then just as mysteriously they would disappear. By this time my neck would be stiff with staring upward, and the cold would be beginning to sink in. I also had a fear that if I stayed out too long without plugging in the vehicle's block heater, I would not be able to get the engine started. At -40° Celsius the internal combustion engine quickly becomes useless. I did get stuck once on a more adventurous trip out along the Road to Nowhere while chasing a particularly spectacular show. A four-wheel-drive SUV is actually not much use when it sinks into 2 or 3 feet of rutted snow. I was eventually rescued by two Inuit hunters travelling home from a trip out on the land. They dug me out and sent me on my way, chastising me in a good-natured way for my foolishness. The temperature was -30° Celsius, and the air was still with no wind chill. Cold but beautiful.

In the past sixty years, change has come to the Arctic with a vengeance. Following the Second World War, the settlement and rapid colonization of the Arctic continued with the establishment of the DEW Line, or Distant Early Warning, posts across the Arctic. Iqaluit, the new capital of Nunavut, was settled as the town of Frobisher Bay because of this military presence, as was Resolute Bay. Relocations of Inuit occurred not only in Canada. The Inughuit of northern Greenland were also moved farther north to their present location of Qaanaaq in order to make way for the gigantic American base in Thule. Canada continued to struggle with issues of sovereignty as the Americans began aggressively moving across the Arctic from Greenland in the East to the Beaufort Sea in the West. Nuclear-powered submarines (both American and Soviet) were believed to be lurking through the Northwest Passage, intercontinental ballistic missiles were aimed in all directions over the North Pole, and extensive oil and gas, mining, and fishing development meant that the Arctic was no longer perceived by national governments as the vast empty wilderness on the edge of the world that it had long been. Today the Northwest Passage, once a northern mirage of grandiose ambitions and insane failure, is being resurrected as a site of ambitious development and a source of potential conflict in international relations. Much of the passage is still inaccessible for most of the year, but this situation is changing. When one reads the descriptions of northern travel during the days of Sir John Franklin, Dr John Rae, Qitdlarssuaq, and even Nuqallaq and then compares them to travel through the relatively long stretches of open water during the summer months that are common now, it is clear that global warming is changing the Arctic in dramatic ways.

What is still not sufficiently acknowledged in the story of Canada's sovereignty in the Arctic is the Inuit role in this process of search and claim. Despite the statement in the preamble of the *Nunavut Land Claims Agreement* of 1993 recognizing the Inuit contribution to Canadian sovereignty,[2] federal government representatives and other international experts consistently fail to see the Inuit or hear what they have to say on northern issues.

The difficulty in getting the Inuit point of view across was brought home to me very clearly at the annual meeting of the Canadian Council on International Law held in Ottawa in October 2010. The conference was dedicated to Arctic issues. But, despite a strong contingent of Inuit and Greenlandic representatives, the international law experts and the Inuit speakers seemed to be talking past each other. The international law experts focused on the law of the sea, sovereignty, security, and resource development, whereas the human dimension consistently emphasized by speakers such as Mary Simon (then president of Inuit Tapiriit Kanatami) and former Nunavut premier Paul Okalik did not seem to engage the attention of non-Inuit participants. It was almost as if the two points of view were being expressed in two different languages that were not being translated. But the Inuit speakers were talking mostly in English, not Inuktitut. Siila Watt-Cloutier relates a similar experience in trying to get non-Inuit to focus on climate change as a human, not just a scientific, political, or economic issue:

I have attended three COPs [UN conferences on climate change]. People rush from meeting to meeting arguing about all sorts of narrow technical points. The bigger picture, the cultural picture, the human picture is being lost. Climate change is not about bureaucrats scurrying around. It is about families, parents, children, and the lives we lead in our communities in the broader environment. We have to regain this perspective if climate change is to be stopped. Inuit understand these connections because we remain a people of the land, ice, and snow. This is why, for us, climate is an issue of our right to exist as an Indigenous people. How can we stand up for ourselves and help others do the same?[3]

The Inuit and their predecessors have, over the course of thousands of years, successfully explored, discovered, and settled the lands and seas of the North. This pre-existing human presence in the Arctic was not however acknowledged by the British as determinative of any kind of sovereignty recognized by international or national law, nor was it in the minds of either British or Canadian officials when formal sovereignty over the islands was transferred in 1880. The Inuit, of course, were not consulted. Yet the reliance on Inuit for survival and the gradual adoption of Inuit means of travel and living in the Arctic were crucial to the eventual success of European, American, and Canadian missions of exploration. The loss of the Franklin Expedition and the search to find it as well as subsequent criminal trials such as that of Nuqallaq, the establishment of a Canadian police presence in the High Arctic, and the removal and resettlement of Inuit in the North have all been important factors in the establishment of dominion and claims of sovereignty by Canada. From Ennadai Lake in the Kivilliq region of Nunavut to the High Arctic, Inuit were moved into settlements or were moved from one settlement to another for the primary purpose of establishing a Canadian presence in the North.

Since 1950 southern "experts," government officials, resource companies, and scientific researchers have moved into the Arctic in ever greater numbers. I myself was one of that number for a while. The constant pressure on Inuit to voice their concerns over and above government and commercial priorities is still a problem. Incoming southerners bring their preconceptions with them and are sometimes unwilling to let these go in the face of Inuit objection. Those who spend little time in the Arctic, or who have never visited there, may be recommending policies that have little to do with the realities on the ground. This is especially true of political or commercial policies formed overseas, as with the 2009 ban imposed by the European Union on the import of seal products.[4] But Canadian government officials can be just as obtuse. Sometimes I wonder if the rest of Canada realizes that Nunavut is a part of this country and that Inuit are Canadian citizens. Even federal government efforts to highlight northern issues seem to be fulfilling several incompatible agendas.

In February 2010 the federal government hosted a meeting of G7 finance ministers in Iqaluit. It was seen as an audacious move, but it at least gave the people of Nunavut an opportunity to show the world's most powerful countries what the Arctic is like. Premier Eva Aariak and Iqaluit mayor Elisapee Sheutiapik, along with Nunavut minister of health Leona Aglukkak, took the opportunity to show the foreign politicians, government officials, diplomats, and media something of life in the Canadian Arctic as it is really lived. The visitors were invited on a dogsled trip. The Inuk singer Lucy Idlout performed a song about domestic violence. Everyone had an opportunity to taste caribou, char, seal meat, and other "country food." Activists opposing the seal hunt were outraged, and the diplomats were a little perplexed by the location of their meeting:

> Sheryl Fink, the director of the Canadian seal campaign for the International Fund for Animal Welfare, notes … "We know they're trying to play up this Inuit thing and portray all commercial [seal] hunting in Canada as Inuit hunting," she said, describing the non-aboriginal hunt as much larger and more wasteful. "It is frustrating for us when we see lines getting blurred between the two because it is a deliberate tactic on the part of the government."
>
> … The European Union office in Ottawa declined comment, as did several other embassies. Some European diplomats, speaking on condition they not be named, were bemused.
>
> "Once we knew the venue, we kind of knew what would be on the menu," said one diplomat.[5]

## Is Greenland a Foreign Country?

Another story might help to illustrate how complex the relationship between Inuit and Canadian sovereignty can be. In 2003 I went on an Arctic voyage that included a stopover in Greenland. One of the special guests on the ship was Kenojuak Ashevak, the celebrated artist from Cape Dorset who has been honoured many times for her magnificent prints and carvings.[6] Until her death in 2013, she was a highly respected elder in her community. She looked like many other female Inuit elders – a small, smiling, quiet woman in practical clothing and the ubiquitous headscarf older Inuit women wear. She spoke little or no English. She was accompanied on the voyage by a companion and interpreter, Mukshowya Niviaqsi, also from Cape Dorset. At the end of the trip, the charter flight from Greenland left the three of us in Iqaluit, and the remaining crew and passengers went on to Ottawa. We encountered an immigration and customs officer at the entrance to the Iqaluit airport. I had my passport, but neither Kenojuak nor Mukshowya had theirs – all they had were their Nunavut identity cards. We spent an extremely uncomfortable hour in the airport's little immigration office explaining to the officer-in-charge why this distinguished Canadian elder and world-class artist from Cape Dorset and her companion should be allowed to enter their own land despite not having the necessary mark of Canadian citizenship. I pointed out to the immigration officer who Kenojuak was – one of the greatest Inuit artists in the North, a member of the Order of Canada, whose work has appeared in galleries and museums all over the world. She had even had works reproduced on Canadian postage stamps! The immigration officer asked me, "Why don't you say she's one of the greatest *Canadian* artists?" My response was that she was both. Eventually, after a phone call to Ottawa, the immigration officer let them both in. Their identification was photocopied for his records, and we were all free to go. At one point Mukshowya asked, "Who are you to decide who comes into our own country?"

I ran into this same immigration officer a few weeks later at a local café. He said he had gone to see a showing of Kenojuak's works at the local museum – and now had a story to tell his grandchildren! The irony is that Kenojuak and Mukshowya did get into Canada without their passports, contrary to Canadian law, precisely because the immigration officer and his superiors in Ottawa were convinced to "bend the rules" for the sake of an elderly

9.1  Kenojuaq Ashevak, Kekkerton Island, Cumberland Sound

Inuit lady and her companion. The experience was nevertheless profoundly disrespectful and disturbing to everyone involved.

Sir John Franklin is now treated as a historical martyr for failing to survive his supposed discovery of a sea passage that was completely useless for commercial travel at the time. Now, 150 years later, when the Northwest Passage is becoming navigable, his failed attempt to transit through the Arctic islands seems to be crucial to Canada's argument that the passage is part of Canada. Dr John Rae's reputation was ruined because he told the truth as told to him by "the Esquimaux." Nuqallaq carried out the laws of his people against a Newfoundland fox trapper, embraced the new Christian religion, and then was himself trapped in the Canadian judicial net being spread across the High Arctic in the early part of the twentieth century. Elisapee Karetak survived her mother's ordeal after being relocated from Ennadai Lake and has told her story in a moving documentary that describes the clash of bureaucratic demands, Canadian criminal law, and her own family's survival.[7] John Amagoalik was moved with his family from the east coast of Hudson Bay to the windy flatlands of Resolute Bay, and the Inuit descendants of the creator of *Nanook of the North* went to Grise Fiord. Kenojuak was both a great Canadian artist and a great Inuit artist – but what this meant to her, to her community, to Nunavut, and to Canadian heritage as a whole still seems very complex. And now Inuit are facing a new dilemma – climate change. Yet again southern demands and theories and supposed solutions seem to overwhelm the knowledge of the people who have always lived in the North.

## Nanuq of the North

The iconic symbol of climate change is the polar bear. To the Inuit the bear is *nanuq*. To marine biologists it is *ursus maritimus* – the sea bear. The polar bear is a marine mammal that relies mainly on hunting seals in direct competition with Inuit hunters, who also rely primarily on seal. The bear is a powerful swimmer and can be seen many miles from shore swimming or happily resting on an ice floe. The bear can range hundreds of miles in a year's travel over ice, land, and sea in search of game, and can cover many thousands of miles during a lifetime of travel over a home range. *Nanuq* fears nothing, certainly not humans, although only a desperately hungry bear would try to take on an adult walrus. Polar bears are much bigger and more dangerous than their cousins to the south, including grizzly bears and the giant brown bears in Alaska. Despite cute cubs on display in European and American zoos polar bears cannot usually be tamed or domesticated. After a few short months of babyhood the animal is much too dangerous to approach. The black bears that beg for handouts by the side of the road in our national parks and raid garbage cans in suburban Vancouver are pesky little scavengers in comparison. Nevertheless, there are stories of Inuit having polar bears as friends or even pets:

> In earlier times Inuit had all kinds of animals as pets and I remember a man named Quviq who had a polar bear as a pet. Sometimes the bear stayed inside his home. I was afraid of it. One day his tent was so crowded with visitors that the bear was sent outside. Although Quviq's dogs were used to the bear, the dogs of Quviq's visitors weren't, and they attacked and killed him. I fondly remember growing up with that

bear. It would follow a person everywhere, sometimes to the point that you would find him bothersome, especially when he wanted to play a game with a ball.[8]

There are about 25,000 polar bears worldwide (possibly more, as the number of bears in Siberia is largely unknown). The largest concentration is in Canada, where different groups, or subpopulations, range from southern Hudson Bay to the High Arctic as far north as eighty-two degrees latitude (northern Greenland and Ellesmere Island). Bears have been spotted close to the North Pole, although travelling on multiyear pack ice is not something they prefer, as seals are hard to find where the ice is too thick. Polar bears need sea ice in order to live, just as Inuit do, since both depend on seals, which live and breed above and below ice. The spring (April) is the time of *nattian* (seal pups), when seals give birth on ice floes, and is a prime hunting season for both bears and humans.

9.2 Polar bears approach the starboard bow of the Los Angeles–class fast attack submarine uss *Honolulu*, surfaced 280 miles from the North Pole. Sighted by a lookout from the bridge of the submarine, the bears investigated the boat for almost two hours before leaving.

To the Inuit all things have an *inua* (soul), which has the shape of a human to remind them of when animals and humans could transform into each other. Killing for food is therefore a dangerous activity, not only because the animal itself might turn and attack the hunter (as a bear or walrus might do) but also because once dead the animal's *inua* continues to exist. If the animal is not treated with respect, it might take revenge on humans by telling other animals not to give themselves to a hunter or a community. Nuliajuk may also take revenge if her children are mistreated. Thus, when a hunter kills a seal, it is considered respectful to pour a little fresh water into the dead seal's mouth. Polar bears are considered to be the closest to humans of all the animals and must be treated with the greatest respect. The elder-in-residence at the Akitsiraq Law School, Lucien Ukaliannuk, used to tell us that we must not talk about bears or say bad things about them. They can hear us and may become angry and take revenge. To someone from the South (including polar researchers and conservationists) this notion may sound silly. But polar bears have acute hearing and can move both quickly and very quietly. If you attract a bear's attention, it can be on you before you know it – and that encounter can be lethal. Even talking about bears when they are not physically present can be seen as disrespectful and dangerous.

*Qimmiit* (dogs) are considered to be *nanuq*'s cousins. Neither has any fear of the other. Bears do not normally prey on dogs and have been known to play with chained sled dogs. But dogs can also be very useful when hunting for bears:

> When the dogs catch up to the polar bear they would start to bark at the bear, which of course is agitating. As the dogs bark at the bear, some would even bite at the polar bear, making the bear panic so that its attention is taken by the dogs, so the polar bear no longer pays attention to the man who would harpoon and catch the bear. So that was the reason why the old polar bear's face was full of scars, as he had been caught time and time again. He would be butchered and once he had been used he would return home among the other polar bears.[9]

Inuit have had a long and colourful relationship with *nanuq*. Oral history records the time when polar bears and humans could transform into each other, as Qitdlarssuaq could do. Powerful shamans like Kiviuq could call on *nanuq* as one of their *tuurngait* (helping spirits) in times of trouble. In his encounter with a bee woman Kiviuq discovers that he needs help. She disguises herself as Arnatiaq ("good beautiful woman") and invites him into her house, where she puts his clothes on her drying rack while she shows him her bed:

> Kiviuq looked around. The bed had a solid wood frame, but it was strung from side to side with human intestines.
>
> And then he saw the skulls, on the floor in a ring around the base of the wall. What was worse was that he recognized them. These were the skulls of his former companions – men who had died at sea.
>
> One of the skulls spoke to him. This was the last shaman who had died at sea, the one Kiviuq had tried to save. "If you don't want to turn out like me, get out of here fast!"
>
> Kiviuq didn't have to be told twice. He reached for his boots and clothes up on the drying rack. But every time he reached, the rack moved higher up in the air. He stretched and jumped but couldn't get his clothes down.
>
> "Come in here and help me!" he called to the woman. But she replied from outside, "I put them up, you get them down!"
>
> Now Kiviuq called on his *tuurngaq*, his powerful shamanic helping spirit. This was the giant polar bear. "Nanurluk, come and get this woman!"
>
> A loud growling and snuffling came from outside. The door flew open and in came Bee Woman. "H-here are your b-boots. H-here are your c-clothes," she said, fearfully.[10]

There is nothing like seeing a polar bear in its natural environment. For me to have had the opportunity to see and photograph this amazing animal in the Arctic has been an unforgettable experience. The largest can measure 12 feet or more from nose to tail. They are more at home in the water than on land, but they can outrun any human unfortunate enough to encounter one unarmed. While working in Iqaluit, and afterward, I was able to travel in parts of the High Arctic where sightings of bears are common. Their coats are not actually white. Each hair is hollow and translucent. Bears in zoos, or those living in southern Hudson Bay, seem to pick up a yellowish tinge from their surroundings. Bears in the High Arctic tend to be a glistening clean white. They are also solitary creatures. Male bears, once they have separated from their mothers, have little contact with other bears except to mate.

There are exceptions to this solitary behaviour. While travelling near Gjoa Haven in 2011 I witnessed an incredible gathering of male bears. There were about two dozen of them along a stretch of low shoreline near the estuary of a small river. They were feasting on at least half a dozen beluga whales. They must have been there for some time, as the carcasses were well picked over. The bears were enormous and hugely fat after days of gorging. These were not the photogenic white bears of nature magazines, the Discovery Channel, or Disney documentaries. Their faces were smeared with blood and animal remains. Two pairs of young males were in the water nearby sparring with each other, play fighting to test their strength and dominance. A lone female and her two cubs were swimming well offshore, waiting for the males to finish feeding.

Female bears raise one, two, or even three cubs. If you see more than one bear, it is almost certainly a mother and her young. Females den during the winter to give birth. Young cubs are tiny, hairless, and blind at birth, cuddling up against their mother's fur and nipple until they are big enough to leave the den in the spring. They will then live and travel with their mothers for two or three years until she has taught them how to fend for themselves. Polar bears are extremely intelligent, curious, sometimes aggressive, always magnificent, and dangerous.

## Are Polar Bears in Danger?

[At a] recent meeting of the IUCN [International Union for Conservation of Nature] Polar Bear Specialist Group (Copenhagen, 2009), scientists reported that of the 19 subpopulations of polar bears, eight are declining, three are stable, one is increasing, and seven have insufficient data on which to base a decision – this is a change from five that were declining in 2005, five that were stable, and two that were increasing. During the meeting, delegates renewed their conclusion from previous meetings that the greatest conservation challenge to the polar bear is ecological change in the Arctic related to climate warming.[11]

9.3 Big male *nanuq* (polar bear) feasting on the remains of a beluga. He was one of about twenty-five bears enjoying a meal near Gjoa Haven. This photo was taken with a long zoom lens.

Management and conservation of polar bears are covered under several national and international laws. The *Agreement on Conservation of Polar Bears* of 1973 requires the five polar bear nations – Canada, Denmark (Greenland), Norway, the United States, and Russia – to protect polar bear habitat, to ban hunting from aircraft or motor boats, to coordinate management and research, and to exchange research data.[12] Polar bears can be killed for scientific purposes, to prevent problems in the management of other resources, and to protect life or property. Local people using traditional methods and exercising their traditional rights may also hunt bears. In 1975 polar bears were listed as "threatened" under the *United Nations Convention on International Trade in Endangered Species of Wild Fauna and Flora*, although hunting and the export of bears or bear parts were still permitted.[13] In 1994 the United States allowed the issuance of permits for American hunters to bring home polar bear trophies under the *Marine Mammal Protection Act* of 1972.[14]

But, in recent years, concerns about polar bear habitat due to climate change have given rise to a tougher approach:

> "Polar bears are being threatened by humans on two fronts: sport hunting and habitat loss due to global warming," said Rep. Inslee, a member of the House Natural Resources Committee and Select Committee on Energy Independence and Global Warming. "We need to address both."
>
> "There is clear, scientific evidence that the habitats of polar bears and other Arctic species are being threatened by global warming. As these irreplaceable species become increasingly endangered, it is our responsibility to make every reasonable effort to protect them," said Congressman LoBiondo, a member of the Congressional Friends of Animals Caucus.[15]

> An estimated 21,500 to 25,000 polar bears remain in the world. Polar bears hunt their primary prey – ringed and other ice seals – on the sea ice during winter, storing the fat they will need for the spring thaw that forces them ashore to fast until the ice returns in autumn. But research has shown that the annual sea ice is now receding earlier and forming later, leaving polar bears with less time to hunt and more time on land where they must fast. This development adversely affects their condition and, ultimately, threatens their survival. If the current rate of ice shrinkage and related weight loss continues, bears may become so thin by 2012 that they may no longer be able to reproduce.[16]

The year 2012 has come and gone, and bears still seem to be reproducing. My own experience of bear sightings from 2003 to 2011 suggests that these predictions are too pessimistic. According to people living in northern communities polar bear sightings have increased substantially in the past ten to twenty years. Nevertheless, as a result of concerted campaigning by environmental groups such as the International Federation for Animal Welfare and the World Wildlife Federation, in 2008 the United States listed polar bears as "endangered" under the *Endangered Species Act*.[17] This act abolished the system of permits under the *Marine Mammal Protection Act*. As a consequence, American hunters may no longer bring home bear parts as trophies. In addition the United States is lobbying the United Nations to put polar bears under the "endangered species" category internationally.

In Canada polar bears are listed as a species of "special concern" under the *Species at Risk Act* of 2002. Such a species "may become a threatened or an endangered species because of a combination of biological character-istics and identified threats."[18] Inuit are allowed to hunt polar bears under international and national legislation. In addition they are allowed to con-duct commercial "sport" hunting by big game enthusiasts as long as the hunt is done in a sustainable way. In Canada provincial and territorial leg-islation also governs protection of wildlife. In Nunavut the harvesting, man-agement, and conservation of animals are protected under article 5 of the *Nunavut Land Claims Agreement.* Under this provision the Nunavut Wildlife Management Board was established to work with Inuit organiza-tions and governments to protect wildlife for the benefit of Inuit and all Canadians. The *Nunavut Wildlife Act* of 2003 regulates all species, including the polar bear.[19]

Big game hunting of polar bears using Inuit guides has been a valuable source of income for Inuit communities since the 1980s. Sport hunting can bring $30,000 per bear into communities where employment opportunities are scarce and cash income is uncertain. Permits for killing bears for subsis-tence are issued on a "raffle system," whereas sport hunting permits are granted to outfitters on a limited basis. Sport hunting permits that are not used are returned to the community for subsistence hunting. Inuit subsis-tence hunters will generally kill all the bears for which they have permits. The reliance on sport hunting of bears is often criticized by outsiders who wonder how this can be squared with the sacred nature of *nanuq.* Some communities do have serious concerns about this contradiction:

> [S]ome Clyde River Inuit believe that sport hunting, and indeed efforts at conservation-management, are antithetical to maintaining an appro-priate ethical relationship between people and polar bears. The concern here is the implied presumption that people can directly influence an-imal behavior, in this case by taking fewer animals than (according to Inuit belief) choose to make themselves available to worthy hunters. Secondarily, it was felt that the establishment of a quota – and indeed even a population census – would cause polar bears to think that

humans were bragging about their own prowess and were consequently being disrespectful to *nanuq*. Such inappropriate human be-
havior would cause the animals to move to areas where humans would
be respectful.[20]

Reports in the media paint a dire picture of the polar bear's survival:

The late formation of Arctic sea ice may be forcing some hungry and
desperate polar bears in northern Manitoba to resort to cannibalism.
Eight cases of mature male polar bears eating bear cubs have been reported this year among the animals around Churchill, according to scientists. Four cases were reported to Manitoba Conservation and four
to Environment Canada. Some tourists on a tundra buggy tour of the
Churchill wildlife management area on Nov. 20 were shaken and
started crying after witnessing a male bear eating a cub, said John
Gunter, general manager for Frontiers North Adventures, an area tour
operator.

"A big male polar bear separated a young cub from its mother and
had its way with the cub," he said. "But the whole time, while that
mother polar bear watched and witnessed, and actually after the big
bears left, she still tried to take care of it. It was difficult for our guests
to witness and it was difficult for me to hear about and learn about. It
was a sombre day on the buggy that's for sure."

In recent years, Manitoba Conservation has received one to two
reports each year about bear cannibalism. Retired Environment Canada
biologist Ian Stirling, who has studied bears all over the arctic, said evidence suggests the cubs are being killed for food, not just so the male
can mate with the sow. The Hudson Bay sea ice, which the bears use
to get at the seals they need to fatten up for winter, isn't appearing until
weeks later than it used to, he said.

However, an Inuit leader in Rankin Inlet, Nunavut said the incidents
are non-events and that it's wrong to connect the bear's behaviour with
starvation.

"It makes the south – southern people – look so ignorant," said
Kivilliq Inuit Association president Jose Kusugak. "A male polar bear
eating a cub becomes a big story and they try to marry it with climate

change and so on, it becomes absurd when it's a normal occurrence," Kusugak said.

Kusugak admitted some communities are having polar bear problems because warmer than average temperatures means sea ice hasn't yet formed properly. But he disagrees that their numbers are dwindling or that polar bears are in other danger because of climate change.[21]

Inuit wildlife officers and hunters are reporting an increase of bears, including mothers with multiple cubs. This is a sign of a healthy bear population. Bears are moving into communities to the point of becoming a dangerous and expensive nuisance:

"They [hunters] are guaranteed to be seeing polar bears at camp," Ikummaq said. "This much we know now. Twenty years back, you went caribou hunting, there was never a time you saw a bear. But in the last six years, that's when polar bear–human encounters have occurred more constantly."

Increasing reports of damaged property caused by polar bears has the Nunavut environment department eyeing a program that would help hunters create bear-proofed cabins and food caches and reduce the number of encounters with humans. Though a spate of bear sightings in Arviat made headlines this past fall, Sarah Medill, a wildlife deterrence specialist with the environment department, said it's a problem throughout the territory. "Basically bears are coming into communities and they're getting access to meat and sealskins," Medill said. "When bears find food they tend to want to come back to food."

Bears in search of food have also been approaching hunters out on the land. And around Igloolik, they've been getting into meat caches near the community, Medill said. In addition to the safety risk posed by bears becoming more comfortable around humans, hunters also face economic losses. They've spent a lot of time and money hunting, making the loss of meat to bears frustrating. They also have to spend time and money fixing cabins ripped open by marauding bears.[22]

Some scientists insist that melting ice is causing bears to resort to town dumps and food caches to feed themselves. It may well be that late freeze-up and early breakup are causing bears to spend more time on land. Human communities with garbage sites, food caches, and wandering pets provide a convenient larder for scavenging bears. But this behaviour does not necessarily mean that bears are starving – rather that they are intelligent and opportunistic. This would seem to agree with Inuit observations of many fat, healthy bears. Bear "cannibalism," which caused such distress in Churchill, is actually a normal occurrence. Male bears will attack and kill cubs if given the opportunity, either to breed with the female or from hunger. Reports of male bears eating cubs occur every year. Mother bears know to stay well away from males, as I observed in Gjoa Haven.

The distress of polar bear researchers, conservationists, and tourists from the South may be partly an aesthetic or sentimental reaction that demonstrates a cultural disconnect with the reality of *nanuq*. Mothers and their cubs are incredibly photogenic, as past Coca-Cola commercials promising small amounts of money for polar bear research and protection demonstrate (the commercials with real bears, not the silly cartoon bears and penguins).[23] But the bears are not so beautiful raiding the town dump or threatening the local children. Bears as pests or menaces present a very different image from bears as magnificent symbols of a disappearing Arctic. Bears who persistently move into communities have to be shot. This is distressing for everyone but essential. They are simply too dangerous. There is no doubt that climate change is increasing contact between humans and polar bears, creating problems for both. But this does not necessarily translate into imminent extinction for bears.

International organizations are beginning to respond to complaints that the Inuit's own information about polar bear populations does not indicate that the numbers are declining. In addition the abolition of permits to import bear parts to the United States is causing economic hardship without doing anything positive for polar bears. Some bear populations may well be at risk from melting ice, particularly the group farthest south in western Hudson Bay near Churchill. Even this southern group may be more numerous than previously feared. Surveys done in 2012 indicate that there are many more bears travelling throughout the southern Hudson Bay region than was previously thought.[24] When food sources become scarce near Churchill these bears seem to be moving north to Arviat and Rankin Inlet, causing major problems for the local population of humans. Other polar bear populations are either stable or increasing according to data collected by the IUCN

Species Survival Commission's Polar Bear Specialist Group[25] (although the group is concerned that its own figures show the situation may be worsening). Further research on polar bears in Davis Strait indicates that the population has increased substantially over the past thirty-five years (probably as a result of a rebound from overhunting in earlier years and an abundance of ring seals in the area) and that the area has probably reached its saturation point of healthy bears (a little over 2,000).[26]

Part of the problem is a tendency to make generalizations about sea ice. Multiyear ice in the High Arctic is melting at an unprecedented rate. This means that winter ice in the High Arctic will tend to be thinner annual ice (ice that freezes over in the autumn and melts in the spring) rather than thicker multiyear ice that stays frozen all year. But thinner annual ice is precisely the type of ice that seals and polar bears like. So a reduction of multiyear ice and an increase in annual ice may actually improve both seal and polar bear numbers, at least in the short term. In addition bears are adaptable. If they are losing opportunities to hunt out on the ice, they will come onto land to find food – from stranded belugas to town garbage dumps.

Isuma Films released the documentary *Qapirangajuk: Inuit Knowledge and Climate Change* in October 2010.[27] One of the topics discussed in the film is the effect of climate change on polar bears. The elders reiterate their belief that polar bear numbers are not decreasing, although they say that the increase of sightings on land may indeed have to do with the lengthening of ice-free seasons in spring and fall. But they also condemn the practices of southern wildlife specialists who tranquillize and tag bears, saying this is harmful and potentially lethal. The collars placed around bears' necks with radio beacons to track them impede their ability to hunt on the ice. Inookie Uqigiuaqsi, an elder from Iqaluit famous for his prowess as a polar bear hunter in his youth, says bears have long necks for a reason – to get at seals through holes in the ice. He has seen bears starve to death because of the collars.[28] Martin Keavy writes,

> The observations made by elders in *Qapirangajuk* challenge scientists in a profound way ... [S]everal elders maintain that it is *the actions of the scientists themselves* that are endangering Arctic wildlife – and Inuit communities. As Nathaniel Kalluk of Resolute Bay observes, polar bears wearing radio collars cannot hunt effectively at seal breathing holes; Simon Idlout, also of Resolute Bay, mentions that the bears'

sensitive hearing has been damaged by the noise of scientists' helicopters. As the bears' ability to hunt is threatened – again, not by reduced sea ice, but by interference of this kind – they cause more and more problems for Inuit on the land and in their communities ... Jamesie Mike, an elder from Pangnirtung, noted that "bears that are tagged and handled act more aggressively." While scientists may believe they are providing data that will lead to policies that protect the "fragile" Arctic environment, Simon Idlout points out that they are in fact breaking a vital Inuit law about the mistreatment of wildlife. As Innusiq Nashalik of Pangnirtung observes, "[Bears] are constantly tampered with, by Southerners, who only know them by what they read and have never interacted with them. We know our wildlife intimately."[29]

Nevertheless, both Inuit and polar bear scientific specialists are concerned about the long-term impact of melting ice. Freeze-up is occurring later, and melting is starting earlier. As of early December 2010 the ice had still not formed on Frobisher Bay near Iqaluit, and during the spring the floe edge was unsafe as early as May. This is an unprecedented period of open water even for South Baffin Island. In the more southerly regions of the Arctic this change is definitely having an impact on the ability of bears to fatten up during the winter and spring in order to get through the summer. Stories and pictures of polar bear distress are mainly coming from the Churchill area of northern Manitoba. Churchill is also the area where non-Inuit people study and watch bears most closely and where tourists come to see bears. Farther north the picture is quite different. Elders indicate their faith in the intelligence of both bears and humans to adapt to climate change. It would be better if scientists, researchers, and Inuit worked together on conservation issues, taking into account human as well as wildlife concerns.

## Protecting the Animals

It is not only that Inuit knowledge about polar bear numbers and conditions is not always heard by well-meaning conservationists who are a long way from the Arctic; also at issue is the ease with which Inuit dependence on bears is ignored. Inuit have had to deal for years with southerners imposing wildlife management that directly impedes the ability of Inuit to manage their own land with their own knowledge. The hunting of muskox was restricted in the early part of the twentieth century to prevent Inughuit from crossing Smith Sound in order to hunt on Ellesmere Island. As a result Inuit who were relocated to Grise Fiord and Resolute Bay were not permitted to kill muskoxen for food. Restrictions on hunting caribou also impeded their ability to feed themselves, but this did not prevent the severe reduction of caribou numbers that led to starvation on the Barren Grounds in the 1950s. Inuit were encouraged by the Hudson's Bay Company and the Government of Canada to set up fox fur traps, causing them to abandon their old hunting camps and to lose their traditional skills. When the fox fur industry collapsed after 1930 because of economic problems to the south, Inuit went hungry. Changes in fur fashions, including the latest anti-fur crusades, do nothing to protect animal populations while causing severe distress to humans. The ongoing battle over sealskin exports is another example.

I do not wish to defend the annual seal hunt on the Atlantic east coast. The rights and wrongs of that issue are well known and have been argued extensively elsewhere. However, as a consequence of that debate, the European Union Parliament decided in May 2009 to ban sealskin products being imported into Europe. For Inuit, the ban is a serious problem. The ban contains a partial exemption for Inuit hunters – but this distinction is not always clear to purchasers of seal products or to anti-sealing activists in Europe or elsewhere. The ban also tends to lump Inuit hunting in with activities that are completely foreign to their culture. The EU ban of 2009 states,

> [F]ollowing an agreement reached with the European Parliament in first reading, the Council adopted a Regulation setting restrictions for the placing on the market of seal products. The Danish, Romanian and Austrian delegations abstained.
>
> More specifically, the regulation permits the placing on the market of seal products only where the seal products result from hunts traditionally conducted by Inuit and other indigenous communities and contribute to their subsistence. This provision applies solely to indigenous peoples in Inuit areas in Alaska, Canada, Greenland and Russia. These conditions shall apply at the time or point of import for imported products.[30]

For most Inuit, the *nattiq* (ring seal) is the foundation of life. The seal provides meat, oil for lamps, bone, skin for making twine and thread, and seal fur for clothing. Every part of the animal is used. In addition, the export of sealskins and the making of clothing from sealskin for sale or export are important to the Inuit economy. Aaju Peter, a graduate of the Akitsiraq Law School, is also a prominent fashion designer in sealskin. Her clothing is internationally recognized for its beautiful combination of the traditional and the modern. She originally comes from Greenland, although she has lived in Canada for many years. She has become a strong and articulate advocate for seal products, the Inuit use of sealskins, and the culture of the Arctic (for which she was made a member of the Order of Canada in 2012):

> My ancestors' country is very, very big. It's an amazing place and we're proud of it. All the Inuit in the Arctic are related – the Greenland Inuit, the Canadian, the American and the Siberian. We all speak the same language – Inuktitut – and we have the same principles of law that apply to nature, to wildlife and to people, so you see how for hundreds of years we've coexisted in the Arctic. Greenlanders come and hunt polar bears – they're not our polar bears, they're just in our region and other Inuit go and hunt and fish in other areas even though they are called Danish territory or Canadian territory. Those territories came long after we had established our relationships.
>
> In terms of sustainability and our resources, we share the animals with other regions and other people. In fact it is an obligation that when an animal gives itself to you, you have to share it. In our culture we believe that if you don't honour the animals by sharing, then they will go somewhere else. For our own sake we don't fight about the region or the animals – we always try to come to a consensus.
>
> ... The European ban on the import of seals will have a devastating effect on our communities. Families can get $30 to $50 for a seal skin to buy food or bullets for hunting. That money makes a lot of difference to Inuit families in remote communities because buying food is expensive – four litres of milk for the children costs $12 to $15 because it has to be flown in or brought by ship. It's very sad to see the ban and it will have a real impact on our way of life.
>
> The most sustainable resource we have in Nunavut is our people.

The Arctic is a vast, vast territory and there are a lot of opportunities in minerals etc., but our wealth is the children.

I have a responsibility for my children and my grandchildren so that they can live in harmony and enjoy the incredibly vast territory that we have. We really have to remind ourselves how blessed we are to live in the Arctic. If the world were to think about the Arctic in a traditional fashion where we will respect nature, the animals and the people that live there, it would be very powerful.[31]

Pictures of former governor general Michaëlle Jean eating raw seal and cutting seal meat with the traditional *ulu* ("woman's knife") were strongly criticized when they were publicized.[32]

To urban dwellers in North America or Europe, who are used to finding food nicely wrapped in plastic at the local supermarket, a traditional kill for food is a disturbing sight. There is blood on the snow. The skin is carefully peeled away from the carcass and the guts are spilled, displaying ribs and spine. A living, breathing creature is dead. From an Inuit perspective, the animal has given itself up to be eaten. Its soul will live on, and the animal will be transformed again and again and again from one living creature to another. Life is interconnected – the hunter (whether human or polar bear) and the hunted (whether seal, polar bear, or sometimes human) are in a relationship essential to the survival of each. The animal's death is not cruel or inhumane – it is a gift.

We have lost touch with our ancestors who hunted and gathered for subsistence. We no longer trust the stories and myths from our own ancient past, dismissing them as "fairy tales" fit only for children. Indigenous peoples are frequently treated as if they themselves were children. The anti-sealing campaigners seem to be mesmerized and horrified by what to them looks like a remnant of our barbaric past, when killing and eating meat were essential for survival. But what we forget is how much we have lost by leaving this past behind, and what a cost we have all paid. Hunters who live off the land know that if animals are not treated with respect, they will disappear. The lessons a hunter learns are matters not only of skill but also of character and spiritual integrity. If a hunter is not patient, humble, and generous, he and his family will starve. The animals we eat also have souls, as do all living things. I am always mystified that so much attention is paid to seal or polar

9.4 Lucien Ukaliannuk, Sandra Omik, and Symatuk "Sam" Itorcheak (from left to right) about to go sailing in Victoria, British Columbia. Lucien and Sam have both since passed away.

bear hunting but so little to the factory farms and slaughter houses where our beef, chicken, mutton, and pork come from. Inuit who are close to the land and sea for their immediate survival recognize the connections between all living things. Urban dwellers, like myself, do not have this daily reminder that our lives depend on what Earth gives us. Traditional hunters such as Inuit are taught conservation and environmental integrity as an essential part of their upbringing. The rest of us, however well intentioned our environmental concerns and reaction to the killing of animals might be, no longer have this connection.

For many people living in southern Canada, the United States, or Europe, the important question about climate change seems to be "Is the Arctic safe for polar bears?" The lonely bear portrayed on the cover of this book conveys this sense of unease. But the question of whether the Arctic is still safe for Inuit seems to get less attention. It is not that polar bears or seals are not important – they are. Although changes in climate do not seem to be causing a reduction in numbers of either bears or seals at the moment, long-term warming of the Arctic will inevitably lead to the need for bears, seals, and humans to adapt. Other species, such as walrus, may well be in greater danger. Polar bears and humans are known for their intelligence and adaptability. But there is every reason to fear that the Arctic ecosystem as a whole is being profoundly altered by climate change. Polar bears, seals, walrus, whales, fish, and humans all exist in an interconnected ecosystem where what is unsafe for one species will inevitably impact everyone and everything else. If the Arctic is not safe for Inuit, it is not safe for seals or polar bears either. Nor is it safe for us.

# Tusaqtittijiit: Messengers

I didn't know much about the Inuit culture. My childhood home
was filled with artefacts that I took for granted and did not
inquire about. I didn't know the first thing about igloos or sled dogs,
hunting or sealing, carving or throat singing.

Heidi Langille[1]

Climate change, sovereignty, and human rights in the Arctic are each part
of the continuing story of ice, sea, and land – and of the life, including human
life, they support. Seals, polar bears, walrus, other marine animals, and
humans have lived on the sea ice in the Arctic for thousands of years. The
northern hemisphere used to be dominated by great sheets of ice 15,000
years ago, and their shadow still lies on the land. Lakes, mountains, and
valleys were scoured by the ice, and giant deposits of rock and earth were
left by the retreating glaciers. The land is still slowly rising from the weight
of the ice as it melts. The glaciers of North America, Europe, and Asia are
the remnants of those great ice sheets. Greenland is a shrinking orphan left
over from the last cycle of ice.

Ice can speak – it crackles and booms as icebergs break off from glaciers.
Falling ice tinkles like glass, and little bergy bits thump up against the hull
of your boat as you move slowly through a slush of icy sea. The churning
noise of crumbling ice sounds like a giant washing machine as a ship moves
through seas of broken pack ice.

Ice moves. Glaciers creep down great valleys through mountains of ice.
Nowadays that creep has become a sprint. Icebergs sail serenely through
Davis Strait down to the North Atlantic, where they can wreak havoc on

10.1  Ice in Ilulissat Harbour, Greenland

shipping, offshore oil rigs, coastal communities, and possibly even the Gulf Stream. The *Titanic* was sunk by an iceberg that originally came from one of Greenland's glaciers.

Every year in Pond Inlet an iceberg gets stuck in the sea ice during freeze-up. It provides a ready source of fresh water for the community all winter. Tea made from glacier ice has a slightly minty taste that brings out the flavour of the tea. Sea ice starts out as salt water, but the freezing gradually leaches the salt from the ice so that it becomes fresh. Water melted on the surface of sea ice is often drinkable. Ice is not always white. The minerals in the ice and the refraction of light through the translucent surface creates a delicate range of colour from deep blue-green to pale aqua. Both glacier ice and icebergs can be black with dirt, and there are occasions when ice can turn blood red, although I have never seen this.

Ice is dangerous. Glaciers can suddenly send a mountain of ice into the water, and icebergs can roll over without warning. Both can kill. Travelling on ice always means ensuring it is thick enough to support weight – a plunge into the cold Arctic Ocean means hypothermia and death within minutes. Cracks can appear suddenly, and pans of ice can separate from the pack,

10.2 Iceberg stained with black carbon, or soot.

leaving anyone on them stranded. Involuntary travellers can drift for days before being found.

Inuit depend on their knowledge of the ice to determine when it is thick enough to travel on and hunt. But the ice also has to be thin enough for seal holes. Hunters travel long distances to find an *allu* (seal's breathing hole). There a hunter will stand bent over, sometimes for many hours, waiting until a seal finally presents itself for a breath of air. The hunter will have placed a single white feather over the tiny hole. When the seal breathes out, the feather flutters. Then the hunter must be quick with either his rifle or his spear, hooking the animal with his *kakivak* (barbed harpoon head) and line before the animal sinks beneath the ice. Sea ice is the primary habitat of polar bears, which also rely on the seals to survive. They too will crouch over *alluit* for hours waiting for an unlucky seal forced to surface in order to breathe. Humans hunt polar bears for their meat and skin – but polar bears will hunt humans if given the opportunity. Each must treat the other with respect.

In November 2009 elder Jimmy Nakoolak and teenager Jupi Angoo-tealuk set off from the community of Coral Harbour in northern Hudson Bay to hunt for polar bear. They did not take a dog team; instead they pulled their *qamutik* (dogsled) with a snowmobile. Inuit do not use dog teams much anymore because of the slaughter of the dogs in the 1950s and 1960s. The hunters' snowmobile broke down. They tried to walk back to land. The elder insisted that Angootealuk carry his rifle and ammunition. Then they tested the ice. It should have been safe but it wasn't. The ice cracked and then cracked again, separating the two men. Nakoolak managed to make it back to shore, but Angootealuk was left stranded on an ice floe that was drifting out into Hudson Bay. He was rescued by a Royal Canadian Air Force search crew a few days later, frostbitten and hungry but otherwise fine. However, if he had not had his rifle, it would have been a different story. He was joined on the ice floe by a mother bear and two cubs who were very curious about this strange-looking seal and were definitely looking for a meal. Angootealuk had to shoot and kill the mother, stranding the two cubs, which would not leave their mother's body. If the two hunters had succeeded in bringing a bear back to the community, its meat and fur would have been shared with everyone. Likewise, if the two men had been using dogs rather than a snowmobile, they may well have been in less trouble. Dog teams don't break down. Dogs are also unafraid of bears and will attack or at least distract them. But the ice was also much thinner than it should have been in November. Inuit in Coral Harbour are convinced this anomaly was a result of climate change. This dramatic story made headlines around the world. As much concern was expressed for the polar bear cubs as for young Angootealuk, who returned to Coral Harbour a community hero.[2] Inuit, polar bears, seals, dogs, and all the other species in the Arctic environment have long lived a symbiotic existence in which neither humans nor animals are superior. All souls are equal and all must be respected.

10.3  Greenlandic *qimmiq* (husky) with puppies, Ilulissat, Greenland

But not all young Inuit live in the Arctic, and not all have the skills taught by the elders. There are urban communities of Inuit in Ottawa, Montreal, Edmonton, and Winnipeg. Families have been migrating to the cities from all over the Arctic from at least the 1950s, and they are still very mobile. Kiviaq, formerly known as Peter Ward, was one of these. Some Inuit were sent to Ottawa during the 1960s in an experimental attempt to put children into white foster homes and schools. Some never returned. Other children are from mixed-heritage families and are subject to their parents' mobility from the North to the South. Two of the students at the Akitsiraq Law School were raised in Ottawa and returned to the North only when Nunavut was created in 1999. One succeeded in regaining much of her language and culture, but the other did not. Several of the Akitsiraq graduates have since migrated south again but will likely return. Wherever they are, they maintain close ties with Nunavut, their families, and friends.

The community in Ottawa is numbered at around 1,000 people, although an exact figure is hard to come by.[3] Inuit have established local organizations that cater to the needs of their community, such as the Inuit Head Start program and the Tungasuvvingat Inuit Community Centre. Many Inuit in Ottawa also participate in political activities through Inuit Tapiriit Kanatami, Nunavut Tunngavik Incorporated, and other national Inuit organizations that maintain offices there. Some Inuit travel back and forth between Ottawa and Nunavut on a regular basis. It is a three-hour flight from Ottawa to Iqaluit, and planes fly back and forth two or three times a day. Many Inuit are die-hard hockey fans and will (if they can) travel to Toronto or Montreal to watch their favourite teams. When Jordin Tootoo, the only Inuk to play in the National Hockey League, had his first game with the Nashville Predators, the plane south was full of hockey fans on their way to Tennessee!

Many Inuit in urban communities in southern Canada have the same problems as other urban Aboriginals – a feeling of alienation, dislocation, poor education, poor job skills, and an experience of growing up in a ghettoized community that is not really part of the city or "back home." But this situation is changing. Inuit in Ottawa are reintroducing their language and culture, not necessarily as Inuit on the land but as an urbanized community that is nevertheless truly Inuit. To be a "real Inuk" does not necessarily mean hunting and fishing "on the land," although many Inuit are also relearning these skills during their trips north. In addition to learning (or relearning) Inuktitut, Inuit are also developing their cultural identity through drum dancing, throat singing, and other truly Inuit activities. The federal government was forced to recognize "Eskimos," or Inuit, as part of federal responsibility under section 91 (24) of the Canadian Constitution after the Supreme Court held in 1939 that they must receive the same attention as "Indians and lands reserved for Indians."[4] But urban Inuit are still given much less attention, something Edmonton's Kiviaq and others are trying to rectify.

Although this book focuses on Inuit of Nunavut and has less to say about Inuvialuit of the Northwest Territories, Nunavimmiut of Nunavik (northern Quebec), and Inuit of Nunatsiavut in Labrador, it is also important to remember that many Inuit travel between these regions and the South whenever their financial situation, employment, or education permits. I can still remember the excitement of flying south with Inuit whose first stop was always "the Mall"! Communities of Inuit are reconnecting with different regions throughout Canada and the Arctic as a whole, regaining a sense of pan-Inuit identity. Geographical boundaries between provinces, territories, and nation-states are beginning to open up again. Inuit have always been great travellers and tellers of tales, as this book has tried to show, and this distinctive trait remains strong. All of the Arctic where Inuit live is known as Nunaat ("many lands"), recognizing the diversity of Inuit communities and their territories as well as the connections between them.

There is no doubt that climate change is dramatically altering the Arctic. Temperatures are rising faster there than anywhere else on Earth. The long-term prospects for all life are uncertain. Melting ice is a fundamental ecological problem that is affecting the entire planet. The problem did not originate in the Arctic, although solutions might be found there if we are willing to listen to what Inuit have to say. The United Nations Intergovernmental Panel on Climate Change (IPCC) can be criticized for being too conservative, and for the long time between reports, but generally the vast majority of scientists agree that it gets the science right. However, the IPCC also does not cover all the potential problems facing the Arctic, such as an increase in the thaw of permafrost, which would cause major infrastructure headaches for northerners and the release of massive quantities of methane. In addition the IPCC does not address all the possible repercussions of melting ice in Greenland and Antarctica.[5] Humans are intelligent and resourceful – like polar bears, we will survive. But the transformations that are occurring now are causing real stress to all life in the Arctic, and are already starting to cause problems planet-wide.

In some ways life in the Arctic is easier than it was for Inuit in the past, but in other ways it is becoming more dangerous. The ice is thinning, and every year hunters are lost while trying to provide for their families and communities. The elders' knowledge is becoming less and less reliable, leading to a diminishment of respect. Meanwhile many young Inuit are simply lost, neither able to cope with the modern ways of the South that have now infiltrated their world nor any longer comfortable with the traditional ways of the past.

During my last winter in Iqaluit I attended two funerals. Both were for young Inuit men, one to suicide and the other to a terrible snowmobile accident. Both men were employed and both had young families. I did not know the young men myself, but I did know their parents and was especially close to the father of the young suicide victim. Both funeral services were wrenching. A young priest, who had obviously performed many of these services before, tried to speak to the guilt of the family of the young suicide victim by asking for their forgiveness on his behalf. The words were simple and stark. I remember driving in the procession from the church to the graveyard. It was a pale grey day in late January when sky, snow, and ice were a seamless milky white. A blustery wind was kicking up snow. It was cold. A backhoe was parked near the shoreline where the grave had been scraped out of the frozen ground and where the wooden coffin would later be covered by icy dirt and snow. I was acutely conscious of how cold and lonely that grave looked against the backdrop of the great white frozen bay behind it. The sense of loss and the grief were painful for me and unimaginably difficult for the families. I never again went down to the graveyard to look at the northern lights.

Maps, postage stamps, supply ships, aircraft, churches, police stations, gold mines, exploratory oil and gas wells, satellite television, CBC North, and now the Internet mark the physical and communication frontiers of *qallunaat* culture in the Arctic. They are the markers of a colonial invasion that is still going on. The Canadian search for sovereign legitimacy in an international setting is fixated on ice-choked passages as if they were navigable waterways, while all the time we are surrounded by a bubble of civilization whose price is a world that is literally melting out from under us. In such a world are the old boundaries even relevant? The irony is that as the ice melts and the waters become navigable, new boundaries are being aggressively championed by nation-states and the supporters of resource extraction, while at the same time old colonial barriers binding Inuit to one nation or community are disappearing. As Aaju Peter says, "We are one people divided by imaginary borders. Why am I telling you all this? Because we're seeing a lot of interest in the Arctic. There is a lot of talk about resources and international law and so on. These things are foreign to us. Even climate change is foreign to us. I say to myself, well this is our backyard. We live here and have lived here for a long time. We have our own laws relating to nature and relating to how to treat other people."[6]

10.4 Iqaluit graveyard

Images of the Canadian Arctic are central to Canada's vision of itself as the "True North strong and free." What could be more iconically Canadian than an *inuksuk*? The 2010 Vancouver Olympic Committee certainly thought so. They chose the Inuit symbol despite the fact that the West Coast of Canada is home to Aboriginal peoples with many talented artists and beautiful traditional designs. The *inuksuk* is prominently displayed on the Nunavut territorial flag. Our national motto is also the subject of a low-key debate – "From Sea to Shining Sea" should be changed to "From Sea to Sea to Sea" in recognition that we are a country surrounded by three oceans, not just two. Canada has the longest coastline of any nation on the planet and by far the longest stretch of that coastline is in the Arctic.

*Inuksuit* are the physical markers of the land in Inuit law – not as fence posts marking proprietary claims but as guideposts and messengers. The word *inuksuk* means "like a person." Children are taught that it is wrong to destroy an *inuksuk*, as it too has an *inua* (soul), which must be respected. There are thousands of them strung across the tundra. They can be guides to places of good fishing or hunting, or warnings that the trail ahead leads to a barren land where there is no food. They were never meant as boundary markers. The Inuit, although living and travelling in wide stretches of territory, did not have firm frontiers between one nation and another. They did not need them.

The Arctic Circle traverses at least six nation-state boundaries. What do these boundaries mean to Inuit travelling between Greenland and Nunavut? A demand for a passport they never thought to carry, an argument over "our land" and what it means, and then an embarrassed official who was willing to bend the rules – common sense prevailing over bureaucratic rigidity? Now that climate change is opening up the ice to longer and less stable periods of melting, both Inuit and non-Inuit need to reassess their commitment to the North and how they will relate to each other and the land. Part of this adjustment has to do with how we think about Earth's environment. Climate change is redrawing the boundaries of what both Inuit and non-Inuit have learned to expect from our world. Because Inuit are closer to their environment than most of us are to ours, and because the Arctic is warming faster than anywhere else on Earth, they are seeing the changes happen more quickly and are more aware of what is happening. They are truly *silaup aalaruqpalianigata tusaqtittijiit* – "witnesses and messengers of climate change."

In Inuktitut the word for "the environment" is *sila*, which can also be a synonym for "weather." Climate change, or *silaup aulaninga* ("our weather is changing"), requires us to think beyond the more limited meaning of *sila*. *Silarjuaq* means "the skies," "the universe," or "the powerful spirit of the air." We need to start moving toward an understanding of *silarjuaq* – the big picture. To do so, we need to be aware of the other meaning of *sila*, "intelligence," or *silatuniq*, "wisdom." In his book *Climate, Culture, Change*, Timothy Leduc quotes Jaypeetee Arnakak:

I truly believe in this *Sila* and the means with which Inuit shamanism accessed its depths and breadth through suffering and fasting. It is through suffering that the phenomenal self lets go and equanimity is achieved, clarity is achieved. Nature is indifferent; it cares nothing for our limited conceptions of "good" and "bad," "evil" and "beneficence." This insight can either kill us or liberate within us unbounded creativity.[7]

Leduc goes onto discuss what this might mean for Inuit as well as non-Inuit:

> Though the shaman's *Silatuniq* allows the community to be brought into a *Sila* relationship that "is fundamentally an ethical one, not economic," Arnakak clarifies that the difficulty is that this *Silatuniq* may contradict dominant cultural assumptions for everyday living. Beyond the narrowing dynamics of cultural assumptions, colonial pressures, and expanding climate impacts, this dialogue suggests a fourth dynamic is limiting the breadth of interdisciplinary and intercultural research on *Sila*'s northern warming: the West's rational rejection of shamanic or spiritual wisdom for socially contextualizing knowledge.[8]

Scientific knowledge needs to be open to a reality beyond the material – something most modern scientists are absolutely unwilling to do. But we also need to avoid both a rejection of Inuit wisdom and a tendency to romanticize what this might be. *Silatuniq* is not some New Age vision. It is very ancient – the second part of the word, *tuniq*, is also the name for a person from the pre-Inuit Dorset culture, an ancient person living on the land before Inuit arrived in their territory. *Silatuniq* may well be the wisdom of the ancient people – the Tuniit – who lived here long before the Thule culture or Europeans arrived.

People living in Arctic Siberia from a time dating back to the last glacial period had to learn how to interrelate and interact with *sila*. Their descendants – including Inuit – carry this knowledge with them in their travels across the Arctic. This knowledge requires close observation and intelligent assessment of everything around them – of *sila*, or the environment. "The etymological explanation for the correlation of these two concepts may be more complex than the conclusion that wisdom is predicated on a knowledge of one's environment, but practically speaking, this seems to be the case."[9] This knowledge, based on close observation, has always had to be very practical, hard-headed, and adaptable. There is little room for error. A polar bear doesn't care if you're an experienced Inuit hunter, a trophy seeker from Texas, an amiable tourist from Vancouver, a dedicated environmentalist, a scientific researcher, or a child playing near the town dump. To him you are one of three things: a source of curiosity, a threat, or prey.

But understanding polar bears is not just about practical knowledge or observation. It also requires more – *silatuniq* – the wisdom that brings one closer to *silarjuaq* both as universe and as spirit. The polar bear is also *nanuq* and has a spiritual as well as a biological or cultural significance. Great shamans could transform themselves into bears, and bears used to be able to become human. The most fearsome spirits of the North often take the shape of bears. This sense of spiritual as well as material connection is fundamentally different from environmental knowledge or commercial images of polar bears. Inuit do not believe in these traditions and stories as mythology, but as messengers of another reality that needs to be respected and even feared. They are part of the "great loneliness," where only suffering can teach, destroy, or liberate.[10]

Inuit Qaujimajatuqangit is not just about cultural traditions or ecological knowledge. It is "the knowledge that the elders have always known and will continue to know." This knowledge or wisdom should not be confined to Inuit or other Indigenous peoples. It directly impacts the lives of those of us in urban environments, even though it may be long forgotten. What I gathered as the basic teaching of this knowledge is that there is no "human" outside of "nature." Humility and cooperation are as much about relationships with animals, plants, the land, the ice, the weather, the universe – *sila* – as they are about consensus decision making or alternative dispute resolution, something young Inuit are also prone to forget. Both civilization and wilderness are human constructs that artificially divide us from the knowledge and wisdom of our ancient past and of our immediate and long-term future on this planet.

The story of Kiviuq is the great odyssey of the North. Elders across the Arctic are retelling this story, and I hope southern readers will come to know it. The story ends with a strange journey south to the land of the *qallunaat*. Kiviuq the shaman travels through a "hole in the world" to find his goose wife, who has flown south with their children, as is the nature of geese:

> Some say Kiviuq and his wife were reunited, others that she was unable to return to her human body. Some say she came out to greet him but she had forgotten a small amulet and the words to the song that she had to sing in order to transform back into a human. And now it was too late. She stayed in the form of a goose, and when the time came, she flew north again with her children.

Kiviuq is now stuck in the warm southern lands ... When John

[Houston] asked Niviuvak Marqniq whether Kiviuq is still alive, she replied, "He must be. If he were not, I would have heard about it."

... Samson Quinangnaq says ... that his face had turned to stone. His spirit is alive on earth, says Madeleine Ivalu, but he has more and more difficulty moving. His body is calcified and his joints stiff. He moves around a bit in the warm days of summer but is almost motionless in the cold days of winter. He is shy about coming out where people can see him, since his face is covered in lichens. Ollie Ittinnuar says he is alive, always changing from one animal to another. When asked if he would ever return north, Niviuvak Marqniq says he would not. Why? "It's too cold for him here!"

Samson Quinangnaq says that when Kiviuq dies there will be no more air to breathe and life on earth will end. But for now, he is still alive and has much to teach us about how to live a good life on this earth.[11]

Kiviuq's lessons are not only about being kind to children, respecting animals, and being wary of evil spirits. They are also about "getting things right the first time"[12] because "there are no second chances in the Arctic."[13] This imperative requires respecting the knowledge of others and moving within realities that go beyond the material or physical. It means being faithful to what Earth teaches.

Most Canadians still live in a thin belt hugging the US-Canada border. If asked where the geographical centre of the country is most Canadians would probably say Winnipeg, Manitoba. It is in fact Baker Lake in the Territory of Nunavut far to the north of most people's experience. The rapid process of colonization of Canada's land and sea north of the 60th parallel has gone almost completely unnoticed by most Canadian citizens until very recently. The creation of the Territory of Nunavut in 1999 triggered some attention, but few Canadians have ever travelled more than a few hundred miles away from the agricultural, industrial, urban thread connecting us to our American neighbours. Nunavut and the Arctic still remain remote and exotic locations on the periphery of Canadian political, economic, and cultural agendas, even as the Canadian government goes through another fit of interest, waking up from years of absence of mind. The race to establish Canadian sovereignty in the Arctic under international law has largely lain in the hands of ambitious Arctic "experts," mapmakers, scientific researchers, and government officials following in the trail of missionaries, Hudson's Bay Company employees, the Royal Canadian Mounted Police, and European explorers searching for a sea passage from one known world to another. Inuit need to be heard.

Any history of the Canadian Arctic must take seriously the interaction between climate, land, sea, wildlife, and people – both Indigenous and non-Indigenous. Abstract concepts of sovereignty at both the national and international levels and worries about the changing Arctic climate are shaped by the realities of human stories as they are lived in geographic space over long periods of time. Recognizing the terrestrial, natural, human, and spiritual realities of sovereignty in the Arctic might help us to avoid making unrealistic demands on those realities.

The strongest claim Canada can make to sovereignty over the Arctic is through "effective occupation." Achieving this objective not only requires an increased military presence, greater monitoring of maritime travel through the Arctic Archipelago, or a much enhanced search and rescue capacity (although the latter is surely needed). Modern state sovereignty, incorporating the international law of human rights, is also about building healthy communities of people living in a healthy environment. As Inuit Tapiriit Kanatami, Nunavut Tunngavik Incorporated, the Nunavut government, the Inuit Circumpolar Council, and many other organizations and individuals have said over and over again, *sovereignty begins at home; it starts with healthy people in healthy communities.*

During my time in Iqaluit, trying to do my job as the northern director of Akitsiraq, I was constantly impressed by the ability of Inuit to respond to and meet incredible challenges. Law school is difficult for anyone, but for these students it came on top of lifetimes of hurdles to overcome. At times very difficult and painful choices had to be made. But most of those who started the program finished it despite many initial doubts expressed by head-shaking commentators in both the North and the South. Graduation day on 21 June 2005 was a proud day for the whole extended family that is Nunavut.

Successes on an individual level are important, but they do not solve systemic problems that have been building for at least the past sixty years. Although the creation of Nunavut was a triumph for Inuit negotiators, it has not ended colonialism in the North. In some ways it has made it clearer. The federal government has been dilatory to the point of gross negligence in failing to address the financial costs of providing for needed services, as it is required to do under the *Nunavut Land Claims Agreement* of 1993.[14]

To those of us from the South, the Arctic appears remote and formidable, but this impression is only a matter of point of view. All global systems – climatic, geographic, biological, and human – necessarily interact. Whether or not we agree with James Lovelock's theory that Earth – Gaia – is a single living entity, there is no doubt that the planet works as a whole.[15] For at least the past 10,000 years we have enjoyed an environment where humans have rapidly evolved to inhabit nearly every mile of Earth's surface and now may well control its ultimate destiny. We modern citizens of the industrialized world have been taught to see ourselves as apart from and superior to this environment, but it is becoming increasingly obvious that we are mistaken. We live in urban centres, taking for granted the development opportunities and conveniences this lifestyle supports (at least for some), but we seem oblivious to the obvious dramatic alterations in the environment that this urban industrialized society has created. We are like fish in water – we don't see where we are because it is all around us. Choosing to leave my own urban, middle-class bubble and live in the Arctic for a while helped me to question and partly shake off these assumptions. But even though we may or may not question our own approaches to nature, our mode of life is altering Earth in such an extravagant way that it is a mystery why so many of us seem not to notice. Urban life seems normal to most of us – but it is in fact a recent and highly artificial addition to Earth's ecosystem. As J.B. MacKinnon says of a day spent observing an abundance of life at a pond near his home in Vancouver,

> The crisis in the natural world is one of awareness as much as any other cause. As a global majority has moved into cities, a feedback loop is increasingly clear. In the city, we tend not to pay attention to nature; for most of us, familiarity with corporate logos and celebrity news really is of more practical day-to-day use than a knowledge of local birds and edible wild plants … A friend pointed out that the scene I witnessed at my local pond might have been more likely to attract people's interest on the internet. I found a number of online videos of eagles hunting ducks, including one with more than 150,000 views, along with a photo series featuring a passerby who fails to notice even

a high-speed mid-air collision between two eagles, one of which crashes into the water.[16]

However, nature is still here and far closer to both urban and rural worlds than we usually imagine. It is possible to hear coyotes yipping in an urban park not far from where I live in Metro Vancouver, and black bears routinely invade garbage bins in city suburbs. Cougar and deer sometimes wander into city centres around the province of British Columbia, and other entrepreneurial creatures like raccoons and skunks prey on the pests of urban living. They have learned to adapt to us in ways we often find annoying and disconcerting. Every urban centre around the world has similar nonhuman residents. In the Arctic polar bears are frequent visitors to the garbage dumps of small communities, and wolves have been known to patrol the outskirts of Iqaluit. Gangs of ravens stake out their territory in every community in the North. Humans cannot ignore or escape the natural world anywhere on Earth. In the Arctic this becomes much more obvious as the earth, sky, ice, and water create a sense of enormity and isolation. When travelling around lonely sites in the High Arctic, it is easy to fall into a reflective mood of awe. But it is also necessary to keep a sharp lookout for bears. To them we are simply large seals dressed in Gore -Tex.

Nunavut is a massive pyramid of geography on the modern map of Canada, representing one-fifth of Canada's overall land mass and the greatest stretch of its coastline. But it is important to remember that the people of Nunavut formed a culturally cohesive community in the Arctic long before any European or Canadian presence was felt. This cohesiveness is not homogenous. Although Inuit speak a common language and share a common culture, there are substantial regional differences. The Inuit of the eastern Arctic (in what are now Nunavut, Nunavik, and Nunatsiavut) may be "Canadian" in a legal sense, but they may or may not be "Canadian" in any sociological or cultural sense. Legal concepts of sovereignty cannot be separated from culture, language, social interaction, and human history. In turn, cultural, linguistic, and social realities are profoundly shaped by the historical development of sovereignty in a legal sense. Although many older Inuit may feel little connection to Canada as their country of citizenship, their children and grandchildren do. This younger generation of Inuit may be much more aware of the disconnection between their culture and the dominant political and economic structures in which they must now survive.

Part of Nunavummiut identity consists of a rejection of Canadian values (the refusal to openly allow political parties to operate in the Legislative Assembly, for example) and at the same time an acceptance of Canadian sovereignty over "our land." In particular many Inuit have served in Canada's military or police forces, assisting in the establishment of Canadian sovereignty over Inuit land and sea. Through this work some have also gained a profound sense of their role as Canadians as well as Inuit in the shaping of the modern North. Nunavut represents both the historical continuity of an ancient geographic and cultural space, in spite of an alien legal concept such as sovereignty, and the vulnerability of this space to the effects of this concept. It also represents the way that Inuit culture and the Inuktitut language have changed, blurring the line between what is "traditional" and what is "modern." The Inuit of Nunavut are not quite the same as the Inuit of Alaska or Greenland, or even of the Northwest Territories, partly because of their historical connection with the region contained within the map of Nunavut. Nor are the people of Nunavut the same as their ancestors, although the continuity of culture can still be seen through the teachings of the elders. Unlike most Indigenous peoples in Canada, Inuit still have access to living libraries of knowledge from a time when the traditional Inuit way of life was lived "on the land." The mapping of Nunavut, crucial evidence of sovereignty's legitimate extent, also shapes the maintenance and transmission of cultural identity both in those regions that lie within the boundaries of the Nunavut land claim area (the Territory of Nunavut) and in those Inuit lands that lie outside those boundaries (as in the Canadian western Arctic or Greenland). But the common connection across these borders also remains.

My own journey involved learning at least as much from the Akitsiraq students and from friends in Nunavut as the students learned from their southern professors, including me. My stay there was in part a great adventure and partly a painful reassessment of my own way of life. It was not easy. But we don't learn from things that are easy. I did get back to Canada the long way round, although my work with the Law School did not turn out to be a good career move in the traditional sense. When I started writing this book seven years ago, I didn't really want it to be about me. But I have come to realize that the only way I can open the door a little to this amazing place and the people who live there is by letting others see it through my eyes, both in words and pictures.

My Arctic education was not a series of clear instructions on where the
boundaries of Inuit and non-Inuit relations lie. Those boundaries are per-
meable, just as all other boundaries in the North are. It is necessary to listen
and try to leave the bubble of southern expectations behind, as hard as that
is. This effort also means sometimes doing and saying the wrong thing, being
misunderstood, and not understanding. It requires an emotional and spiritual, as well as a physical and intellectual, journey. Canada and its Arctic
neighbours need to learn more about environmental stewardship from the
Inuit and other Indigenous peoples of the North. As Lucien Ukaliannuk and
other elders teach us, there can be no learning and no good life without listening and keeping an open mind and heart. The Inuit are willing to share
their knowledge, their stories, and their land – but they are not willing to
be ignored or passed over. We need to see the North as a place of guideposts
and messengers where souls, not boundaries, can lead us all into our collective future.

Beneath the debate over climate change, Inuit rights, and Canadian
sovereignty in the Arctic lies a rich and complex mosaic of geography and
history. Much of this intersection between space and time is laden with
passion, death, ignorance, and loss. It is also powerfully beautiful. There is
a natural phenomenon in the North similar to a desert mirage called the
Fata Morgana – a refraction of light that often makes distant objects loom
into view or small icebergs rear up like skyscrapers. Ships can seem to float
in the air or disappear without a trace. The hidden sun or moon may suddenly blossom just over the horizon and then disappear before rising again.
Nothing is as it seems.

Even when the Arctic light is not playing tricks the most barren landscape
can hide small miracles of persistent flowering beauty. The long dark of winter can slowly lighten into a flush of pink and lavender where before there
was only cold dark snow. Travelling to the floe edge on the spring ice means
moving and standing above an oceanic world of animals and plants as rich
as any tropical coral reef. For the adventurous traveller or searcher for
wilderness beauty, the Arctic is a place where belugas sing like canaries and
birds called thick-billed murres dive into the sea depths as easily as tiny
whales. For most people living in "the South," the Arctic is an exotic space
on the edge of our maps of the modern world. For Canadians of European
descent, both English and French, our belief in the conquest and control of
a vast hinterland has determined who we are as a culture and a people – as

10.5 Shooting into the sun, Bylot Island.

a sovereign state, if not as a unified nation. This in turn fuels the Canadian government's desire to establish secure claims of legal sovereignty over the Arctic up to and including the North Pole.

For the Inuit, this is their home.

# Appendices

# Inuit Circumpolar Council, A *Circumpolar Inuit Declaration on Sovereignty in the Arctic*

We, the Inuit of Inuit Nunaat, declare as follows:

1. Inuit and the Arctic

1.1 *Inuit live in the Arctic.* Inuit live in the vast, circumpolar region of land, sea and ice known as the Arctic. We depend on the marine and terrestrial plants and animals supported by the coastal zones of the Arctic Ocean, the tundra and the sea ice. The Arctic is our home.

1.2 *Inuit have been living in the Arctic from time immemorial.* From time immemorial, Inuit have been living in the Arctic. Our home in the circumpolar world, *Inuit Nunaat*, stretches from Greenland to Canada, Alaska and the coastal regions of Chukotka, Russia. Our use and occupation of Arctic lands and waters pre-dates recorded history. Our unique knowledge, experience of the Arctic, and language are the foundation of our way of life and culture.

1.3 *Inuit are a people.* Though Inuit live across a far-reaching circumpolar region, we are united as a single people. Our sense of unity is fostered and celebrated by the Inuit Circumpolar Council (ICC), which represents the Inuit of Denmark/Greenland, Canada, USA and Russia. As a people, we enjoy the rights of all peoples. These include the rights recognized in and by various international instruments and institutions, such as the *Charter of the United Nations*; the *International Covenant on Economic, Social and Cultural Rights*; the *International Covenant on Civil and Political Rights*; the *Vienna Declaration and Programme of Action*; the Human Rights Council; the Arctic Council; and the Organization of American States.

1.4    *Inuit are an indigenous people*. Inuit are an indigenous people with the rights and responsibilities of all indigenous peoples. These include the rights recognized in and by international legal and political instruments and bodies, such as the recommendations of the UN Permanent Forum on Indigenous Issues, the UN Expert Mechanism on the Rights of Indigenous Peoples, the 2007 UN *Declaration on the Rights of Indigenous Peoples (UNDRIP)*, and others.

Central to our rights as a people is the right to *self-determination*. It is our right to freely determine our political status, freely pursue our economic, social, cultural and linguistic development, and freely dispose of our natural wealth and resources. States are obligated to respect and promote the realization of our right to self-determination. (See, for example, the *International Covenant on Civil and Political Rights [ICCPR]*, Art. 1.)

Our rights as an indigenous people include the following rights recognized in the *United Nations Declaration on the Rights of Indigenous Peoples (UNDRIP)*, all of which are relevant to sovereignty and sovereign rights in the Arctic: the right to self-determination, to freely determine our political status and to freely pursue our economic, social and cultural, including linguistic, development (Art. 3); the right to internal autonomy or self-government (Art. 4); the right to recognition, observance and enforcement of treaties, agreements and other constructive arrangements concluded with states (Art. 37); the right to maintain and strengthen our distinct political, legal, economic, social and cultural institutions, while retaining the right to participate fully in the political, economic, social and cultural life of states (Art. 5); the right to participate in decision-making in matters which would affect our rights and to maintain and develop our own indigenous decision-making institutions (Art. 18); the right to own, use, develop and control our lands, territories and resources and the right to ensure that no project affecting our lands, territories or resources will proceed without our free and informed consent (Art. 25-32); the right to peace and security (Art. 7); and the right to conservation and protection of our environment (Art. 29).

1.5 *Inuit are an indigenous people of the Arctic.* Our status, rights and responsibilities as a people among the peoples of the world, and as an indigenous people, are exercised within the unique geographic, environmental, cultural and political context of the Arctic. This has been acknowledged in the eight-nation Arctic Council, which provides a direct, participatory role for Inuit through the permanent participant status accorded the Inuit Circumpolar Council (Art. 2).

1.6 *Inuit are citizens of Arctic states.* As citizens of Arctic states (Denmark, Canada, USA and Russia), we have the rights and responsibilities afforded all citizens under the constitutions, laws, policies and public sector programs of these states. These rights and responsibilities do not diminish the rights and responsibilities of Inuit as a people under international law.

1.7 *Inuit are indigenous citizens of Arctic states.* As an indigenous people within Arctic states, we have the rights and responsibilities afforded all indigenous peoples under the constitutions, laws, policies and public sector programs of these states. These rights and responsibilities do not diminish the rights and responsibilities of Inuit as a people under international law.

1.8 *Inuit are indigenous citizens of each of the major political subunits of Arctic states (states, provinces, territories and regions).* As an indigenous people within Arctic states, provinces, territories, regions or other political subunits, we have the rights and responsibilities afforded all indigenous peoples under the constitutions, laws, policies and public sector programs of these subunits. These rights and responsibilities do not diminish the rights and responsibilities of Inuit as a people under international law.

2.    The Evolving Nature of Sovereignty in the Arctic

2.1   "Sovereignty" is a term that has often been used to refer to the absolute and independent authority of a community or nation both internally and externally. Sovereignty is a contested concept, however, and does not have a fixed meaning. Old ideas of sovereignty are breaking down as different governance models, such as the European Union, evolve. Sovereignties overlap and are frequently divided within federations in creative ways to recognize the right of peoples. For Inuit living within the states of Russia, Canada, the USA and Denmark/ Greenland, issues of sovereignty and sovereign rights must be examined and assessed in the context of our long history of struggle to gain recognition and respect as an Arctic indigenous people having the right to exercise self-determination over our lives, territories, cultures and languages.

2.2   Recognition and respect for our right to self-determination is developing at varying paces and in various forms in the Arctic states in which we live. Following a referendum in November 2008, the areas of self-government in Greenland will expand greatly and, among other things, Greenlandic (Kalaallisut) will become Greenland's sole official language. In Canada, four land claims agreements are some of the key building blocks of Inuit rights; while there are conflicts over the implementation of these agreements, they remain of vital relevance to matters of self-determination and of sovereignty and sovereign rights. In Alaska, much work is needed to clarify and implement the rights recognized in the *Alaska Native Claims Settlement Act (ANCSA)* and the *Alaska National Interest Lands Conservation Act (ANILCA)*. In particular, subsistence hunting and self-government rights need to be fully respected and accommodated, and issues impeding their enjoyment and implementation need to be addressed and resolved. And in Chukotka, Russia, a very limited number of administrative processes have begun to secure recognition of Inuit rights. These developments will provide a foundation on which to construct future, creative governance arrangements tailored to diverse circumstances in states, regions and communities.

2.3 In exercising our right to self-determination in the circumpolar Arctic, we continue to develop innovative and creative jurisdictional arrangements that will appropriately balance our rights and responsibilities as an indigenous people, the rights and responsibilities we share with other peoples who live among us, and the rights and responsibilities of states. In seeking to exercise our rights in the Arctic, we continue to promote compromise and harmony with and among our neighbours.

2.4 International and other instruments increasingly recognize the rights of indigenous peoples to self-determination and representation in intergovernmental matters, and are evolving beyond issues of internal governance to external relations. (See, for example: *ICCPR*, Art. 1; *UNDRIP*, Art. 3; *Draft Nordic Saami Convention*, Art. 17, 19; *Nunavut Land Claims Agreement*, Art. 5.9).

2.5 Inuit are permanent participants at the Arctic Council with a direct and meaningful seat at discussion and negotiating tables (See 1997 Ottawa Declaration on the Establishment of the Arctic Council).

2.6 In spite of a recognition by the five coastal Arctic states (Norway, Denmark, Canada, USA and Russia) of the need to use international mechanisms and international law to resolve sovereignty disputes (see 2008 *Ilulissat Declaration*), these states, in their discussions of Arctic sovereignty, have not referenced existing international instruments that promote and protect the rights of indigenous peoples. They have also neglected to include Inuit in Arctic sovereignty discussions in a manner comparable to Arctic Council deliberations.

3.  Inuit, the Arctic and Sovereignty: Looking Forward

*The foundations of action*

3.1   The actions of Arctic peoples and states, the interactions between them, and the conduct of international relations must be anchored in the rule of law.

3.2   The actions of Arctic peoples and states, the interactions between them, and the conduct of international relations must give primary respect to the need for global environmental security, the need for peaceful resolution of disputes, and the inextricable linkages between issues of sovereignty and sovereign rights in the Arctic and issues of self-determination.

*Inuit as active partners*

3.3   The inextricable linkages between issues of sovereignty and sovereign rights in the Arctic and Inuit self-determination and other rights require states to accept the presence and role of Inuit as partners in the conduct of international relations in the Arctic.

3.4   A variety of other factors, ranging from unique Inuit knowledge of Arctic ecosystems to the need for appropriate emphasis on sustainability in the weighing of resource development proposals, provide practical advantages to conducting international relations in the Arctic in partnership with Inuit.

3.5   Inuit consent, expertise and perspectives are critical to progress on international issues involving the Arctic, such as global environmental security, sustainable development, militarization, commercial fishing, shipping, human health, and economic and social development.

3.6   As states increasingly focus on the Arctic and its resources, and as climate change continues to create easier access to the Arctic, Inuit inclusion as active partners is central to all national and international deliberations on Arctic sovereignty and related questions, such as who owns the Arctic, who has the right to traverse the Arctic, who has the right to develop the Arctic, and who will be responsible for the social and environmental impacts increasingly facing the Arctic. We have unique knowledge and experience to bring to these deliberations. The inclusion of Inuit as active partners in all future deliberations on Arctic sovereignty will benefit both the Inuit community and the international community.

3.7 The extensive involvement of Inuit in global, trans-national and indigenous politics requires the building of new partnerships with states for the protection and promotion of indigenous economies, cultures and traditions. Partnerships must acknowledge that industrial development of the natural resource wealth of the Arctic can proceed only insofar as it enhances the economic and social well-being of Inuit and safeguards our environmental security.

*The need for global cooperation*

3.8 There is a pressing need for enhanced international exchange and cooperation in relation to the Arctic, particularly in relation to the dynamics and impacts of climate change and sustainable economic and social development. Regional institutions that draw together Arctic states, states from outside the Arctic, and representatives of Arctic indigenous peoples can provide useful mechanisms for international exchange and cooperation.

3.9 The pursuit of global environmental security requires a coordinated global approach to the challenges of climate change, a rigorous plan to arrest the growth in human-generated carbon emissions, and a far-reaching program of adaptation to climate change in Arctic regions and communities.

3.10 The magnitude of the climate change problem dictates that Arctic states and their peoples fully participate in international efforts aimed at arresting and reversing levels of greenhouse gas emissions and enter into international protocols and treaties. These international efforts, protocols and treaties cannot be successful without the full participation and cooperation of indigenous peoples.

*Healthy Arctic communities*

3.11  In the pursuit of economic opportunities in a warming Arctic, states must act so as to: (1) put economic activity on a sustainable footing; (2) avoid harmful resource exploitation; (3) achieve standards of living for Inuit that meet national and international norms and minimums; and (4) deflect sudden and far-reaching demographic shifts that would overwhelm and marginalize indigenous peoples where we are rooted and have endured.

3.12  The foundation, projection and enjoyment of Arctic sovereignty and sovereign rights all require healthy and sustainable communities in the Arctic. In this sense, "sovereignty begins at home."

*Building on today's mechanisms for the future*

3.13  We will exercise our rights of self-determination in the Arctic by building on institutions such as the Inuit Circumpolar Council and the Arctic Council, the Arctic-specific features of international instruments, such as the ice-covered-waters provision of the *United Nations Convention on the Law of the Sea*, and the Arctic-related work of international mechanisms, such as the United Nations Permanent Forum on Indigenous Issues, the office of the United Nations Special Rapporteur on the Rights and Fundamental Freedoms of Indigenous Peoples, and the UN *Declaration on the Rights of Indigenous Peoples*.

4.    A Circumpolar Inuit Declaration on Sovereignty in the Arctic

4.1   At the first Inuit Leaders' Summit, 6–7 November 2008, in Kuujjuaq, Nunavik, Canada, Inuit leaders from Greenland, Canada and Alaska gathered to address Arctic sovereignty. On 7 November, International Inuit Day, we expressed unity in our concerns over Arctic sovereignty deliberations, examined the options for addressing these concerns, and strongly committed to developing a formal declaration on Arctic sovereignty. We also noted that the 2008 *Ilulissat Declaration* on Arctic sovereignty by ministers representing the five coastal Arctic states did not go far enough in affirming the rights Inuit have gained through international law, land claims and self-government processes.

4.2 The conduct of international relations in the Arctic and the resolution of international disputes in the Arctic are not the sole preserve of Arctic states or other states; they are also within the purview of the Arctic's indigenous peoples. The development of international institutions in the Arctic, such as multi-level governance systems and indigenous peoples' organizations, must transcend Arctic states' agendas on sovereignty and sovereign rights and the traditional monopoly claimed by states in the area of foreign affairs.

4.3 Issues of sovereignty and sovereign rights in the Arctic have become inextricably linked to issues of self-determination in the Arctic. Inuit and Arctic states must, therefore, work together closely and constructively to chart the future of the Arctic.

We, the Inuit of Inuit Nunaat, are committed to this Declaration and to working with Arctic states and others to build partnerships in which the rights, roles and responsibilities of Inuit are fully recognized and accommodated.

On behalf of Inuit in Greenland, Canada, Alaska, and Chukotka
Adopted by the Inuit Circumpolar Council, April 2009

[Signed by Patricia A.L. Cochran, ICC chair; Edward S. Itta, ICC vice chair, Alaska; Tatiana Achirgina, ICC vice chair, Chukotka; Duane R. Smith, ICC vice chair, Canada; and Aqqaluk Lynge, ICC vice chair, Greenland]

# Appendix 2
# Inuit Circumpolar Council, *A Circumpolar Inuit Declaration on Resource Development Principles in Inuit Nunaat*

Preamble

Recognizing the Arctic's great resource wealth, the increasing global demand for the Arctic's minerals and hydrocarbons, the scope and depth of climate change and other environmental pressures and challenges facing the Arctic;

Mindful of the core rights of Inuit as recognized in the *United Nations Declaration on the Rights of Indigenous Peoples*, as provided for in a variety of other legal and political instruments and mechanisms, including land rights settlement legislation, land claims agreements (treaties), and self-government, intergovernmental and constitutional arrangements, and as asserted in *A Circumpolar Inuit Declaration on Sovereignty in the Arctic*; and

Respectful of the ingenuity, resilience and wisdom of previous generations of Inuit, confident of the ability of every generation of Inuit to adapt to change, and determined to provide for the material and cultural well-being of Inuit into the future;

We, the Inuit of *Inuit Nunaat*, declare:

- Healthy communities and households require both a healthy environment and a healthy economy.
- Economic development and social and cultural development must go hand in hand.
- Greater Inuit economic, social and cultural self-sufficiency is an essential part of greater Inuit political self-determination.
- Renewable resources have sustained Inuit from the time preceding recorded history to the present. Future generations of Inuit will continue to rely on Arctic foods for nutritional, social, cultural and economic purposes.
- Responsible non-renewable resource development can also make an important and durable contribution to the well-being of current and future generations of Inuit. Managed under *Inuit Nunaat* governance structures, non-renewable resource development can contribute to Inuit economic and social development through both private sector channels (employment, incomes, businesses) and public sector channels (revenues from publicly owned lands, tax revenues, infrastructure).
- The pace of resource development has profound implications for Inuit. A proper balance must be struck. Inuit desire resource development at a rate sufficient to provide durable and diversified economic growth, but constrained enough to forestall environmental degradation and an overwhelming influx of outside labour.
- Resource development results in environmental and social impacts as well as opportunities for economic benefits. In the weighing of impacts and benefits, those who face the greatest and longest-lasting impacts must have the greatest opportunities, and a primary place in the decision-making. This principle applies between *Inuit Nunaat* and the rest of the world, and within *Inuit Nunaat*.
- All resource development must contribute actively and significantly to improving Inuit living standards and social conditions, and non-renewable resource development, in particular, must promote economic diversification through contributions to education and other forms of social development, physical infrastructure, and non-extractive industries.
- Inuit welcome the opportunity to work in full partnership with resource developers, governments and local communities in the sustainable devel-

opment of resources of *Inuit Nunaat*, including related policy-making, to
the long-lasting benefit of Inuit and with respect for baseline environmental and social responsibilities.

In further detail, we declare:

1. Candour, Clarity and Transparency

1.1 The world's peoples and their social, cultural and economic systems
are becoming more interconnected, the pace of change is accelerating,
the challenges faced by the world are escalating in complexity, and the
risks associated with human activities are of increasing significance.

1.2 To prosper under these circumstances, the peoples and states of the
world must conduct their relations cooperatively with candour, clarity and transparency – an approach in keeping with Inuit culture and
custom.

1.3 It is our desire to declare our key understandings, positions and in-
tentions in relation to resource development, recognizing that doing
so will benefit Inuit and the global community.

1.4 While the focus of this Declaration is on the development of non-renewable resources, it must be understood that (a) issues surrounding
the appropriate use of non-renewable and renewable resources are
inextricably linked, and (b) the principles set out in this Declaration
are, in many ways, applicable to the use of renewable resources.

2. United Nations Declaration on the Rights of Indigenous Peoples

2.1 Resource development in *Inuit Nunaat* must be grounded in the
*United Nations Declaration on the Rights of Indigenous Peoples*.

2.2 The UN *Declaration* recognizes the right of indigenous peoples to self-
determination. Under that right, Inuit have the right to freely determine
collectively our political, social, economic, and cultural development.
Resource development in *Inuit Nunaat* directly engages our right to
self-determination, and many other provisions of the UN *Declaration*.

2.3 Our rights as an indigenous people, including our right to self-determination, may be exercised in a practical way through governance
structures that combine both Inuit and non-Inuit constituents. No
matter what level or form of self-determination the Inuit of any par-

ticular region have achieved, resource development in *Inuit Nunaat* must proceed only with the free, prior, and informed consent of the Inuit of that region.

2.4 Private sector resource developers, and governments and public bodies charged with the public management of resource development, must all conduct themselves in concert with the UN *Declaration*. Respect for the UN *Declaration* should be open and transparent, and be subject to independent and impartial review.

3. A Circumpolar Inuit Declaration on Sovereignty in the Arctic

3.1 Resource development in *Inuit Nunaat* must be grounded in *A Circumpolar Inuit Declaration on Sovereignty in the Arctic*, adopted by the Inuit Circumpolar Council in April 2009.

3.2 *A Circumpolar Inuit Declaration on Sovereignty in the Arctic* identified many principles that are relevant to the governance and carrying out of resource development in *Inuit Nunaat*, including the importance of the rule of law and recognition of the rights of Inuit as an Arctic indigenous people under both international and domestic law.

4. Inuit as Partners in Policy Making and Decision Making

4.1 Central to *A Circumpolar Inuit Declaration on Sovereignty in the Arctic* is the requirement that Inuit must be active and equal partners in policy-making and decision-making affecting *Inuit Nunaat*.

4.2 Partnerships with Inuit in relation to resource development will have different characteristics depending on the circumstances, but the spirit and substance of partnership must extend to both public sector governance and private sector enterprise.

4.3 Partnerships must include the meaningful engagement and active participation of Inuit in local communities who are most directly affected by resource development in *Inuit Nunaat*.

4.4 Partnerships must draw upon the growing capacity and aspirations of Inuit businesses and enterprises through use of vehicles such as joint ventures, commercial mechanisms for facilitating equity participation, and the issuance of land and resource rights through licences, leases and similar instruments.

4.5 Inuit recognize the need within *Inuit Nunaat* to create and implement inter-Inuit consultation mechanisms to ensure that approval of major resource development projects in one Inuit region, with major environmental and other implications for one or more adjacent Inuit regions, is accompanied by sufficient opportunity for an informed exchange of information and opinion between or among the Inuit regions.

5.   Global Environmental Security

5.1   Inuit and others – through their institutions and international instruments – have a shared responsibility to evaluate the risks and benefits of their actions through the prism of global environmental security.

5.2   Resource development in *Inuit Nunaat* must contribute to, and not detract from, global, national and regional efforts to curb greenhouse emissions and should always be seen through the reality of climate change.

5.3   In their implementation of mechanisms for adaptation to climate change, states and the international community as a whole must commit to paying the cost of climate change adaptation measures and the upgrading of fuel-related infrastructure in *Inuit Nunaat* regions and communities.

5.4   Resource development projects must not exacerbate the climate change–related stresses on the survival of Arctic wildlife.

5.5   To minimize risk to global environmental security, the pace of resource development in the Arctic must be carefully considered.

6.   Healthy Communities in a Healthy Environment

6.1   The physical and mental health of human communities and individuals cannot be separated from the health of the natural environment.

6.2   Resource development proposals for *Inuit Nunaat* must be assessed holistically, placing human needs at the centre.

6.3   Resource development in *Inuit Nunaat* must promote the physical and mental health of communities and individuals within *Inuit Nunaat*.

6.4   Resource development must enhance, not detract from, Inuit food security.

6.5   In a contemporary context, healthy communities in the Arctic require the establishment, maintenance and improvement of core infrastructure needs, including housing, education, health care and social service delivery infrastructure, and core transportation and communications networks that facilitate both public sector activities and private sector entrepreneurship.

7. Economic Self-Sufficiency and the Sustainable Development of Resources in *Inuit Nunaat*

7.1 Inuit seek to make use of the economic opportunities available through long-term development of the resources of *Inuit Nunaat*.

7.2 Resource development in *Inuit Nunaat* must be sustainable. It must serve the needs of Inuit today without compromising the ability of Inuit [to] meet their needs of tomorrow.

7.3 The proponent of a resource development project bears the burden of demonstrating that the proposed development is sustainable.

7.4 In determining the sustainability of a resource development initiative, the best available scientific and Inuit knowledge and standards must be determined and employed.

7.5 International standard-setting bodies must seek and secure direct and meaningful input from Inuit. National, regional and local bodies, such as offshore and land management regimes, must be designed and operated to be effective, transparent and accountable, thereby gaining and sustaining the confidence of the Inuit public at all times.

7.6 Sustainability standards must emphasize the need for the demonstrated support of those communities directly affected by a resource development proposal.

8. Impact Assessment, Prevention and Mitigation

8.1 Notwithstanding property rights or government rights-granting regimes, there is no free-standing or unqualified "right" to proceed with non-renewable resource development in *Inuit Nunaat*. Projects must be scrutinized by Inuit and proved to be in the best interests of Inuit and the wider public.

8.2 Land and offshore management regimes must include (a) long-term land use plans that set out ground rules for development applicable to specific projects, and (b) robust impact assessment processes to gauge the likely impacts of specific projects.

8.3 Management, land use planning and impact assessment regimes must address the cumulative impacts of existing and potential projects and, where prudent, limit the number and scope of projects permitted.

8.4   Impact assessments covering broad geographic areas are important and necessary management tools, and their completion in advance of specific project proposals should be encouraged.

8.5   Impact assessments should examine all potential environmental, socio-economic and cultural impacts anticipated both during the project and after the project is completed or abandoned.

8.6   In accordance with relevant provisions of the *Rio Declaration on Environment and Development*, the precautionary principle and the polluter pays principle must be applied in all stages of project planning, assessment, implementation and reclamation.

8.7   Reclamation and recovery of habitat and affected lands and waters must be thoroughly planned and fully funded in advance of and throughout project implementation.

8.8   All development in *Inuit Nunaat* must adhere to the most developed and demanding environmental standards taking Arctic conditions fully into account. (For example, mining operations and offshore hydro-carbon development should entail zero-volume discharge onto land and into Arctic waters.)

8.9   Preventing spills offshore and eliminating release of toxic substances to land and waters are paramount. Prevention efforts should be viewed as investments that pay dividends in cost avoidance.

8.10  Response to spills, contamination of lands or waters, and mining emergencies must meet the highest technological standards and be anchored in proven cleanup technologies with full Inuit participation.

8.11  Proposals for spill response in Arctic waters must include a proven demonstration of the industry's ability to retrieve spilled oil in frozen, broken and refreezing ice conditions. Allowing resource development without such a demonstration would be fundamentally irresponsible.

8.12  Effective oil spill prevention and response in Arctic waters requires active monitoring of vessel traffic and swift and effective emergency response in the event of mishap. Public authorities and developers with relevant responsibilities must commit to increased investment in navigation aids, vessel traffic management, ship compliance inspections, security considerations, emergency response capability, and overall port and harbour infrastructure.

8.13 Standards and requirements for Arctic marine pilots must be carefully conceived and strictly applied.

8.14 An international liability and compensation regime for contamination of lands, waters and marine areas resulting from offshore oil exploration and exploitation must be established.

8.15 Respecting the Arctic Council's "Arctic Offshore Oil and Gas Guidelines" as minimum standards.

9. Improving Inuit Living Standards and Expanding Inuit Governance

9.1 Inuit expect that new resource development projects will contribute to an improvement in our material well-being. This expectation is well-rooted in the fundamental features of relevant international indigenous and human rights laws and standards, in the underlying constitutional constructs and political values of the four Arctic States in which Inuit live, and in the application of fairness and reason.

9.2 Through a variety of mechanisms – land rights settlement legislation, land claims agreements (treaties), self-government arrangements, and intergovernmental and Constitutional provisions – Inuit have acquired critical means and levels of control over the governance of *Inuit Nunaat*. Many of these mechanisms provide for direct Inuit participation in specialized resource management bodies, including planning, project review, and regulatory bodies.

9.3 While this trend is primarily a result of Inuit effort and determination, it has often been assisted and welcomed as healthy and normative by and within the four Arctic States.

9.4 Accordingly, resource development projects must take into account the trend toward greater Inuit self-governance and, to the extent possible, advance it.

9.5 Public sector revenues derived from all phases of resource development should be distributed in a fair and visible way according to the following hierarchy of priorities: (1) providing security against unplanned or unintended environmental consequences, (2) compensating for negative community and regional impacts, (3) contributing to the improvement of community and regional living standards and overall well-being, and (4) contributing to the fiscal health and stability of institutions and mechanisms of Inuit governance. Only after the legitimate needs of the Inuit of *Inuit Nunaat* are met, should public sector revenues contribute to the coffers of central State treasuries.

9.6 Inuit employment at all levels must be maximized in resource development activities in *Inuit Nunaat*.

9.7 Independent of the rate of resource development, Inuit must derive direct and substantial employment income benefit from resource development projects. Accordingly, an Inuit education fund should be established in each of Canada, Greenland, Russia and the U.S.A. with public sector investments.

10. Promoting and Accommodating a Dynamic Inuit Culture

10.1 Many international law principles and standards in relation to indigenous peoples are rooted in the strong conviction that the development and preservation of human cultural diversity is both a responsibility and a benefit for all humanity. The UN *Declaration on the Rights of Indigenous Peoples* acknowledges that indigenous peoples have the right to maintain, control, protect and develop their language, traditional knowledge and cultural heritage and expressions.

10.2 Inuit culture is both well-rooted and dynamic. Inuit are committed to ensuring that resource development projects must be planned and implemented in such a way as to support and enhance Inuit culture, rather than subvert or overwhelm it.

10.3 Inuit are committed to safe-guarding Inuit culture against excess adverse pressures and impacts that could be brought on by an overly ambitious, ill timed, or poorly planned and implemented staging of major resource development projects, particularly insofar as such a scenario precipitated a major influx of non-Inuit while failing to impart the technologies, skills and training, and business opportunities needed by Inuit.

10.4 Governments, public bodies and private sector actors in *Inuit Nunaat* must share in these commitments.

We, the Inuit of *Inuit Nunaat*, are committed to the principles on resource development in *Inuit Nunaat* set out in this Declaration. Inuit invite – and are entitled to expect – all those who have or seek a role in the governance, management, development, or use of the resources of *Inuit Nunaat* to conduct themselves within the letter and spirit of this Declaration.

[Adopted by the Inuit Circumpolar Council, 11 May 2011. Signed by Aqqaluk Lynge, chair, Inuit Circumpolar Council; Jim Stotts, vice chair, Alaska; Tatiana Achirgina, vice chair, Chukotka; Duane Smith, vice chair, Canada; and Carl Christian Olsen, vice chair, Greenland]

# United Nations, *United Nations Declaration on the Rights of Indigenous Peoples*

*The General Assembly,*

*Guided* by the purposes and principles of the Charter of the United Nations, and good faith in the fulfilment of the obligations assumed by States in accordance with the Charter,

*Affirming* that indigenous peoples are equal to all other peoples, while recognizing the right of all peoples to be different, to consider themselves different, and to be respected as such,

*Affirming also* that all peoples contribute to the diversity and richness of civilizations and cultures, which constitute the common heritage of humankind,

*Affirming further* that all doctrines, policies and practices based on or advocating superiority of peoples or individuals on the basis of national origin or racial, religious, ethnic or cultural differences are racist, scientifically false, legally invalid, morally condemnable and socially unjust,

*Reaffirming* that indigenous peoples, in the exercise of their rights, should be free from discrimination of any kind,

*Concerned* that indigenous peoples have suffered from historic injustices as a result of, inter alia, their colonization and dispossession of their lands, territories and resources, thus preventing them from exercising, in particular, their right to development in accordance with their own needs and interests,

*Recognizing* the urgent need to respect and promote the inherent rights of indigenous peoples which derive from their political, economic and social structures and from their cultures, spiritual traditions, histories and philosophies, especially their rights to their lands, territories and resources,

*Recognizing also* the urgent need to respect and promote the rights of indigenous peoples affirmed in treaties, agreements and other constructive arrangements with States,

*Welcoming* the fact that indigenous peoples are organizing themselves for political, economic, social and cultural enhancement and in order to bring to an end all forms of discrimination and oppression wherever they occur,

*Convinced* that control by indigenous peoples over developments affecting them and their lands, territories and resources will enable them to maintain and strengthen their institutions, cultures and traditions, and to promote their development in accordance with their aspirations and needs,

*Recognizing* that respect for indigenous knowledge, cultures and traditional practices contributes to sustainable and equitable development and proper management of the environment,

*Emphasizing* the contribution of the demilitarization of the lands and territories of indigenous peoples to peace, economic and social progress and development, understanding and friendly relations among nations and peoples of the world,

*Recognizing in particular* the right of indigenous families and communities to retain shared responsibility for the upbringing, training, education and well-being of their children, consistent with the rights of the child,

*Considering* that the rights affirmed in treaties, agreements and other constructive arrangements between States and indigenous peoples are, in some situations, matters of international concern, interest, responsibility and character,

*Considering also* that treaties, agreements and other constructive arrangements, and the relationship they represent, are the basis for a strengthened partnership between indigenous peoples and States,

*Acknowledging* that the Charter of the United Nations, the International Covenant on Economic, Social and Cultural Rights and the International Covenant on Civil and Political Rights, as well as the Vienna Declaration and Programme of Action, affirm the fundamental importance of the right to self-determination of all peoples, by virtue of which they freely determine their political status and freely pursue their economic, social and cultural development,

*Bearing in mind* that nothing in this Declaration may be used to deny any peoples their right to self-determination, exercised in conformity with international law,

*Convinced* that the recognition of the rights of indigenous peoples in this Declaration will enhance harmonious and cooperative relations between the State and indigenous peoples, based on principles of justice, democracy, respect for human rights, non-discrimination and good faith,

*Encouraging* States to comply with and effectively implement all their obligations as they apply to indigenous peoples under international instruments, in particular those related to human rights, in consultation and cooperation with the peoples concerned,

*Emphasizing* that the United Nations has an important and continuing role to play in promoting and protecting the rights of indigenous peoples,

*Believing* that this Declaration is a further important step forward for the recognition, promotion and protection of the rights and freedoms of indigenous peoples and in the development of relevant activities of the United Nations system in this field,

*Recognizing and reaffirming* that indigenous individuals are entitled without discrimination to all human rights recognized in international law, and that indigenous peoples possess collective rights which are indispensable for their existence, well-being and integral development as peoples,

*Recognizing* that the situation of indigenous peoples varies from region to region and from country to country and that the significance of national and regional particularities and various historical and cultural backgrounds should be taken into consideration,

*Solemnly proclaims* the following United Nations Declaration on the Rights of Indigenous Peoples as a standard of achievement to be pursued in a spirit of partnership and mutual respect:

*Article 1*
Indigenous peoples have the right to the full enjoyment, as a collective or as individuals, of all human rights and fundamental freedoms as recognized in the Charter of the United Nations, the Universal Declaration of Human Rights and international human rights law.

*Article 2*
Indigenous peoples and individuals are free and equal to all other peoples and individuals and have the right to be free from any kind of discrimination, in the exercise of their rights, in particular that based on their indigenous origin or identity.

*Article 3*
Indigenous peoples have the right to self-determination. By virtue of that right they freely determine their political status and freely pursue their economic, social and cultural development.

*Article 4*

Indigenous peoples, in exercising their right to self-determination, have the right to autonomy or self-government in matters relating to their internal and local affairs, as well as ways and means for financing their autonomous functions.

*Article 5*

Indigenous peoples have the right to maintain and strengthen their distinct political, legal, economic, social and cultural institutions, while retaining their right to participate fully, if they so choose, in the political, economic, social and cultural life of the State.

*Article 6*

Every indigenous individual has the right to a nationality.

*Article 7*

1. Indigenous individuals have the rights to life, physical and mental integrity, liberty and security of person.
2. Indigenous peoples have the collective right to live in freedom, peace and security as distinct peoples and shall not be subjected to any act of genocide or any other act of violence, including forcibly removing children of the group to another group.

*Article 8*

1. Indigenous peoples and individuals have the right not to be subjected to forced assimilation or destruction of their culture.
2. States shall provide effective mechanisms for prevention of, and redress for:

   (*a*) Any action which has the aim or effect of depriving them of their integrity as distinct peoples, or of their cultural values or ethnic identities;
   (*b*) Any action which has the aim or effect of dispossessing them of their lands, territories or resources;
   (*c*) Any form of forced population transfer which has the aim or effect of violating or undermining any of their rights;
   (*d*) Any form of forced assimilation or integration;
   (*e*) Any form of propaganda designed to promote or incite racial or ethnic discrimination directed against them.

*Article 9*

Indigenous peoples and individuals have the right to belong to an indigenous community or nation, in accordance with the traditions and customs of the community or nation concerned. No discrimination of any kind may arise from the exercise of such a right.

*Article 10*

Indigenous peoples shall not be forcibly removed from their lands or territories. No relocation shall take place without the free, prior and informed consent of the indigenous peoples concerned and after agreement on just and fair compensation and, where possible, with the option of return.

*Article 11*

1. Indigenous peoples have the right to practise and revitalize their cultural traditions and customs. This includes the right to maintain, protect and develop the past, present and future manifestations of their cultures, such as archaeological and historical sites, artefacts, designs, ceremonies, technologies and visual and performing arts and literature.

2. States shall provide redress through effective mechanisms, which may include restitution, developed in conjunction with indigenous peoples, with respect to their cultural, intellectual, religious and spiritual property taken without their free, prior and informed consent or in violation of their laws, traditions and customs.

*Article 12*

1. Indigenous peoples have the right to manifest, practise, develop and teach their spiritual and religious traditions, customs and ceremonies; the right to maintain, protect, and have access in privacy to their religious and cultural sites; the right to the use and control of their ceremonial objects; and the right to the repatriation of their human remains.

2. States shall seek to enable the access and/or repatriation of ceremonial objects and human remains in their possession through fair, transparent and effective mechanisms developed in conjunction with indigenous peoples concerned.

*Article 13*

1. Indigenous peoples have the right to revitalize, use, develop and transmit to future generations their histories, languages, oral traditions, philosophies, writing systems and literatures, and to designate and retain their own names for communities, places and persons.

2. States shall take effective measures to ensure that this right is protected and also to ensure that indigenous peoples can understand and be understood in political, legal and administrative proceedings, where necessary through the provision of interpretation or by other appropriate means.

*Article 14*

1. Indigenous peoples have the right to establish and control their educational systems and institutions providing education in their own languages, in a manner appropriate to their cultural methods of teaching and learning.

2. Indigenous individuals, particularly children, have the right to all levels and forms of education of the State without discrimination.

3. States shall, in conjunction with indigenous peoples, take effective measures, in order for indigenous individuals, particularly children, including those living outside their communities, to have access, when possible, to an education in their own culture and provided in their own language.

*Article 15*

1. Indigenous peoples have the right to the dignity and diversity of their cultures, traditions, histories and aspirations which shall be appropriately reflected in education and public information.

2. States shall take effective measures, in consultation and cooperation with the indigenous peoples concerned, to combat prejudice and eliminate discrimination and to promote tolerance, understanding and good relations among indigenous peoples and all other segments of society.

*Article 16*

1. Indigenous peoples have the right to establish their own media in their own languages and to have access to all forms of non-indigenous media without discrimination.

2. States shall take effective measures to ensure that State-owned media duly reflect indigenous cultural diversity. States, without prejudice to ensuring

full freedom of expression, should encourage privately owned media to adequately reflect indigenous cultural diversity.

*Article 17*

1. Indigenous individuals and peoples have the right to enjoy fully all rights established under applicable international and domestic labour law.

2 States shall in consultation and cooperation with indigenous peoples take specific measures to protect indigenous children from economic exploitation and from performing any work that is likely to be hazardous or to interfere with the child's education, or to be harmful to the child's health or physical, mental, spiritual, moral or social development, taking into account their special vulnerability and the importance of education for their empowerment.

3. Indigenous individuals have the right not to be subjected to any discriminatory conditions of labour and, inter alia, employment or salary.

*Article 18*

Indigenous peoples have the right to participate in decision-making in matters which would affect their rights, through representatives chosen by themselves in accordance with their own procedures, as well as to maintain and develop their own indigenous decision-making institutions.

*Article 19*

States shall consult and cooperate in good faith with the indigenous peoples concerned through their own representative institutions in order to obtain their free, prior and informed consent before adopting and implementing legislative or administrative measures that may affect them.

*Article 20*

1. Indigenous peoples have the right to maintain and develop their political, economic and social systems or institutions, to be secure in the enjoyment of their own means of subsistence and development, and to engage freely in all their traditional and other economic activities.

2. Indigenous peoples deprived of their means of subsistence and development are entitled to just and fair redress.

*Article 21*

1. Indigenous peoples have the right, without discrimination, to the improvement of their economic and social conditions, including, inter alia, in the areas of education, employment, vocational training and retraining, housing, sanitation, health and social security.

2. States shall take effective measures and, where appropriate, special measures to ensure continuing improvement of their economic and social conditions. Particular attention shall be paid to the rights and special needs of indigenous elders, women, youth, children and persons with disabilities.

*Article 22*

1. Particular attention shall be paid to the rights and special needs of indigenous elders, women, youth, children and persons with disabilities in the implementation of this Declaration.

2. States shall take measures, in conjunction with indigenous peoples, to ensure that indigenous women and children enjoy the full protection and guarantees against all forms of violence and discrimination.

*Article 23*

Indigenous peoples have the right to determine and develop priorities and strategies for exercising their right to development. In particular, indigenous peoples have the right to be actively involved in developing and determining health, housing and other economic and social programmes affecting them and, as far as possible, to administer such programmes through their own institutions.

*Article 24*

1. Indigenous peoples have the right to their traditional medicines and to maintain their health practices, including the conservation of their vital medicinal plants, animals and minerals. Indigenous individuals also have the right to access, without any discrimination, to all social and health services.

2. Indigenous individuals have an equal right to the enjoyment of the highest attainable standard of physical and mental health. States shall take the necessary steps with a view to achieving progressively the full realization of this right.

*Article 25*

Indigenous peoples have the right to maintain and strengthen their distinctive spiritual relationship with their traditionally owned or otherwise occupied and used lands, territories, waters and coastal seas and other resources and to uphold their responsibilities to future generations in this regard.

*Article 26*

1. Indigenous peoples have the right to the lands, territories and resources which they have traditionally owned, occupied or otherwise used or acquired.

2. Indigenous peoples have the right to own, use, develop and control the lands, territories and resources that they possess by reason of traditional ownership or other traditional occupation or use, as well as those which they have otherwise acquired.

3. States shall give legal recognition and protection to these lands, territories and resources. Such recognition shall be conducted with due respect to the customs, traditions and land tenure systems of the indigenous peoples concerned.

*Article 27*

States shall establish and implement, in conjunction with indigenous peoples concerned, a fair, independent, impartial, open and transparent process, giving due recognition to indigenous peoples' laws, traditions, customs and land tenure systems, to recognize and adjudicate the rights of indigenous peoples pertaining to their lands, territories and resources, including those which were traditionally owned or otherwise occupied or used. Indigenous peoples shall have the right to participate in this process.

*Article 28*

1. Indigenous peoples have the right to redress, by means that can include restitution or, when this is not possible, just, fair and equitable compensation, for the lands, territories and resources which they have traditionally owned or otherwise occupied or used, and which have been confiscated, taken, occupied, used or damaged without their free, prior and informed consent.

2. Unless otherwise freely agreed upon by the peoples concerned, compensation shall take the form of lands, territories and resources equal in quality,

size and legal status or of monetary compensation or other appropriate redress.

## Article 29

1. Indigenous peoples have the right to the conservation and protection of
the environment and the productive capacity of their lands or territories and
resources. States shall establish and implement assistance programmes for
indigenous peoples for such conservation and protection, without discrimination.

2. States shall take effective measures to ensure that no storage or disposal
of hazardous materials shall take place in the lands or territories of indigenous peoples without their free, prior and informed consent.

3. States shall also take effective measures to ensure, as needed, that programmes for monitoring, maintaining and restoring the health of indigenous
peoples, as developed and implemented by the peoples affected by such materials, are duly implemented.

## Article 30

1. Military activities shall not take place in the lands or territories of indigenous peoples, unless justified by a relevant public interest or otherwise freely
agreed with or requested by the indigenous peoples concerned.

2. States shall undertake effective consultations with the indigenous peoples
concerned, through appropriate procedures and in particular through their
representative institutions, prior to using their lands or territories for military activities.

## Article 31

1. Indigenous peoples have the right to maintain, control, protect and develop their cultural heritage, traditional knowledge and traditional cultural
expressions, as well as the manifestations of their sciences, technologies and
cultures, including human and genetic resources, seeds, medicines, knowledge of the properties of fauna and flora, oral traditions, literatures, designs,
sports and traditional games and visual and performing arts. They also have
the right to maintain, control, protect and develop their intellectual property
over such cultural heritage, traditional knowledge, and traditional cultural
expressions.

2. In conjunction with indigenous peoples, States shall take effective measures to recognize and protect the exercise of these rights.

*Article 32*

1. Indigenous peoples have the right to determine and develop priorities and strategies for the development or use of their lands or territories and other resources.

2. States shall consult and cooperate in good faith with the indigenous peoples concerned through their own representative institutions in order to obtain their free and informed consent prior to the approval of any project affecting their lands or territories and other resources, particularly in connection with the development, utilization or exploitation of mineral, water or other resources.

3. States shall provide effective mechanisms for just and fair redress for any such activities, and appropriate measures shall be taken to mitigate adverse environmental, economic, social, cultural or spiritual impact.

*Article 33*

1. Indigenous peoples have the right to determine their own identity or membership in accordance with their customs and traditions. This does not impair the right of indigenous individuals to obtain citizenship of the States in which they live.

2. Indigenous peoples have the right to determine the structures and to select the membership of their institutions in accordance with their own procedures.

*Article 34*

Indigenous peoples have the right to promote, develop and maintain their institutional structures and their distinctive customs, spirituality, traditions, procedures, practices and, in the cases where they exist, juridical systems or customs, in accordance with international human rights standards.

*Article 35*

Indigenous peoples have the right to determine the responsibilities of individuals to their communities.

*Article 36*
1. Indigenous peoples, in particular those divided by international borders, have the right to maintain and develop contacts, relations and cooperation, including activities for spiritual, cultural, political, economic and social purposes, with their own members as well as other peoples across borders.
2. States, in consultation and cooperation with indigenous peoples, shall take effective measures to facilitate the exercise and ensure the implementation of this right.

*Article 37*
1. Indigenous peoples have the right to the recognition, observance and enforcement of treaties, agreements and other constructive arrangements concluded with States or their successors and to have States honour and respect such treaties, agreements and other constructive arrangements.
2. Nothing in this Declaration may be interpreted as diminishing or eliminating the rights of indigenous peoples contained in treaties, agreements and other constructive arrangements.

*Article 38*
States, in consultation and cooperation with indigenous peoples, shall take the appropriate measures, including legislative measures, to achieve the ends of this Declaration.

*Article 39*
Indigenous peoples have the right to have access to financial and technical assistance from States and through international cooperation, for the enjoyment of the rights contained in this Declaration.

*Article 40*
Indigenous peoples have the right to access to and prompt decision through just and fair procedures for the resolution of conflicts and disputes with States or other parties, as well as to effective remedies for all infringements of their individual and collective rights. Such a decision shall give due consideration to the customs, traditions, rules and legal systems of the indigenous peoples concerned and international human rights.

### Article 41

The organs and specialized agencies of the United Nations system and other intergovernmental organizations shall contribute to the full realization of the provisions of this Declaration through the mobilization, inter alia, of financial cooperation and technical assistance. Ways and means of ensuring participation of indigenous peoples on issues affecting them shall be established.

### Article 42

The United Nations, its bodies, including the Permanent Forum on Indigenous Issues, and specialized agencies, including at the country level, and States shall promote respect for and full application of the provisions of this Declaration and follow up the effectiveness of this Declaration.

### Article 43

The rights recognized herein constitute the minimum standards for the survival, dignity and well-being of the indigenous peoples of the world.

### Article 44

All the rights and freedoms recognized herein are equally guaranteed to male and female indigenous individuals.

### Article 45

Nothing in this Declaration may be construed as diminishing or extinguishing the rights indigenous peoples have now or may acquire in the future.

### Article 46

1. Nothing in this Declaration may be interpreted as implying for any State, people, group or person any right to engage in any activity or to perform any act contrary to the Charter of the United Nations or construed as authorizing or encouraging any action which would dismember or impair, totally or in part, the territorial integrity or political unity of sovereign and independent States.

2. In the exercise of the rights enunciated in the present Declaration, human rights and fundamental freedoms of all shall be respected. The exercise of the rights set forth in this Declaration shall be subject only to such limitations as are determined by law and in accordance with international human

rights obligations. Any such limitations shall be non-discriminatory and strictly necessary solely for the purpose of securing due recognition and respect for the rights and freedoms of others and for meeting the just and most compelling requirements of a democratic society.

3. The provisions set forth in this Declaration shall be interpreted in accordance with the principles of justice, democracy, respect for human rights, equality, non-discrimination, good governance and good faith.

# Acknowledgments

I owe thanks to a great many people. This of course includes all those authors of books and articles, filmmakers, webmasters, public speakers, friends, and storytellers upon whose work so much of my own depends. I have not met all the Inuit elders on whose words I rely in this book, and some I will never meet, as they have passed away, but without their willingness to share their stories, much of what I have learned about the Arctic would have been lost, not only to me but to everyone. In particular I would like to acknowledge Inooki Uqigjuaqsi Adamie, John Amagoalik, Leah Aqpik, Simionie Aqpik, Kenojuaq Ashevak, Mariano Aupilaarjuk, Udjualuk Etidloi, Emile Imaruittuq, Piita Irniq, Madeleine Ivalu, Akisu Joamie, Alice Joamie, Mark Kalluak, George Agiaq Kappianaq, Teresa Kimmaliadjuk, Jose Kusugak, Jamesie Mike, Qaunaq Mikkigak, Lucassie Nutaraaluk, Cornelius Nutaraq, Mary Qulitalik, Sarah Takolik, Marie Tulimaaq, and Lucien Ukaliannuk. Ukaliannuk was the elder-in-residence for both the Akitsiraq Law School and the Nunavut Department of Justice, among many other things. It was from him that I learned most of what little I know about Inuit culture and language.

I would also like to thank all those people with whom I have worked in Nunavut, including Naullaq Arnaqaq, Simon Awa, Beverley Browne, Michael Byers, Anne Crawford, Gary Crowe, Heather Daley, Kelly-Ann Fenney, Lalena Flaherty, Steven Foulds, previous northern director Kelly Gallagher-McKay, Susan Hardy, Gwen Healey, former commander of "V" Division John Henderson, Liina Ivic, Leslie Kemp, Alexina Kublu, Cindy Kudloo, Judge Earl Johnson, Shirley Johnson, Elisapee Karetak, Nancy Karetak-Lindell, Suzanne Lalonde, Brian Lanman, Bernie and Maria Lodge, Marion Love, Mick Mallon, Cam and Cathy McGregor, Brian McLeod, Stephanie McTaggart, Joan Mercredi, Richard Meredith, John Merritt, Meeka Mike, former premier of Nunavut Paul Okalik, Judith Paradis-Pastori, Marcelo Parungao, Garry Pon, Mireille Provost, Leonie Qaumariaq, Nigel Qaumariaq, Anthony Saez, Nora Sanders, Neil Sharkey, Mary Simon, Susan Switch, Nanci Tagalik, Lorraine Thomas, Tom Thompson, Bonnie Tulloch, John Walsh, Siila Watt-Cloutier, Rebekah Uqi Williams, and Mary Wilman, as well as southern directors Don Galloway and Kim Hart, Dean (now President) Andrew Petter of Simon Fraser University, everyone at the University of Victoria, and all those professors of law, judges, and lawyers who came north to teach at the Akitsiraq Law School, especially Catherine Bell, John Borrows, Justice Constance Hunt, Justice James Igloliorte, John McLaren, and Heather Raven.

I owe special thanks to the first northern director, Andrejs Berzins, and to Lorraine Berzins, who together introduced me to the North and were always there when I needed them. Thank you to Matthew Swan, Cedar Bradley-Swan, everyone at Adventure Canada, and all the wonderful elders, experts, and visitors who shared our travels, including Ann and Nigel Way (William Edward Parry's great grandson) for sharing an early edition of the *North Georgia Gazette and Winter Chronicle* with me. Without the Akitsiraq Law School and Adventure Canada, I would never have seen much of the Arctic that appears in these pages. And finally, many thanks to Symatuk "Sam" Itorcheak, with whom I worked and shared an office for two and a half years. She was unfailingly helpful and a good friend. She passed away a few years ago, much too young.

Thank you to the 2005 graduates of the Akitsiraq Law School and their families for teaching me more about life in the Arctic than I could ever have imagined. They are (by the names they used as students) Lillian Aglukark,

Siobhan Arnatsiaq-Murphy, Henry Coman, Susan Enuaraq, Sandra Inutiq, Connie Merkosak, Sandra Omik, Aaju Peter, Madeleine Redfern, Qajaq Robinson, and Naomi Wilman.

I also wish to thank all those who took the time to read all or part of this manuscript at various stages in its development, including Liz Attebury, Jon Dudley, Piita Irniq, Elisapee Karetak, Suzanne Lalonde, Ken McGoogan, Sandra Omik, Chris Scotnicki, Siila Watt-Cloutier, and Rob Wright. Thanks also to John Amagoalik, Martha Flaherty, Piita Irniq, Elisapee Karetak, Zacharias Kunuk, Mukshowya Niviaqsi, and Sam and Sandra Omik for allowing me to share part of their stories. Finally I would like to thank Silaqqi Ashevak (on behalf of her late mother Kenojuaq Ashevak), the estate of Richard Harrington and the Stephen Bulger Gallery in Toronto, Norman Cohn, Susan Enuaraq, David Gladders, Kim Hart, Gwen Healey, Carol Heppenstall, Piita Irniq, Elisapee Karetak, Jayson Kunnuk, Zacharias Kunuk, Library and Archives Canada, Lillian Lundrigan, Connie Merkosak, Meeka Mike, Qaunaq Mikkigak, the National Snow and Ice Data Center and the National Oceanic and Atmospheric Administration (Earth System Research Laboratory Sciences Division), Matthew Nuqingaq, Sandra Omik, Leesee Papatsie, Aaju Peter, Dave Sheehan, Karla Jensen Williamson, and the United States Navy for allowing me to use their photographs, images, words, charts, and graphs. Thanks also to Batty Levely for the maps.

I worked in several libraries while writing this book. I am especially grateful to Library and Archives Canada both in Ottawa and online as well as libraries at the University of British Columbia, University of Victoria, and Nunavut Arctic College. Thanks to the Powell River Public Library and Breakwater Books and Cafe for free WiFi and to Nancy's Bakery in Lund, British Columbia, for the great food during the final edit of this book. I would also like to thank my family and friends for putting up with authorship woes for a very long time. And finally I have to thank all the folks at McGill-Queen's University Press, especially Jacqueline Mason, for making publication of this book possible.

The information contained in this book is current up to 31 October 2013. To obtain further information about the book and the topics it covers (including updates), as well as more colour illustrations and photographs, links to helpful websites (including McGill-Queen's), contacts, questions, and discussions, please see http://www.sikuvut.ca.

Short edited portions of this book were included in the article "Inuit Perspectives on Governance in the Canadian Arctic," in *Polar Oceans Governance in an Era of Environmental Change*, edited by Tim Stephens and David L. VanderZwaag (Edward Elgar, Cheltenham, UK, 2014) 189–212.

# Notes

CHAPTER ONE

1  Cited in Bennett and Rowley, eds, *Uqalurait*, 310.
2  Scoffield, "Arctic Ice Melt in 2012 Was Fastest, Widest in Recent History."
3  Gillis, "Ending Its Summer Melt, Arctic Sea Ice Sets a New Low That Leads to Warnings."
4  Naam, "Arctic Sea Ice."
5  Cited in Brahic, "Arctic Ice Low Heralds End of Three-Million-Year Cover."
6  United Nations, Intergovernmental Panel on Climate Change, *Fifth Assessment Report: Climate Change 2013: The Physical Science Basis: Summary for Policymakers*, 12.
7  Austin, "Tourists Rescued after Nearly Two Days Stranded in Canadian Arctic."
8  Sandra Omik, Facebook communication, 30 June 2013.
9  Nash, *Wilderness and the American Mind*, 389.
10  Waldie, "Signs of Warming Earth 'Unmistakable.'"
11  Gillis, "The Threats to a Crucial Canopy."
12  *Agreement between the Inuit of the Nunavut Settlement Area and Her Majesty the Queen in Right of Canada [Nunavut Land Claims Agreement]*.
13  Cited in Baikie, "Inuit Perspectives on Recent Climate Change."

CHAPTER TWO

1  Aupilaarjuk et al., *Interviewing Inuit Elders*, 13.
2  Kunuk, dir., *Atanarjuat*; Kunuk and Cohn, dirs, *The Journals of Knud Rasmussen*; Cousineau and Ivalu, dirs, *Before Tomorrow*.
3  Fossett, *In Order to Live Untroubled*, 9–10.
4  McGhee, "When and Why Did the Inuit Move to the Eastern Arctic?" 155–63.
5  Hamilton, "The Medieval Norse on Baffin Island."

6  Ibid.
7  Pringle, "Vikings and Native Americans."
8  Armstrong, "Vikings in Canada?"
9  Gregg, dir., *The Norse.*
10 Sutherland, "Dorset-Norse Interactions in the Canadian Eastern Arctic."
11 Butler, "Cold Comfort."
12 Canadian Broadcasting Corporation, "Silence of the Labs."
13 Radford and Thompson, dirs, *Inuit Odyssey.*
14 Cited in MacDonald, *The Arctic Sky,* 97–8.
15 Kalluak, *Unipkaaqtuat Arvianit,* 11–20.
16 Inuit Circumpolar Council, *A Circumpolar Inuit Declaration on Sovereignty in the Arctic.*
17 Arctic Institute of North America, "Tusaqtuut."
18 Government of Nunavut, Office of the Language Commissioner, *Official Languages Act,* RSNWT 1988, c. O-1, http://langcom.nu.ca/nunavuts-official-languages/official-languages-act.
19 Government of Nunavut, Office of the Languages Commissioner, *Nunavut's Official Languages.*
20 Brody, *The Other Side of Eden,* 284–5.
21 Spalding and Kusugaq, *Inuktitut,* 111–12.
22 Bennett and Rowley, eds, *Uqalurait,* 3.
23 Cited in ibid.
24 Cited in Alia, "Inuit Names," 252–3.
25 Cited in ibid, 252.
26 Kunuk, dir., *Kiviaq v. Canada.*
27 Cited in Bennett and Rowley, eds, *Uqalurait,* 4.
28 See Houston, dir., *Nuliajuk.*
29 Kappianaq and Nutaraq, *Inuit Perspectives on the 20th Century,* vol. 2, *Travelling and Surviving on Our Land,* 79.
30 Cited in Rasmussen, *Across Arctic America,* 30–1.

CHAPTER THREE
1  Rogers, *Northwest Passage.*
2  See Cameron and Groves, *Bones, Stones and Molecules*; Flannery, *The Weather Makers*; and Gibbons, "Clocking the Human Exodus out of Africa."
3  Sankararaman et al., "The Date of Interbreeding between Neandertals and Modern Humans."
4  Hofreiter, "Drafting Human Ancestry."
5  O'Rourke and Raff, "The Human Genetic History of the Americas."
6  See Meltzer, *First Peoples in a New World,* esp. chs 4–6, 95–207, which contain an exhaustive review of the evidence with no clear conclusions.
7  Broecker, "Was the Medieval Warm Period Global?"
8  See Behringer, *A Cultural History of Climate,* 74–84; Fagan, *The Great Warming*; and Xing, "Paleoclimate of China."
9  Cited in McGhee, *The Last Imaginary Place,* 54.
10 Spalding and Kusugaq, "tuniq," in *Inuktitut,* 168.
11 Martin, *Stories in a New Skin,* 29.
12 I am not alone in this conjecture. See Agger and Maschner, "Medieval Norse

and the Bidirectional Spread of Epidemic Disease between Europe and North-eastern America."

13  Magnusson and Palsson, trans, *The Vinland Sagas*.

14  Phelpstead, ed., *A History of Norway and the Passion and Miracles of the Blessed Olafr*, 3.

15  Rink, *Tales and Traditions of the Eskimo*, 319.

16  Folger, "Viking Weather," 59.

17  *Legal Status of South-Eastern Territory of Greenland (Nor. v. Den.)*, 1932 PCIJ (ser. A/B), no. 53 (order of Aug. 3), http://www.worldcourts.com/pcij/eng/decisions/1932.08.03_greenland.htm.

18  Inookie Adamie, cited in Eber, *Encounters on the Passage*, 3–4.

19  Ross, *A Voyage of Discovery*, 172–5, cited in Fleming, *Barrow's Boys*, 47–8.

20  Sabine, ed., *North Georgia Gazette and Winter Chronicle*, 1.

21  William Edward Parry as "Amicus," letter, in ibid., 56.

22  This transfer was effected by an order-in-council and subsequently confirmed in the *Imperial Colonial Boundaries Act*, 1895, Regnal. 58 and 59 Vict., c. 34. See also Kindred, et al., *International Law Chiefly as Interpreted and Applied in Canada*, 455.

23  Beattie and Geiger, *Frozen in Time*, 141.

24  Rae, "The Arctic Expedition."

25  Rae, *John Rae's Correspondence with the Hudson's Bay Company on Arctic Exploration, 1844–1855*, 286–7.

26  McGoogan, *Lady Franklin's Revenge*, 339.

27  Dickens, "The Lost Arctic Voyagers," 362. See also McGoogan, *Fatal Passage*, 227.

28  Rae, "The Lost Arctic Voyagers."

29  Walker, dir., *Passage*. For a synopsis of this film, see http://www.onf-nfb.gc.ca/eng/collection/film/?id=54861.

30  Shortly before his death in 1999, the shaman Nicholas Qayutinuaq told this story to Tommy Anguttitauruq, cited in Eber, *Encounters on the Passage*, 76–8.

CHAPTER FOUR

1   Cited in Rasmussen, *Across Arctic America*, 381.

2   Van Deusen, *Kiviuq*, 3.

3   A version of the story that is similar to what Rasmussen heard is recounted by Anna Kappianaq in Tulugarjuk and Arnakak, eds, *Unikkaaqtuat Qikiqtanin-ngaaqtut*, vol. 1, *Arctic Bay and Igloolik*, 99–105.

4   Houston, dir., *Kiviuq*; *Kiviuq's Journey* website, http://www.unipka.ca.

5   John Houston, communication with author, 31 August 2012.

6   Van Deusen, *Kiviuq*, 343–7.

7   Aupilaarjuk et al., *Interviewing Inuit Elders*, 193.

8   Kimmaliadjuk, "The Goose-Wife Told by Theresa Kimmaliadjuk."

9   Cited in "Comments from Nunavut Elders on Storytelling."

10  Van Deusen, *Kiviuq*, 348.

11  Ibid., 337.

12  Cited in ibid., 336.

13  Cited in ibid., 157. See also Mariano Aupilardjuk, cited in "Comments from Nunavut Elders on Storytelling."

14 Tulugarjuk and Arnakak, eds, *Unikkaaqtuat Qikiqtaninngaaqtut*, vol. 1, *Arctic Bay and Igloolik*, 6.
15 Cited in Dick, *Muskox Land*, 99.
16 Mary-Rousselière, *Qitdlarssuaq*, 42.
17 Cited in Rasmussen, *People of the Polar North*, 27.
18 Tulugarjuk and Arnakak, eds, *Unikkaaqtuat Qikiqtaninngaaqtut*, vol. 1, *Arctic Bay and Igloolik*, 6.
19 Kunuk, dir., *Atanarjuat*.
20 Wissink, "The Qitdlarssuaq Chronicles, Part 1," 2.
21 Cited in Rasmussen, *People of the Polar North*, 28.
22 Mary-Rousselière, *Qitdlarssuaq*, 42.
23 Cited in Rasmussen, *People of the Polar North*, 29.
24 Cited in ibid., 32.
25 Cited in ibid., 33–4.
26 In Smith and Szucs, dirs, *Vanishing Point*.
27 See Wissink, "The Qitdlarssuaq Chronicles, Parts 1–4."
28 Mary-Rousselière, *Qitdlarssuaq*, 160–1.
29 Ehrlich, *This Cold Heaven*, 53.
30 Rasmussen, *Across Arctic America*, 21–5.
31 Ibid., 381–6.

CHAPTER FIVE
1 Cited in Bennett and Rowley, eds, *Uqalurait*, 431.
2 Nansen, "Preface," v.
3 O'Fallon and Fehren-Schmitz, "Native Americans Experienced a Strong Population Bottleneck Coincident with European Contact."
4 Aupilaarjuk et al., *Interviewing Inuit Elders*, 98.
5 Pelly and Minty, "Dundas Harbour."
6 Bernier, *Master Mariner and Arctic Explorer*, 343–4.
7 MacMillan, *Paris 1919*, 44–9.
8 Heron, *The Workers' Revolt in Canada, 1917–1925*.
9 King, *Defiant Spirits*.
10 Titley, *A Narrow Vision*, 50.
11 *Northwest Game Act*, SC 1917, c. 36, RSC 1927, c. 141, http://www.justice.gov.nt.ca/Legal/documents/AuthoritiesVol1-21.pdf.
12 Pelly, *Sacred Hunt*, 106.
13 Aupilaarjuk et al., *Interviewing Inuit Elders*, 34.
14 Reaney, "Pond Inlet Graves Moved."
15 See "La mort violente de l'oncle Victor, dans l'Extrême Nord canadien."
16 Briggs, "To the Ragged Edge of the World (Devon Island 1998)."
17 Cited in Grant, *Arctic Justice*, 229.
18 Cited in ibid., 154.
19 Cited in ibid., 159.
20 "RCMP Annual Report for the Year Ending March 1924," cited in ibid., 163.
21 *Reference re Secession of Quebec*, [1998] 2 SCR 217, http://scc-csc.lexum.com/decisia-scc-csc/scc-csc/scc-csc/en/item/1643/index.do.
22 *Constitution Act*, 1982, being Schedule B to the *Canada Act 1982* (UK), 1982, c. 11, s. 35 (1), http://www.canlii.org/en/ca/const/const1982.html.

23 Ibid., s. 35 (2), s. 35 (3).

24 George, *Lament for Confederation*, quoted in Henderson, *First Nations Jurisprudence and Aboriginal Rights*, 17.

25 Borrows, *Canada's Indigenous Constitution*, 282–3.

26 *Alaska Native Claims Settlement Act*, [1971] 43 USC 1601, c. 33, http://www.law.cornell.edu/uscode/text/43/chapter-33.

27 Government of the United States, *Treaty Concerning the Cession of the Russian Possessions in North America by His Majesty the Emperor of All the Russias to the United States of America.*

28 *Rupert's Land Act*, 1868, 31–32 Vict., c. 105 (UK), http://caid.ca/RupLan Act1868.pdf, confirmed in the *Imperial Colonial Boundaries Act*, 1895, 58–59 Vict., c. 34 (UK), http://www.legislation.gov.uk/ukpga/1895/34/pdfs/ukpga_18950034_en.pdf.

29 Currie, *Public International Law*, 229.

30 Ibid., 237.

31 Ibid., 241.

32 Secretariat of the Antarctic Treaty, *The Antarctic Treaty.*

33 *Agreement Governing the Activities of States on the Moon and Other Celestial Bodies*, 5 December 1979, 1363 UNTS 3.

34 Parliament of Canada, Senate, *Debates*, 20 February 1907, 271.

35 Byers and Lalonde, "Who Controls the Northwest Passage?"; Killaby, "'Great Game in a Cold Climate'"; Pharand, *Canada's Arctic Waters in International Law.*

36 *North Sea Continental Shelf Cases (Federal Republic of Germany v. Denmark and v. Netherlands)*, [1969] ICJ Rep. 3.

37 *Fisheries Case (United Kingdom v. Norway)*, [1951] ICJ Rep. 116; United Nations, *United Nations Convention on the Law of the Sea.*

38 *Corfu Channel Case (United Kingdom v. Albania)*, [1949] ICJ Rep. 4.

39 Pharand, *Canada's Arctic Waters in International Law*, 224.

40 Ibid.

41 Ibid., 225.

42 Byers, "Canada's Arctic Nightmare Just Came True."

43 Dawson, "Canada Suspends Military Operations Near Disputed Hans Island."

44 Government of Canada, Fisheries and Oceans Canada, "United Nations Convention on the Law of the Sea."

45 Stewart, "(Almost) Everyone Agrees."

46 Suthren, *The Island of Canada*, 326.

47 United Nations, *United Nations Convention on the Law of the Sea*, art. 234.

48 Government of Canada, Transport Canada, *Arctic Waters Pollution Prevention Act*, RSC 1985, c. A-12, http://www.tc.gc.ca/eng/marinesafety/debs-arctic-acts-regulations-awppa-494.htm.

49 See Canadian Coast Guard, "Northern Canada Vessel Traffic Services Zone (NORDREG)."

50 Inuit Circumpolar Council, *A Circumpolar Inuit Declaration on Sovereignty in the Arctic.* See appendix 1 for the full text.

51 *Agreement between the Inuit of the Nunavut Settlement Area and Her Majesty the Queen in Right of Canada [Nunavut Land Claims Agreement].*

52 Byers, *Who Owns the Arctic?* 126.

53  Ibid., 50–1.
54  Inuit Tapiriit Kanatami, *An Integrated Arctic Strategy.*
55  Lackenbauer, *The Canadian Rangers.*
56  Tobias, *Living Proof*, 53. See also the Nunavut Planning Commission website, http://www.nunavut.ca.
57  Pharand, *Canada's Arctic Waters in International Law*, 252.
58  *Legal Status of Eastern Greenland (Den. v. Nor.)*, 1933 PCIJ (ser. A/B), no. 53 (Apr. 5), http://www.worldcourts.com/pcij/eng/decisions/1933.04.05_greenland.htm.
59  For a good review of the issues, see Spector, "Western Sahara and the Self-Determination Debate."
60  *Advisory Opinion on the Western Sahara*, [1975] ICJ Rep. 12, paras 152, 162.
61  *United Nations International Covenant on Civil and Political Rights*, 19 December 1966, 999 UNTS 171 (entered into force 23 March 1976), art. 1; *United Nations International Covenant on Economic, Social and Cultural Rights*, 19 December 1966, 993 UNTS 3 (entered into force 3 January 1976), art. 1.
62  United Nations, *United Nations Declaration on the Rights of Indigenous Peoples*, art. 3. See appendix 3 for the full text.
63  Ibid., art. 1.
64  See Daschuk, *Clearing the Plains.*
65  Saul, "Listen to the North," 4.
66  Ibid., 3.
67  Cited in "Harper on Arctic."
68  Flaherty, dir., *Nanook of the North.*
69  Saul, *A Fair Country*, 286.

CHAPTER SIX

1  Inuit Circumpolar Council, *A Circumpolar Inuit Declaration on Sovereignty in the Arctic*, art. 2.1. See appendix 1 for the full text.
2  Mowat, *Walking on the Land*, 13.
3  See Laugrand, Oosten, and Serkoak, "Relocating the Ahiarmiut from Ennadai Lake to Arviat (1950–1958)," for an excellent review of the Ahiarmiut relocations based on the workshop "Survival and Angakkuuniq," with Ahiarmiut elders Job and Eva Muqyunnik and Luke and Mary Anautalik, held in Arviat, Nunavut, 2003.
4  Mowat, *Walking on the Land*, 49.
5  Cited in Tassinan, dir., *Broken Promises.*
6  Ibid.
7  Cited in Tester and Kulchyski, *Tammarniit (Mistakes)*, 236.
8  Cited in ibid., 139.
9  Amagoalik, *Changing the Face of Canada*, 18–19.
10  Cited in Marcus, *Out in the Cold*, 18.
11  Cited in ibid., 17.
12  Cited in Tester and Kulchyski, *Tammarniit (Mistakes)*, 140.
13  Amagoalik, *Changing the Face of Canada*, 19.
14  Cited in Tester and Kulchyski, *Tammarniit (Mistakes)*, 145.
15  Cited in ibid., 140.
16  Cited in McGrath, *Long Exile*, 186.

17  Cited in Tester and Kulchyski, *Tammarniit (Mistakes)*, 152.
18  Amagoalik, *Changing the Face of Canada*, 28, 31.
19  Cited in Government of Canada, Royal Commission on Aboriginal Peoples, *The High Arctic Relocation*, 30.
20  McGrath, *Long Exile*, 216–20.
21  Cited in Marcus, *Relocating Eden*, 98.
22  Martha Flaherty, personal communication with author, 15 January 2014.
23  In Tassinan, dir., *Broken Promises*.
24  In ibid.
25  *Agreement between the Inuit of the Nunavut Settlement Area and Her Majesty the Queen in Right of Canada [Nunavut Land Claims Agreement]*.
26  Government of Canada, Royal Commission on Aboriginal Peoples, *The High Arctic Relocation*.
27  Government of Canada, Aboriginal Affairs and Northern Development Canada, "Government of Canada Apologizes for Relocation of Inuit Families to the High Arctic."
28  George, "Special Claim for Nunavut's Ennadai Lake Relocatees Moves Ahead."
29  John Amagoalik, personal communication with author, April 2005.
30  Grygier, *A Long Way from Home*. See also Pilon, *Ce qu'il faut pour vivre*, a moving film drama about an Inuit man and boy, and their experiences in a sanatorium in Quebec during the early 1950s.
31  Erasmus, "Interview with Elisapee Karetak," 3.
32  Qikiqtani Truth Commission, "Analysis of the RCMP Sled Dog Report" and "Qimmiliriniq: Inuit Sled Dogs in Qikiqtaaluk," in *Thematic Reports and Special Studies, 1950 to 1975*, 7–66, 323–82.
33  There is a large and growing literature on residential schools in Canada, although relatively little of it focuses on the Inuit experience. See Pauktuutit Inuit Women's Association of Canada, *Sivumuapallianiq*. See also Truth and Reconciliation Commission of Canada, *Canada, Aboriginal Peoples, and Residential Schools*; *Interim Report*; and "Northern National Event." See also Fontaine, *Broken Circle*; Haig-Brown, *Resistance and Renewal*; Miller, *Shingwauk's Vision*; Milloy, *A National Crime*; and Regan, *Unsettling the Settler Within*.
34  Truth and Reconciliation Commission of Canada, *Canada, Aboriginal Peoples, and Residential Schools*, 77–9.
35  Government of Canada, Aboriginal Affairs and Northern Development Canada, "Prime Minister Harper Offers Full Apology on Behalf of Canadians for the Indian Residential Schools System."
36  Qikiqtani Truth Commission, *Community Histories, 1950 to 1975*.
37  Excerpt of video testimony by Peter Irniq, in IsumaTV, *Truth and Reconciliation*, reproduced with permission.
38  Amagoalik, *Changing the Face of Canada*, 43.
39  Kreelak, dir., *Kikkik E1-472*.

CHAPTER SEVEN
 1  Cited in Bennett and Rowley, eds, *Uqalurait*, 118.
 2  Kingwatsiaq, "Country Food Shouldn't Be Sold," cited in Gombay, *Making a Living*, 15.

3  Cone, *Silent Snow.*

4  Munro, "'Unprecedented' Ozone Hole Opens over Canadian Arctic."

5  Mercer, *Claiming Nunavut, 1971–1999,* 21.

6  Cited in ibid., 22–3.

7  For a useful summary of constitutional history since 1867, see Dodek *The Canadian Constitution.*

8  See Reid, *Louis Riel and the Creation of Modern Canada*; and Waiser and Stonechild, *Loyal to Death.*

9  Daschuk, *Clearing the Plains,* 79–158.

10  *Indian Act,* RSC 1985, c. I-5 (amended; first passed in 1876), http://laws.justice. gc.ca/eng/acts/I-5.

11  A detailed history of contact and conflict between Aboriginals, whites, and Chinese in central British Columbia is hard to find. Most histories of this period say little or nothing about Aboriginal resistance to the incursion of miners and settlers. See Barman, *The West beyond the West,* which is the authoritative history of the province but contains only sparse references to Indigenous resistance. See also Forsythe and Dickson, *The Trail of 1858*; and Griffin, *Radical Roots,* esp. ch. 7, 91–104.

12  See Ladner and Simpson, *This is an Honour Song*; and Swain, *Oka.*

13  *Agreement between the Inuit of the Nunavut Settlement Area and Her Majesty the Queen in Right of Canada [Nunavut Land Claims Agreement].*

14  Government of Canada, Aboriginal Affairs and Northern Development Canada, *Statement of the Government of Canada on Indian policy (The White Paper, 1969).*

15  See, for example, Cardinal, *The Unjust Society.*

16  *The James Bay and Northern Quebec Agreement,* 13 February 1975, http://www.gcc.ca/pdf/LEG000000006.pdf.

17  *Alaska Native Claims Settlement Act,* [1971] 43 USC 1601, c. 33, http://www.law.cornell.edu/uscode/text/43/chapter-33. See also Jones, *Alaska Native Claims Settlement Act of 1971 (Public Law 92-203).*

18  Amagoalik, *Changing the Face of Canada,* 73–4.

19  Alfred, *Wasáse,* 122.

20  Rasmussen, *Across Arctic America,* 126–7.

21  For information on the transliteration of Inuktitut syllabics into English, see http://www.translitteration.com/transliteration/en/inuktitut/canadian-aboriginal-syllabics.

22  *Bill C-38* is also called the *Civil Marriage Act,* or *An Act Respecting Certain Aspects of Legal Capacity for Marriage for Civil Purposes,* SC 2005, c. 33.

23  Bell, "Nunavut's MP Says Yes to Same-Sex Marriage."

24  Williamson, "'Arnaasiaq' and 'Angutaasiaq' People Deserve Love and Tolerance."

25  Tait, "Chevron, Statoil Set a Course for Arctic Exploration."

26  CBC *News,* "Oil Companies Seek to Drill in Deep Beaufort Sea."

27  Varga, "Oil and Gas Pose Big Questions for Baffin Region Inuit," 1.

28  Macalister, "Greenland Halts New Oil Drilling Licences."

29  *Nunavut Land Claims Agreement,* art. 12.

30  Ibid., arts 12.2.6, 12.2.24.

31  Ibid., arts 12.2.24 to 12.2.27.

32  Ibid., art. 12.2.2.
33  Ibid., art. 12.2.3.
34  Ibid., art. 12.5.
35  Ibid., art. 12.3.
36  Ibid., art. 12.6.
37  CBC *News*, "Sabina Buys Bathurst Inlet Port and Road Project."
38  Bathurst Inlet Port and Road Project, NWT *Community Consultation.*
39  See Bathurst Inlet Port and Road Project, "Executive Summary."
40  Herman, "Port and Road Project Delay."
41  Thorpe et al., *Thunder on the Tundra.* See also Flanders et al., *Caribou Land-scape Vulnerability Mapping for the Proposed Bathurst Inlet Port and Road.* My thanks to David Gladders, a co-author of the latter report, for allowing me access to this document.
42  Nunavut Impact Review Board, *Final Hearing Report.*
43  Government of Canada, Aboriginal Affairs and Northern Development Canada, "Government of Canada Approves Baffinland Mary River Project."
44  Nunavut Impact Review Board, *Final Hearing Report,* x.
45  The following information on the Mary River Project is from notes taken by the author while listening to the oral evidence presented during the five days of the NIRB's public hearing, unless otherwise indicated by a note.
46  For a summary of the Baffinland Iron Mines Corporation's presentation, see Baffinland, "NIRB Final Hearings for Mary River Project."
47  Professor Enuaraq was speaking at the NIRB's public hearing as a private citizen, not as a representative of Arctic College.
48  See Qikiqtani Inuit Association, *The Mary River Project Inuit Impact and Benefit Agreement.*
49  Mukshowya Niviaqsi, communication with author, Vancouver, 5 September 2012.
50  In IsumaTV, *Zacharias Kunuk with Lloyd Lipsett.* For information on Kunuk's work, see Evans, *Isuma*; and the IsumaTV website, http://www.isuma.tv/hi/en.
51  Jordan, "Baffinland Iron Mines Sharply Scales back Mary River Project."
52  Waldie, "Baffinland CEO Says No to Northwest Passage."
53  Inuit Circumpolar Council, *A Circumpolar Inuit Declaration on Resource Development Principles in Inuit Nunaat.* See appendix 2 for the full text.
54  Cited in Bennett and Rowley, eds, *Uqalurait,* 118.
55  CBC *News*, "Arctic Leaders."
56  *Qikiqtani Inuit Association v. Canada (Minister of Natural Resources), Attorney General of Canada, Nunavut (Minister Responsible for the Arctic College), the Commissioner of Nunavut,* 2010 NUCJ 12, http://www.nunatsiaqonline.ca/pub/docs/QIA_decision.pdf.
57  The Nunavut Court of Justice cited *Constitution Act, 1982,* being Schedule B to the *Canada Act 1982* (UK), 1982, c. 11, s. 35; *Haida Nation v. British Columbia (Minister of Forests),* [2004] 3 SCR 511, [2005] 1 CNLR 72; *Little Salmon/Carmacks First Nation v. Yukon (Director, Agriculture Branch, Department of Energy, Mines and Resources),* 2008 YKCA 13, [2008] 4 CNLR 25; and *Mikisew Cree First Nation v. Canada (Minister of Canadian Heritage),* [2005] 3 SCR 388, [2006] 1 CNLR 78.
58  Qikiqtani Inuit Association, *Tallurutiup Tariunga Inulik.*

59  Galloway, "Ottawa Sets up Arctic Marine Park."
60  *Constitution Act, 1982*, being Schedule B to the *Canada Act 1982* (UK), 1982, c. 11, s. 35.
61  Newman, *The Duty to Consult*, 16. See also *Taku River Tlingit First Nation v. British Columbia (Project Assessment Director)*, 2003 SCC 74, [2004] 3 SCR 550.
62  See *Mikisew Cree First Nation v. Canada (Minister of Canadian Heritage)*, [2005] 3 SCR 388, [2006] 1 CNLR 78.
63  In Yaffe, "Resource Sector about to Witness New Era of Native Empowerment." See also Gallagher, *Resource Rulers.*
64  See United Nations, *United Nations Declaration on the Rights of Indigenous Peoples*, esp. arts 10, 19, 28, 29, 32, as well as provisions on consultation and accommodation in relation to land use and other rights. The full text of the declaration is in appendix 3.
65  Government of Canada, Aboriginal Affairs and Northern Development Canada, "Backgrounder."
66  See Taracena, "Implementing the *Declaration*"; and Joffe, "Canada's Opposition to the UN *Declaration.*"
67  Branswell, "Death, Suicide Rates among Inuit Kids Soar over Rest of Canada."
68  Inuit Tapiriit Kanatami, *Health Indicators of Inuit Nunangat within the Canadian Context, 1994–1998 and 1999–2003.*
69  Nunavut Tunngavik Incorporated, *Backgrounder.*
70  Tarasuk, Mitchell, and Dachner, *Household Food Insecurity in Canada, 2011.*
71  Inuit Tapiriit Kanatami, *Inuit and Cancer.*
72  Inuit Tapiriit Kanatami, *Health Indicators*; Statistics Canada, "Infant Mortality Rates, by Province and Territory."
73  Government of Canada, Department of Justice, *Background Information.*
74  Kappianaq and Nutaraq, *Inuit Perspectives on the 20th Century*, vol. 2, *Travelling and Surviving on Our Land*, 160–1.

CHAPTER EIGHT

1  Watt-Cloutier and Hassan, "Planet Earth."
2  Arctic Climate Impact Assessment, *Impacts of a Warming Arctic*, "Executive Summary," 2.
3  Ibid.
4  Ibid., 10, 11.
5  Stott, "Global-Average Temperature Records."
6  National Oceanic and Atmospheric Administration (NOAA), "Climate."
7  See, for example, Hansen et al., "Global Climate Changes as Forecast by Goddard Institute for Space Studies Three-Dimensional Model," 9341–64.
8  NOAA, "Globe Had Eighth Warmest August on Record."
9  NOAA, *Arctic Report Card.*
10  NOAA, National Climatic Data Center, *Global Climate Change Indicators.*
11  Farnell, "Why the IPCC Climate Change Report Is Flawed."
12  United Nations, Intergovernmental Panel on Climate Change (IPCC), *Fifth Assessment Report: Climate Change 2013: The Physical Science Basis: Summary for Policymakers*, 3.
13  IPCC, *Fifth Assessment Report: Climate Change 2013: The Physical Science Basis*, ch. 9, 3.

14  IPCC, *Fifth Assessment Report: Climate Change 2013: The Physical Science Basis: Summary for Policymakers*, 3.

15  North Pole Environmental Observatory, webcam, 22 July 2013, http://psc.apl.washington.edu/northpole/NPEO2013/webcam2.html.

16  Ahmed, "White House Warned on Imminent Arctic Ice Death Spiral."

17  National Aeronautic and Space Administration, "Warm Ocean Rapidly Melting Antarctic Ice Shelf from Below."

18  Homer-Dixon and Weaver, "Climate Uncertainty Shouldn't Mean Inaction."

19  Meehl et al., "Model-Based Evidence of Deep-Ocean Heat Uptake during Surface-Temperature Hiatus Periods."

20  Harvey, "Climate Change Slowdown Is Due to Warming of Deep Oceans, Say Scientists."

21  IPCC, *Fifth Assessment Report: Climate Change 2013: The Physical Science Basis: Summary for Policymakers*, 4.

22  Lloyd, "Twenty-Year Hiatus in Rising Temperatures Has Climate Scientists Puzzled."

23  Mohan, "Carbon Dioxide Levels in Atmosphere Pass 400 Milestone, Again."

24  Fagan, *The Great Warming*, 230.

25  Ruddiman, *Plows, Plagues, and Petroleum*, 137–8.

26  See the extensive documentation at the IPCC website, http://www.ipcc.ch.

27  Hansen, *Storms of My Grandchildren*, 250–1.

28  Kappianaq and Nutaraq, *Inuit Perspectives on the 20th Century*, vol. 2, *Travelling and Surviving on Our Land*, 152–3.

29  Fox, "When the Weather Is Uggianaqtuq."

30  Arctic Climate Impact Assessment, *Impacts of a Warming Arctic*, ch. 3, 82.

31  Ibid.

32  Ibid., ch. 3, 83.

33  Ibid., ch. 3, 84.

34  Leah Aqpik, Uqigjuaqsi Adamie Inookie, and Qaunaq Mikkigak, oral presentations at Arctic Institute of North America, "Tusaqtuut"; Houston, dir., *Diet of Souls*; Kunuk and Mauro, dirs, *Qapirangajuk*.

35  Both the screening of the film *Qapirangajuk* and the follow-up commentary were streamed live from Toronto. See the discussion of what the filmmakers discovered in the making of the film at http://www.youtube.com/watch?v=kOhaoliLow4. For more information, see http://www.isuma.tv/inuit-knowledge-and-climate-change.

36  Inuit Circumpolar Council, "Inuit Petition Inter-American Commission on Human Rights to Oppose Climate Change Caused by the United States of America"; Inuit Circumpolar Council, *Petition to the Inter-American Commission on Human Rights Seeking Relief from Violations Resulting from Global Warming Caused by Acts and Omissions of the United States*.

37  Inter-American Commission on Human Rights, *Mary and Carrie Dann v. United States*, 2002, case no. 11.140, resolution no. 75/02; Inter-American Commission on Human Rights, *Maya Indigenous Communities of the Toledo District (Belize Maya)*, 2004, case no. 12.053, resolution no. 40/04; Inter-American Commission on Human Rights, *Yanomami Community v. Brazil*, 1985, case no. 7615, resolution no. 12/85; Inter-American Court of Human Rights, *Mayagna (Sumo) Awas Tingni Community v. Nicaragua*, 2001, ser. C, no. 79.

38  Osofsky, "Complexities of Addressing the Impacts of Climate Change on Indigenous Peoples through International Law Petitions," 325.
39  Cited in ibid., 314.
40  Inuit Circumpolar Council, *Petition to the Inter-American Commission on Human Rights*, paras 75-95.
41  Inter-American Commission on Human Rights, *American Declaration of the Rights and Duties of Man*.
42  Organization of American States, *American Convention on Human Rights*.
43  Inuit Circumpolar Council, *Petition to the Inter-American Commission on Human Rights*, para. 18.
44  See, in particular, *United Nations International Covenant on Civil and Political Rights* (ICCPR), 19 December 1966, 999 UNTS 171 (entered into force 23 March 1976).
45  *Chief Bernard Ominayak and the Lubicon Lake Band v. Canada*, 1990 UNHRC, doc. CCPR/C/38/D/167/1984.
46  *ICCPR*, art. 27.
47  Inter-American Court of Human Rights, *Mayagna (Sumo) Awas Tingni Community v. Nicaragua*, 2001, ser. C, no. 79.
48  Inter-American Commission on Human Rights, *Maya Indigenous Communities of the Toledo District (Belize Maya)* (2004), case no. 12.053, resolution no. 40/04; Inter-American Commission on Human Rights, *Yanomami Community v. Brazil* (1985), case no. 7615, resolution no. 12/85.
49  Inter-American Commission on Human Rights, *Report on the Situation of Human Rights of a Segment of the Nicaraguan Population of Miskito Origin*, 76, cited in Inuit Circumpolar Council, *Petition to the Inter-American Commission on Human Rights*, para. 75.
50  *ICCPR*, art. 1; *United Nations International Covenant on Economic, Social and Cultural Rights*, 19 December 1966, 993 UNTS 3 (entered into force 3 January 1976), art. 1.
51  United Nations, *United Nations Declaration on the Rights of Indigenous Peoples*, art. 3.
52  Government of Canada, Aboriginal Affairs and Northern Development Canada, "Backgrounder."
53  Canada's statement of acceptance is similar to those of Australia and the United States. New Zealand's statement accepted the declaration as affirming international and national law on Maori rights.
54  There is an enormous literature on self-determination. For a small sample, see Anaya, *Indigenous Peoples in International Law*; Brownlie, *Principles of Public International Law*; Cassese, *Self-Determination of Peoples*; Charlesworth and Chinkin, *The Boundaries of International Law*; Henderson, *Indigenous Diplomacy and the Rights of Peoples*; Joffe, "Canada's Opposition to the UN Declaration"; Knop, *Diversity and Self-Determination in International Law*; and Venne, *Our Elders Understand Our Rights*.
55  *Reference re Secession of Quebec*, [1998] 2 SCR 217, http://scc-csc.lexum.com/decisia-scc-csc/scc-csc/scc-csc/en/item/1643/index.do.
56  *Constitution Act*, 1982, being Schedule B to the *Canada Act 1982* (UK), 1982, c. 11, s. 35. See also Government of Canada, Aboriginal Affairs and Northern Development Canada, *The Government of Canada's Approach to Implementa-*

*tion of the Inherent Right and the Negotiation of Aboriginal Self*-Government;
and Borrows, *Canada's Indigenous Constitution*.

57  *Agreement between the Inuit of the Nunavut Settlement Area and Her Majesty
    the Queen in Right of Canada [Nunavut Land Claims Agreement]*.

58  See Christie, "Aboriginal Nationhood and the Inherent Right to Self-
    Government."

59  United Nations, Permanent Forum on Indigenous Issues, "Climate Change."

60  Davis, "Climate Change Impacts to Aboriginal and Torres Strait Islander
    Communities in Australia," 498.

61  *Native Village of Kivalina and City of Kivalina v. ExxonMobil Corporation et
    al.*, [2008] 28 USC 1331, 2201, http://www.climatelaw.org/cases/country/us/
    kivalina/Kivalina%20Complaint.pdf.

62  See Government of New Zealand, Department of Immigration, "How Do I
    Qualify for Residence under the 2012 Pacific Access Category?"

63  McAdam, *Climate Change, Forced Migration, and International Law*.

65  National Round Table on the Environment and the Economy (Canada), *Paying
    the Price*.

65  Ibid., 69.

66  Curry and McCarthy, "Canada Formally Abandons Kyoto Protocol on Climate
    Change."

CHAPTER NINE

1   Cited in Wiebe, *Playing Dead*, 125.

2   *Agreement between the Inuit of the Nunavut Settlement Area and Her Majesty
    the Queen in Right of Canada [Nunavut Land Claims Agreement]*.

3   Watt-Cloutier, "Presentation by Sheila Watt-Cloutier, Chair, Inuit Circumpolar
    Conference, Eleventh Conference of Parties to the UN Framework Convention
    on Climate Change, Montreal, December 7, 2005," cited in Osofsky, "Com-
    plexities of Addressing the Impacts of Climate Change on Indigenous Peoples
    through International Law Petitions," 336.

4   Regulation (EC) no. 1007/2009 of the European Parliament and of the Council
    of 16 September 2009 on Trade in Seal Products, http://eur-lex.europa.eu/
    smartapi/cgi/sga_doc?smartapi!celexplus!prod!CELEXnumdoc&lg=EN&
    numdoc=32009R1007.

5   Curry and Clarke, "Canada Using Inuit as Political Tool at Summit, Critics
    Say."

6   See Feeney, dir., *Eskimo Artist*.

7   See Kreelak, dir., *Kikkik E1-472*.

8   Elizabeth Nutarakittuq, cited in Bennett and Rowley, eds, *Uqalurait*, 48.

9   Peter Tatigat Arnatsiaq, cited in Bennett and Rowley, eds, *Uqalurait*, 44.

10  Van Deusen, *Kiviuq*, 25.

11  Polar Bears International, *Polar Bear Facts and Information*.

12  *Agreement on Conservation of Polar Bears*, Oslo, Norway, 15 November 1973,
    http://sedac.ciesin.org/entri/texts/polar.bears.1973.html.

13  United Nations, *United Nations Convention on International Trade in Endan-
    gered Species of Wild Fauna and Flora*.

14  *Marine Mammal Protection Act*, [1972] 16 USC, c. 31, http://www.nmfs.noaa.
    gov/pr/laws/mmpa/text.htm.

15  International Fund for Animal Welfare, "Animal Welfare and Conservation Groups Urge Congress to Protect Polar Bears from Trophy Hunting."

16  World Wildlife Federation, Conservation Action Network, "Polar Bear Seas Protection Act Gains Cosponsors."

17  *Endangered Species Act*, [1973] 7 USC 136, 16 USC 1531, http://www.fws.gov/endangered/laws-policies/index.html.

18  *Species at Risk Act*, SC 2002, c. 29, s. 2 (1), http://laws.justice.gc.ca/eng/S-15.3/index.html.

19  *Nunavut Wildlife Act*, SNU 2003, c. 26, http://www.canlii.org/en/nu/laws/stat/snu-2003-c-26/latest/snu-2003-c-26.html.

20  Wenzel and Dowsley, "Economic and Cultural Aspects of Polar Bear Sport Hunting in Nunavut, Canada," 43.

21  CBC *News*, "Hungry Polar Bears Resorting to Cannibalism."

22  Windeyer, "Influx of Bears a Nuisance across Nunavut."

23  Coca Cola's Christmas campaign (2011) partnered with the World Wildlife Fund to highlight the impact of climate change on polar bears. See the long version of the commercial at http://www.youtube.com/watch?v=hSBDFifNDuA.

24  Waldie, "Healthy Polar Bear Count Confounds Doomsayers."

25  IUCN/SSC Polar Bear Specialist Group, "Summary of Polar Bear Population Status per 2010."

26  Peacock et al., "Population Ecology of Polar Bears in Davis Strait, Canada and Greenland."

27  Kunuk and Mauro, dirs, *Qapirangajuk*.

28  Oral presentation at Arctic Institute of North America, "Tusaqtuut."

29  Martin, *Stories in a New Skin*, 1–2.

30  Regulation (EC) no. 1007/2009 of the European Parliament and of the Council of 16 September 2009 on Trade in Seal Products, http://eur-lex.europa.eu/smartapi/cgi/sga_doc?smartapi!celexplus!prod!CELEXnumdoc&lg=EN&numdoc=3 2009R1007.

31  Peter, speech presented at Canada House, Canadian High Commission, London.

32  See Potter, "Row Erupts over Governor General's Seal Taste."

CHAPTER TEN

1   Cited in Patrick et al., "'Regaining the Childhood I Should Have Had,'" 79.

2   Kennedy, "Missing Canadian Teenager Survives Three Days on Ice Floe." (The names of the two Inuit appear to be wrongly cited in this article.)

3   Patrick et al., "'Regaining the Childhood,'" 72.

4   *Re Eskimos (sub nom. Re Term "Indians")*, [1939] 2 DLR 417, [1939] SCR 104.

5   "Fiddling While the World Warms."

6   Peter, speech presented at Canada House, Canadian High Commission, London.

7   Cited in Leduc, *Climate, Culture, Change*, 36.

8   Ibid., 37.

9   Martin, *Stories in a New Skin*, 5.

10  Igjugarjuk of the Padlermiut (Caribou Inuit), cited in Rasmussen, *Across Arctic America*, 83-4, cited in Leduc, *Climate, Culture, Change*, 34.

11  Van Deusen, *Kiviuq*, 308, 310.

12  Ibid., 337.

13 Philip Paniaq, cited in ibid., 336.
14 *Agreement between the Inuit of the Nunavut Settlement Area and Her Majesty the Queen in Right of Canada [Nunavut Land Claims Agreement].*
15 Lovelock, *Gaia.*
16 MacKinnon, *The Once and Future World,* 77.

# Bibliography

Abate, Randall S., and Elizabeth Ann Kronk, eds. *Climate Change and Indigenous Peoples: The Search for Legal Remedies*. Cheltanham, UK: Edward Elgar, 2013.

Abele, Frances, Thomas J. Courchene, Leslie F. Seidle, and France St Hilaire, eds. *The Art of the State*. Vol. 4, *Northern Exposure: Peoples, Powers and Prospects in Canada's North*. Montreal: Institute for Research on Public Policy, 2009.

Abram, David. *Becoming Animal: An Earthly Cosmology*. New York: Pantheon, 2010.

*Agreement between the Inuit of the Nunavut Settlement Area and Her Majesty the Queen in Right of Canada [Nunavut Land Claims Agreement]*. 1993. http://www.nucj.ca/library/bar_ads_mat/Nunavut_Land_Claims_Agreement.pdf.

Agger, William A., and Herbert Maschner. "Medieval Norse and the Bidirectional Spread of Epidemic Disease between Europe and Northeastern America: A New Hypothesis." In *The Northern World, AD 900–1400*, ed. Herbert Maschner, Owen Mason, and Robert McGhee, 321–37. Salt Lake City: University of Utah Press, 2009.

Ahmed, Nafeez. "White House Warned on Imminent Arctic Ice Death Spiral." *Guardian* (London), 2 May 2013. http://www.guardian.co.uk/environment/earth-insight/2013/may/02/white-house-arctic-ice-death-spiral.

Alfred, Taiaiake. *Wasáse: Indigenous Pathways of Action and Freedom*. Peterborough, ON: Broadview, 2005.

Alia, Valerie. "Inuit Names: The People Who Love You." In *Hidden in Plain Sight: Contributions of Aboriginal Peoples to Canadian Identity and Culture*, ed. David Newhouse, Cora Voyageur, and Dan Beavon, 251–66. Toronto: University of Toronto Press, 2005.

– *Names and Nunavut: Culture and Identity in the Inuit Homeland*. New York: Berghahn, 2009.

Amagoalik, John. *Changing the Face of Canada: The Life Story of John Amagoalik*. Ed. Louis McComber. Iqaluit, NU: Nunavut Arctic College, 2007.

Anaya, S. James. *Indigenous Peoples in International Law*. 2nd ed. Oxford: Oxford University Press, 2004.

Arctic Climate Impact Assessment. *Impacts of a Warming Arctic*. Cambridge, UK: Cambridge University Press, 2004. http://www.acia.uaf.edu/default.html and http://amap.no/acia.

Arctic Institute of North America. "Tusaqtuut: The Peoples' Time for Sharing." Seminar with South Baffin (Uqqurmiut) Inuit elders, University of Calgary, 5 November 2010.

Armstrong, Jane. "Vikings in Canada?" *Maclean's Magazine*, 20 November 2012. http://www2.macleans.ca/2012/11/20/a-twist-in-time.

Aupilaarjuk, Mariano, Marie Tulimaaq, Akisu Joamie, Emile Imaruittuq, and Lucassie Nutaraaluk. *Interviewing Inuit Elders: Perspectives on Traditional Law*. Ed. Jarich Oosten, Frédéric Laugrand, and Wim Rasing. Iqaluit, NU: Nunavut Arctic College, 1999.

Austin, Henry. "Tourists Rescued after Nearly Two Days Stranded in Canadian Arctic." NBC *World News*, 27 June 2013. http://worldnews.nbcnews.com/_news/2013/06/27/19169774-tourists-rescued-after-nearly-2-days-stranded-in-canadian-arctic?lite.

Baffinland. "NIRB Final Hearings for Mary River Project." 11 September 2012. http://www.baffinland.com/uncategorized/nirb-final-hearings-for-mary-river-project/?lang=en.

Baikie, Caitlyn. "Inuit Perspectives on Recent Climate Change." *Skeptical Science*, 27 September 2012. http://www.skepticalscience.com/Inuit-Climate-Change.html.

Balog, James. *Extreme Ice Now: Vanishing Glaciers and Changing Climate – A Progress Report*. Washington, DC: National Geographic Society, 2009.

Banerjee, Subhankar, ed. *Arctic Voices: Resistance at the Tipping Point*. New York: Seven Stories Press, 2012.

Barman, Jean. *The West beyond the West: A History of British Columbia*. 3rd ed. Toronto: University of Toronto Press, 2007.

Bathurst Inlet Port and Road Project. "Executive Summary." In *Draft Environmental Impact Statement*, i-xix. ftp://ftp.nirb.ca/02-REVIEWS/ACTIVE%20REVIEWS/03UN114-BIPR/02-REVIEW/07-DRAFT%20EIS/01-DEIS/Executive%20Summaries/Executive%20Summary%20-%20English.pdf.

– NWT *Community Consultation*. 28 May 2013. http://www.miningnorth.com/wp-content/uploads/2013/05/BIPR-NWT-May-28-2013.pdf.

Beattie, Owen, and John Geiger. *Frozen in Time: The Fate of the Franklin Expedition*. Vancouver: Greystone, 1987.

Behringer, Wolfgang. *A Cultural History of Climate*. Cambridge, UK: Polity, 2010.

Bell, Catherine, and Robert K. Paterson. *Protection of First Nations Cultural Heritage: Laws, Policy and Reform*. Vancouver: UBC Press, 2009.

Bell, Jim. "Nunavut's MP Says Yes to Same-Sex Marriage: GN Won't Do Gay Weddings until Federal Law Passes." *Nunatsiaq News*, 22 April 2005. http://www.nunatsiaqonline.ca/stories/article/nunavuts_mp_says_yes_to_same-sex_marriage.

Bennett, John, and Susan Rowley, eds. *Uqalurait: An Oral History of Nunavut.* Montreal and Kingston: McGill-Queen's University Press, 2004.

Bernier, Joseph E. *Master Mariner and Arctic Explorer: A Narrative of Sixty Years at Sea from the Logs and Yarns of Captain J.E. Bernier.* Ottawa: Le Droit, 1939.

Borrows, John. *Canada's Indigenous Constitution.* Toronto: University of Toronto Press, 2010.

Brahic, Catherine, "Arctic Ice Low Heralds End of Three-Million-Year Cover." Editorial. *New Scientist,* 31 August 2012. http://www.newscientist.com/article/mg21528802.200-arctic-ice-low-heralds-end-of-3millionyear-cover.html.

Brandt, Anthony. *The Man Who Ate His Boots: The Tragic History of the Search for the Northwest Passage.* New York: Knopf Doubleday, 2010.

Branswell, Helen. "Death, Suicide Rates among Inuit Kids Soar over Rest of Canada." *Globe and Mail,* 18 July 2012. http://www.theglobeandmail.com/news/national/death-suicide-rates-among-inuit-kids-soar-over-rest-of-canada/article4426600.

Briggs, Sandy. "To the Ragged Edge of the World (Devon Island 1998)." N.d. http://www.tinoxygentungsten.com/Arctic/Sledding1.htm.

Brody, Hugh. *The Other Side of Eden: Hunters, Farmers, and the Shaping of the World.* New York: North Point, 2000.

– *The People's Land: Whites and the Eastern Arctic.* Harmondsworth, UK: Penguin, 1975.

Broecker, Wallace S. "Was the Medieval Warm Period Global?" *Science,* 23 February 2001, 1497–9.

Brownlie, Ian. *Principles of Public International Law.* 6th ed. Oxford: Clarendon, 2003.

Bunyan, Ian, Jenni Calder, Dale Idiens, and Bryce Wilson. *No Ordinary Journey: John Rae, Arctic Explorer, 1813-1893.* Montreal and Kingston: McGill-Queen's University Press, 1993.

Burt, Page. *Barrenland Beauties: Showy Plants of the Canadian Arctic.* Yellowknife, NT: Outcrop Northern Publishers, 2004.

Butler, Don. "Cold Comfort: Recognition for Research into Viking Presence in the Arctic Comes Too Late for a Fired Ottawa Archeologist." *Ottawa Citizen,* 22 November 2012, C1.

Byers, Michael. "Canada's Arctic Nightmare Just Came True: The Northwest Passage Is Commercial." *Globe and Mail,* 20 September 2013. http://www.theglobeandmail.com/commentary/canadas-arctic-nightmare-just-came-true-the-northwest-passage-is-commercial/article14432440.

– *Who Owns the Arctic? Understanding Sovereignty Disputes in the North.* Vancouver: Douglas and McIntyre, 2009.

Byers, Michael, and Suzanne Lalonde. "Who Controls the Northwest Passage?" *Vanderbilt Journal of Transnational Law,* October 2009, 1133–1210.

Cameron, David W., and Colin P. Groves. *Bones, Stones and Molecules: "Out of Africa" and Human Origins.* London: Elsevier Academic Press, 2004.

Canadian Broadcasting Corporation. "Silence of the Labs." *The Fifth Estate,* season 39, episode 10, 10 January 2014.

Canadian Coast Guard. "Northern Canada Vessel Traffic Services Zone (NORDREG)." N.d. http://www.ccg-gcc.gc.ca/eng/MCTS/Vtr_Arctic_Canada.

Cardinal, Harold. *The Unjust Society*. 1969. Reprint, Vancouver: Douglas and McIntyre, 1999.

Cassese, Antonio. *Self-Determination of Peoples: A Legal Reappraisal*. Cambridge, UK: Cambridge University Press, 1995.

CBC *News*. "Arctic Leaders: Lancaster Sound Plans in Conflict." 19 April 2010. http:www.cbc.ca/news/canada/north/story/2010/04/19/lancaster-sound-seismic. html.

– "Hungry Polar Bears Resorting to Cannibalism." 3 December 2009. http://www.cbc.ca/news/canada/manitoba/hungry-polar-bears-resorting-to-cannibalism-1.817518.

– "Oil Companies Seek to Drill in Deep Beaufort Sea: Imperial Oil Canada, Exxon Mobil and BP Jointly File for Arctic Offshore Drilling." 27 September 2013. http://www.cbc.ca/news/canada/north/oil-companies-seek-to-drill-in-deep-beaufort-sea-1.1871343.

– "Sabina Buys Bathurst Inlet Port and Road Project." 11 January 2012. http://www.cbc.ca/news/canada/north/story/2012/01/11/north-sabina-bathurst-inlet.html.

Charlesworth, Hilary, and Christine Chinkin. *The Boundaries of International Law: A Feminist Analysis*. Manchester, UK: Manchester University Press, 2000.

Christie, Gordon. "Aboriginal Nationhood and the Inherent Right to Self-Government." Research paper for the National Centre for First Nations Governance. May 2007. http://fngovernance.org/ncfng_research/gordon_christie.pdf.

– ed. *Aboriginality and Governance: A Multidisciplinary Approach*. Penticton, BC: Theytus, 2006.

Coates, Ken S. *A Global History of Indigenous Peoples: Struggle and Survival*. Basingstoke, UK: Palgrave MacMillan, 2004.

Coates, Ken S., P. Whitney Lackenbauer, William R. Morrison, and Greg Poelzer. *Arctic Front: Defending Canada in the Far North*. Toronto: Thomas Allen, 2008.

"Comments from Nunavut Elders on Storytelling." In *Kiviuq's Journey*. http://www.unipka.ca/quotes.html.

Cone, Marla. *Silent Snow: The Slow Poisoning of the Arctic*. New York: Grove, 2005.

Cousineau, Marie-Hélène, and Madeline Ivalu, dirs. *Before Tomorrow*. Feature film. Isuma Productions, 2008.

Couture, Pauline. *Ice: Beauty, Danger, History*. Toronto: McArthur and Company, 2005.

Cruikshank, Julie. *Do Glaciers Listen? Local Knowledge, Colonial Encounters, and Social Imagination*. Vancouver: UBC Press, 2005.

Currie, John. *Public International Law*. Toronto: Irwin Law, 2001.

Curry, Bill, and Campbell Clarke. "Canada Using Inuit as Political Tool at Summit, Critics Say: Government Accused of Attempting to Overturn EU's Ban of Seal Hunt through Promotion of Seal Products at G7 Meeting." *Globe and Mail*, 2 February 2010. http://www.theglobeandmail.com/news/politics/canada-using-inuit-as-political-tool-at-summit-critics-say/article1453893.

Curry, Bill, and Shawn McCarthy. "Canada Formally Abandons Kyoto Protocol on Climate Change." *Globe and Mail*, 12 December 2011. http://www.theglobeand mail.com/news/politics/canada-formally-abandons-kyoto-protocol-on-climate-change/article4180809.

Dahl, Jens, Jack Hicks, and Peter Jull. *Nunavut: Inuit Regain Control of Their Lands and Their Lives*. Copenhagen, Denmark: International Work Group for Indigenous Affairs, 2000.

Daschuk, James. *Clearing the Plains: Disease, Politics of Starvation, and the Loss of Aboriginal Life*. Regina, SK: University of Regina Press, 2013.

Davis, Megan, "Climate Change Impacts to Aboriginal and Torres Strait Islander Communities in Australia." In *Climate Change and Indigenous Peoples: The Search for Legal Remedies*, ed. Randall S. Abate and Elizabeth Ann Kronk, 493–507. Cheltanham, UK: Edward Elgar, 2013.

Dawson, Tyler. "Canada Suspends Military Operations Near Disputed Hans Island." 7 June 2013. http://o.canada.com/news/261064.

de Coccola, Raymond, with Paul King. *Ayorama: That's the Way It Is*. 1955. Reprint, Ottawa: Novalis, 2007.

Delgado, James P. *Across the Top of the World: The Quest for the Northwest Passage*. Vancouver: Douglas and McIntyre, 1999.

– *Dauntless St. Roch: The Mounties' Arctic Schooner*. Victoria, BC: Horsdal and Schubart, 1992.

Diamond, Jared. *Collapse: How Societies Choose to Fail or Succeed*. New York: Penguin, 2005.

Dick, Lyle. *Muskox Land: Ellesmere Island in the Age of Contact*. Calgary: University of Calgary Press, 2001.

Dickens, Charles. "The Lost Arctic Voyagers." *Household Words* 10, no. 245 (2 December 1854): 361–5.

Dickson, Frances Jewel. *The DEW Line Years: Voices from the Coldest Cold War*. Lawrencetown Beach, NS: Pottersfield, 2007.

Diubaldo, Richard J. *Stefansson and the Canadian Arctic*. Montreal and Kingston: McGill-Queen's University Press, 1978.

Dixon, Homer, ed. *Carbon Shift: How Peak Oil and the Climate Crisis Will Change Canada (and Our Lives)*. Toronto: Vintage Canada, 2010.

Dodek, Adam. *The Canadian Constitution*. Toronto: Dundurn, 2013.

Dorais, Louis-Jacques. *The Language of the Inuit: Syntax, Semantics and Society in the Arctic*. Montreal and Kingston: McGill-Queen's University Press, 2010.

Douglas, Chris, Leena Evik, Myna Ishulutak, Gavin Nesbitt, and Jeela Palluq, eds. *Inuktitut Essentials: A Phrasebook*. Iqaluit, NU: Pirurvik, 2009.

Eber, Dorothy Harley. *Encounters on the Passage: Inuit Meet the Explorers*. Toronto: University of Toronto Press, 2008.

– *When the Whalers Were Up North: Inuit Memories from the Eastern Arctic*. Montreal and Kingston: McGill-Queen's University Press, 1989.

Ehrlich, Gretel. *This Cold Heaven: Seven Seasons in Greenland*. New York: Vintage, 2001.

Ehrlich, Paul, and Anne H. Ehrlich. *The Dominant Animal: Human Evolution and the Environment*. Washington, DC: Island Press and Shearwater Books, 2008.

Emerson, Charles. *The Future History of the Arctic*. Philadelphia, PA: PublicAffairs, 2010.

English, John. *Ice and Water: Politics, Peoples, and the Arctic Council*. Toronto: Allen Lane, 2013.

Erasmus, Naomi. "Interview with Elisapee Karetak." *Indigenous Times* 1, no. 1 (Fall 2004): 2–7.

Evans, Michael Robert. *The Fast Runner: Filming the Legend of Atanarjuat.* Lincoln: University of Nebraska Press, 2010.

– *Isuma: Inuit Video Art.* Montreal and Kingston: McGill-Queen's University Press, 2008.

Fagan, Brian. *The Great Warming: Climate Change and the Rise and Fall of Civilizations.* New York: Bloomsbury, 2008.

Farnell, Anthony. "Why the IPCC Climate Change Report Is Flawed." *Global News,* 29 September 2013. http://globalnews.ca/news/868787/why-the-ipcc-climate-change-report-is-flawed.

Feeney, John, dir. *Eskimo Artist: Kenojuak.* Documentary. National Film Board of Canada, 1963.

"Fiddling While the World Warms: Assessments of Climate Change Must Come Faster and More Frequently." Editorial. *Scientific American,* October 2013, 12.

Flaherty, Robert J., dir. *Nanook of the North: A Story of Life and Love in the Actual Arctic.* Feature film. Revillon Frères, 1922.

Flanders, David, Anne Gunn, Petr Cizek, and David Gladders. *Caribou Landscape Vulnerability Mapping for the Proposed Bathurst Inlet Port and Road.* Submitted by the Canadian Arctic Resources Committee to the Nunavut Impact Review Board as part of the CACR Technical Presentation, December 2009.

Flannery, Tim. *Here on Earth: An Argument for Hope.* Melbourne, Australia: Text Publishing Company, 2010.

– *The Weather Makers: The History and Future Impact of Climate Change.* Melbourne, Australia: Text Publishing Company, 2005.

Fleming, Fergus. *Barrow's Boys: The Original Extreme Adventurers.* London: Granta Books, 2001.

Folger, Tim. "Viking Weather: Greenland's Changing Face." *National Geographic,* June 2010, 48–67.

Fontaine, Theodore. *Broken Circle: The Dark Legacy of Indian Residential Schools – A Memoir.* Vancouver: Heritage House, 2010.

Forsythe, Mark, and Greg Dickson. *The Trail of 1858: British Columbia's Gold Rush Past.* Madeira Park, BC: Harbour, 2007.

Fossett, Renée. *In Order to Live Untroubled: Inuit of the Central Arctic, 1550 to 1940.* Winnipeg: University of Manitoba Press, 2001.

Fox, Shari. "When the Weather Is Uggianaqtuq: Linking Inuit and Scientific Observations of Recent Environmental Change in Nunavut, Canada." PhD diss., University of Colorado, 2004.

Franklin, Jane. *As Affecting the Fate of My Absent Husband: Selected Letters of Lady Franklin Concerning the Search for the Lost Franklin Expedition, 1848–1860.* Ed. Erika Behrisch Elce. Montreal and Kingston: McGill-Queen's University Press, 2009.

Freeman, Milton M.R., Robert J. Hudson, and Lee Foote, eds. *Conservation Hunting: People and Wildlife in Canada's North.* Edmonton: Canadian Circumpolar Institute, 2005.

Fu, Congbin, Zhihong Jiang, Zhaoyong Guan, Jinhai He, and Zhongfeng Xu, eds. *Regional Climate Studies of China.* Berlin, Germany: Springer-Verlag, 2008.

Gallagher, Bill. *Resource Rulers: Fortune and Folly on Canada's Road to Resources.* Waterloo, ON: Bill Gallagher, 2012.

Galloway, Gloria. "Ottawa Sets up Arctic Marine Park." *Globe and Mail,* 6 Decem-

ber 2010. http://www.theglobeandmail.com/news/politics/ottawa-notebook/
ottawa-sets-up-arctic-marine-park/article1826548/?service=mobile.

George, Dan. *Lament for Confederation.* Performance with drums and chanting,
Empire Stadium, Vancouver, 1 July 1967.

George, Jane. "Special Claim for Nunavut's Ennadai Lake Relocatees Moves
Ahead." *Nunatsiaq News,* 4 April 2013. http://www.nunatsiaqonline.ca/stories/
article/656/4special_claim_for_nunavuts_ennadai_lake_relocatees_moves_ahead.

Gibbons, Ann. "Clocking the Human Exodus out of Africa." *Science Now,* 21
March 2013. http://news.sciencemag.org/sciencenow/2013/03/clocking-the-
human-exodus-out-of.html.

Gillis, Justin. "Ending Its Summer Melt, Arctic Sea Ice Sets a New Low That Leads
to Warnings." *New York Times,* 19 September 2012. http://www.nytimes.com/
2012/09/20/science/earth/arctic-sea-ice-stops-melting-but-new-record-low-is-
set.html?_r=0.

– "The Threats to a Crucial Canopy: Deaths of Forests May Weaken Controls on
Heat-Trapping Gas." *New York Times,* 1 October 2011.

Gombay, Nicole. *Making a Living: Place, Food and Economy in an Inuit Community.* Saskatoon, SK: Purich, 2010.

Gore, Al. *Our Choice: A Plan to Solve the Climate Crisis.* New York: Rodale and
Melcher Media, 2009.

Government of Australia. *Statement on the United Nations Declaration on the
Rights of Indigenous Peoples.* 3 April 2009. http://www.un.org/esa/socdev/
unpfii/documents/Australia_official_statement_endorsement_UNDRIP.pdf.

Government of Canada. *Canada's Northern Strategy.* http://www.northernstrategy.
gc.ca/index-eng.asp.

Government of Canada, Aboriginal Affairs and Northern Development Canada.
"Backgrounder: Canada's Endorsement of the United Nations Declaration on the
Rights of Indigenous Peoples." 12 November 2010. http://www.aadnc-aandc.gc.
ca/eng/1292353979814/1292354016174.

– *Conciliator's Final Report: Nunavut Land Claims Agreement Implementation
Planning Contract Negotiations for the Second Planning Period.* 1 March 2006.
http://www.aadnc-aandc.gc.ca/eng/1100100030982/1100100030985.

– "Government of Canada Apologizes for Relocation of Inuit Families to the High
Arctic." 18 August 2010. http://www.aadnc-aandc.gc.ca/eng/1100100015397/
1100100015404.

– "Government of Canada Approves Baffinland Mary River Project." 3 December
2012. http://www.aadnc-aandc.gc.ca/eng/1354555214335/1354555258461.

– *The Government of Canada's Approach to Implementation of the Inherent Right
and the Negotiation of Aboriginal Self-Government.* 1995. http://www.aadnc-aandc.
gc.ca/eng/1100100031843/1100100031844.

– "Prime Minister Harper Offers Full Apology on Behalf of Canadians for the Indian Residential Schools System." 11 June 2008. http://www.aadnc-aandc.gc.ca/
eng/1100100015644/1100100015649.

– *Statement of the Government of Canada on Indian policy (The White Paper,
1969).* http://www.ainc-inac.gc.ca/ai/arp/ls/pubs/cp1969/cp1969-eng.asp.

Government of Canada, Department of Justice. *Background Information: Nunavut
and the Nunavut Legal Services Board.* October 2002. http://canada.justice.gc.ca/
eng/rp-pr/aj-ja/rro3_la14-rro3_aj14/p2.html.

Government of Canada, Environment Canada. "Conservation of Polar Bears in
    Canada." 2012. http://www.ec.gc.ca/default.asp?lang=En&xml=9FAB1921-
    CE0F-4B9A-90CE-B4ED209842DF.
Government of Canada, Fisheries and Oceans Canada. "United Nations Conven-
    tion on the Law of the Sea." http://www.dfo-mpo.gc.ca/international/media/
    bk_unclos-eng.htm.
Government of Canada, Royal Commission on Aboriginal Peoples. *The High Arctic
    Relocation: A Report on the 1953–55 Relocation*. Ottawa: Canada Communica-
    tion Group, 1994.
Government of New Zealand. *Statement of Acceptance of United Nations Declara-
    tion on the Rights of Indigenous Peoples*. N.d. The full text is contained in Pita
    Sharples, "Supporting UN Declaration Restores NZ's Mana," 20 April 2010,
    http://www.beehive.govt.nz/release/supporting-un-declaration-restores-nz039s-
    mana.
Government of New Zealand, Department of Immigration. "How Do I Qualify for
    Residence under the 2012 Pacific Access Category?" 30 July 2012.
    http://www.immigration.govt.nz/migrant/stream/live/pacificaccess/residence.
Government of Nunavut, Department of Environment, Environmental Protection
    Division. *Inuit Qaujimajatuqangit of Climate Change in Nunavut: A Sample of
    Inuit Experiences of Recent Climate and Environmental Changes in Pangnirtung
    and Iqaluit, Nunavut*. November 2005. http://env.gov.nu.ca/sites/default/files/
    South%20Baffin%20English.pdf.
Government of Nunavut, Office of the Languages Commissioner. *Nunavut's Official
    Languages*. N.d. http://www.langcom.nu.ca/nunavuts-official-languages.
Government of the United States. *Announcement of U.S. Support for the United
    Nations Declaration on the Rights of Indigenous Peoples: Initiatives to Promote
    the Government-to-Government Relationship and Improve the Lives of Indige-
    nous Peoples*. N.d. http://usun.state.gov/documents/organization/153239.pdf.
– *Treaty Concerning the Cession of the Russian Possessions in North America by
    His Majesty the Emperor of All the Russias to the United States of America*.
    30 March 1867. http://memory.loc.gov/cgi-bin/ampage?collId=llsl&fileName
    =015/llsl015.db&recNum=572.
Grace, Sherrill E. *Canada and the Idea of North*. Montreal and Kingston: McGill-
    Queen's University Press, 2001.
Grant, Shelagh D. *Arctic Justice: On Trial for Murder, Pond Inlet, 1923*. Montreal
    and Kingston: McGill-Queen's University Press, 2002.
– *Polar Imperative: A History of Arctic Sovereignty in North America*. Vancouver:
    Douglas and McIntyre, 2010.
Gregg, Andrew, dir. *The Norse: An Arctic Mystery*. Documentary. Broadcast by the
    Canadian Broadcasting Corporation on the television program *The Nature of
    Things*, 13 June 2013.
Griffin, Harold. *Radical Roots: The Shaping of British Columbia*. Vancouver: Com-
    monwealth Fund, 1999.
Griffiths, Tom. *Slicing the Silence: Voyaging to Antarctica*. Sydney, Australia: Uni-
    versity of New South Wales Press, 2007.
Grygier, Pat Sandiford. *A Long Way from Home: The Tuberculosis Epidemic among
    the Inuit*. Montreal and Kingston: McGill-Queen's University Press, 1994.

Haig-Brown, Celia. *Resistance and Renewal: Surviving the Indian Residential School.* Vancouver: Arsenal Pulp, 1988.

Hallendy, Norman. *Tukiliit: The Stone People Who Live in the Wind – An Introduction to Inuksuit and Other Stone Figures of the North.* Vancouver: Douglas and McIntyre, 2009.

Hamilton, Andrew. "The Medieval Norse on Baffin Island." 8 February 2013. http://www.counter-currents.com/2013/02/the-medieval-norse-on-baffin-island.

Hansen, James. *Storms of My Grandchildren: The Truth about the Coming Climate Catastrophe and Our Last Chance to Save Humanity.* New York: Bloomsbury, 2009.

Hansen, James, I. Fung, A. Lacis, D. Rind, S. Lebedeff, R. Ruedy, G. Russell, and P. Stone. "Global Climate Changes as Forecast by Goddard Institute for Space Studies Three-Dimensional Model." *Journal of Geophysical Research* 93, no. D8 (20 August 1988): 9341–64.

Harper, Kenn. *Give Me My Father's Body: The Life of Minik, the New York Eskimo.* 1986. Reprint, Vermont: Steerforth, 2000.

"Harper on Arctic – 'Use It or Lose It': Canada Will Build up to Eight Arctic Patrol Vessels to Reassert the Country's Northern Sovereignty, Prime Minister Stephen Harper Said in Esquimalt Yesterday." *Victoria Times Colonist,* 10 July 2007. http://www.canada.com/topics/news/story.html?id=7ca93d97-3b26-4dd1-8d92-8568f9b7cc2a&k=73323.

Hartley, Jackie, Paul Joffe, and Jennifer Preston, eds. *Realizing the UN Declaration on the Rights of Indigenous Peoples: Triumph, Hope, and Action.* Saskatoon, SK: Purich, 2010.

Harvey, Fiona. "Climate Change Slowdown Is Due to Warming of Deep Oceans, Say Scientists." *Guardian* (London), 22 July 2013. http://www.guardian.co.uk/science/2013/jul/22/climate-change-slowdown-warming-oceans.

Hayes, Derek. *Historical Atlas of the Arctic.* Vancouver: Douglas and McIntyre, 2003.

Henderson, James Youngblood. *First Nations Jurisprudence and Aboriginal Rights: Defining the Just Society.* Saskatoon, SK: Native Law Centre, University of Saskatchewan, 2006.

– *Indigenous Diplomacy and the Rights of Peoples: Achieving UN Recognition.* Saskatoon, SK: Purich, 2008.

Hensley, William L. Iggiagruk. *Fifty Miles from Tomorrow: A Memoir of Alaska and the Real People.* New York: Picador, 2009.

Herman, Lyndsay. "Port and Road Project Delay: Port Relocation Puts the Breaks on Proposed Bathurst Inlet Port and Road." 13 July 2013. *Northern News Services.* http://nnsl.com/northern-news-services/stories/papers/jul15_13baf41.html.

Heron, Craig, ed. *The Workers' Revolt in Canada, 1917-1925.* Toronto: University of Toronto Press, 1998.

Hofreiter, Michael. "Drafting Human Ancestry: What Does the Neanderthal Genome Tell Us about Hominid Evolution? Commentary on Green et al. (2010)." *Human Biology* 83, no. 1 (February 2011): 1–11.

Homer-Dixon, Thomas, and Andrew Weaver. "Climate Uncertainty Shouldn't Mean Inaction." *Globe and Mail,* 7 October 2013. http://www.theglobeandmail.com/globe-debate/uncertainty-shouldnt-mean-inaction/article14707217.

Houston, James. *Canadian Eskimo Art*. Ottawa: Minister of Northern Affairs and National Resources, 1954.

– *Confessions of an Igloo Dweller: The Story of the Man Who Brought Inuit Art to the Outside World*. Toronto: McClelland and Stewart, 1995.

– *Kiviok's Magic Journey: An Eskimo Legend*. Don Mills, ON: Longman Canada, 1973.

Houston, John, dir. *Diet of Souls*. Documentary. Triad Film Productions, 2004.

– dir. *Kiviuq*. Feature film. Drumsong Communications and Kiviuq Film Productions, 2006.

– dir. *Nuliajuk: Mother of the Sea Beasts*. Feature film. Triad Film Productions, 2001.

Howard, Heather A., and Craig Proulx, eds. *Aboriginal Peoples in Canadian Cities: Transformations and Continuities*. Waterloo, ON: Wilfrid Laurier University Press, 2011.

Huebert, Rob. "U.S. Arctic Policy: The Reluctant Arctic Power." In *The Fast-Changing Arctic: Rethinking Arctic Security for a Warmer World*, ed. Barry Scott Zellen, 189–226. Calgary: University of Calgary Press, 2013.

Hulan, Renée. *Northern Experience and the Myth of Canadian Culture*. Montreal and Kingston: McGill-Queen's University Press, 2002.

Hulme, Mike. *Why We Disagree about Climate Change: Understanding Controversy, Inaction and Opportunity*. Cambridge, UK: Cambridge University Press, 2009.

Hutchins, Peter W. "Power and Principle: State-Indigenous Relations across Time and Space." In *Aboriginal Title and Indigenous Rights: Canada, Australia and New Zealand*, ed. Louis A. Knafla and Haijo Westra, 214–28. Vancouver: UBC Press, 2010.

*Ilulissat Declaration*. 28 May 2008. http://www.oceanlaw.org/downloads/arctic/Ilulissat_Declaration.pdf.

Ingstad, Helge, and Anne Stine Ingstad. *The Viking Discovery of America: The Excavation of a Norse Settlement in L'Anse aux Meadows, Newfoundland*. New York: Checkmark, 2001.

Inter-American Commission on Human Rights. *American Declaration of the Rights and Duties of Man*. 1948. http://www.cidh.oas.org/Basicos/English/Basic2. American%20Declaration.htm.

– *Report on the Situation of Human Rights of a Segment of the Nicaraguan Population of Miskito Origin*. 1983. http://www.cidh.oas.org/countryrep/Miskitoeng/toc. htm.

International Fund for Animal Welfare. "Animal Welfare and Conservation Groups Urge Congress to Protect Polar Bears from Trophy Hunting." 15 May 2007. http://www.ifaw.org/united-states/node/11416.

Inuit Circumpolar Council. *A Circumpolar Inuit Declaration on Resource Development Principles in Inuit Nunaat*. 11 May 2011. http://inuitcircumpolar.com/files/uploads/icc-files/Declaration_on_Resource_Development_A3_FINAL.pdf.

– *A Circumpolar Inuit Declaration on Sovereignty in the Arctic*. April 2009. http://inuitcircumpolar.com/files/uploads/icc-files/declaration12x18vicechairs signed.pdf.

– "Inuit Petition Inter-American Commission on Human Rights to Oppose Climate

Change Caused by the United States of America." Press release. 7 December 2005. http://www.inuitcircumpolar.com/index.php?Lang=En&ID=316.

– *Petition to the Inter-American Commission on Human Rights Seeking Relief from Violations Resulting from Global Warming Caused by Acts and Omissions of the United States.* Submitted 7 December 2005. http://www.inuitcircumpolar.com/files/uploads/icc-files/FINALPetitionICC.pdf.

Inuit Tapiriit Kanatami. *Health Indicators of Inuit Nunangat within the Canadian Context, 1994–1998 and 1999–2003.* 13 July 2010. https://www.itk.ca/publication/health-indicators-inuit-nunangat-within-canadian-context.

– *An Integrated Arctic Strategy.* January 2008. http://www.itk.ca/sites/default/files/Integrated-Arctic-Stratgey.pdf.

– *Inuit and Cancer: Fact Sheets.* February 2009. https://www.itk.ca/publication/inuit-and-cancer-fact-sheets.

IsumaTV. *Truth and Reconciliation.* Video interviews with Inuit residential school survivors. http://www.isuma.tv/hi/en/truth-and-reconciliation.

– *Zacharias Kunuk with Lloyd Lipsett, Formal Intervention, NIRB Technical Hearing, July 23, 2012, Igloolik, Part 1/2 3:13 English Version.* Video. http://www.isuma.tv/en/jons-working-channel/zacharias-kunuk-nirb-presentation-english-part-1-0.

IUCN/SSC Polar Bear Specialist Group. "Summary of Polar Bear Population Status per 2010." 11 May 2010. http://pbsg.npolar.no/en/status/status-table.html.

Jenness, Diamond. *The People of the Twilight.* 1928. Reprint, Chicago, IL: Phoenix Books and University of Chicago Press, 1959.

Joffe, Paul. "Canada's Opposition to the UN *Declaration*: Legitimate Concerns or Ideological Bias?" In *Realizing the UN Declaration on the Rights of Indigenous Peoples: Triumph, Hope, and Action,* ed. Jackie Hartley, Paul Joffe, and Jennifer Preston, 70–9. Saskatoon, SK: Purich, 2010.

Jones, Richard S. *Alaska Native Claims Settlement Act of 1971 (Public Law 92-203): History and Analysis Together with Subsequent Amendments.* 1 June 1981. http://www.alaskool.org/projects/ancsa/rePorts/rsjones1981/ancsa_history71.htm.

Jordan, Pav. "Baffinland Iron Mines Sharply Scales back Mary River Project." *Globe and Mail,* 11 January 2013. http://www.theglobeandmail.com/globe-investor/baffinland-iron-mines-sharply-scales-back-mary-river-project/article7227358.

Kalluak, Mark. *Unipkaaqtuat Arvianit: Traditional Inuit Stories from Arviat.* Vol. 2. Iqaluit, NU: Inhabit Media, 2010.

Kunuk, Zacharias, dir. *Atanarjuat: The Fast Runner.* Feature film. Isuma Productions and National Film Board of Canada, 2001.

– dir. *Kiviaq v. Canada.* Documentary. Kunuk-Cohn Productions and Isuma Productions, 2006. Press kit at http://www.catbirdproductions.ca/wp-content/files_mf/1255722069kiviaq_presskit.pdf.

– dir. *Nanugiurutiga (My First Polar Bear).* Documentary. IsumaTV, n.d. http://www.isuma.tv/hi/en/isuma-productions/nanugiurutiga-my-first-polar-bear.

Kunuk, Zacharias, and Norman Cohn, dirs. *The Journals of Knud Rasmussen.* Feature film. Isuma Productions, 2005.

Kunuk, Zacharias, and Ian Mauro, dirs. *Qapirangajuk: Inuit Knowledge and Climate Change.* Documentary. Isuma Productions, 2010.

Kappianaq, George Agiaq, and Cornelius Nutaraq. *Inuit Perspectives on the 20th Century*. Vol. 2, *Travelling and Surviving on Our Land*. Ed. Jarich Oosten and Frédéric Laungrand. Iqaluit, NU: Nunavut Arctic College, 2001. http://traditional-knowledge.ca/english/pdf/Travelling-And-Surviving-On-Our-Land-E.pdf.

Kennedy, Maeve. "Missing Canadian Teenager Survives Three Days on Ice Floe: Search Team Finds Teenager Jupi Nakoolak 'in Decent Shape' after Drifting in -15C Temperatures with Polar Bears." *Guardian* (London), 10 November 2009. http://www.theguardian.com/world/2009/nov/10/canada-teenager-alive-on-ice.

Kenney, Gerard. *Dangerous Passage: Issues in the Arctic*. Toronto: Natural Heritage Books, 2006.

Killaby, Guy. "'Great Game in a Cold Climate': Canada's Arctic Sovereignty in Question." *Canadian Military Journal* (Winter 2005–06). http://www.journal.forces.gc.ca/vo6/no4/north-nord-01-eng.asp.

Kimmaliadjuk, Theresa. "The Goose-Wife Told by Theresa Kimmaliadjuk." In *Kiviuq's Journey*. http://www.unipka.ca/Stories/Goose_Wife.html.

Kindred, Hugh M., et al. *International Law Chiefly as Interpreted and Applied in Canada*. 7th ed. Toronto: Montgomery, 2006.

King, Ross. *Defiant Spirits: The Modernist Revolution of the Group of Seven*. Vancouver: Douglas and McIntyre, 2010.

Kingwatsiaq, Pilitsi. "Country Food Shouldn't Be Sold." Letter to the editor. *Nunatsiaq News*, 10 August 2001.

Knafla, Louis A., and Haijo Westra, eds. *Aboriginal Title and Indigenous Rights: Canada, Australia and New Zealand*. Vancouver: UBC Press, 2010.

Knop, Karen. *Diversity and Self-Determination in International Law*. Cambridge, UK: Cambridge University Press, 2002.

Kolbert, Elizabeth. *The Arctic: An Anthology*. London: Granta, 2007.

Kreelak, Martin, dir. *Kikkik E1-472*. Documentary. Inuit Broadcasting Corporation, 2003.

Kulchyski, Peter, and Frank James Tester. *Kiumajut (Talking Back): Game Management and Inuit Rights, 1900–70*. Vancouver: UBC Press, 2007.

"La mort violente de l'oncle Victor, dans l'Extrême Nord canadien." 5 July 2010. http://www.benoitlaporte.com/2320/la-mort-violente-de-l%E2%80%99oncle-victor-dans-l%E2%80%99extreme-nord-canadien.

Ladner, Keira L., and Leanne Simpson. *This Is an Honour Song: Twenty Years since the Blockades*. Winnipeg: Arbeiter Ring, 2010.

Lambert, Andrew. *Franklin: Tragic Hero of Polar Navigation*. London: Faber and Faber, 2009.

Lackenbauer, P. Whitney. *The Canadian Rangers: A Living History*. Vancouver: UBC Press, 2013.

Larsen, Henry. *The Northwest Passage, 1940-1942 and 1944: The Famous Voyages of the Royal Canadian Mounted Police Schooner "St. Roch."* Winnipeg: Royal Canadian Mounted Police, 1984.

Laugrand, Frédéric, and Jarich Oosten. *Inuit Shamanism and Christianity: Transitions and Transformations in the Twentieth Century*. Montreal and Kingston: McGill-Queen's University Press, 2010.

Laugrand, Frédéric, Jarich Oosten, and David Serkoak. "Relocating the Ahiarmiut from Ennadai Lake to Arviat (1950–1958)." In *Orality in the 21st Century: Inuit Discourse and Practices: Proceedings of the 15th Inuit Studies Conference*, ed. B.

Collignon and M. Therrien, 1-34. Paris, France: INALCO, 2009. http://www.inuitoralityconference.com/art/Laugrand.pdf.

Leduc, Timothy B. *Climate, Culture, Change: Inuit and Western Dialogues with a Warming North*. Ottawa: University of Ottawa Press, 2010.

Lepage, Marquise, dir. *Martha of the North*. Documentary. Les Productions Virage and National Film Board of Canada, 2008.

Lloyd, Graham. "Twenty-Year Hiatus in Rising Temperatures Has Climate Scientists Puzzled." *The Australian*, 30 March 2013. http://www.theaustralian.com.au/news/features/twenty-year-hiatus-in-rising-temperatures-has-climate-scientists-puzzled/story-e6frg6z6-1226609140980.

Lopez, Barry. *Arctic Dreams: Imagination and Desire in a Northern Landscape*. Toronto: Bantam, 1986.

Loukacheva, Natalia. *The Arctic Promise: Legal and Political Autonomy of Greenland and Nunavut*. Toronto: University of Toronto Press, 2007.

Lovelock, James. *Gaia: A New Look at Life on Earth*. Oxford: Oxford University Press, 1979.

– *The Vanishing Face of Gaia: A Final Warning*. London: Allen Lane, 2009.

Macalister, Terry. "Greenland Halts New Oil Drilling Licences." *Guardian* (London), 27 March 2013. http://www.theguardian.com/world/2013/mar/27/greenland-halts-oil-drilling-licences.

MacDonald, John. *The Arctic Sky: Inuit Astronomy, Star Lore, and Legend*. Toronto and Iglulik, NU: Royal Ontario Museum and Nunavut Research Institute, 2000.

MacKinnon, J.B. *The Once and Future World: Nature as It Was, as It Is, as It Could Be*. Toronto: Random House, 2013.

MacMillan, Margaret. *Paris 1919: Six Months that Changed the World*. New York: Random House, 2003.

Magnusson, Magnus, and Hermann Palsson, trans. *The Vinland Sagas: The Norse Discovery of America – Graenlendinga Saga and Eirik's Saga*. London: Penguin, 1965.

Malaurie, Jean. *Ultima Thule: Explorers and Natives in the Polar North*. New York: Norton, 2003.

Mancini Billson, Janet, and Kyra Mancini. *Inuit Women: Their Powerful Spirit in a Century of Change*. Lanham, MD: Rowman and Littlefield, 2007.

Mann, Michael E. *The Hockey Stick and the Climate Wars: Dispatches from the Front Lines*. New York: Columbia University Press, 2012.

Marcus, Alan Rudolph. *Out in the Cold: The Legacy of Canada's Inuit Relocation Experiment in the High Arctic*. Copenhagen, Denmark: International Work Group for Indigenous Affairs, 1992.

– *Relocating Eden: The Image and Politics of Inuit Exile in the Canadian Arctic*. Hanover: University Press of New England, 1995.

Martin, Keavy. *Stories in a New Skin: Approaches to Inuit Literature*. Winnipeg: University of Manitoba Press, 2012.

Mary-Rousselière, Guy. *Qitdlarssuaq: The Story of a Polar Migration*. Trans. Alan Cooke. Winnipeg: Wuerz, 1991.

Maschner, Herbert, Owen Mason, and Robert McGhee, eds. *The Northern World, AD 900–1400*. Salt Lake City: University of Utah Press, 2009.

McAdam, Jane. *Climate Change, Forced Migration, and International Law*. Oxford: Oxford University Press, 2011.

McGhee, Robert. *Ancient People of the Arctic*. Vancouver: UBC Press, 1996.

– *The Arctic Voyages of Martin Frobisher: An Elizabethan Adventure*. Montreal and Kingston: McGill-Queen's University Press, 2001.

– *The Last Imaginary Place: A Human History of the Arctic World*. Toronto: Key Porter, 2004.

– "When and Why Did the Inuit Move to the Eastern Arctic?" In *The Northern World, AD 900–1400*, ed. Herbert Maschner, Owen Mason, and Robert McGhee, 155–63. Salt Lake City: University of Utah Press, 2009.

McGoogan, Ken. *Fatal Passage: The Untold Story of John Rae, the Arctic Adventurer Who Discovered the Fate of Franklin*. Toronto: HarperPerennial Canada, 2001.

– *Lady Franklin's Revenge: A True Story of Ambition, Obsession and the Remaking of Arctic History*. Toronto: HarperCollins, 2005.

McGrath, Melanie. *The Long Exile: A True Story of Deception and Survival among the Inuit of the Canadian Arctic*. London: Fourth Estate, 2006.

McGregor, Heather E. *Inuit Education and Schools in the Eastern Arctic*. Vancouver: UBC Press, 2010.

Meehl, Gerald A., et al. "Model-Based Evidence of Deep-Ocean Heat Uptake during Surface-Temperature Hiatus Periods." *Nature Climate Change* 1 (18 September 2011): 360–4. http://www.nature.com/nclimate/journal/v1/n7/full/nclimate1229.html.

Meltzer, David J. *First Peoples in a New World: Colonizing Ice Age America*. Berkeley: University of California Press, 2009.

Mercer, Stephen A. *Claiming Nunavut, 1971–1999*. Victoria, BC: Trafford, 2008.

Miller, J.R. *Shingwauk's Vision: A History of Native Residential Schools*. Toronto: University of Toronto Press, 1996.

Milloy, John S. *A National Crime: The Canadian Government and the Residential School System, 1879 to 1986*. Winnipeg: University of Manitoba Press, 1999.

Mohan, Geoffrey. "Carbon Dioxide Levels in Atmosphere Pass 400 Milestone, Again." *Los Angeles Times*, 20 March 2013. http://articles.latimes.com/2013/may/20/science/la-sci-sn-carbon-dioxide-400-20130520.

Monbiot, George. *Feral: Rewilding the Land, the Sea and Human Life*. London: Allen Lane, 2013.

Morrison, William R. *Showing the Flag: The Mounted Police and Canadian Sovereignty in the North, 1894–1925*. Vancouver: UBC Press, 1985.

Mowat, Farley. *Canada North Now: The Great Betrayal*. Toronto: McLelland and Stewart, 1967.

– *The Desperate People*. 1959. Reprint, Toronto: Key Porter, 2005.

– *The People of the Deer*. 1952. Reprint, Toronto: Bantam, 1981.

– *Walking on the Land*. Toronto: Key Porter, 2000.

Munro, Margaret "'Unprecedented' Ozone Hole Opens over Canadian Arctic." *National Post*, 2 Oçtober 2011. http://news.nationalpost.com/2011/10/02/unprecedented-ozone-hole-opens-over-canadian-arctic.

Murphy, David. *The Arctic Fox: Francis Leopold McClintock*. Toronto: Dundurn, 2004.

Naam, Ramez. "Arctic Sea Ice: What, Why and What Next." *Scientific American*, 21 September 2012. http://blogs.scientificamerican.com/guest-blog/2012/09/21/arctic-sea-ice-what-why-and-what-next.

Nansen, Fridtjof. "Preface." In *The People of the Twilight*, by Diamond Jenness, i–xii. Chicago, IL: Phoenix Books and University of Chicago Press, 1959.

Nash, Roderick Frazier. *Wilderness and the American Mind*. 4th ed. New Haven, CT: Yale University Press, 2001.

National Aeronautic and Space Administration. "Warm Ocean Rapidly Melting Antarctic Ice Shelf from Below." 12 September 2013. http://www.nasa.gov/content/goddard/warm-ocean-rapidly-melting-antarctic-ice-shelf-from-below/#.UkoKdr5rapo.

National Oceanic and Atmospheric Administration. *Arctic Report Card: Update for 2012 – Executive Summary*. 21 January 2013. http://www.arctic.noaa.gov/reportcard/exec_summary.html.

– "Climate." http://www.noaa.gov/climate.html.

– "Globe Had Eighth Warmest August on Record." 15 September 2011. http://www.noaanews.noaa.gov/stories2011/20110915_globalstats.html.

National Oceanic and Atmospheric Administration, National Climatic Data Center. *Global Climate Change Indicators*. 30 July 2010. http://www.ncdc.noaa.gov/indicators.

National Round Table on the Environment and the Economy (Canada). *Paying the Price: The Economic Impacts of Climate Change for Canada*. September 2011. http://coastalchange.ca/download_files/external_reports/NRTEE_(2011)_%20ClimateProsperity_1.pdf.

Newbury, Nick. *Iqaluit*. Iqaluit, NU: Royal Canadian Legion Branch No. 168 and Nortext, 2009.

Newhouse, David, Cora Voyageur, and Dan Beavon, eds. *Hidden in Plain Sight: Contributions of Aboriginal Peoples to Canadian Identity and Culture*. Toronto: University of Toronto Press, 2005.

Newman, Dwight G. *The Duty to Consult: New Relationships with Aboriginal Peoples*. Saskatoon, SK: Purich, 2009.

Newman, Peter C. *Company of Adventurers: How the Hudson's Bay Empire Determined the Destiny of a Continent*. Toronto: Penguin, 2005.

Nunavut Impact Review Board. *Final Hearing Report*. Report on Mary River Project, Baffinland Iron Mines Corporation. File no. 08MN053. September 2012.

Nunavut Tunngavik Incorporated. *Backgrounder: Thomas Berger's Final Report on the Implementation of the Nunavut Land Claims Agreement*. 5 April 2006. http://www.tunngavik.com/blog/2006/04/05/backgrounder-thomas-bergers-final-report-on-the-implementation-of-the-nunavut-land-claims-agreement.

O'Fallon, Brendan D., and Lars Fehren-Schmitz. "Native Americans Experienced a Strong Population Bottleneck Coincident with European Contact." *Proceedings of the National Academy of Sciences* 108, no. 51 (20 December 2011). http://www.pnas.org/content/108/51/20444.full.

Organization of American States. *American Convention on Human Rights*. 1969. http://www.oas.org/juridico/english/treaties/b-32.html.

O'Rourke, Dennis H., and Jennifer A. Raff. "The Human Genetic History of the Americas: The Final Frontier." *Current Biology* 20, no. 4 (23 February 2010):

R202–R207. http://www.sciencedirect.com/science/article/pii/S0960982209
020661.

Osofsky, Hari M. "Complexities of Addressing the Impacts of Climate Change on
Indigenous Peoples through International Law Petitions: A Case Study of the Inuit
Petition to the Inter-American Commission on Human Rights." In *Climate
Change and Indigenous Peoples: The Search for Legal Remedies*, ed. Randall S.
Abate and Elizabeth Ann Kronk, 313–37. Cheltenham, UK: Edward Elgar, 2013.

Paehlke, Robert C. *Some Like It Cold: The Politics of Climate Change in Canada*.
Toronto: Between the Lines, 2008.

Parks, Jennifer. *Canada's Arctic Sovereignty: Resources, Climate and Conflict*.
Edmonton: Lone Pine, 2010.

Patrick, Donna, Julie-Ann Tomiak, Lynda Brown, Heidi Langille, and Mihaela
Vieru. "'Regaining the Childhood I Should Have Had': The Transformation of
Inuit Identities, Institutions, and Community in Ottawa." In *Aboriginal Peoples in
Canadian Cities: Transformations and Continuities*, ed. Heather A. Howard and
Craig Proulx, 69–86. Waterloo, ON: Wilfrid Laurier University Press, 2011.

Pauktuutit Inuit Women's Association of Canada. *Sivumuapallianiq: Journey Forward: National Inuit Residential Schools Healing Strategy*. Iqaluit, NU: Pauktuutit
Inuit Women's Association of Canada, 2007.

Peacock, E., M.K. Taylor, J. Laake, and I. Stirling. "Population Ecology of Polar
Bears in Davis Strait, Canada and Greenland." *Journal of Wildlife Management*
77 (2013): 463–76.

Pelly, David F. *Sacred Hunt: A Portrait of the Relationship between Seals and Inuit*.
Vancouver: Greystone, 2001.

Pelly, David F., and Dennis Minty. "Dundas Harbour: Keeping Watch over the
Northwest Passage." *Above and Beyond: Canada's Arctic Journal* (July/August
2013): 15–18.

Peter, Aaju. Speech presented at Canada House, Canadian High Commission, London, Summer 2009.

Petrone, Penny, ed. *Northern Voices: Inuit Writing in English*. Toronto: University
of Toronto Press, 1992.

Pharand, Donat. *Canada's Arctic Waters in International Law*. Cambridge, UK:
Cambridge University Press, 1988.

Phelpstead, Carl, ed. *A History of Norway and the Passion and Miracles of the
Blessed Olafr*. Trans. Devra Kunin. London: Viking Society for Northern Research, University College, 2001.

Pielou, E.C. *A Naturalist's Guide to the Arctic*. Chicago, IL: University of Chicago
Press, 1994.

Pilon, Benoit, dir. *Ce qu'il faut pour vivre – The Necessities of Life*. Feature film. Les
Films Séville and Arico Film Communication, 2008.

Polar Bears International. *Polar Bear Facts and Information*. N.d. http://www.polar
bearsinternational.org/bear-facts.

Potter, Mitch. "Row Erupts over Governor General's Seal Taste." *Toronto Star*,
26 May 2009. http://www.thestar.com/news/canada/article/640588.

Pringle, Heather. "Vikings and Native Americans." *National Geographic*, November
2012. http://ngm.nationalgeographic.com/2012/11/vikings-and-indians/pringle-
text.

Qikiqtani Inuit Association. *The Mary River Project Inuit Impact and Benefit*

*Agreement: A Plain Language Guide.* 6 September 2013. http://www.isuma.tv/en/
DID/news/mary-river-project-iiba.
– *Tallurutiup Tariunga Inulik: Inuit Participation in Determining the Future of
Lancaster Sound.* February 2012. http://www.qia.ca/apps/authoring/dspPage.
aspx?page=lancaster.
Qikiqtani Truth Commission. *Community Histories, 1950 to 1975.* Toronto:
Inhabit Media, 2013.
– *Thematic Reports and Special Studies, 1950 to 1975.* Toronto: Inhabit Media,
2013.
Radford, Tom, and Niobe Thompson, dirs. *Inuit Odyssey.* Documentary. Clearwater
Films, 2012.
Radmore, Caludia Coutu, ed. *Arctic Twilight: Leonard Budgell and Canada's
Changing North.* Toronto: Blue Butterfly, 2009.
Rae, John. "The Arctic Expedition." Letter. *Times* (London), 23 October 1854, 7.
– *John Rae's Correspondence with the Hudson's Bay Company on Arctic Explo-
ration, 1844–1855.* Ed. E.E. Rich. London: Hudson's Bay Record Society, 1953.
– "The Lost Arctic Voyagers." *Household Words* 10, no. 248 (23 December 1854):
233–7.
Rasmussen, Knud. *Across Arctic America: Narrative of the Fifth Thule Expedition.*
1927. Reprint, Fairbanks: University of Alaska Press, 1999.
– *The People of the Polar North: A Record.* Ed. G. Herring. Philadelphia, PA: J.B.
Lippincott, 1908.
Reaney, Brent. "Pond Inlet Graves Moved." *Northern News Services,* 13 September
2004. http://www.nnsl.com/frames/newspapers/2004-09/sep13_04grv.html.
Regan, Paulette. *Unsettling the Settler Within: Indian Residential Schools, Truth
Telling, and Reconciliation in Canada.* Vancouver: UBC Press, 2010.
Reid, Jennifer. *Louis Riel and the Creation of Modern Canada: Mythic Discourse.*
Santa Fe: University of New Mexico Press, 2008.
Rink, Henrik. *Tales and Traditions of the Eskimo.* 1875. Reprint, London: C.
Hurst, 1974.
Robbins, Lisa L., et al. "Baseline Monitoring of the Western Arctic Ocean Estimates
20% of Canadian Basin Surface Waters Are Undersaturated with Respect to Arag-
onite." *PLOS ONE* 8, no. 9 (2013). http://www.plosone.org/article/info%3Adoi%
2F10.1371%2Fjournal.pone.0073796.
Rogers, Stan. *Northwest Passage.* Song. http://www.mp3lyrics.org/s/stan-rogers/
northwest-passage.
Ross, John. *A Voyage of Discovery … for the Purpose of Exploring Baffin's Bay and
Inquiring into the Probability of a North-West Passage.* London: John Murray,
1819.
Rothwell, Donald R., and Tim Stephens. *The International Law of the Sea.* Oxford:
Hart, 2010.
Rowley, Graham W. *Cold Comfort: My Love Affair with the Arctic.* Montreal and
Kingston: McGill-Queen's University Press, 1996.
Royal Canadian Mounted Police. *Reports and Other Papers Relating to the Two
Voyages of the RCMP Schooner "St. Roch" through the North West Passage from
(1) Vancouver, B.C. to Sydney, N.S. (1940–42) (2) Dartmouth, N.S. to Vancouver,
B.C. (1944) under the Command of Regimental Number 10407, Staff Sergeant
H.A. Larsen (now Sub-Inspector).* Ottawa: King's Printer, 1945.

Ruddiman, William F. *Plows, Plagues, and Petroleum: How Humans Took Control of Climate*. Princeton, NJ: Princeton University Press, 2010.

Sabine, Edward, ed. *North Georgia Gazette and Winter Chronicle*. 2nd ed. London: John Murray, 1822.

Saint-Pierre, Marjolaine. *Joseph-Elzéar Bernier: Champion of Canadian Arctic Sovereignty*. Trans. William Barr. Montreal: Baraka, 2009.

Sandiford, Mark, dir. *Qallunaat: Why White People Are Funny*. Documentary. National Film Board of Canada, 2006.

Sankararaman, S., N. Patterson, H. Li, S. Pääbo, and D. Reich. "The Date of Interbreeding between Neandertals and Modern Humans." *PLOS Genetics* 8, no. 10 (2012). http://www.plosgenetics.org/article/info%3Adoi%2F10.1371%2Fjournal.pgen.1002947.

Saul, John Ralston. *A Fair Country: Telling Truths about Canada*. Toronto: Penguin, 2008.

– "Listen to the North: Cramming Northerners' Needs into a Southern Model Just Isn't Working." *Literary Review of Canada* l17, no. 8 (October 2009): 3–5.

Scoffield, Heather. "Arctic Ice Melt in 2012 Was Fastest, Widest in Recent History." *Toronto Star*, 19 September 2012. http://www.thestar.com/news/canada/article/1259382-arctic-ice-melt-in-2012-was-fastest-widest-in-recent-history.

Secretariat of the Antarctic Treaty. *The Antarctic Treaty*. 1961. http://www.ats.aq/index_e.htm.

Sharples, Pita. "Supporting UN Declaration Restores NZ's Mana." 20 April 2010. http://www.beehive.govt.nz/release/supporting-un-declaration-restores-nz039s-mana.

Sissons, Jack. *Judge of the Far North: The Memoirs of Jack Sissons*. Toronto: McLelland and Stewart, 1968.

Smith, Stephen A., and Julia Szucs, dirs. *Vanishing Point*. Documentary. Meltwater Media and the National Film Board of Canada, 2012.

Spalding, Alex, and Thomas Kusugaq. *Inuktitut: A Multi-Dialectal Outline Dictionary*. Iqaluit, NU: Nunavut Arctic College, 1998.

Spector, Samuel J. "Western Sahara and the Self-Determination Debate." *Middle East Quarterly* 16, no. 3 (Summer 2009): 33–43. http://www.meforum.org/2400/western-sahara-self-determination.

Statistics Canada. "Infant Mortality Rates, by Province and Territory." Table. http://www.statcan.gc.ca/tables-tableaux/sum-som/l01/cst01/health21a-eng.htm.

Steckley, John L. *White Lies about the Inuit*. Peterborough, ON: Broadview, 2008.

Steele, Harwood. *Policing the Arctic: The Story of the Conquest of the Arctic by the Royal Canadian (Formerly North-West) Mounted Police*. Toronto: Ryerson, 1935.

Stewart, Patrick M. "(Almost) Everyone Agrees: The US Should Ratify the Law of the Sea Treaty." *The Atlantic*, 10 June 2012. http://www.theatlantic.com/international/archive/2012/06/-almost-everyone-agrees-the-us-should-ratify-the-law-of-the-sea-treaty/258301.

Stott, Peter. "Global-Average Temperature Records." Met Office, United Kingdom. N.d. http://www.metoffice.gov.uk/climate-change/guide/science/explained/temp-records.

Struzik, Edward. *The Big Thaw: Travels in the Melting North*. Mississauga, ON: John Wiley, 2009.

Struzik, Edward, and Mike Beedell. *Northwest Passage: The Quest for an Arctic Route to the East*. London: Blandford, 1991.

Sutherland, Patricia D. "Dorset-Norse Interactions in the Canadian Eastern Arctic." In *Identities and Cultural Contacts in the Arctic: Proceedings from a Conference at the Danish National Museum, Copenhagen, November 30 to December 2, 1999*, ed. Martin Appelt, Joel Berglund, and Hans Christian Gulløv. Copenhagen, Denmark: Danish National Museum and Danish Polar Center, 2000. http://www.civilization.ca/research-and-collections/research/resources-for-scholars/ essays-1/archaeology-1/patricia-sutherland/dorset-norse-interactions in the canadian-eastern-arctic.

Suthren, Victor. *The Island of Canada: How Three Oceans Shaped Our Nation.* Toronto: Thomas Allen, 2009.

Suzuki, David, and Dave Robert Taylor. *The Big Picture: Reflections on Science, Humanity, and a Quickly Changing Planet.* Vancouver: Greystone, 2009.

Swain, Harry. *Oka: A Political Crisis and Its Legacy.* Vancouver: Douglas and McIntyre, 2010.

Tait, Carrie. "Chevron, Statoil Set a Course for Arctic Exploration." In "Report on Business," *Globe and Mail*, 13 January 2012.

Tape, Ken D. *The Changing Arctic Landscape.* Fairbanks: University of Alaska Press, 2010.

Tassinan, Patricia V., dir. *Broken Promises: The High Arctic Relocation.* Documentary. Nutaaq Média and the National Film Board of Canada, 1995.

Taracena, Connie. "Implementing the *Declaration*: A State Representative Perspective." In *Realizing the UN Declaration on the Rights of Indigenous Peoples: Triumph, Hope, and Action*, ed. Jackie Hartley, Paul Joffe, and Jennifer Preston, 60–75. Saskatoon, SK: Purich, 2010.

Tarasuk, Valerie, Andy Mitchell, and Naomi Dachner. *Household Food Insecurity in Canada, 2011.* Toronto: PROOF, 2013. http://nutritionalsciences.lamp. utoronto.ca/wp-content/uploads/2013/07/Household-Food-Insecurity-in-Canada-2011.pdf.

Tester, Frank James, and Peter Kulchyski. *Tammarniit (Mistakes): Inuit Relocation in the Eastern Arctic, 1939–63.* Vancouver: UBC Press, 1994.

Theberge, John, and Mary Theberge. *The Ptarmigan's Dilemma: An Exploration into How Life Organizes and Supports Itself.* Toronto: McClelland and Stewart, 2010.

Thorpe, Natasha, Naikak Hakongak, Sandra Eyegetok, and Kitikmeot Elders. *Thunder on the Tundra: Inuit Qaujimajatuqangit of the Bathurst Caribou.* Cambridge Bay, NU: Tuktu and Nogak Project, 2001.

Timpson, Annis May, ed. *First Nations, First Thoughts: The Impact of Indigenous Thought in Canada.* Vancouver: UBC Press, 2009.

Titley, E. Brian. *A Narrow Vision: Duncan Campbell Scott and the Administration of Indian Affairs in Canada.* Vancouver: UBC Press, 1986.

Tobias, Terry N. *Living Proof: The Essential Data-Collection Guide for Indigenous Use-and-Occupancy Map Surveys.* Vancouver: Ecotrust Canada and Union of British Columbia Indian Chiefs, 2009.

Toronto Public Library. *Frozen Ocean: Search for the Northwest Passage.* Virtual exhibition. http://ve.torontopubliclibrary.ca/frozen_ocean/index.htm.

Truth and Reconciliation Commission of Canada. *Canada, Aboriginal Peoples, and Residential Schools: They Came for the Children.* 2012. http://www.attendance marketing.com/~attmk/TRC_jd/ResSchoolHistory_2012_02_24_Webposting.pdf.

– *Interim Report*. 2012. http://www.attendancemarketing.com/~attmk/TRC_jd/ Interim_report_English_electronic_copy.pdf.

– "Northern National Event." Inuvik, Northwest Territories, 28 June to 1 July 2011. http://www.trcnationalevents.ca/websites/Northern/index.php?p=213.

Tulugarjuk, Leo, and Jaypeetee Arnakak, eds. *Unikkaaqtuat Qikiqtaninngaaqtut: Traditional Stories from the Qikiqtani Region*. Vol. 1, *Arctic Bay and Igloolik*. Iqaluit, NU: Niutaq Cultural Institute and Qikiqtani Inuit Association, 2007.

United Nations. *United Nations Convention on International Trade in Endangered Species of Wild Fauna and Flora*. 3 March 1973. Amended 22 June 1979. http://www.cites.org/eng/disc/text.php#texttop.

– *United Nations Convention on the Law of the Sea*. 10 December 1982. http://www.un.org/Depts/los/convention_agreements/texts/unclos/closindx.htm.

– *United Nations Declaration on the Rights of Indigenous Peoples*. 13 September 2007. http://www.un.org/esa/socdev/unpfii/documents/DRIPS_en.pdf.

United Nations, Intergovernmental Panel on Climate Change. *Fifth Assessment Report: Climate Change 2013: The Physical Science Basis*. 27 September 2013. http://www.ipcc.ch/report/ar5/wg1/#.UkdaIb5rapo.

– *Fifth Assessment Report: Climate Change 2013: The Physical Science Basis: Summary for Policymakers*. 27 September 2013. http://www.climatechange2013. org/images/uploads/WGI_AR5_SPM_brochure.pdf.

United Nations, Permanent Forum on Indigenous Issues. "Climate Change." http://undesadspd.org/IndigenousPeoples/ThematicIssues/Environment/ ClimateChange.aspx.

University of British Columbia. "UN Declaration on the Rights of Indigenous Peoples." 2009. http://indigenousfoundations.arts.ubc.ca/home/global-indigenous- issues/un-declaration-on-the-rights-of-indigenous-peoples.html.

Van Deusen, Kira. *Kiviuq: An Inuit Hero and His Siberian Cousins*. Montreal and Kingston: McGill-Queen's University Press, 2009.

Varga, Peter. "Oil and Gas Pose Big Questions for Baffin Region Inuit." *Nunatsiaq News*, 25 October 2013.

Venne, Sharon Helen. *Our Elders Understand Our Rights: Evolving International Law with Regards to Indigenous Peoples*. Penticton, BC: Theytus Books, 1998.

Von Finckenstein, Maria, ed. *Nuvisavik: The Place Where We Weave*. Montreal and Kingston: Canadian Museum of Civilization and McGill-Queen's University Press, 2002.

Wachowich, Nancy, in collaboration with Apphia Agalakti Awa, Rhoda Kaukjak Katsak, and Sandra Pikujak Katsak. *Saqiyuq: Stories from the Lives of Three Inuit Women*. Montreal and Kingston: McGill-Queen's University Press, 1999.

Wadden, Marie. *Where the Pavement Ends: Canada's Aboriginal Recovery Movement and the Urgent Need for Reconciliation*. Vancouver: Douglas and McIntyre, 2008.

Waiser, Bill, and Blair Stonechild. *Loyal to Death: Indians and the Northwest Rebellion*. Markham, ON: Fifth House, 2010.

Waldie, Paul. "Baffinland CEO Says No to Northwest Passage." *Globe and Mail*, 18 October 2013. http://www.globeadvisor.com/servlet/ArticleNews/story/gam/ 20131018/RBARCTICBAFFINLANDWALDIEATL.

– "Healthy Polar Bear Count Confounds Doomsayers." *Globe and Mail*, 4 April 2012. http://www.theglobeandmail.com/news/national/healthy-polar-bear-count- confounds-doomsayers/article4099460.

– "Signs of Warming Earth 'Unmistakable.'" *Globe and Mail*, 29 July 2010. http://embamex.sre.gob.mx/canada_eng/index.php?option=com_content&view=article&id=869:signs-of-warming-earth-unmistakable-the-globe-and-mail&catid=102:jueves-29-julio-2010.

Walk, Ansgar. *Kenojuak: The Life Story of an Inuit Artist*. Trans. Timothy B. Spence. Newcastle, ON: Penumbra, 1999.

Walker, John, dir. *Passage*. Documentary. PTV Productions, John Walker Productions, and National Film Board of Canada, 2008.

Watt-Cloutier, Siila (Sheila). "Presentation by Sheila Watt-Cloutier, Chair, Inuit Circumpolar Conference, Eleventh Conference of Parties to the UN Framework Convention on Climate Change, Montreal, December 7, 2005." http://www.inuit circumpolar.com/index.php?ID=318&Lang=En.

Watt-Cloutier, Siila (Sheila), and Mohamed H.A. Hassan. "Planet Earth: Living On It, Changing It, Sustaining It." Keynote address, Fifth Science Centre World Congress, Toronto, 18 June 2010.

Weaver, Andrew. *Keeping Our Cool: Canada in a Warming World*. Toronto: Penguin, 2008.

Wenzel, George W., and Martha Dowsley. "Economic and Cultural Aspects of Polar Bear Sport Hunting in Nunavut, Canada." In *Conservation Hunting: People and Wildlife in Canada's North*, ed. Milton M.R. Freeman, Robert J. Hudson, and Lee Foote, 37–48. Edmonton: Canadian Circumpolar Institute, 2005.

White, Rodney. *Climate Change in Canada*. Toronto: Oxford University Press, 2010.

Wiebe, Rudy. *Playing Dead: A Contemplation Concerning the Arctic*. Edmonton: NeWest, 2003.

Williamson, Karla Jensen. "'Arnaasiaq' and 'Angutaasiaq' People Deserve Love and Tolerance." *Nunatsiaq News*, 29 April 2005. http://www.nunatsiaqonline.ca/archives/50429/opinionEditorial/editorial.html.

Windeyer, Chris. "Influx of Bears a Nuisance across Nunavut." *Nunatsiaq News*, 18 January 2010. http://www.nunatsiaqonline.ca/stories/article/23567_influx_of_bears_a_nuisance_across_nunavut.

Wissink, Renee. "The Qitdlarssuaq Chronicles, Part 1." *The Fan Hitch: Official Newsletter of the Inuit Sled Dog International* 5, no. 1 (December 2002). http://thefanhitch.org/V5N1/V5N1Qitdlarssaug.html.

– "The Qitdlarssuaq Chronicles, Part 2." *The Fan Hitch: Official Newsletter of the Inuit Sled Dog International* 5, no. 2 (March 2003). http://thefanhitch.org/V5N2/V5N2Qitdlarssuaq.html.

– "The Qitdlarssuaq Chronicles, Part 3." *The Fan Hitch: Official Newsletter of the Inuit Sled Dog International* 5, no. 3 (June 2003). http://thefanhitch.org/V5N3/V5N3Qitdlarssuaq.html.

– "The Qitdlarssuaq Chronicles, Part 4." *The Fan Hitch: Official Newsletter of the Inuit Sled Dog International* 5, no. 4 (September 2003). http://thefanhitch.org/V5N4/V5N4Qitdlarssauq.html.

World Wildlife Federation. *Polar Bear*. http://www.worldwildlife.org/species/finder/polarbear/polarbear.html.

World Wildlife Federation, Conservation Action Network. "Polar Bear Seas Protection Act Gains Cosponsors." N.d. http://wwf.worldwildlife.org/site/PageServer?pagename=can_results_polar_bear_seas&AddInterest=1081.

Wright, Shelley. *International Human Rights, Decolonisation and Globalisation: Becoming Human.* London: Routledge, 2001.

Xing, Chen. "Paleoclimate of China." In *Regional Climate Studies of China,* ed. Congbin Fu, Zhihong Jiang, Zhaoyong Guan, Jinhai He, and Zhongfeng Xu, 49–98. Berlin, Germany: Springer-Verlag, 2008.

Yaffe, Barbara. "Resource Sector about to Witness New Era of Native Empowerment." *Vancouver Sun,* 22 January 2014. http://www.vancouversun.com/business/resources/Resource+sector+about+witness+native+empowerment/9418598/story.html.

Zellen, Barry Scott, ed. *The Fast-Changing Arctic: Rethinking Arctic Security for a Warmer World.* Calgary: University of Calgary Press, 2013.

WEBSITES

Arctic Climate Impact Assessment. http://www.acia.uaf.edu.

Arctic Institute of North America. http://www.arctic.ucalgary.ca.

Blueberries and Polar Bears. Cookbook series. http://www.blueberriesandpolarbears.com/index.htm.

Feeding My Family. http://www.feedingmyfamily.org.

Government of Nunavut. http://www.gov.nu.ca.

Government of Nunavut, Office of the Languages Commissioner. http://www.langcom.nu.ca.

Houston North Gallery. http://www.houston-north-gallery.ns.ca.

Inuit Gallery of Vancouver. http://inuit.com.

Inuit Tapiriit Kanatami. http://www.itk.ca.

Isuma Productions. http://www.isuma.tv/isuma-productions.

IsumaTV. http://www.isuma.tv/hi/en.

*Kiviuq's Journey.* http://www.unipka.ca.

Learning Inuktitut Online. http://www.tusaalanga.ca.

NASA Earth Observatory. http://earthobservatory.nasa.gov.

North Pole Environmental Observatory. Webcam. http://psc.apl.washington.edu/northpole/NPEO2013/webcam2.html.

Nunavut Planning Commission. http://www.nunavut.ca.

Nunavut Tunngavik Incorporated. http://www.tunngavik.com.

Nunavut Wildlife Management Board. http://www.nwmb.com.

*On Thin Ice: Polar Bears in a Climate of Change.* http://onthinice.ca.webhosting.pathcom.com/index.htm.

Organization of American States, Inter-American Commission on Human Rights. http://www.cidh.oas.org/DefaultE.htm.

Statistics Canada. http://www.statcan.gc.ca/start-debut-eng.html.

Truth and Reconciliation Commission of Canada. http://www.trc.ca/websites/trcinstitution/index.php?p=3.

United Nations, Intergovernmental Panel on Climate Change. http://www.ipcc.ch.

United Nations, Permanent Forum on Indigenous Issues. http://undesadspd.org/IndigenousPeoples.aspx.

# Index

Aariak, Eva, 261
Aboriginal, 136, 155, 166; children, 166–7; communities, 188; deprivation, 183; groups, 170; issues, 188; land claims or title to land, 189, 209, 210; minorities, 117; observers, 167; organizations, 187; people or peoples, 117, 130, 167, 182–8, 208, 247, 251, 289; population, 132; premier, 187; rights and treaty rights, 117, 187, 194, 208–10, 248; self–government, 187, 248; settlement, 189; students, 13; voices, 117; writers and leaders, 185, 188
Aboriginals and Torres Strait Islanders (Australia), 81, 251
abuse: child, elder, and spousal, 166, 178–9, 212; and neglect, 166–7; residential schools, 166–7, 194; sexual, 150, 194; substance, 17, 176, 204, 212
Adventure Canada, 23, 82, 211–12
Aglukark, Susan, 18
Aglukkak, Leona, 261
agreements or treaties: Aboriginal, 117,

182, 187, 208, 248, 306, 312, 319; European (seal products), 277; international, 123, 126, 269, 304, 323–4, 334
Ahiarmiut (Inuit of the Barren Grounds), 143–52, 166
Akitsiraq: elder-in-residence, 80, 184, 194, 212, 266 (*see also* Ukaliannuk, Lucien); graduates, 18–19, 190, 278, 286; graduation, 18–19, 36, 294; law school, 13–15, 17–18, 33–6, 148, 190, 194, 211–12, 294; northern director, 13, 41, 148, 184, 190, 294; students, 35–6, 41, 148, 172, 175, 190, 212, 278, 285–6, 297
Alaska, 15, 33, 116, 119–20, 122–3, 195, 264, 277, 297, 303, 310–11, 321; climate change, 238, 243, 251; European exploration, 57; Fifth Thule Expedition, 95–7; Inuit migration, 25, 44, 48, 74, 79, 81, 102, 197; resource development, 205
*Alaska Native Claims Settlement Act*, 120, 185, 306
albedo effect, 7, 219